Enchanter

enchant

2

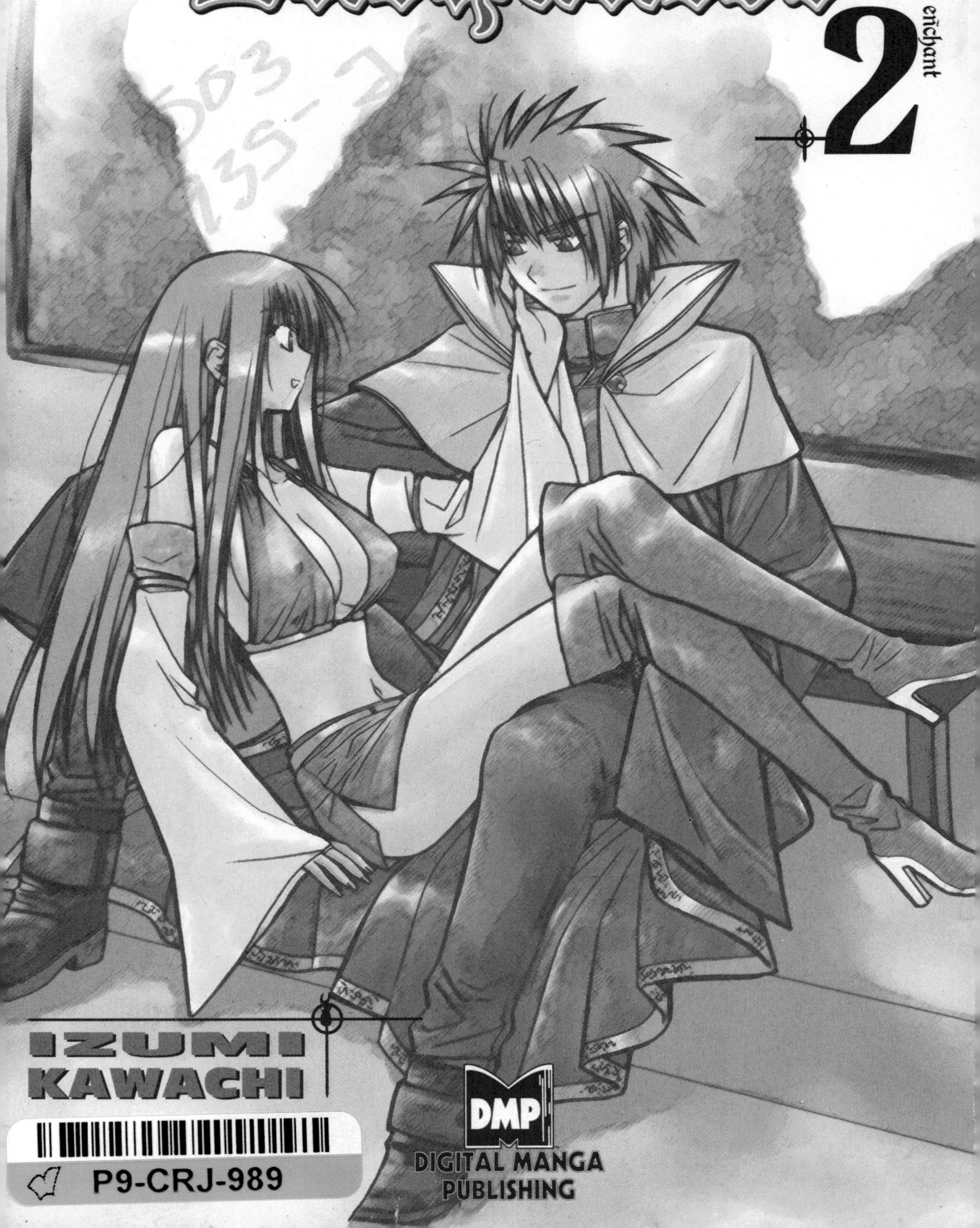

IZUMI KAWACHI

DMP

DIGITAL MANGA PUBLISHING

CONTENTS

Translation	Sachiko Sato
Lettering	IHL
Graphic Design	Fred Lui / Wendy Lee
Editing	Stephanie Donnelly
Editor in Chief	Fred Lui
Publisher	Hikaru Sasahara

English Edition Published by
DIGITAL MANGA PUBLISHING
A division of DIGITAL MANGA, Inc.
1487 W 178th Street, Suite 300
Gardena, CA 90248

www.dmpbooks.com

First Edition: November 2006
ISBN-10: 1-56970-865-7
ISBN-13: 978-1-56970-865-1

1 3 5 7 9 10 8 6 4 2

Printed in China

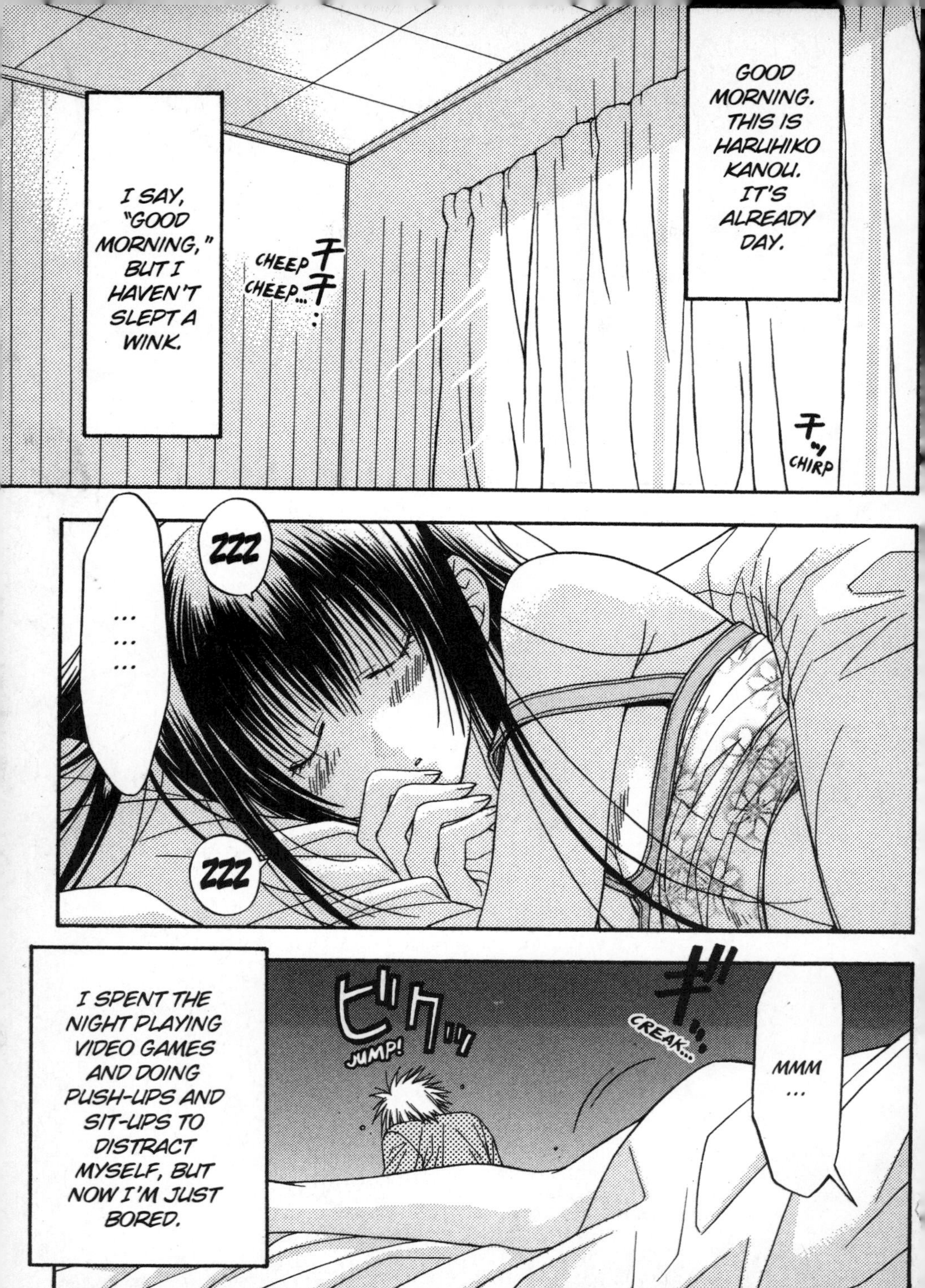
GOOD MORNING. THIS IS HARUHIKO KANOU. IT'S ALREADY DAY.
CHEEP CHEEP...
I SAY, "GOOD MORNING," BUT I HAVEN'T SLEPT A WINK.
CHIRP
ZZZ
...
...
...
ZZZ
MMM ...
CREAK...
JUMP!
I SPENT THE NIGHT PLAYING VIDEO GAMES AND DOING PUSH-UPS AND SIT-UPS TO DISTRACT MYSELF, BUT NOW I'M JUST BORED.

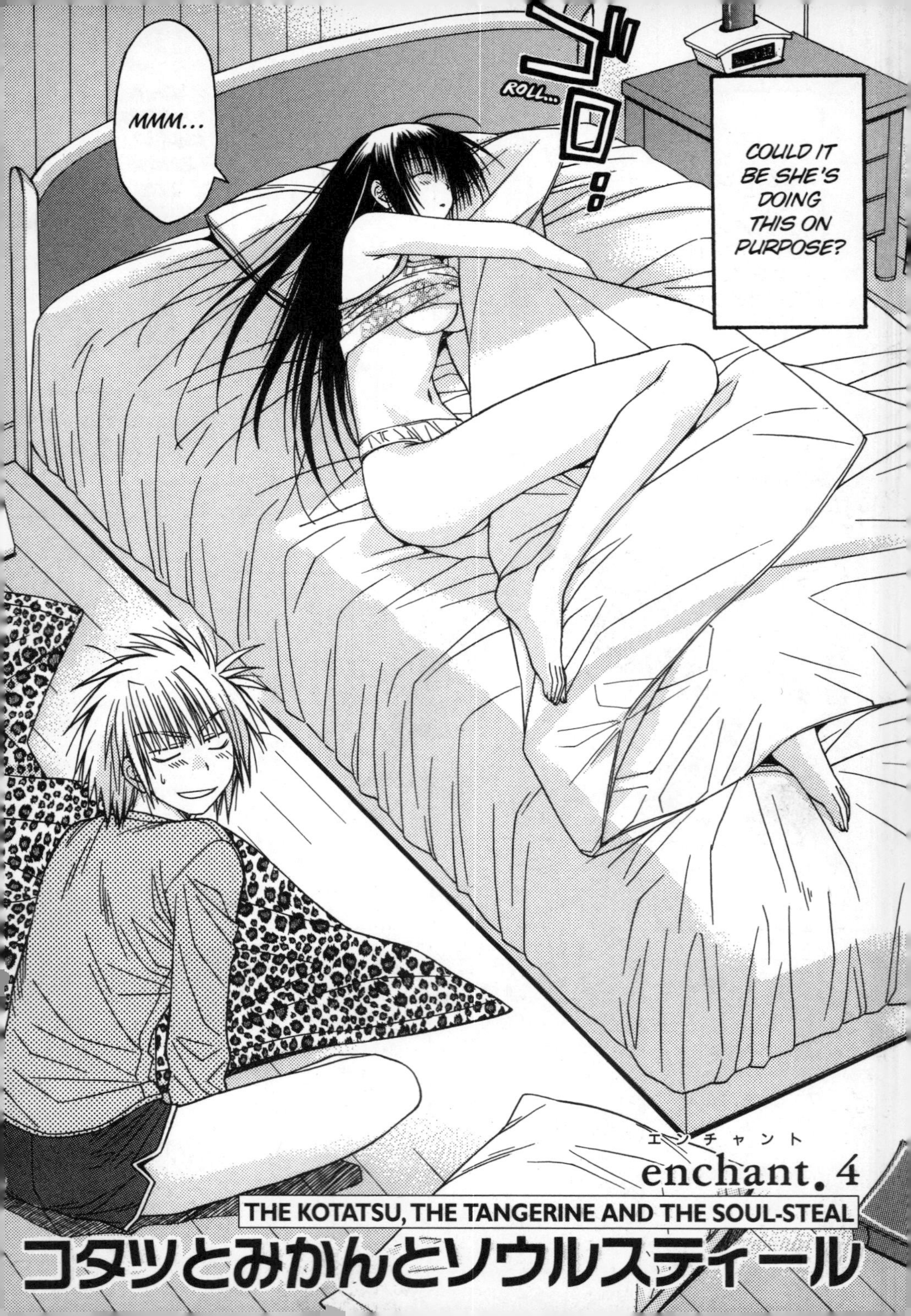
COULD IT BE SHE'S DOING THIS ON PURPOSE?
ゴロ
ROLL...
MMM...
エンチャント
enchant. 4
THE KOTATSU, THE TANGERINE AND THE SOUL-STEAL
コタツとみかんとソウルスティール

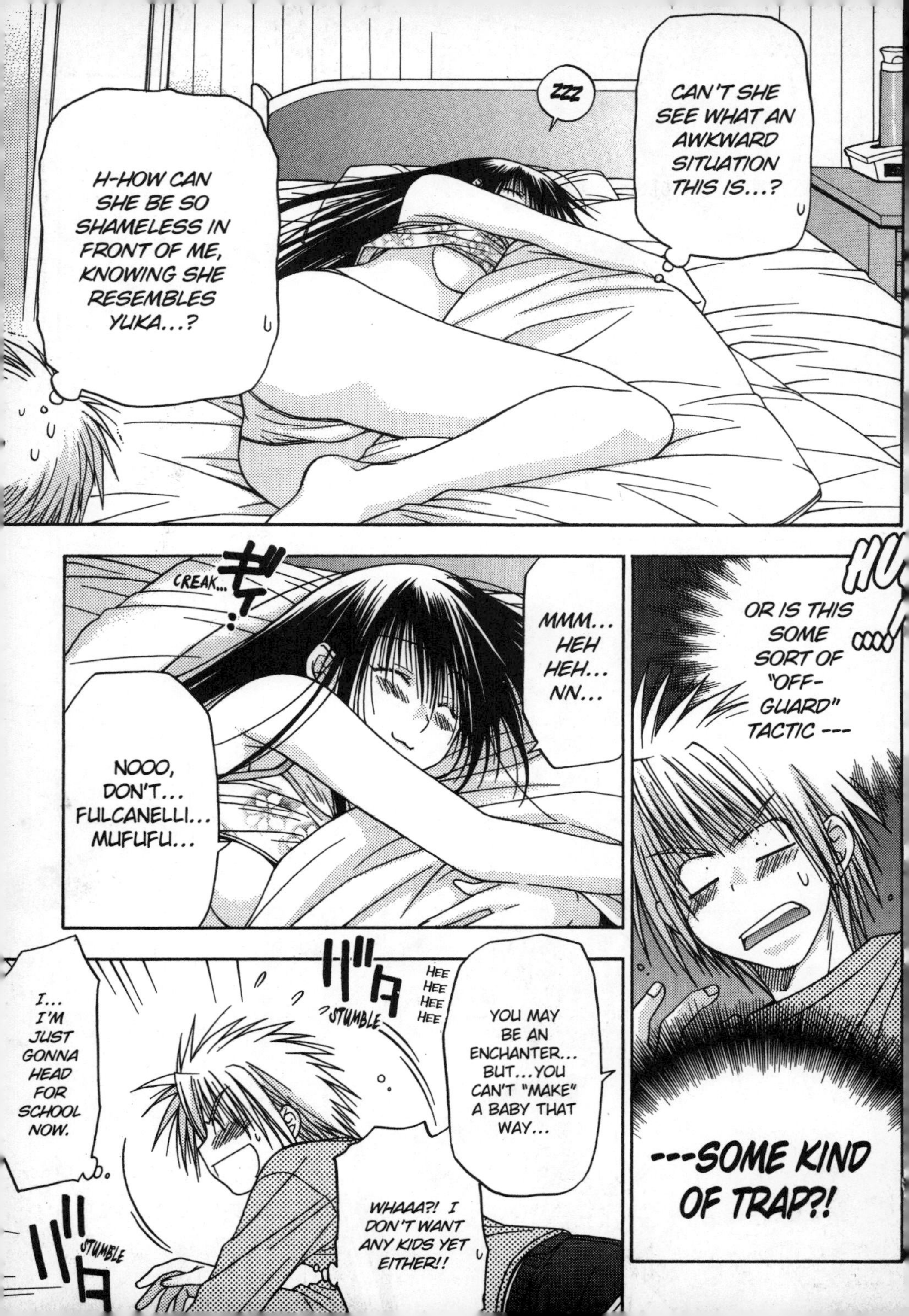

CAN'T SHE SEE WHAT AN AWKWARD SITUATION THIS IS...?
ZZZ
H-HOW CAN SHE BE SO SHAMELESS IN FRONT OF ME, KNOWING SHE RESEMBLES YUKA...?
OR IS THIS SOME SORT OF "OFF-GUARD" TACTIC ---
---SOME KIND OF TRAP?!
CREAK...
MMM... HEH HEH... NN...
NOOO, DON'T... FULCANELLI... MUFUFU...
HEE HEE HEE HEE
YOU MAY BE AN ENCHANTER... BUT...YOU CAN'T "MAKE" A BABY THAT WAY...
STUMBLE
I... I'M JUST GONNA HEAD FOR SCHOOL NOW.
WHAAA?! I DON'T WANT ANY KIDS YET EITHER!!
STUMBLE

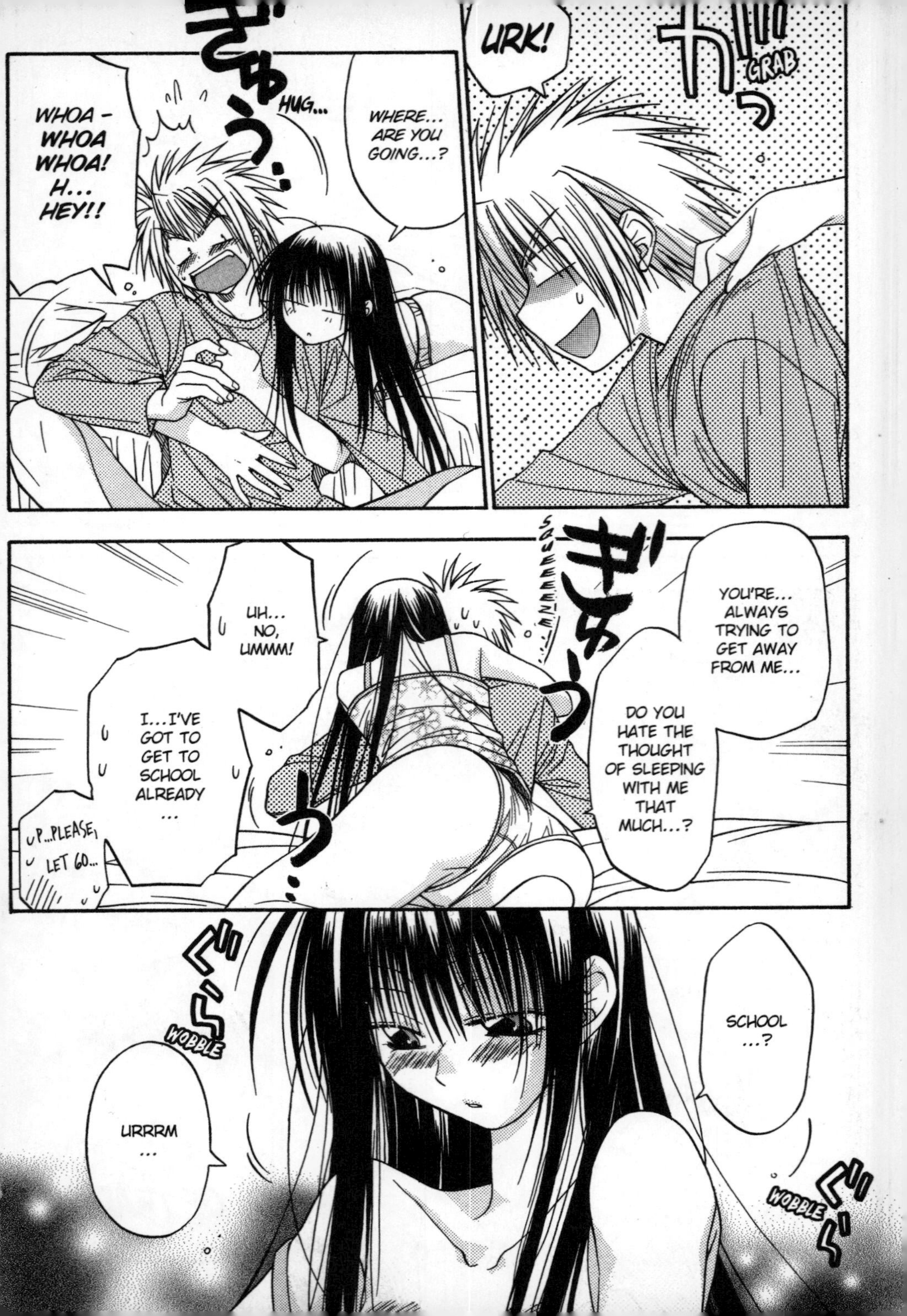
URK!
GRAB
WHERE... ARE YOU GOING...?
HUG...
WHOA - WHOA WHOA! H... HEY!!
YOU'RE... ALWAYS TRYING TO GET AWAY FROM ME...
DO YOU HATE THE THOUGHT OF SLEEPING WITH ME THAT MUCH...?
SQUEEEEZE!!
UH... NO, UMMM!
I...I'VE GOT TO GET TO SCHOOL ALREADY ...
P...PLEASE, LET GO...
SCHOOL ...?
WOBBLE
URRRM ...
WOBBLE

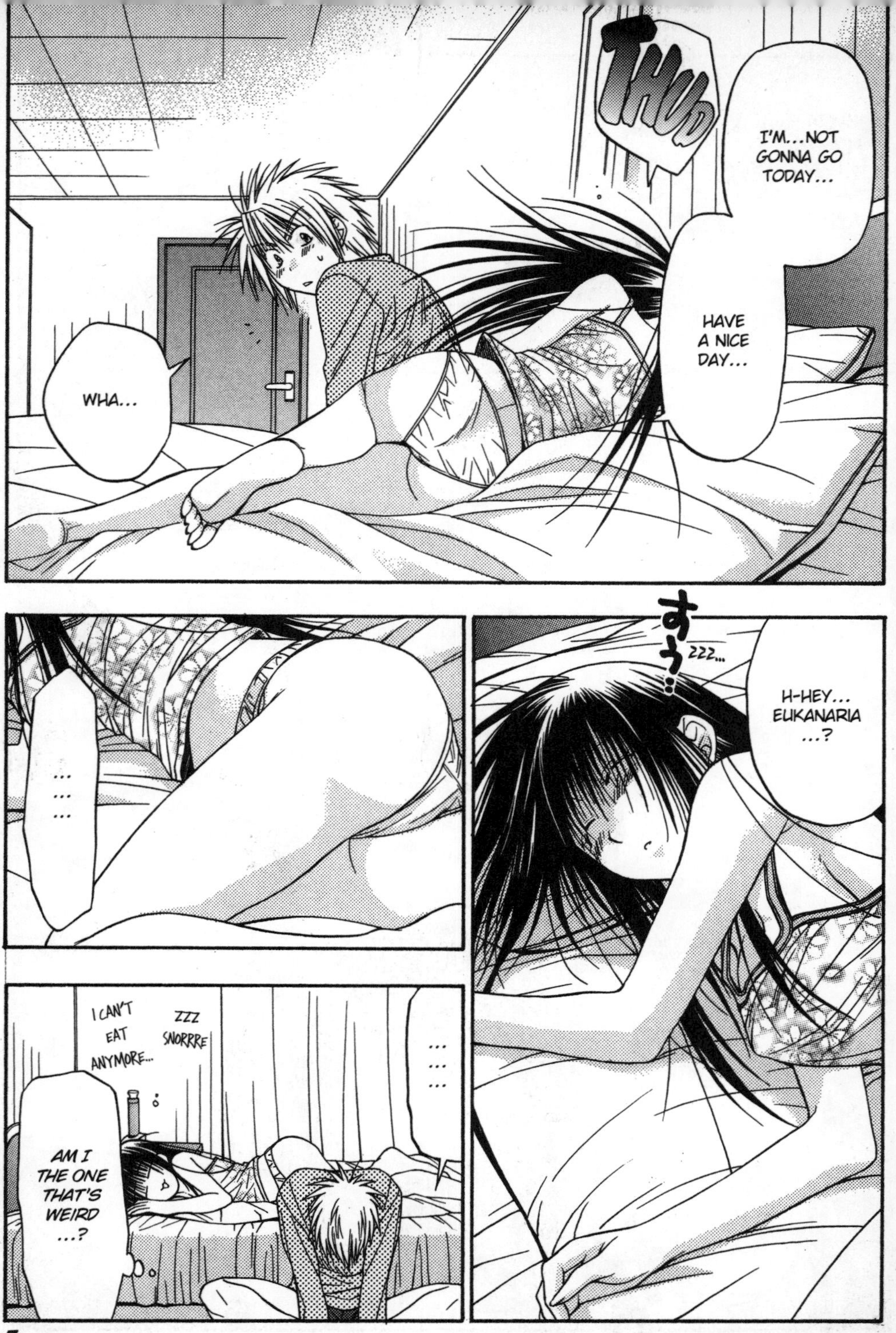
THUD
I'M...NOT GONNA GO TODAY...
HAVE A NICE DAY...
WHA...
すう
ZZZ...
H-HEY... EUKANARIA ...?
... ...
... ...
ZZZ SNORRRE
I CAN'T EAT ANYMORE...
AM I THE ONE THAT'S WEIRD ...?

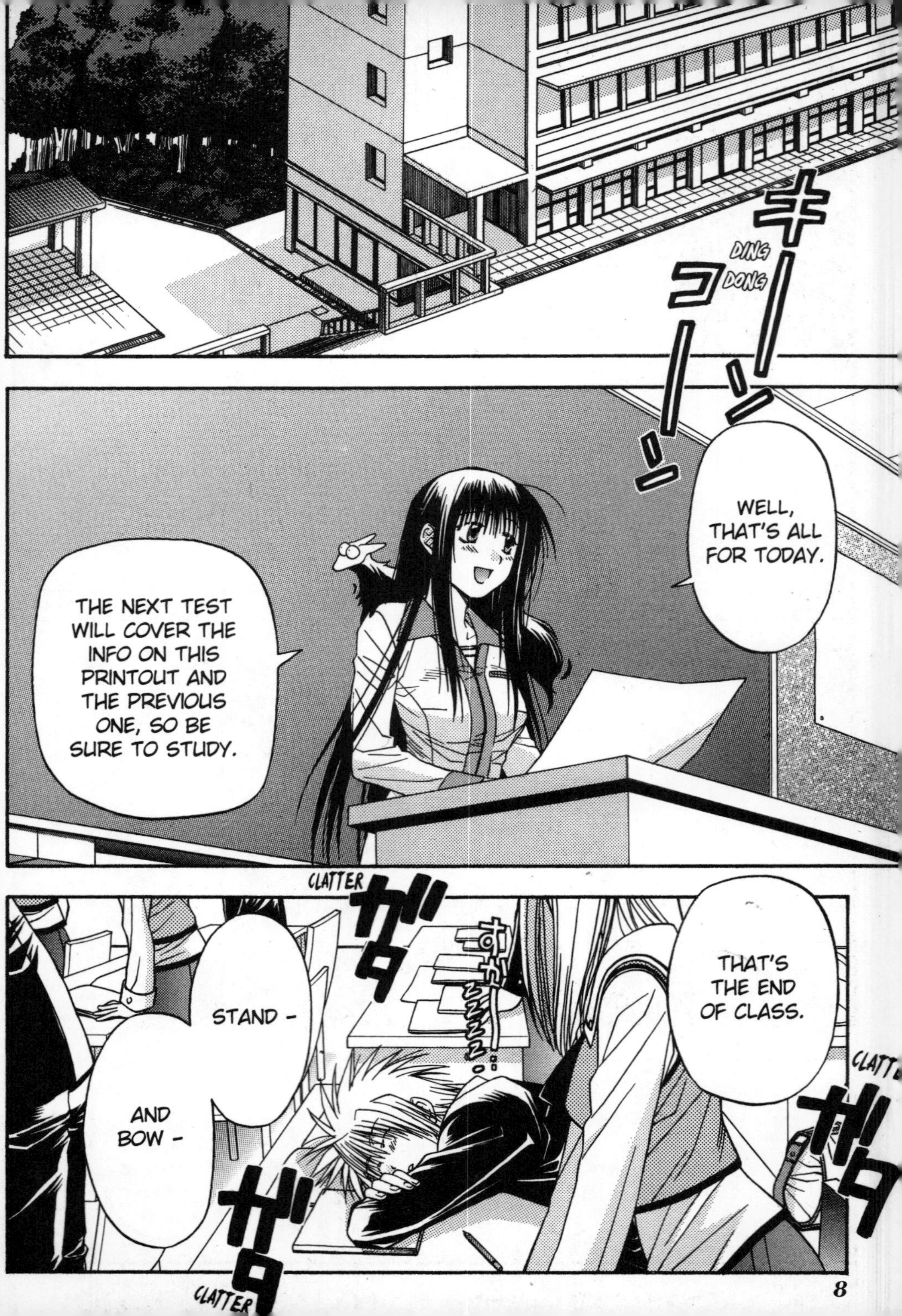
DING
DONG
WELL, THAT'S ALL FOR TODAY.
THE NEXT TEST WILL COVER THE INFO ON THIS PRINTOUT AND THE PREVIOUS ONE, SO BE SURE TO STUDY.
THAT'S THE END OF CLASS.
CLATTER
CLATTER
STAND -
AND BOW -
CLATTER

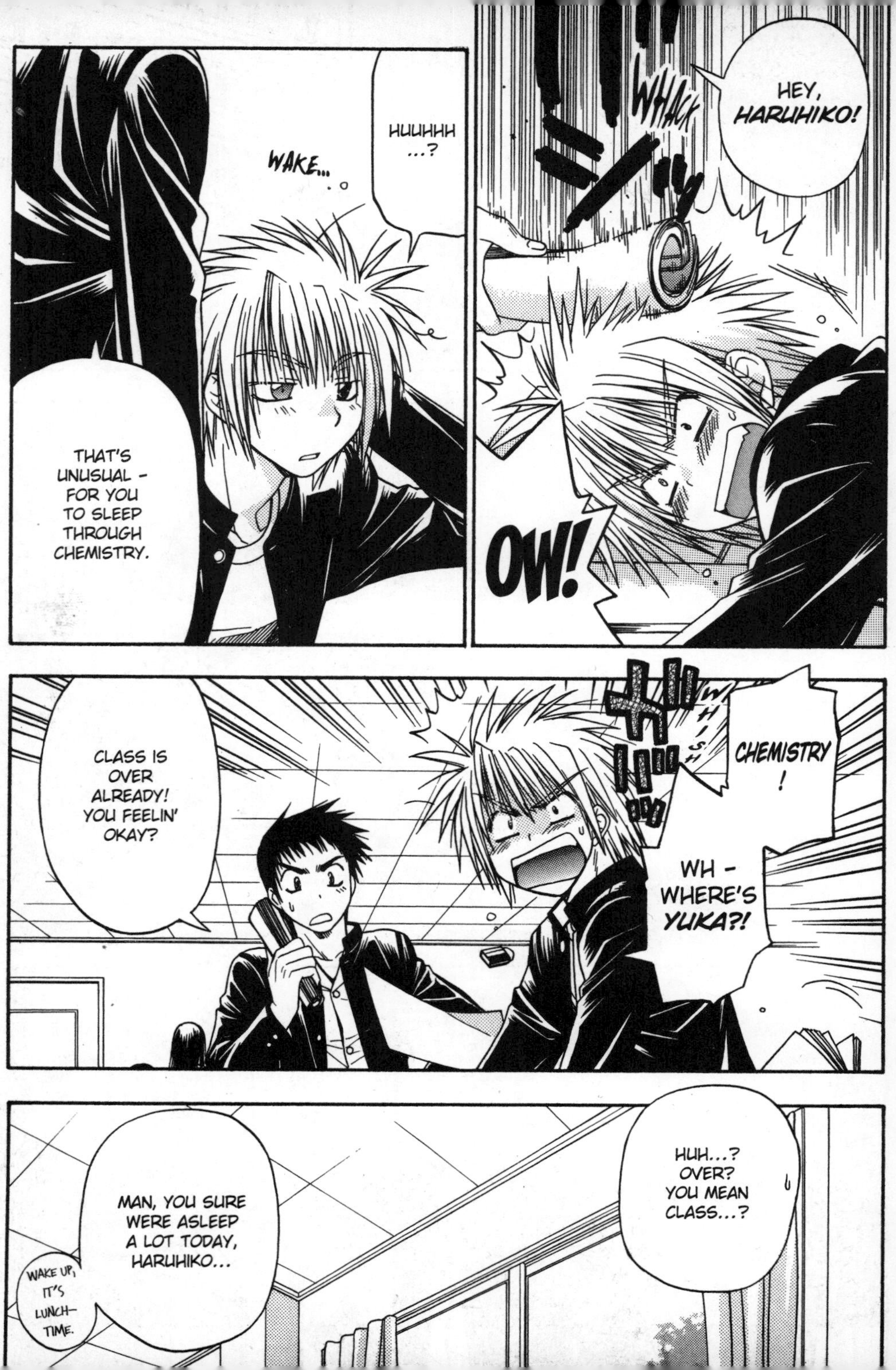
HEY, HARUHIKO!
WHACK
OW!
HUUHHH ...?
WAKE...
THAT'S UNUSUAL - FOR YOU TO SLEEP THROUGH CHEMISTRY.
CHEMISTRY !
WHISH
WH - WHERE'S YUKA?!
CLASS IS OVER ALREADY! YOU FEELIN' OKAY?
HUH...? OVER? YOU MEAN CLASS...?
MAN, YOU SURE WERE ASLEEP A LOT TODAY, HARUHIKO...
WAKE UP, IT'S LUNCH-TIME.

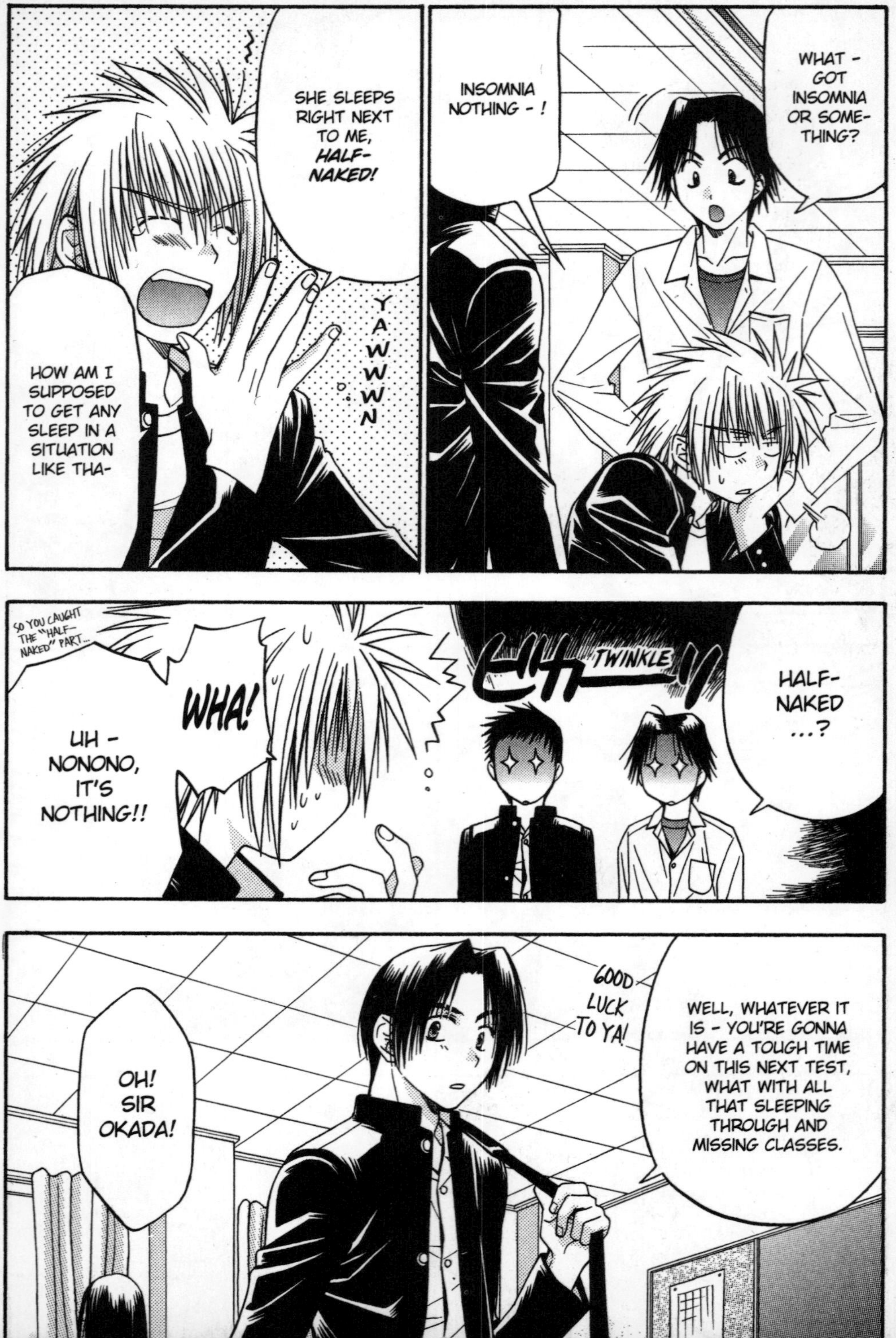
WHAT - GOT INSOMNIA OR SOMETHING?
INSOMNIA NOTHING - !
SHE SLEEPS RIGHT NEXT TO ME, HALF-NAKED!
YAWWWN
HOW AM I SUPPOSED TO GET ANY SLEEP IN A SITUATION LIKE THA-
HALF-NAKED ...?
TWINKLE
SO YOU CAUGHT THE "HALF-NAKED" PART...
WHA!
UH - NONONO, IT'S NOTHING!!
WELL, WHATEVER IT IS - YOU'RE GONNA HAVE A TOUGH TIME ON THIS NEXT TEST, WHAT WITH ALL THAT SLEEPING THROUGH AND MISSING CLASSES.
GOOD LUCK TO YA!
OH! SIR OKADA!

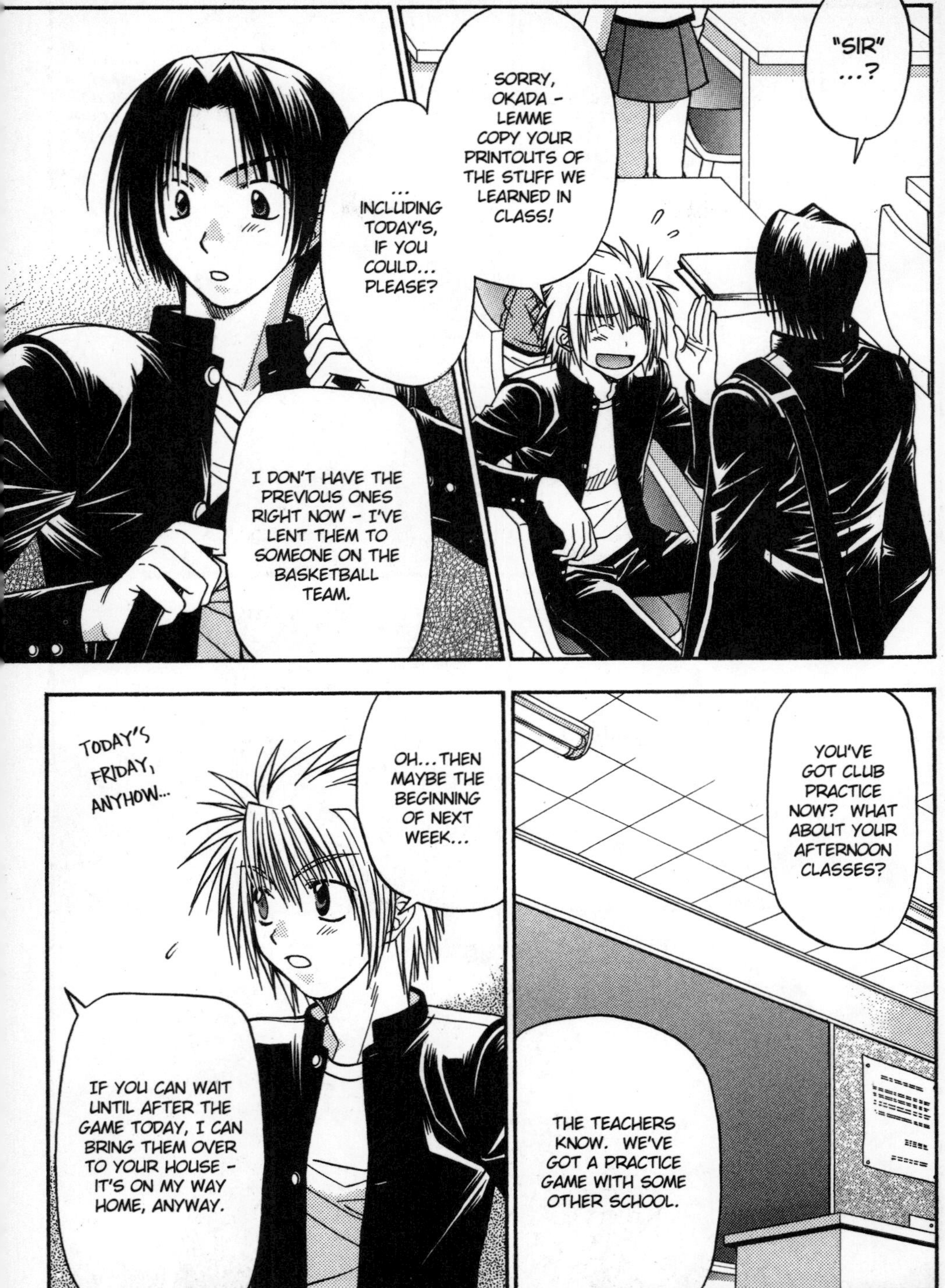
"SIR" ...?
SORRY, OKADA - LEMME COPY YOUR PRINTOUTS OF THE STUFF WE LEARNED IN CLASS!
... INCLUDING TODAY'S, IF YOU COULD... PLEASE?
I DON'T HAVE THE PREVIOUS ONES RIGHT NOW - I'VE LENT THEM TO SOMEONE ON THE BASKETBALL TEAM.
YOU'VE GOT CLUB PRACTICE NOW? WHAT ABOUT YOUR AFTERNOON CLASSES?
THE TEACHERS KNOW. WE'VE GOT A PRACTICE GAME WITH SOME OTHER SCHOOL.
OH...THEN MAYBE THE BEGINNING OF NEXT WEEK...
TODAY'S FRIDAY, ANYHOW...
IF YOU CAN WAIT UNTIL AFTER THE GAME TODAY, I CAN BRING THEM OVER TO YOUR HOUSE - IT'S ON MY WAY HOME, ANYWAY.

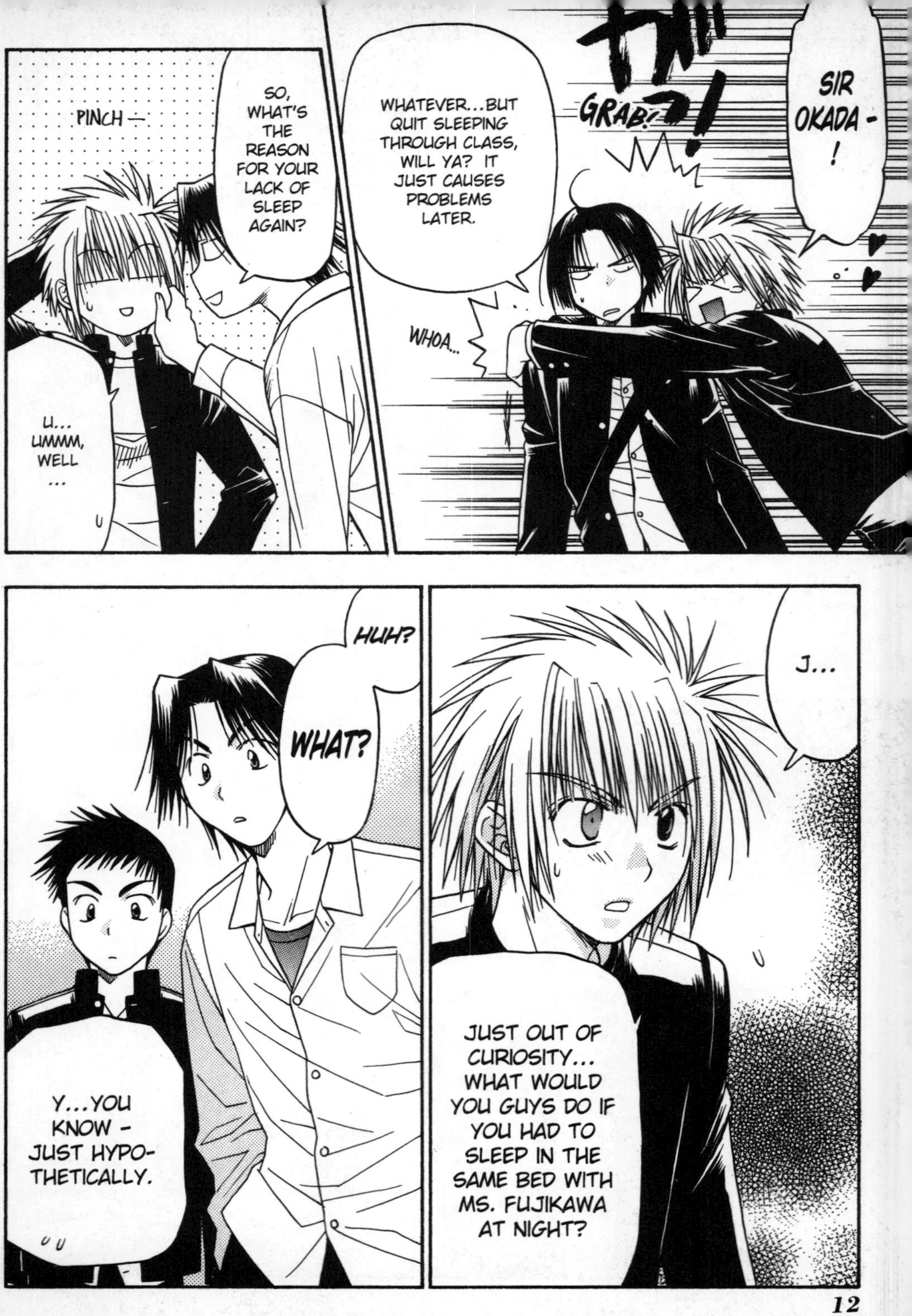
SIR OKADA - !
GRAB!
WHATEVER...BUT QUIT SLEEPING THROUGH CLASS, WILL YA? IT JUST CAUSES PROBLEMS LATER.
WHOA...
SO, WHAT'S THE REASON FOR YOUR LACK OF SLEEP AGAIN?
PINCH —
U... UMMM, WELL ...
J...
JUST OUT OF CURIOSITY... WHAT WOULD YOU GUYS DO IF YOU HAD TO SLEEP IN THE SAME BED WITH MS. FUJIKAWA AT NIGHT?
HUH?
WHAT?
Y...YOU KNOW - JUST HYPO-THETICALLY.

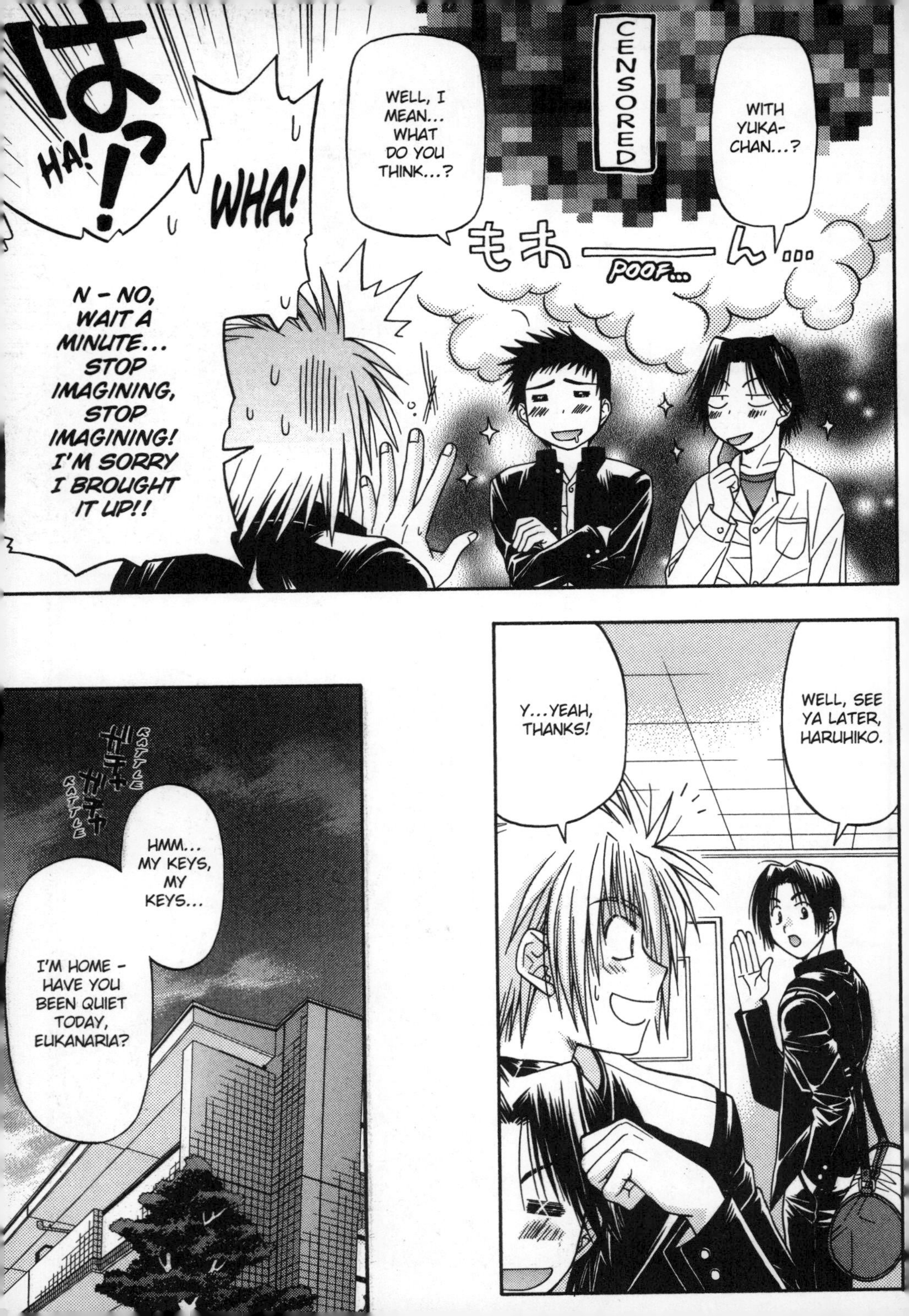
CENSORED
WITH YUKA-CHAN...?
WELL, I MEAN... WHAT DO YOU THINK...?
もわーーん...
POOF...
はっ!
HA!
WHA!
N - NO, WAIT A MINUTE... STOP IMAGINING, STOP IMAGINING! I'M SORRY I BROUGHT IT UP!!
WELL, SEE YA LATER, HARUHIKO.
Y...YEAH, THANKS!
ガチャ ガチャ
RATTLE RATTLE
HMM... MY KEYS, MY KEYS...
I'M HOME - HAVE YOU BEEN QUIET TODAY, EUKANARIA?

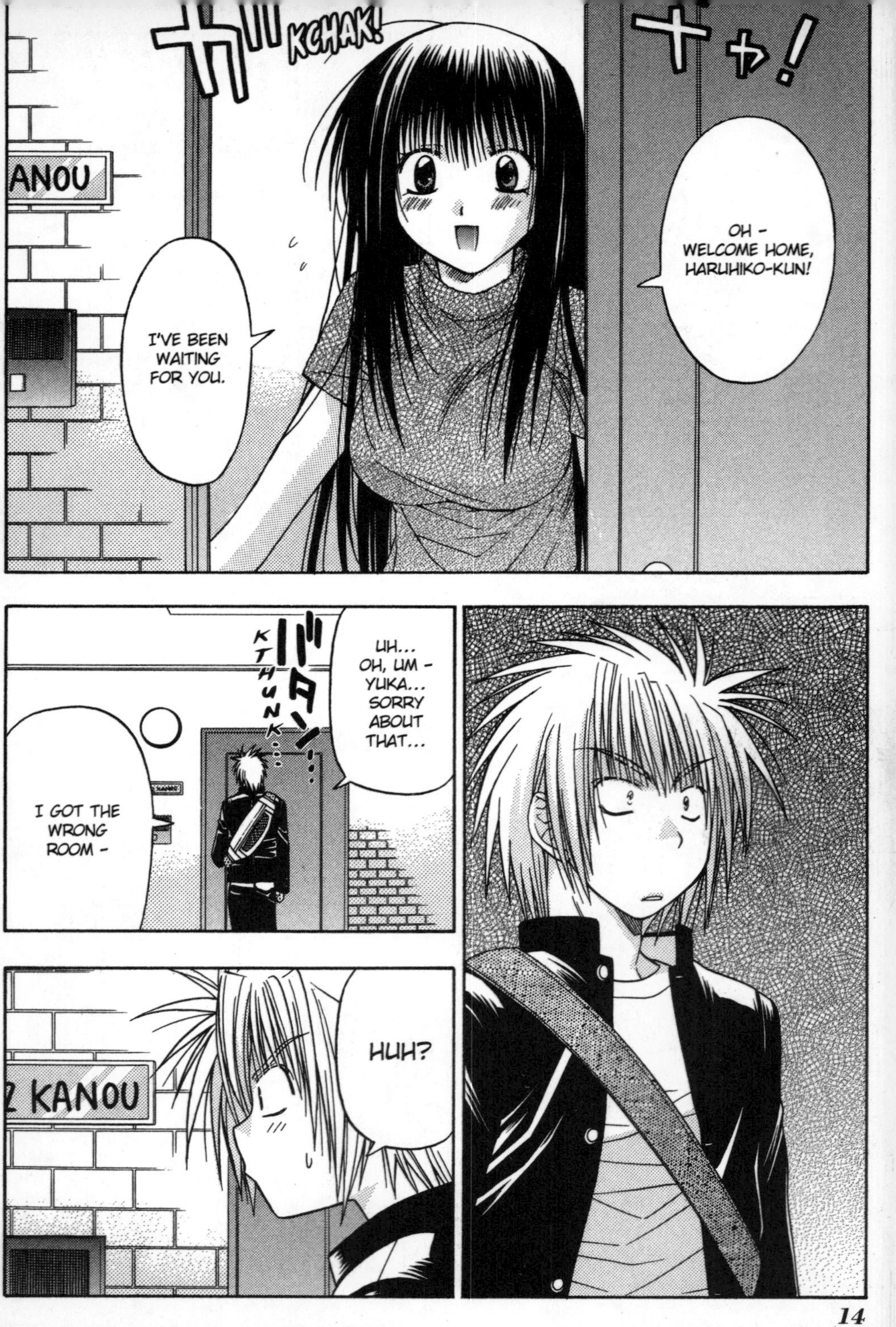
KCHAK!
OH - WELCOME HOME, HARUHIKO-KUN!
ANOU
I'VE BEEN WAITING FOR YOU.
UH... OH, UM - YUKA... SORRY ABOUT THAT...
KTHUNK
I GOT THE WRONG ROOM -
HUH?
2 KANOU

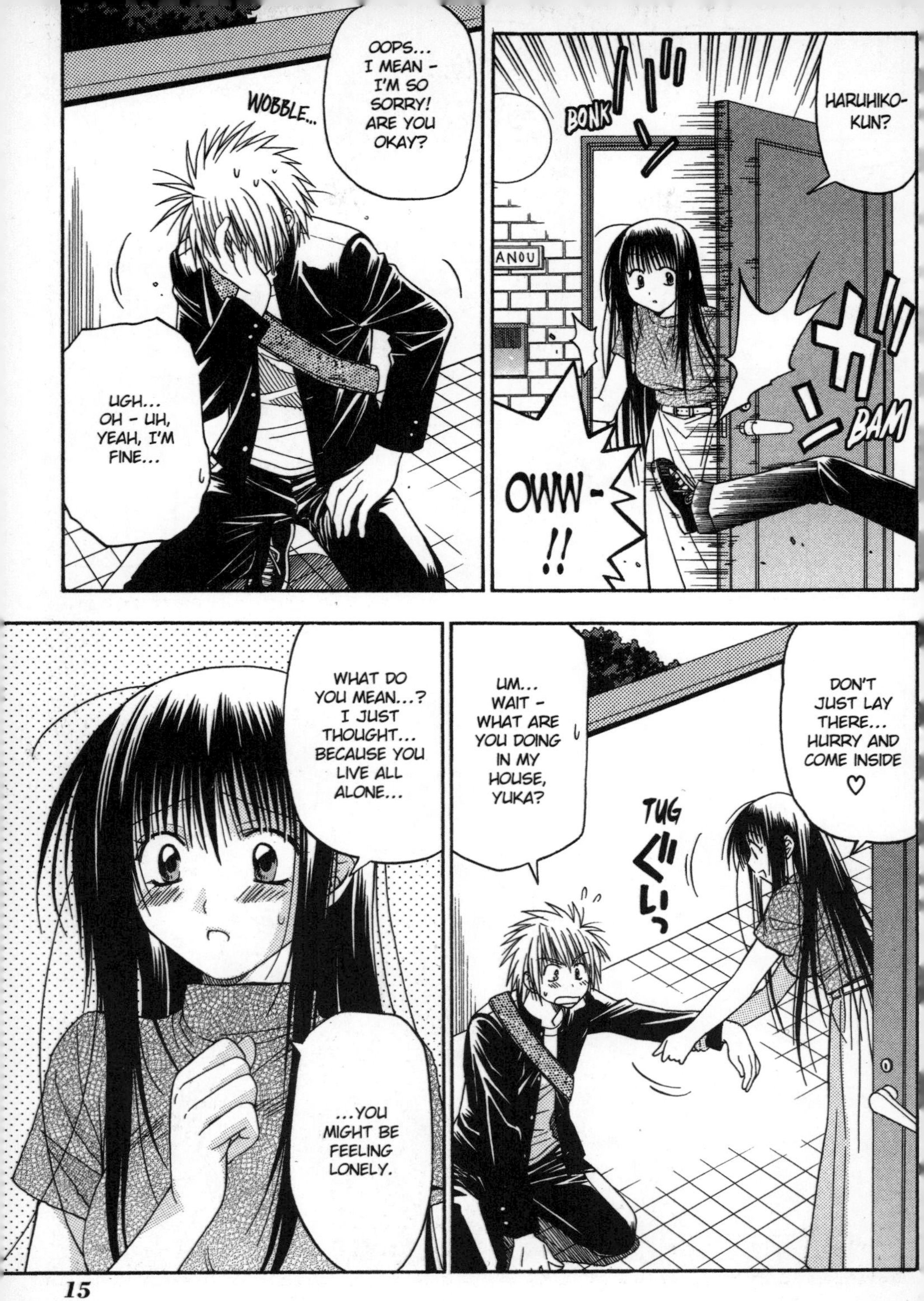
HARUHIKO-KUN?
BONK
ANOU
BAM
OWW- !!
OOPS... I MEAN - I'M SO SORRY! ARE YOU OKAY?
WOBBLE...
UGH... OH - UH, YEAH, I'M FINE...
DON'T JUST LAY THERE... HURRY AND COME INSIDE ♡
UM... WAIT - WHAT ARE YOU DOING IN MY HOUSE, YUKA?
TUG
ぐいっ
WHAT DO YOU MEAN...? I JUST THOUGHT... BECAUSE YOU LIVE ALL ALONE...
...YOU MIGHT BE FEELING LONELY.

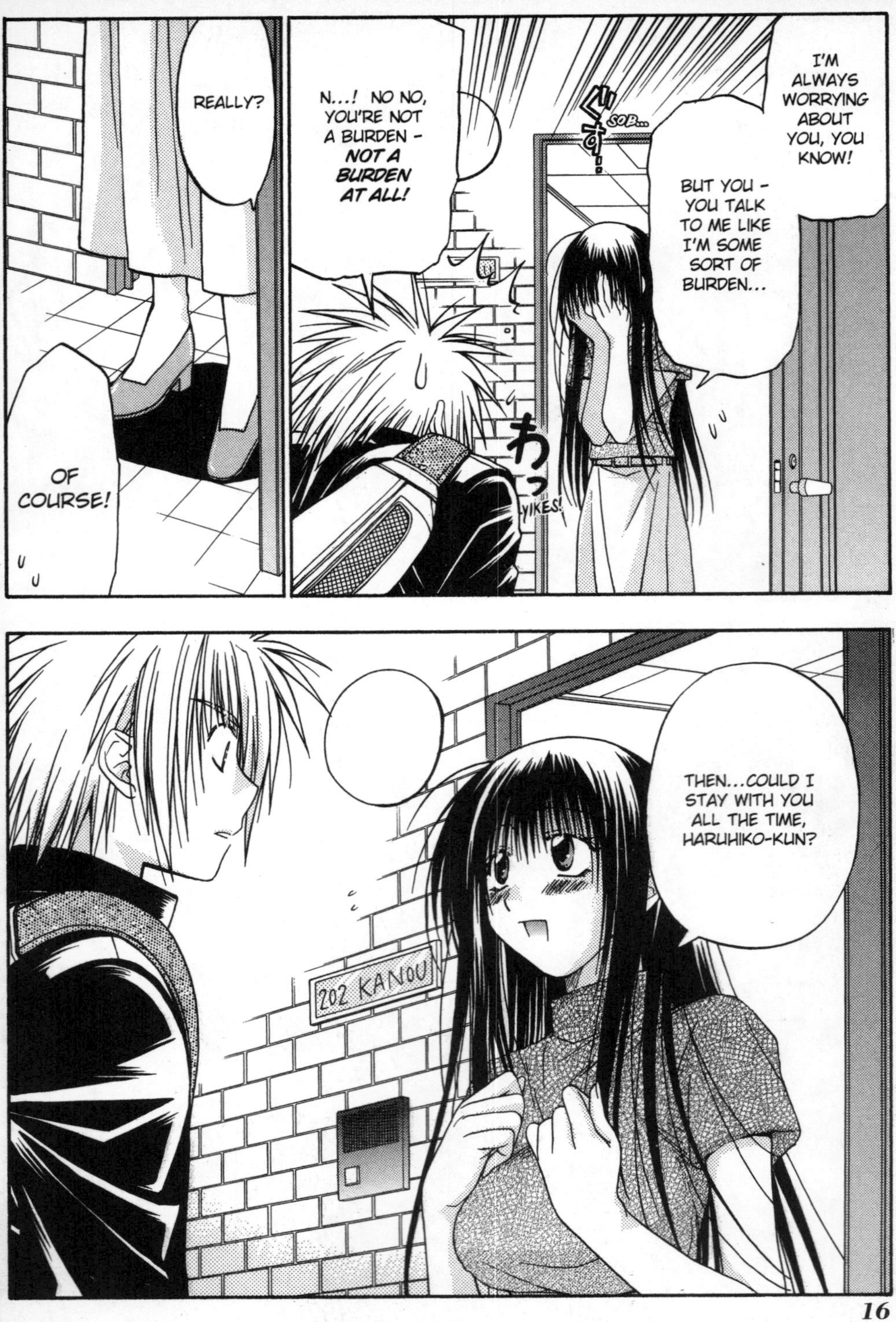

I'M ALWAYS WORRYING ABOUT YOU, YOU KNOW!
SOB...
BUT YOU - YOU TALK TO ME LIKE I'M SOME SORT OF BURDEN...
YIKES!
N...! NO NO, YOU'RE NOT A BURDEN - NOT A BURDEN AT ALL!
REALLY?
OF COURSE!
THEN...COULD I STAY WITH YOU ALL THE TIME, HARUHIKO-KUN?
202 KANOU

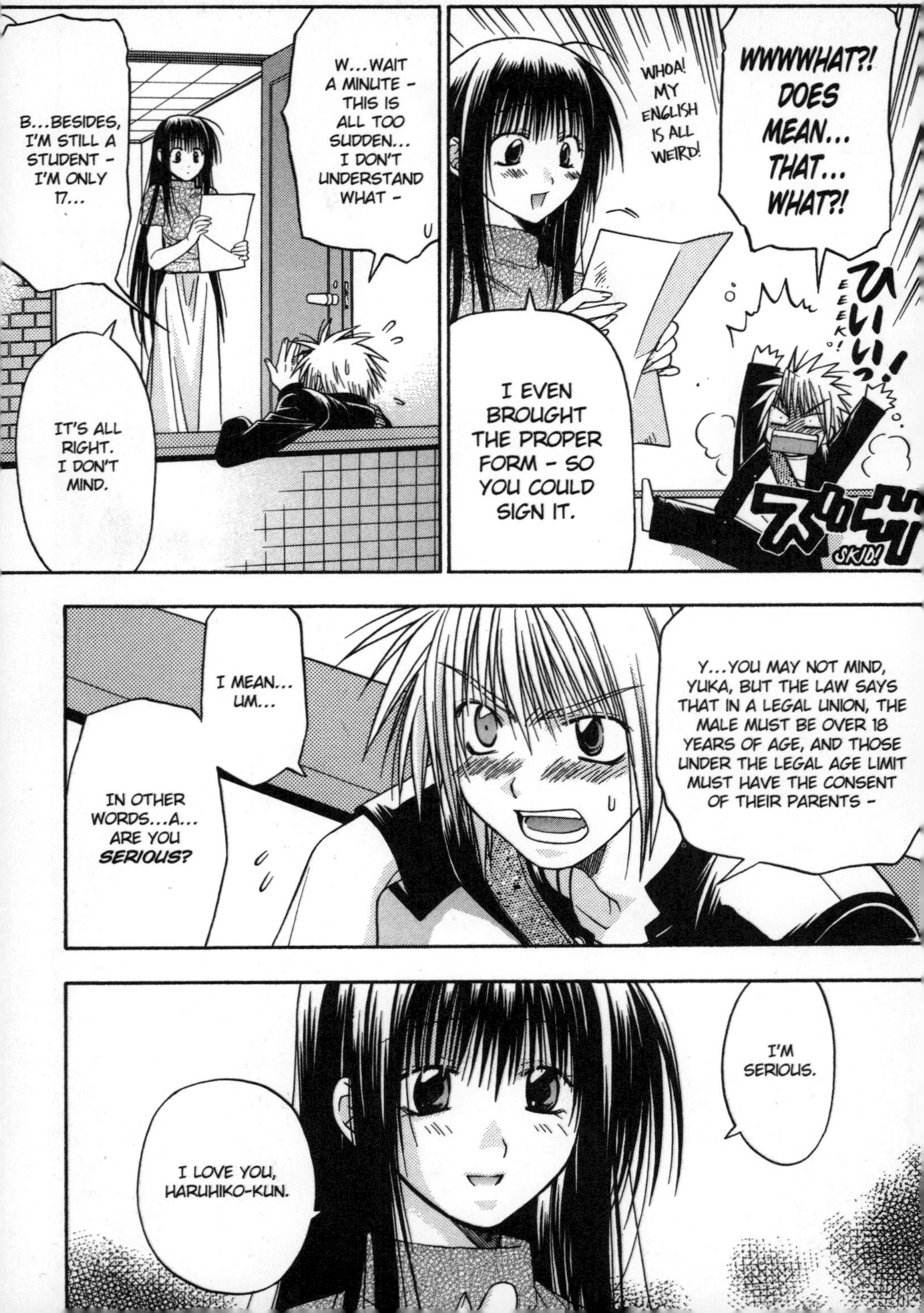
WWWWHAT?! DOES MEAN... THAT... WHAT?!
WHOA! MY ENGLISH IS ALL WEIRD!
I EVEN BROUGHT THE PROPER FORM - SO YOU COULD SIGN IT.
EEEEK!
SKID!
W...WAIT A MINUTE - THIS IS ALL TOO SUDDEN... I DON'T UNDERSTAND WHAT -
B...BESIDES, I'M STILL A STUDENT - I'M ONLY 17...
IT'S ALL RIGHT. I DON'T MIND.
Y...YOU MAY NOT MIND, YUKA, BUT THE LAW SAYS THAT IN A LEGAL UNION, THE MALE MUST BE OVER 18 YEARS OF AGE, AND THOSE UNDER THE LEGAL AGE LIMIT MUST HAVE THE CONSENT OF THEIR PARENTS -
I MEAN... UM...
IN OTHER WORDS...A... ARE YOU SERIOUS?
I'M SERIOUS.
I LOVE YOU, HARUHIKO-KUN.

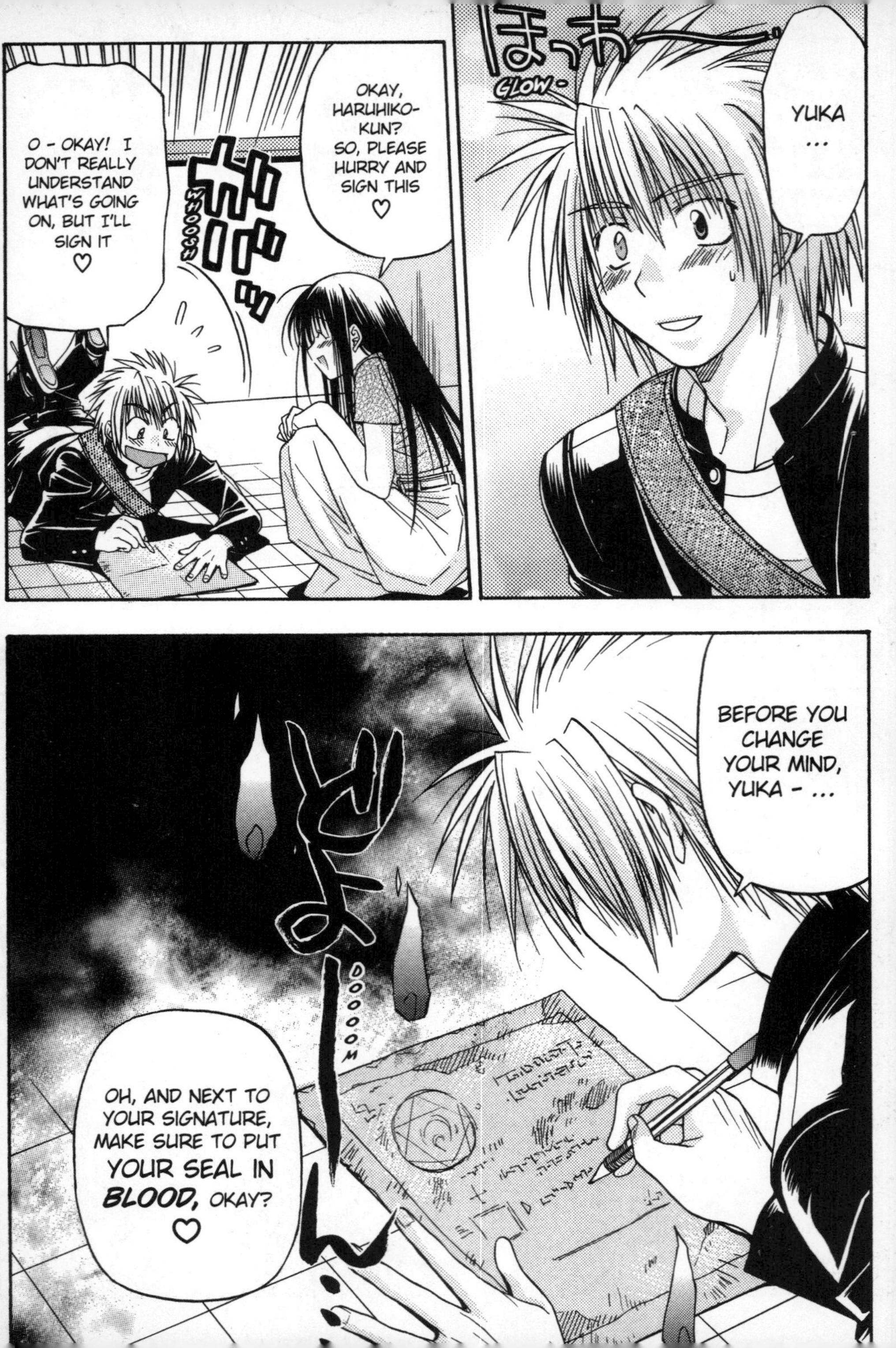
GLOW
YUKA ...
OKAY, HARUHIKO-KUN? SO, PLEASE HURRY AND SIGN THIS ♡
WHOOSH
O - OKAY! I DON'T REALLY UNDERSTAND WHAT'S GOING ON, BUT I'LL SIGN IT ♡
BEFORE YOU CHANGE YOUR MIND, YUKA - ...
DOOOOOM
OH, AND NEXT TO YOUR SIGNATURE, MAKE SURE TO PUT YOUR SEAL IN BLOOD, OKAY? ♡

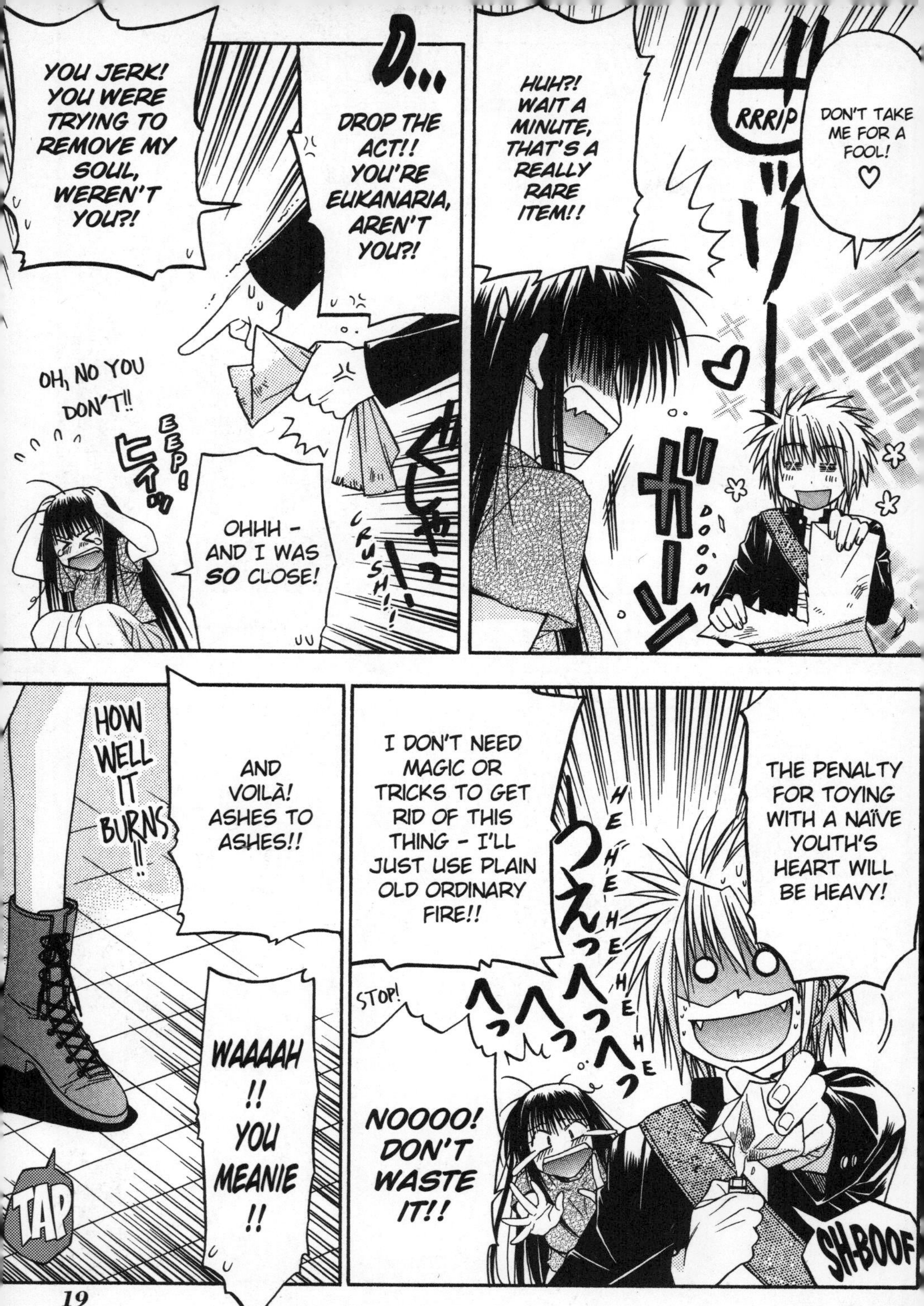
DON'T TAKE ME FOR A FOOL! ♡
RRRIP
HUH?! WAIT A MINUTE, THAT'S A REALLY RARE ITEM!!
DOOOOM
D...
DROP THE ACT!! YOU'RE EUKANARIA, AREN'T YOU?!
YOU JERK! YOU WERE TRYING TO REMOVE MY SOUL, WEREN'T YOU?!
OH, NO YOU DON'T!!
EEP!
OHHH - AND I WAS SO CLOSE!
CRUSH!!
THE PENALTY FOR TOYING WITH A NAÏVE YOUTH'S HEART WILL BE HEAVY!
I DON'T NEED MAGIC OR TRICKS TO GET RID OF THIS THING - I'LL JUST USE PLAIN OLD ORDINARY FIRE!!
HEHEHEHEHEHE
STOP!
NOOOO! DON'T WASTE IT!!
SH-BOOF
AND VOILÀ! ASHES TO ASHES!!
HOW WELL IT BURNS!!
WAAAAH!! YOU MEANIE!!
TAP

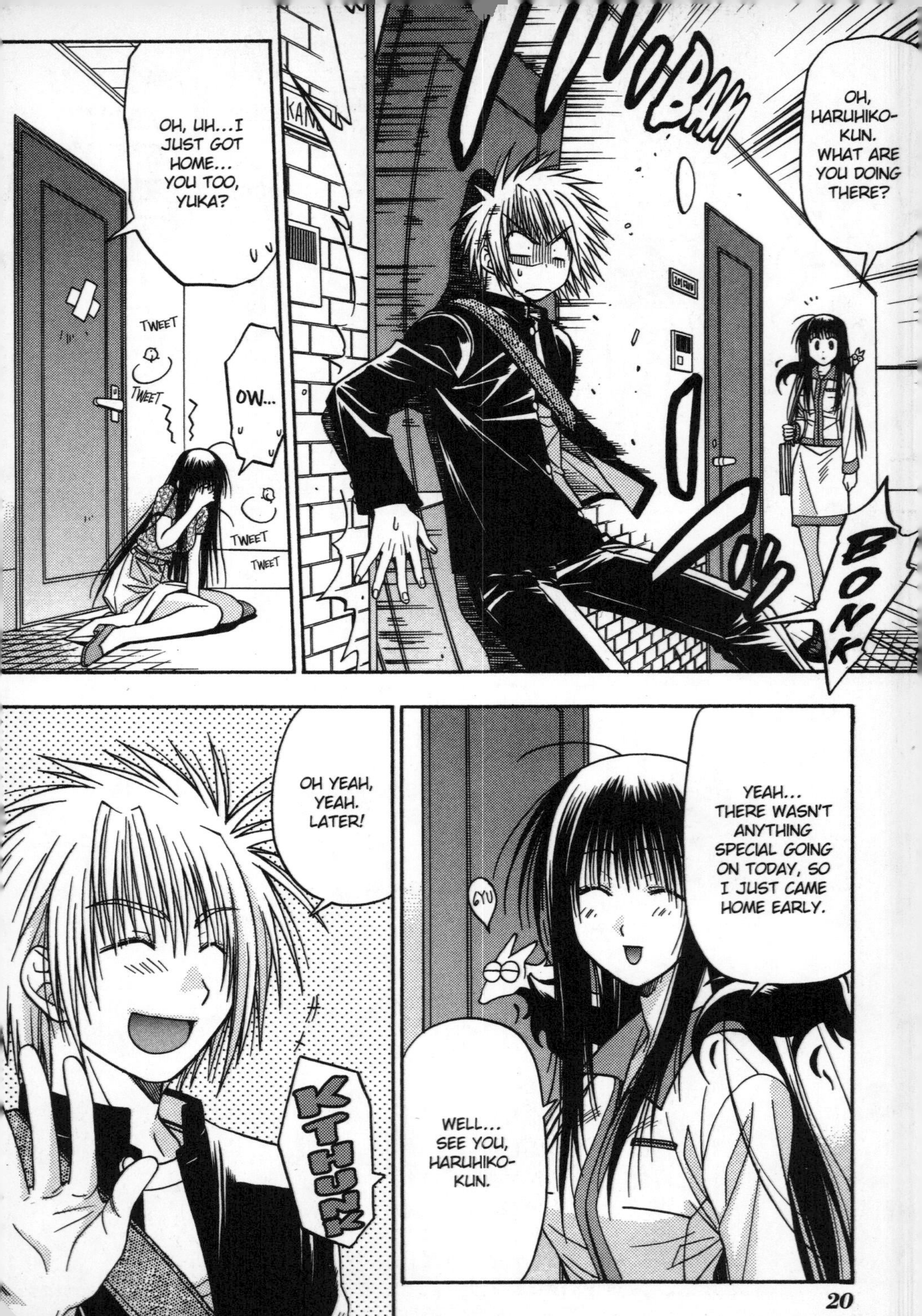
OH, HARUHIKO-KUN. WHAT ARE YOU DOING THERE?
BAM
BONK
OH, UH...I JUST GOT HOME... YOU TOO, YUKA?
TWEET
TWEET
OW...
TWEET
TWEET
YEAH... THERE WASN'T ANYTHING SPECIAL GOING ON TODAY, SO I JUST CAME HOME EARLY.
GYU
WELL... SEE YOU, HARUHIKO-KUN.
OH YEAH, YEAH. LATER!
KTHUNK

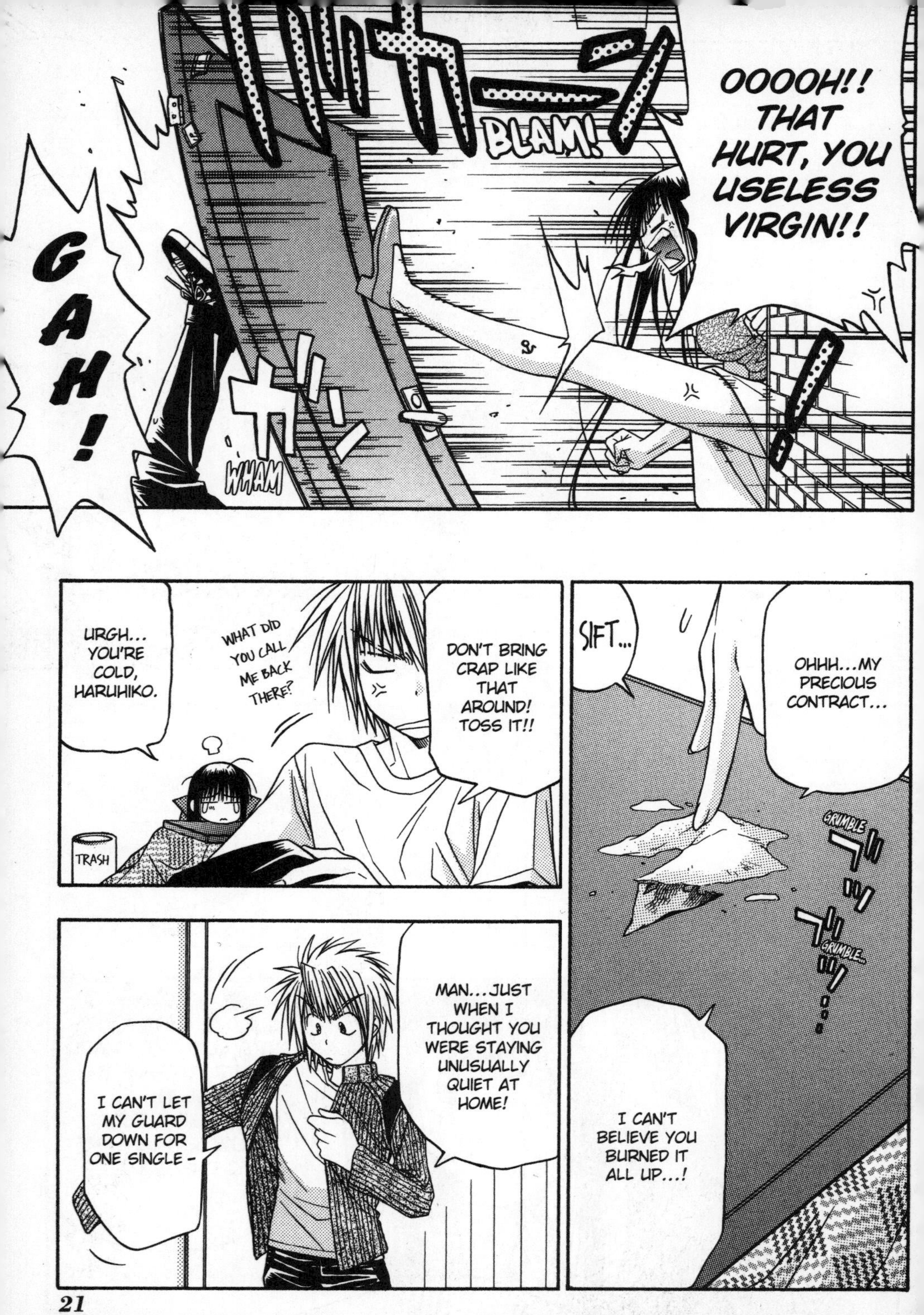
OOOOH!! THAT HURT, YOU USELESS VIRGIN!!
BLAM!
GAH!
WHAM
OHHH...MY PRECIOUS CONTRACT...
SIFT...
GRUMBLE
GRUMBLE...
I CAN'T BELIEVE YOU BURNED IT ALL UP...!
DON'T BRING CRAP LIKE THAT AROUND! TOSS IT!!
WHAT DID YOU CALL ME BACK THERE?
URGH... YOU'RE COLD, HARUHIKO.
TRASH
MAN...JUST WHEN I THOUGHT YOU WERE STAYING UNUSUALLY QUIET AT HOME!
I CAN'T LET MY GUARD DOWN FOR ONE SINGLE-

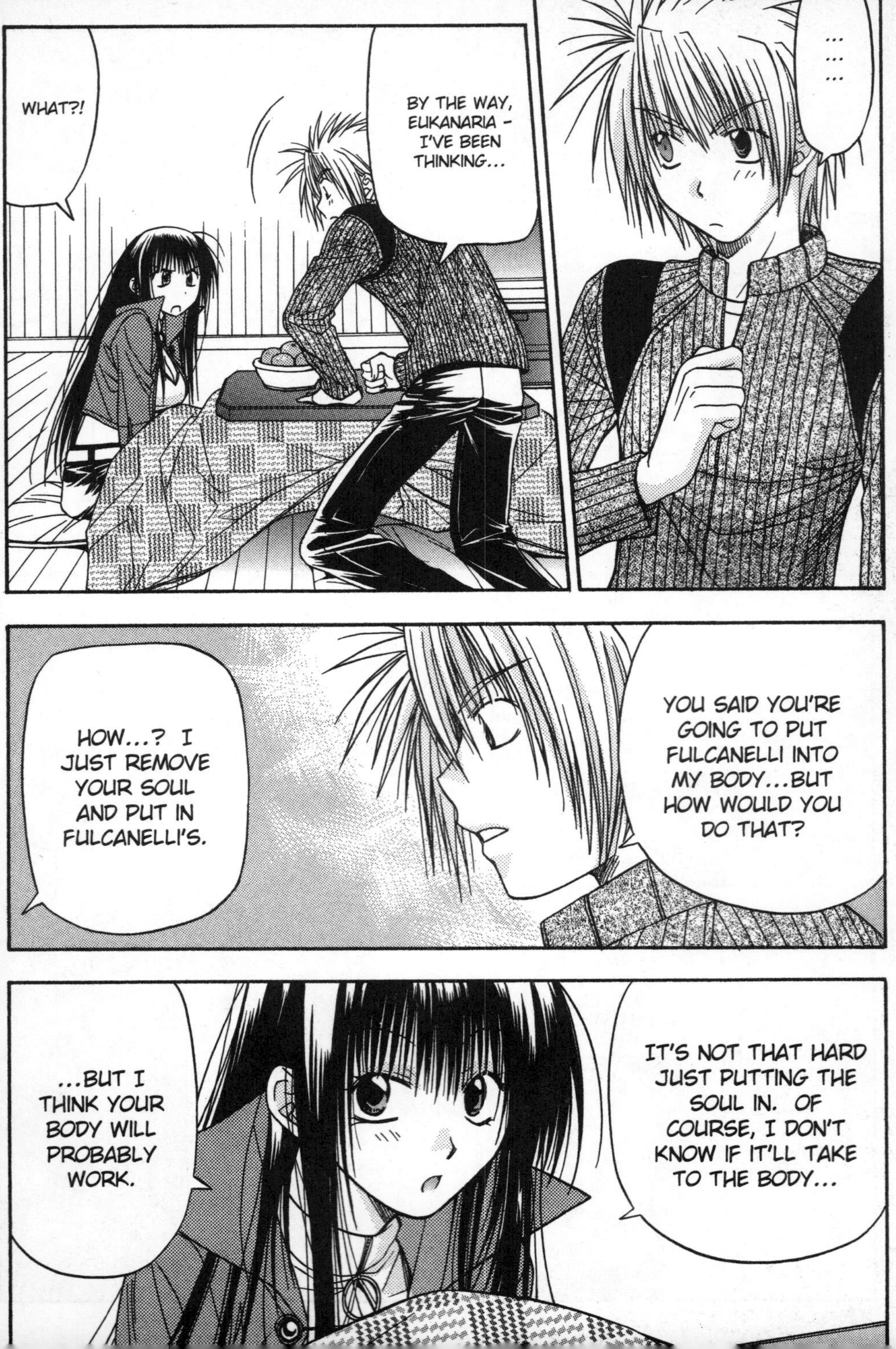
... ...
BY THE WAY, EUKANARIA - I'VE BEEN THINKING...
WHAT?!
YOU SAID YOU'RE GOING TO PUT FULCANELLI INTO MY BODY...BUT HOW WOULD YOU DO THAT?
HOW...? I JUST REMOVE YOUR SOUL AND PUT IN FULCANELLI'S.
IT'S NOT THAT HARD JUST PUTTING THE SOUL IN. OF COURSE, I DON'T KNOW IF IT'LL TAKE TO THE BODY...
...BUT I THINK YOUR BODY WILL PROBABLY WORK.

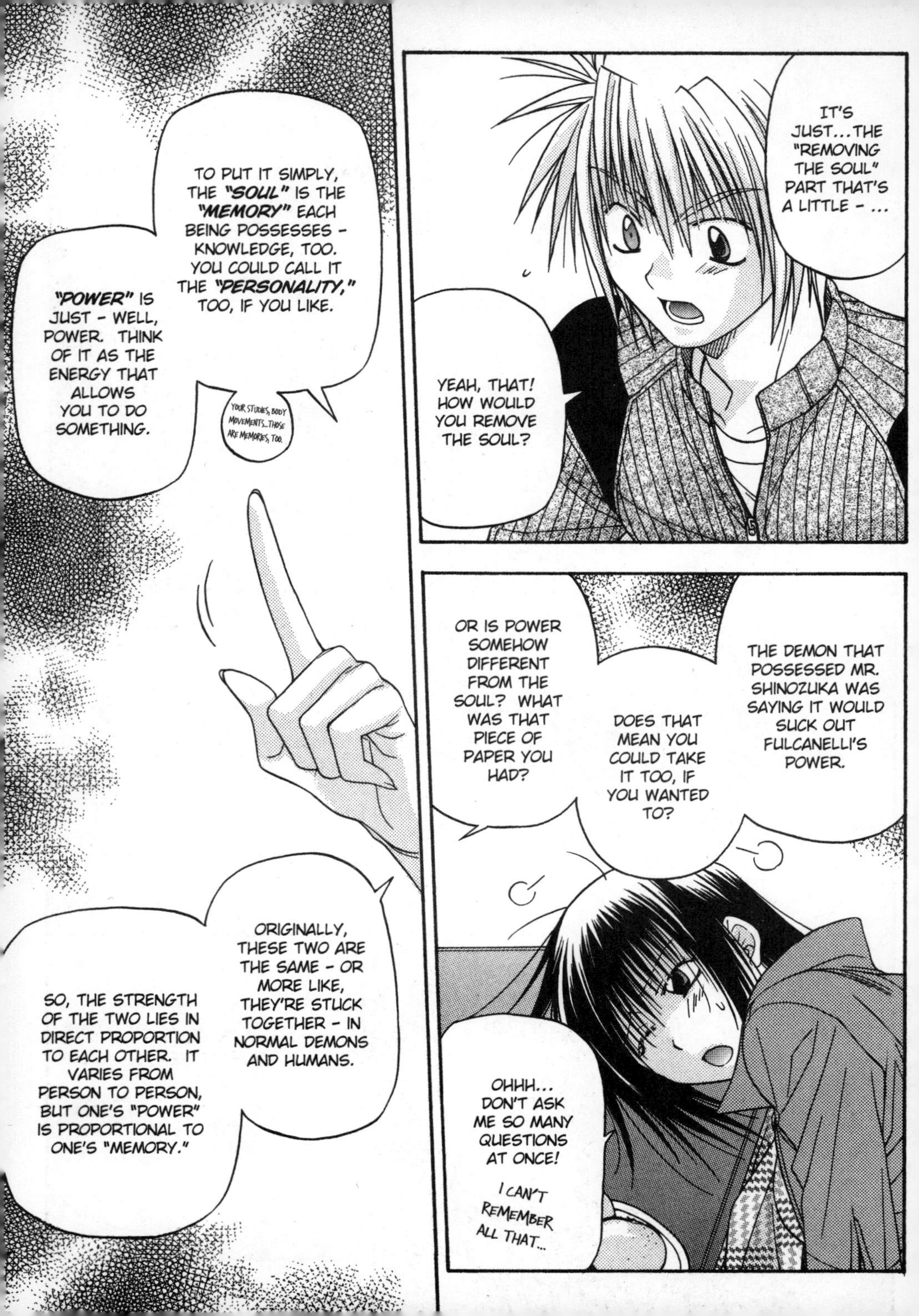
IT'S JUST...THE "REMOVING THE SOUL" PART THAT'S A LITTLE - ...
YEAH, THAT! HOW WOULD YOU REMOVE THE SOUL?
THE DEMON THAT POSSESSED MR. SHINOZUKA WAS SAYING IT WOULD SUCK OUT FULCANELLI'S POWER.
DOES THAT MEAN YOU COULD TAKE IT TOO, IF YOU WANTED TO?
OR IS POWER SOMEHOW DIFFERENT FROM THE SOUL? WHAT WAS THAT PIECE OF PAPER YOU HAD?
OHHH... DON'T ASK ME SO MANY QUESTIONS AT ONCE!
I CAN'T REMEMBER ALL THAT...
TO PUT IT SIMPLY, THE "SOUL" IS THE "MEMORY" EACH BEING POSSESSES - KNOWLEDGE, TOO. YOU COULD CALL IT THE "PERSONALITY," TOO, IF YOU LIKE.
"POWER" IS JUST - WELL, POWER. THINK OF IT AS THE ENERGY THAT ALLOWS YOU TO DO SOMETHING.
YOUR STUDIES, BODY MOVEMENTS...THOSE ARE MEMORIES, TOO.
ORIGINALLY, THESE TWO ARE THE SAME - OR MORE LIKE, THEY'RE STUCK TOGETHER - IN NORMAL DEMONS AND HUMANS.
SO, THE STRENGTH OF THE TWO LIES IN DIRECT PROPORTION TO EACH OTHER. IT VARIES FROM PERSON TO PERSON, BUT ONE'S "POWER" IS PROPORTIONAL TO ONE'S "MEMORY."

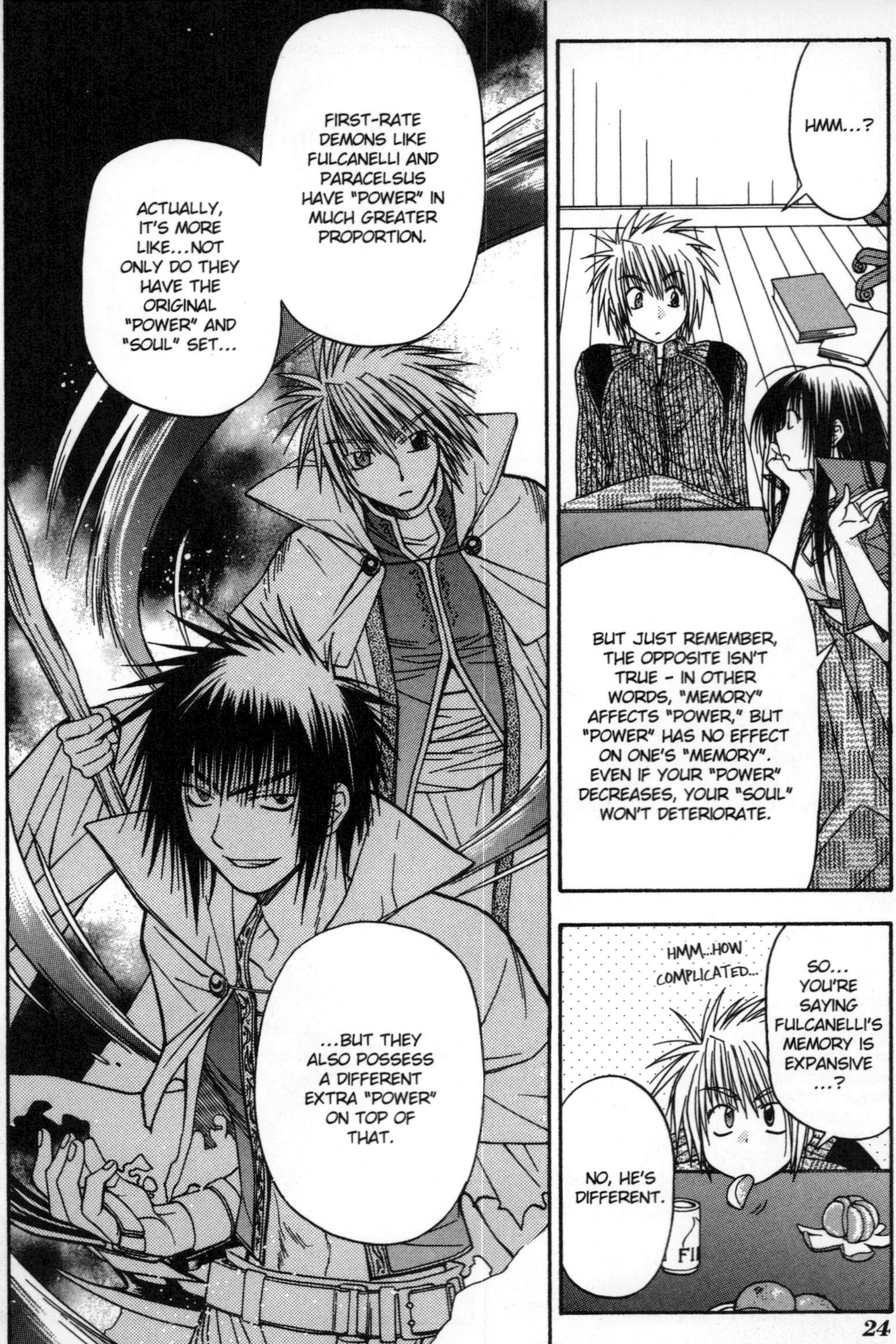
HMM...?
BUT JUST REMEMBER, THE OPPOSITE ISN'T TRUE - IN OTHER WORDS, "MEMORY" AFFECTS "POWER," BUT "POWER" HAS NO EFFECT ON ONE'S "MEMORY". EVEN IF YOUR "POWER" DECREASES, YOUR "SOUL" WON'T DETERIORATE.
SO... YOU'RE SAYING FULCANELLI'S MEMORY IS EXPANSIVE ...?
HMM...HOW COMPLICATED...
NO, HE'S DIFFERENT.
FIRST-RATE DEMONS LIKE FULCANELLI AND PARACELSUS HAVE "POWER" IN MUCH GREATER PROPORTION.
ACTUALLY, IT'S MORE LIKE...NOT ONLY DO THEY HAVE THE ORIGINAL "POWER" AND "SOUL" SET...
...BUT THEY ALSO POSSESS A DIFFERENT EXTRA "POWER" ON TOP OF THAT.

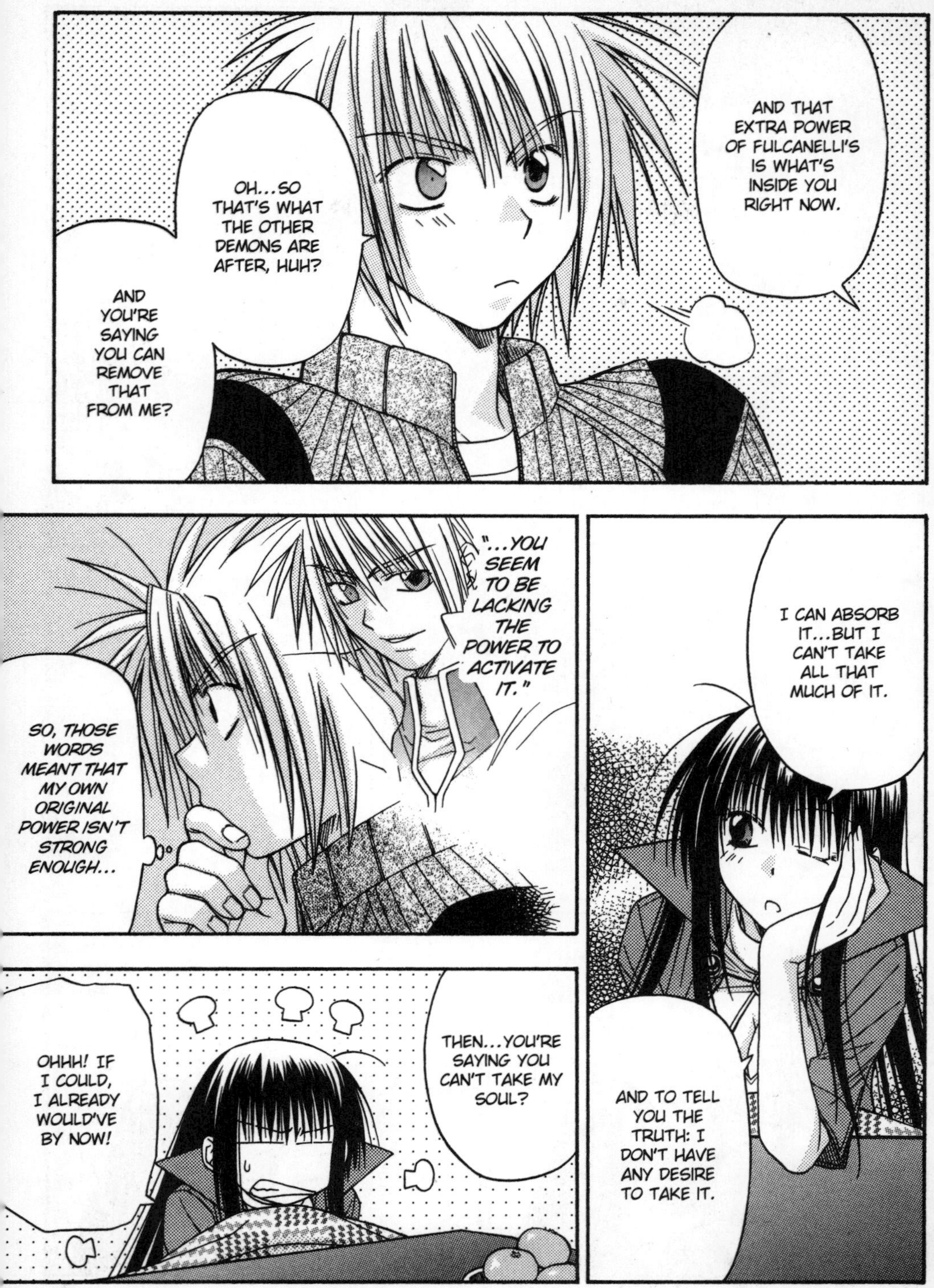
AND THAT EXTRA POWER OF FULCANELLI'S IS WHAT'S INSIDE YOU RIGHT NOW.
OH...SO THAT'S WHAT THE OTHER DEMONS ARE AFTER, HUH?
AND YOU'RE SAYING YOU CAN REMOVE THAT FROM ME?
I CAN ABSORB IT...BUT I CAN'T TAKE ALL THAT MUCH OF IT.
AND TO TELL YOU THE TRUTH: I DON'T HAVE ANY DESIRE TO TAKE IT.
"...YOU SEEM TO BE LACKING THE POWER TO ACTIVATE IT."
SO, THOSE WORDS MEANT THAT MY OWN ORIGINAL POWER ISN'T STRONG ENOUGH...
THEN...YOU'RE SAYING YOU CAN'T TAKE MY SOUL?
OHHH! IF I COULD, I ALREADY WOULD'VE BY NOW!

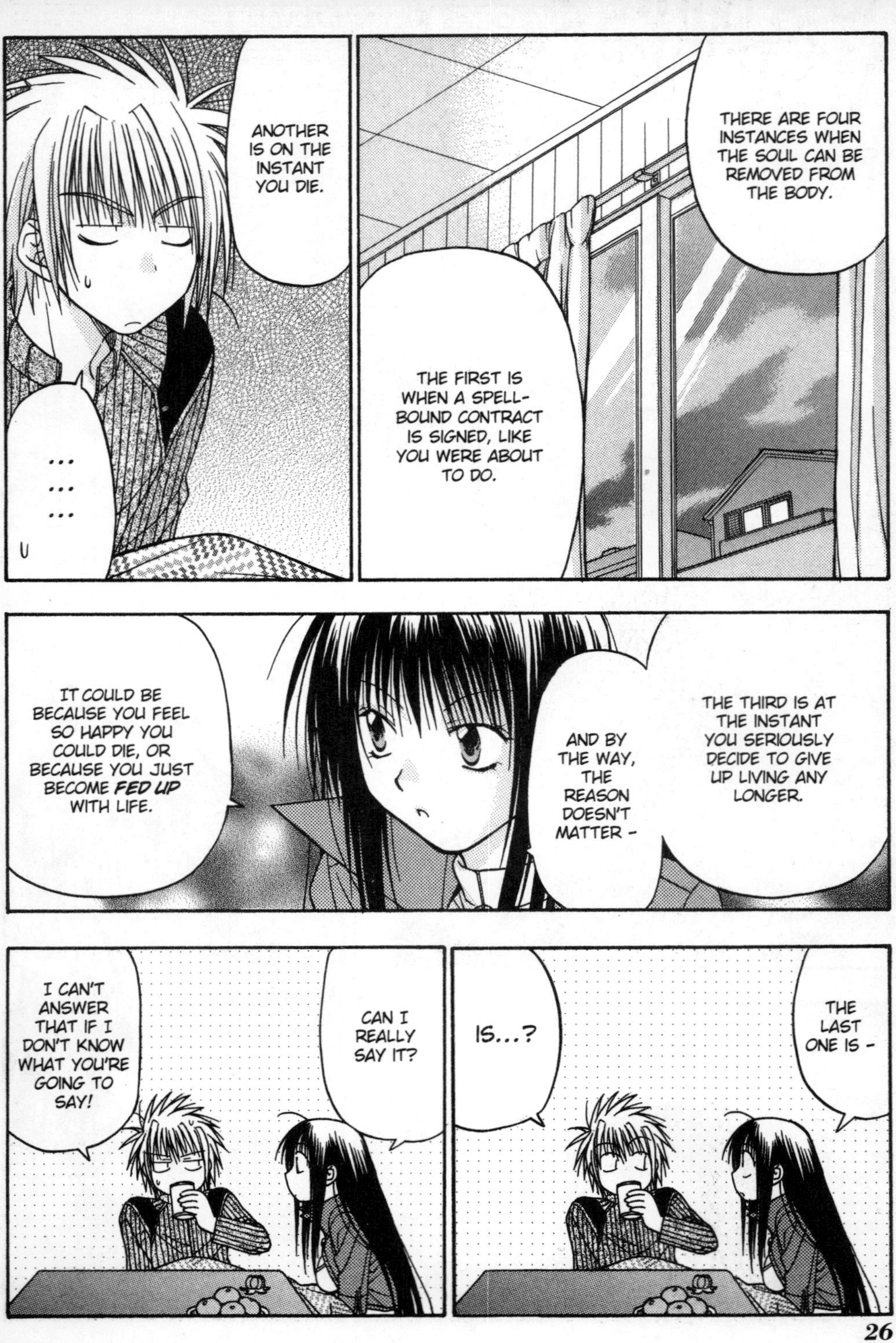
THERE ARE FOUR INSTANCES WHEN THE SOUL CAN BE REMOVED FROM THE BODY.
THE FIRST IS WHEN A SPELL-BOUND CONTRACT IS SIGNED, LIKE YOU WERE ABOUT TO DO.
ANOTHER IS ON THE INSTANT YOU DIE.
... ...
THE THIRD IS AT THE INSTANT YOU SERIOUSLY DECIDE TO GIVE UP LIVING ANY LONGER.
AND BY THE WAY, THE REASON DOESN'T MATTER -
IT COULD BE BECAUSE YOU FEEL SO HAPPY YOU COULD DIE, OR BECAUSE YOU JUST BECOME *FED UP* WITH LIFE.
THE LAST ONE IS -
IS...?
CAN I REALLY SAY IT?
I CAN'T ANSWER THAT IF I DON'T KNOW WHAT YOU'RE GOING TO SAY!

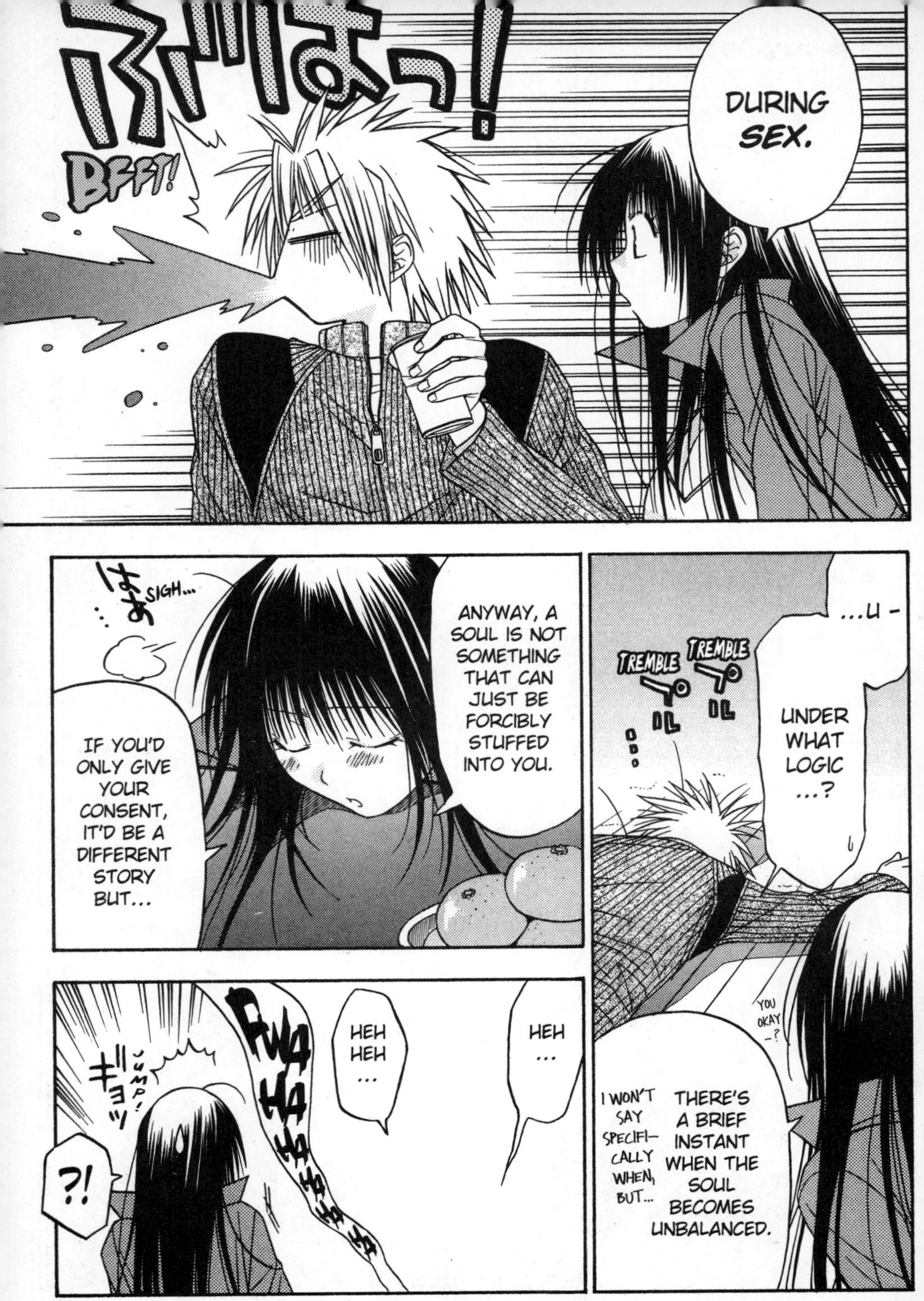
DURING SEX.
ふはっっ!
BFFT!
...U-
TREMBLE TREMBLE
UNDER WHAT LOGIC ...?
YOU OKAY-?
THERE'S A BRIEF INSTANT WHEN THE SOUL BECOMES UNBALANCED.
I WON'T SAY SPECIFICALLY WHEN, BUT...
ANYWAY, A SOUL IS NOT SOMETHING THAT CAN JUST BE FORCIBLY STUFFED INTO YOU.
IF YOU'D ONLY GIVE YOUR CONSENT, IT'D BE A DIFFERENT STORY BUT...
はあ SIGH...
HEH ...
HEH HEH ...
BWAHAHAHAHAHAHA
ギョッ JUMP!
?!

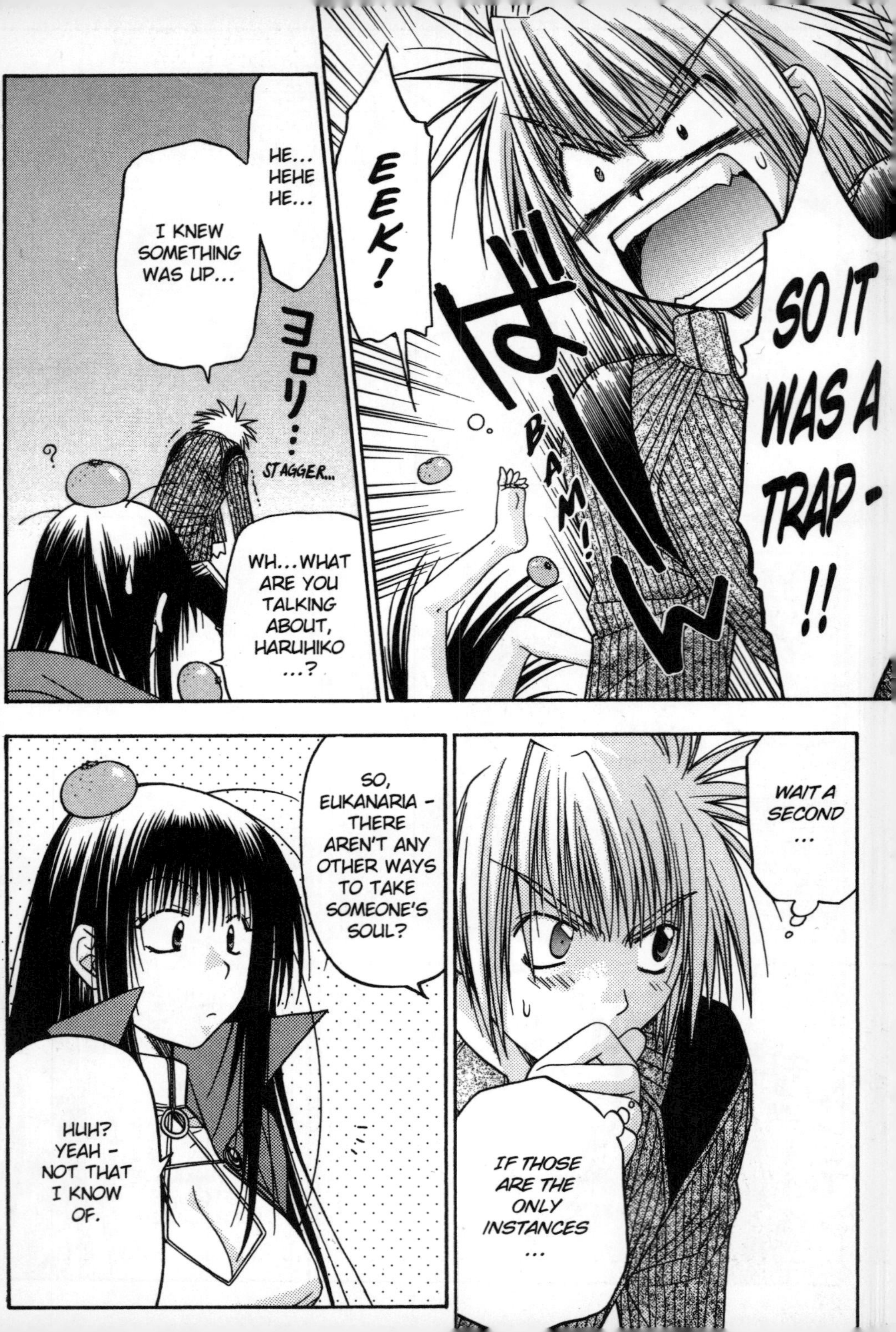
SO IT WAS A TRAP - !!
EEK!
BAM!
HE... HEHE HE...
I KNEW SOMETHING WAS UP...
ヨロリ・・・
STAGGER...
WH...WHAT ARE YOU TALKING ABOUT, HARUHIKO ...?
WAIT A SECOND ...
IF THOSE ARE THE ONLY INSTANCES ...
SO, EUKANARIA - THERE AREN'T ANY OTHER WAYS TO TAKE SOMEONE'S SOUL?
HUH? YEAH - NOT THAT I KNOW OF.

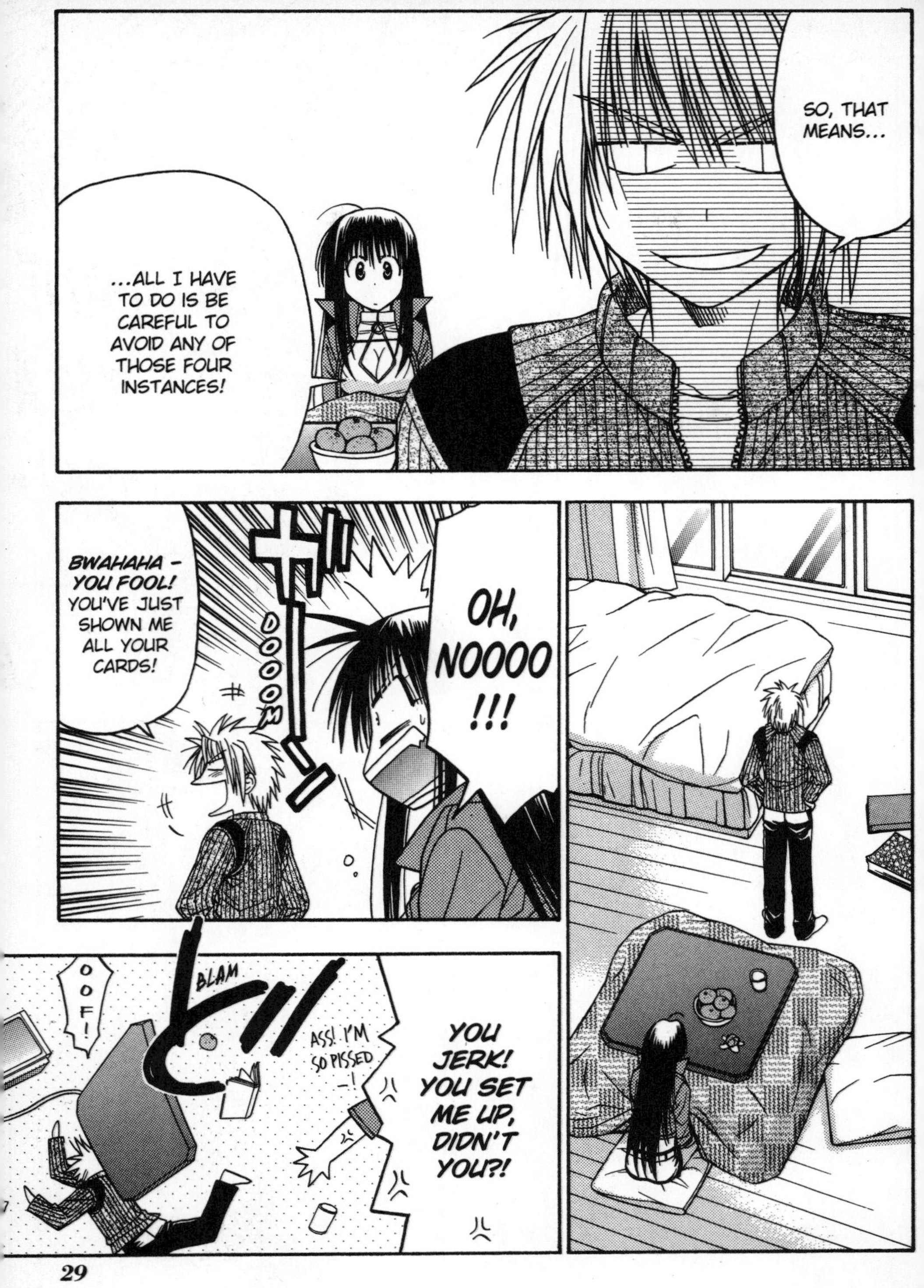
SO, THAT MEANS...
...ALL I HAVE TO DO IS BE CAREFUL TO AVOID ANY OF THOSE FOUR INSTANCES!
OH, NOOOO!!!
DOOOOM
BWAHAHA - YOU FOOL! YOU'VE JUST SHOWN ME ALL YOUR CARDS!
YOU JERK! YOU SET ME UP, DIDN'T YOU?!
ASS! I'M SO PISSED—!
BLAM
OOF!

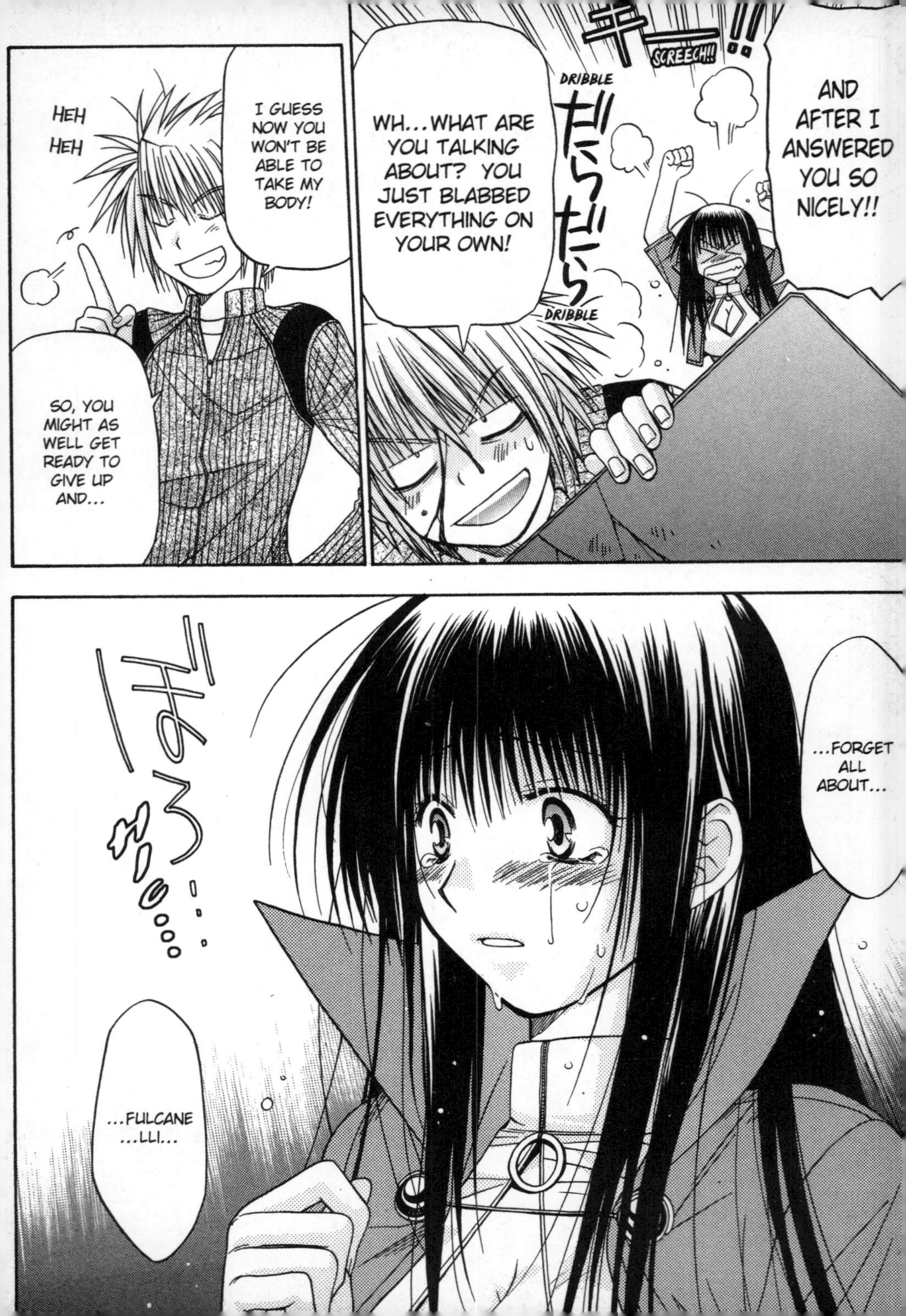
SCREECH!!
AND AFTER I ANSWERED YOU SO NICELY!!
DRIBBLE
DRIBBLE
WH...WHAT ARE YOU TALKING ABOUT? YOU JUST BLABBED EVERYTHING ON YOUR OWN!
I GUESS NOW YOU WON'T BE ABLE TO TAKE MY BODY!
HEH HEH
SO, YOU MIGHT AS WELL GET READY TO GIVE UP AND...
...FORGET ALL ABOUT...
...FULCANE ...LLI...

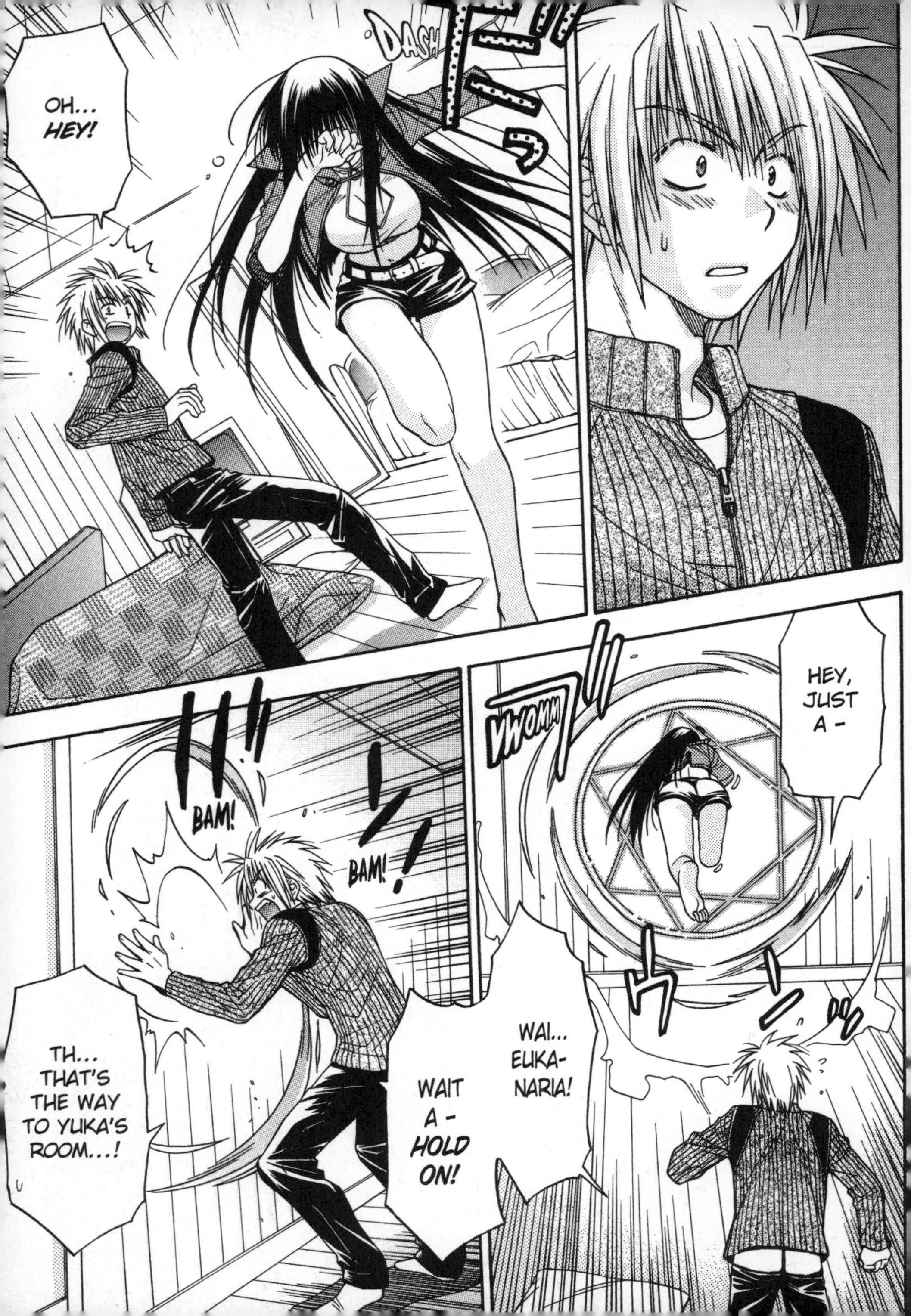
DASH
OH... HEY!
HEY, JUST A -
VWOMM
WAI... EUKA-NARIA!
BAM!
BAM!
WAIT A - HOLD ON!
TH... THAT'S THE WAY TO YUKA'S ROOM...!

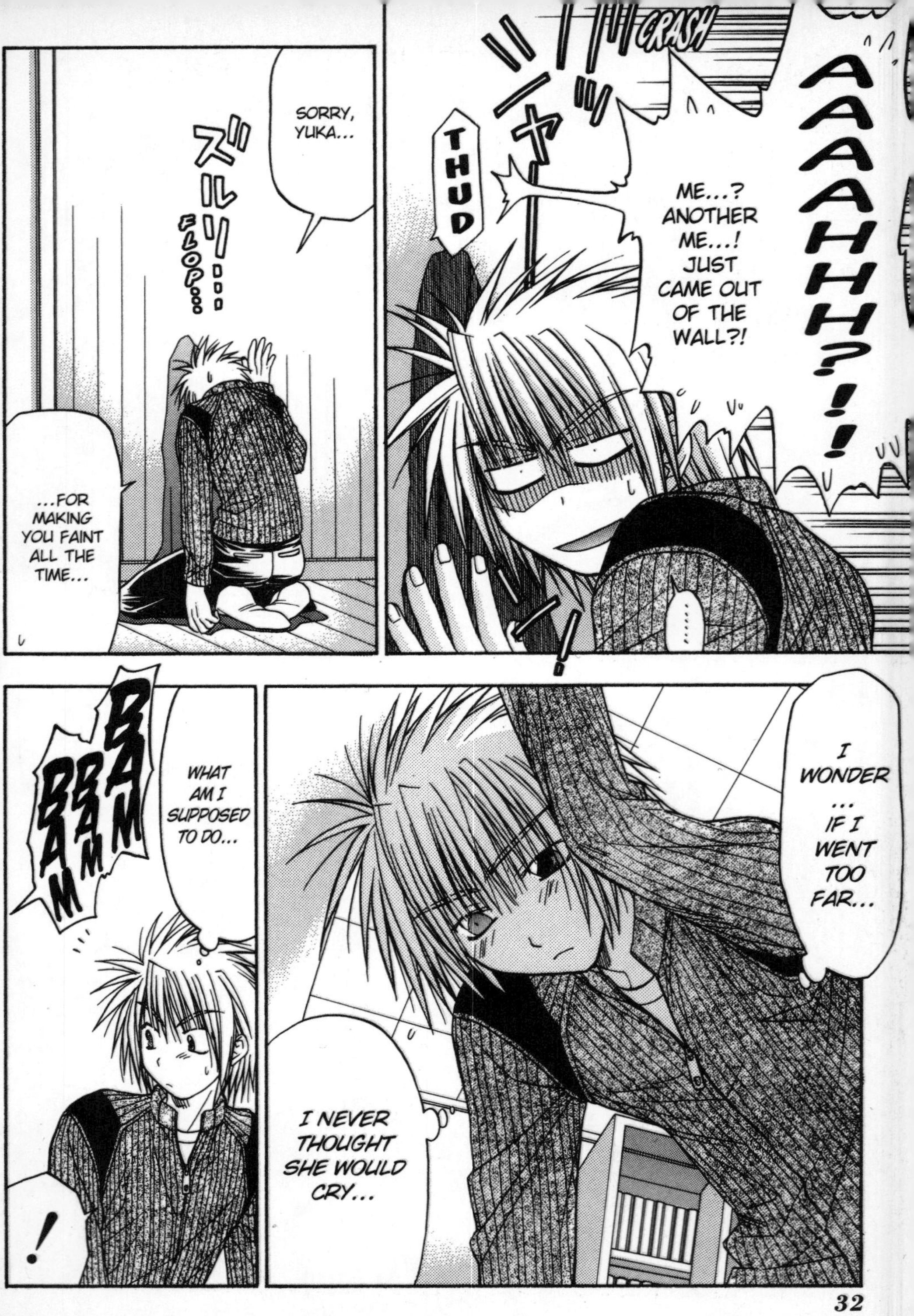
AAAAAHHH?!!
CRASH
THUD
ME...? ANOTHER ME...! JUST CAME OUT OF THE WALL?!
......
!
SORRY, YUKA...
ズルー
FLOP...
...FOR MAKING YOU FAINT ALL THE TIME...
I WONDER ... IF I WENT TOO FAR...
I NEVER THOUGHT SHE WOULD CRY...
BAM BAM BAM
WHAT AM I SUPPOSED TO DO...
!

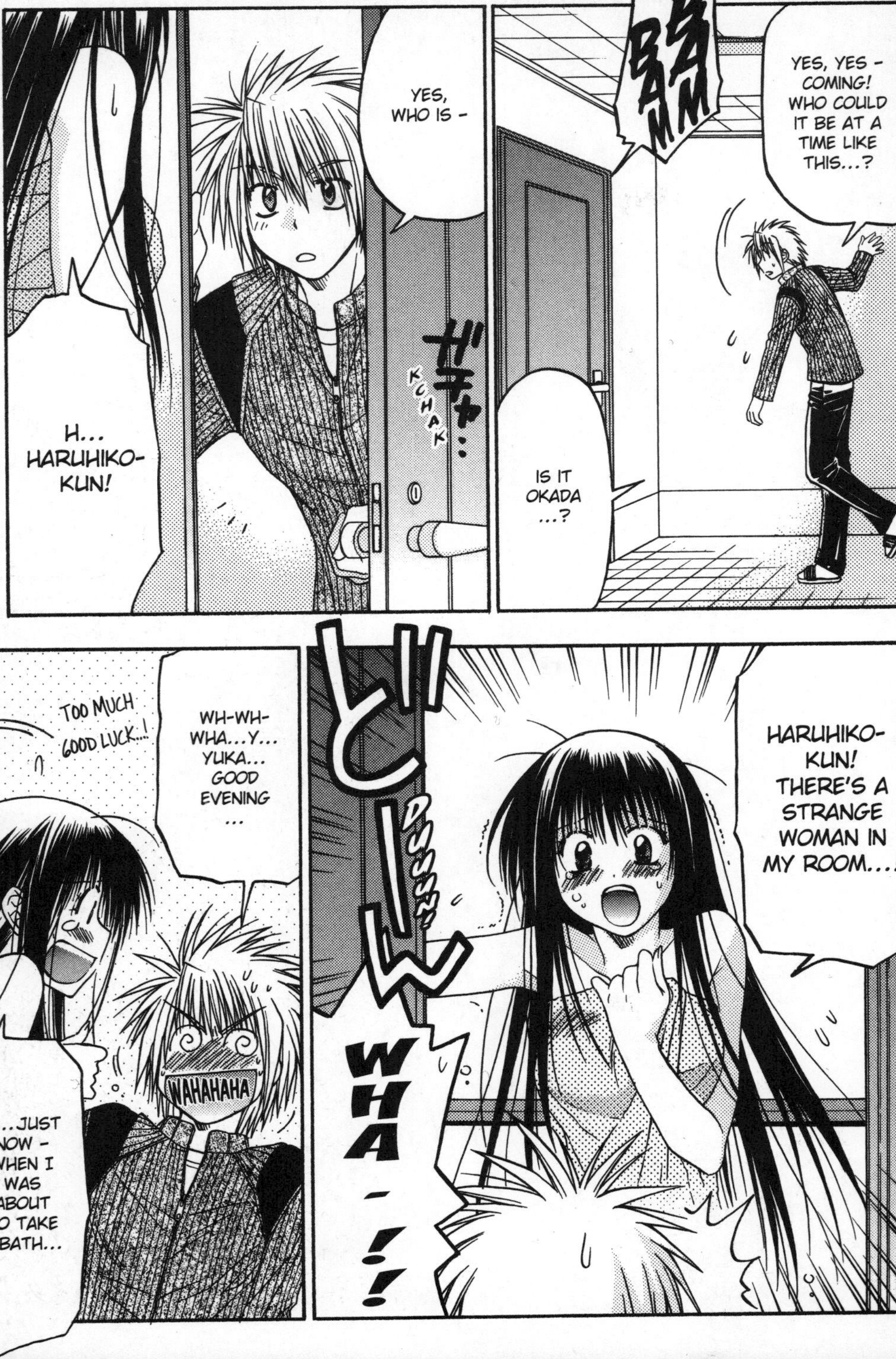
BAMM
YES, YES - COMING! WHO COULD IT BE AT A TIME LIKE THIS...?
IS IT OKADA ...?
YES, WHO IS -
ガチャ…
KCHAK
H... HARUHIKO-KUN!
HARUHIKO-KUN! THERE'S A STRANGE WOMAN IN MY ROOM...!
どーん
DUUUN!
WHA - !!!
WH-WH-WHA...Y... YUKA... GOOD EVENING ...
TOO MUCH GOOD LUCK...!
WAHAHAHA
J...JUST NOW - WHEN I WAS ABOUT TO TAKE A BATH...

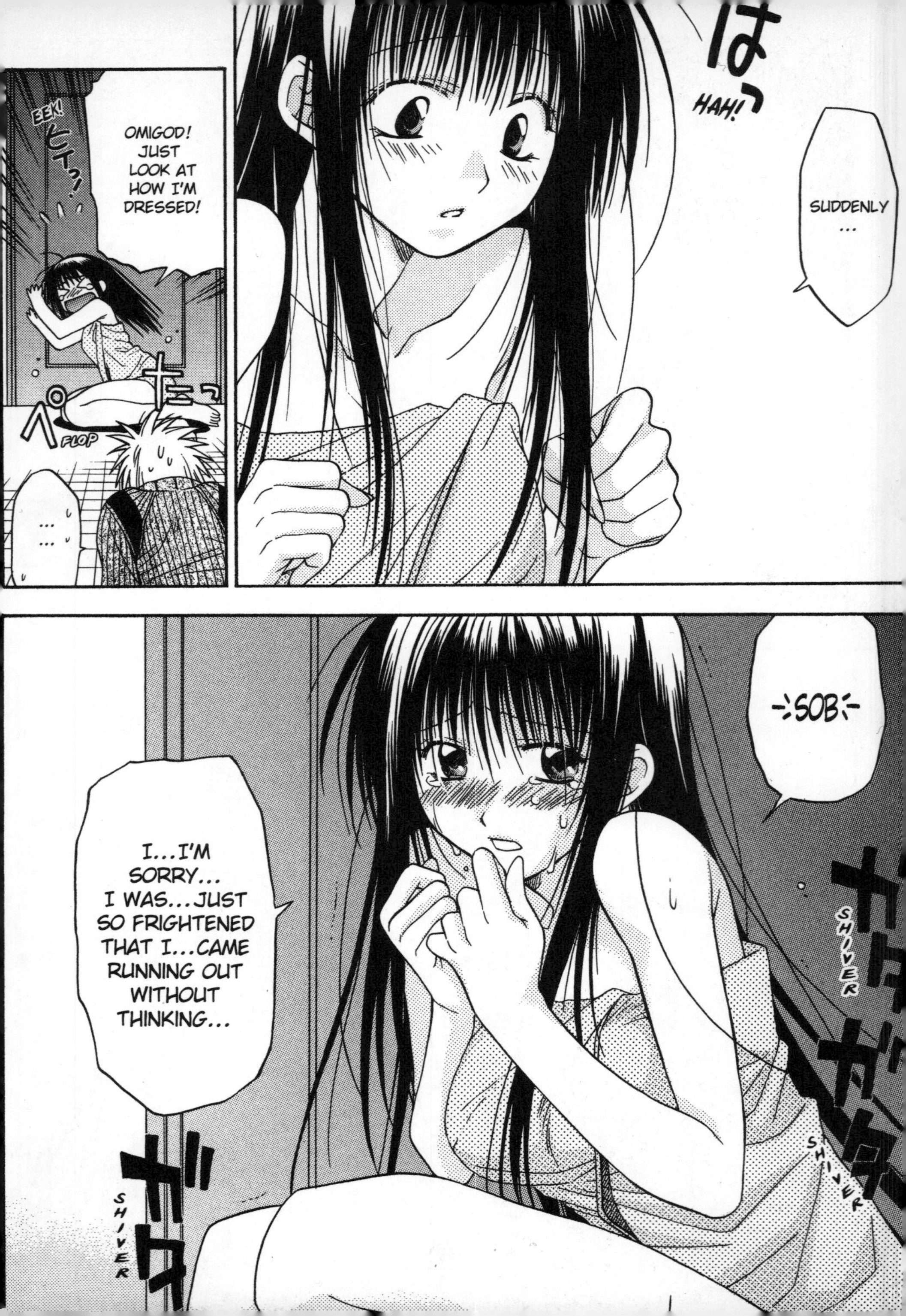
はっ
HAH!
SUDDENLY ...
EEK!
OMIGOD! JUST LOOK AT HOW I'M DRESSED!
FLOP
......
-SOB-
I...I'M SORRY... I WAS...JUST SO FRIGHTENED THAT I...CAME RUNNING OUT WITHOUT THINKING...
SHIVER
SHIVER
SHIVER

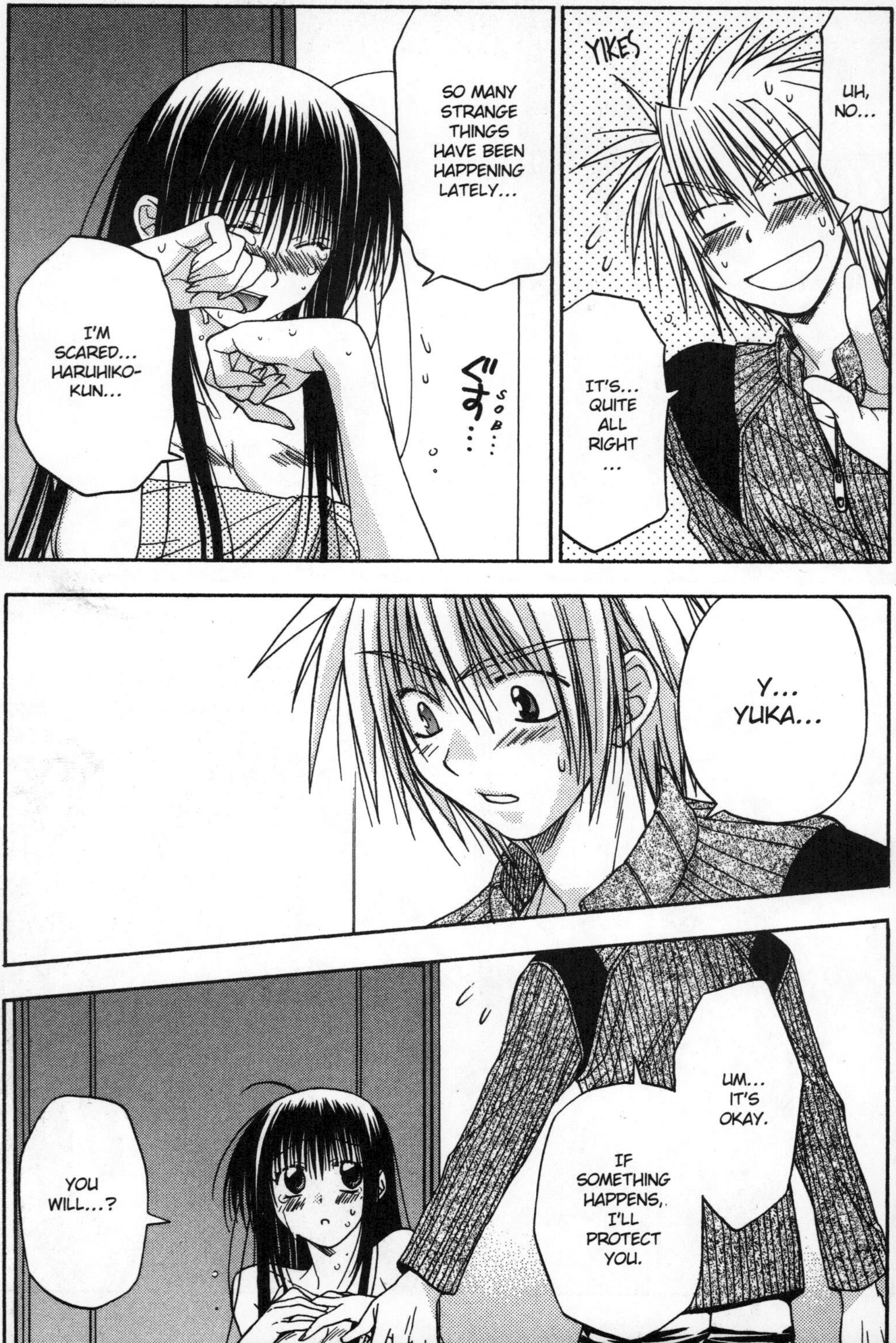
YIKES
UH, NO...
IT'S... QUITE ALL RIGHT ...
SO MANY STRANGE THINGS HAVE BEEN HAPPENING LATELY...
ぐす...
SOB...
I'M SCARED... HARUHIKO-KUN...
Y... YUKA...
UM... IT'S OKAY.
IF SOMETHING HAPPENS, I'LL PROTECT YOU.
YOU WILL...?

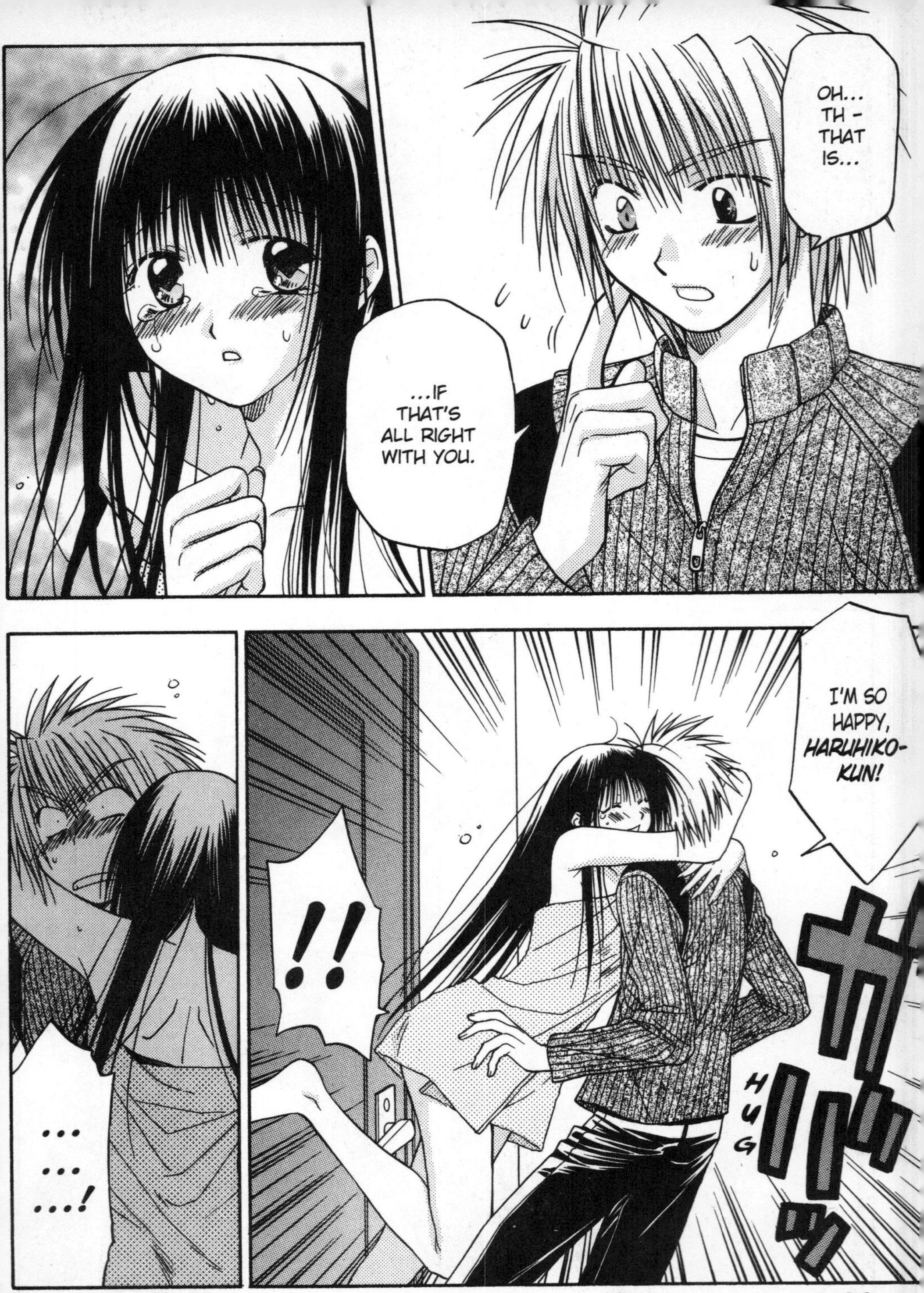
OH... TH - THAT IS...
...IF THAT'S ALL RIGHT WITH YOU.
I'M SO HAPPY, HARUHIKO-KUN!
HUG
!!
... ...!

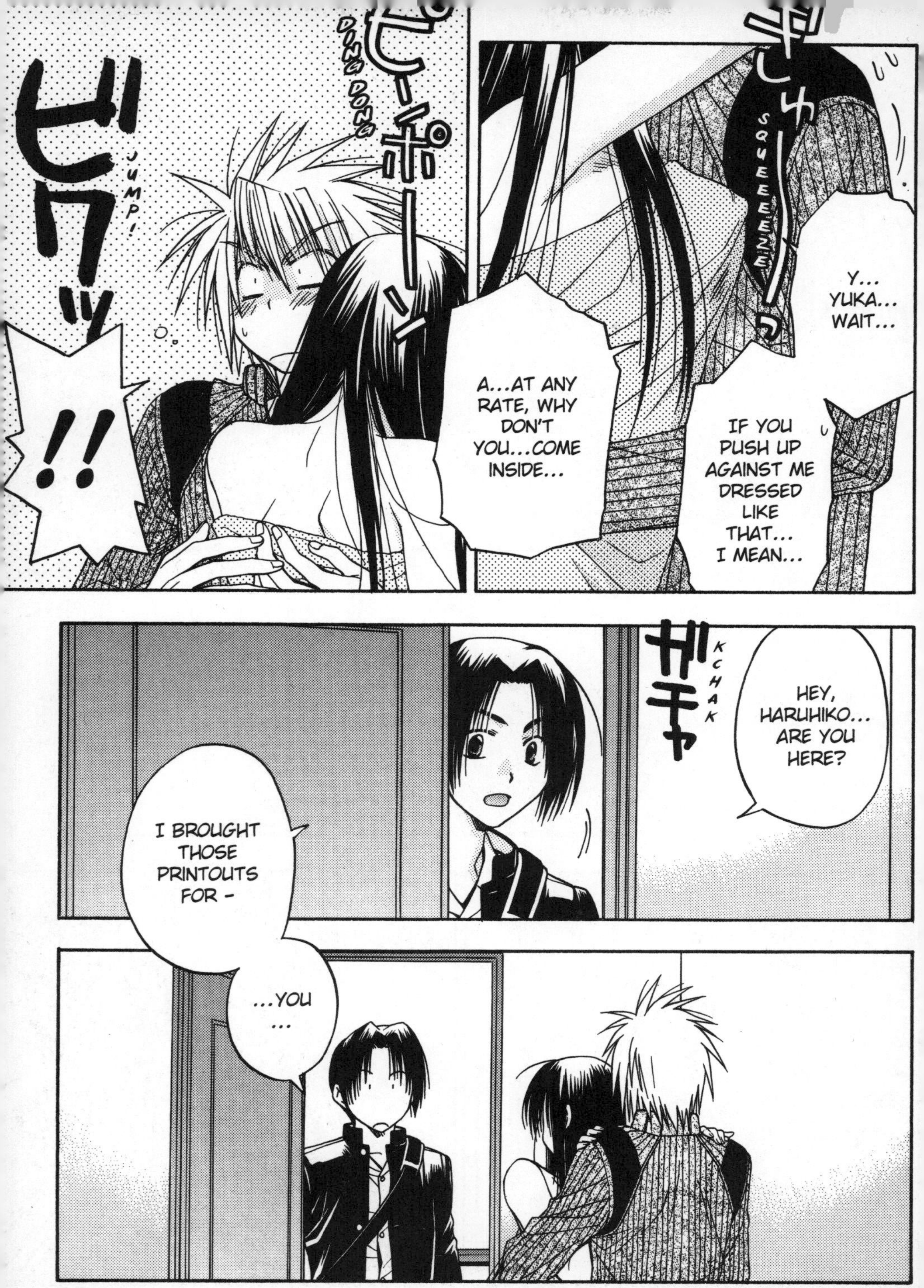
Y... YUKA... WAIT...
ぎゅーっ
SQUEEEEZE
IF YOU PUSH UP AGAINST ME DRESSED LIKE THAT... I MEAN...
A...AT ANY RATE, WHY DON'T YOU...COME INSIDE...
ピンポーン
DING DONG
ビクッ
JUMP!
!!
ガチャ
KCHAK
HEY, HARUHIKO... ARE YOU HERE?
I BROUGHT THOSE PRINTOUTS FOR -
...YOU ...

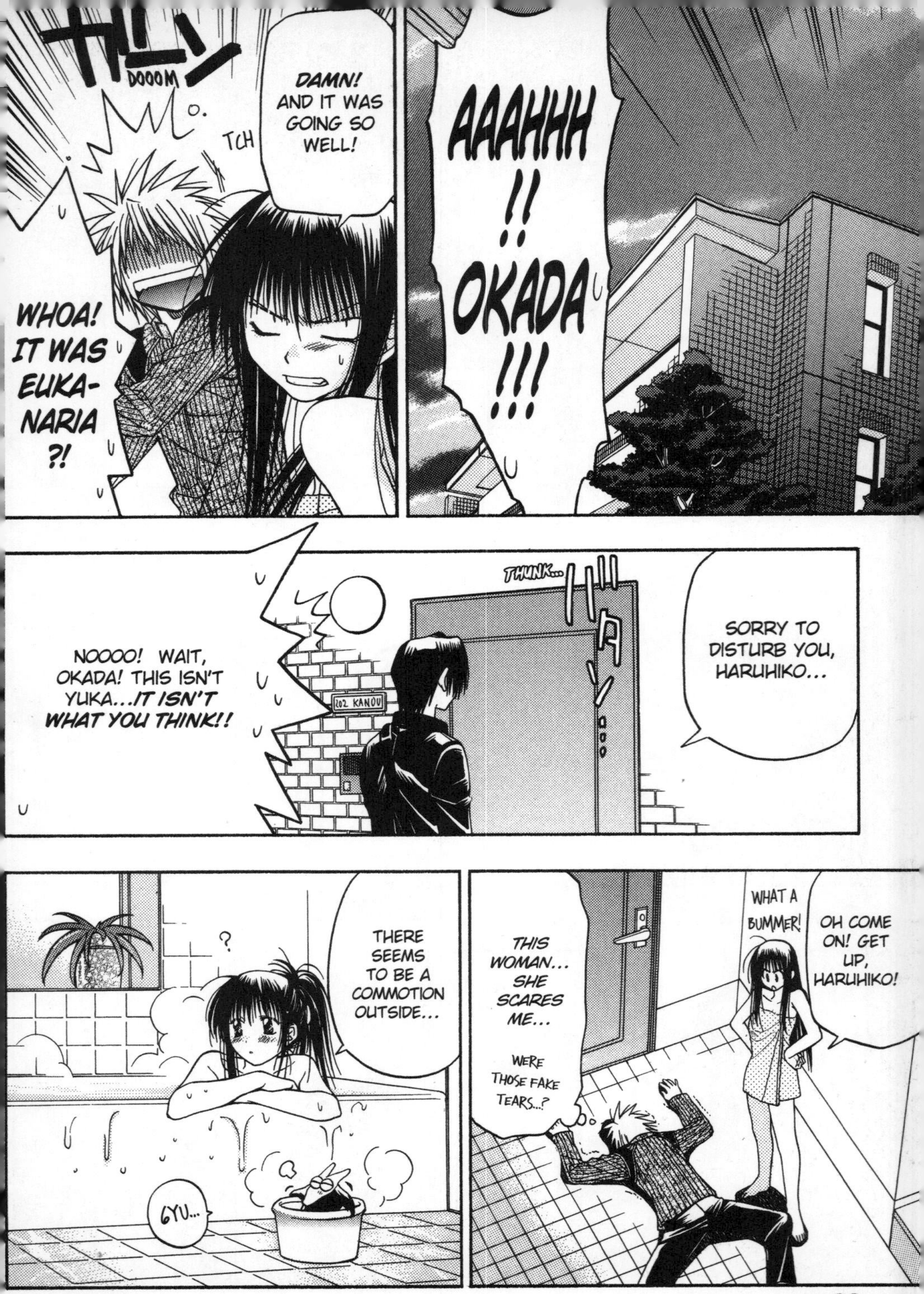
AAAHHH!! OKADA!!!
DAMN! AND IT WAS GOING SO WELL!
DOOOM
TCH
WHOA! IT WAS EUKA-NARIA?!
SORRY TO DISTURB YOU, HARUHIKO...
THUNK...
202 KANOU
NOOOO! WAIT, OKADA! THIS ISN'T YUKA...IT ISN'T WHAT YOU THINK!!
OH COME ON! GET UP, HARUHIKO!
WHAT A BUMMER!
THIS WOMAN... SHE SCARES ME...
WERE THOSE FAKE TEARS...?
THERE SEEMS TO BE A COMMOTION OUTSIDE...
?
GYU...

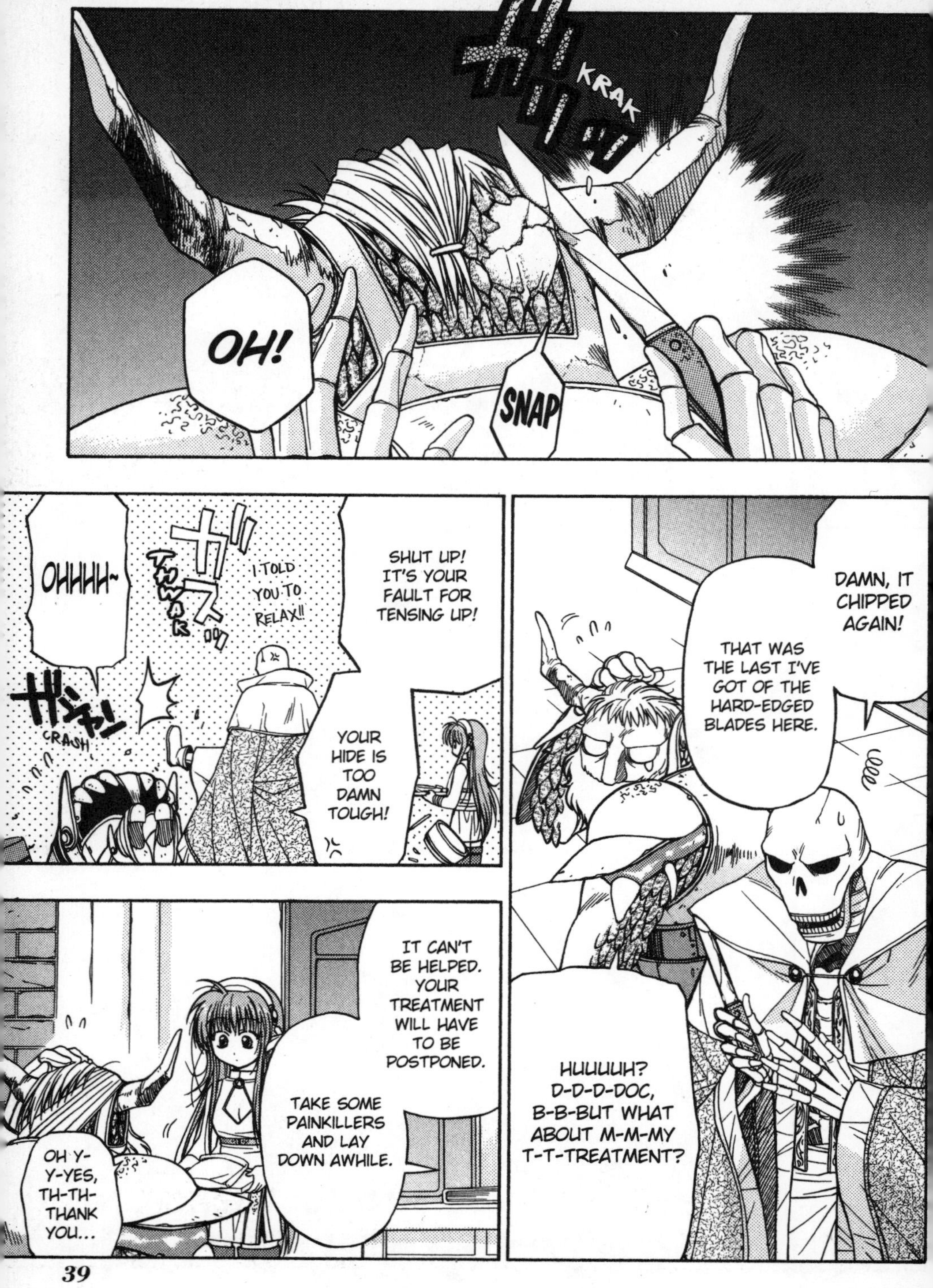
KRAK
SNAP
OH!
DAMN, IT CHIPPED AGAIN!
THAT WAS THE LAST I'VE GOT OF THE HARD-EDGED BLADES HERE.
HUUUUH? D-D-D-DOC, B-B-BUT WHAT ABOUT M-M-MY T-T-TREATMENT?
SHUT UP! IT'S YOUR FAULT FOR TENSING UP!
YOUR HIDE IS TOO DAMN TOUGH!
I TOLD YOU TO RELAX!!
THWAK
OHHHH~
CRASH
IT CAN'T BE HELPED. YOUR TREATMENT WILL HAVE TO BE POSTPONED.
TAKE SOME PAINKILLERS AND LAY DOWN AWHILE.
OH Y-Y-YES, TH-TH-THANK YOU...

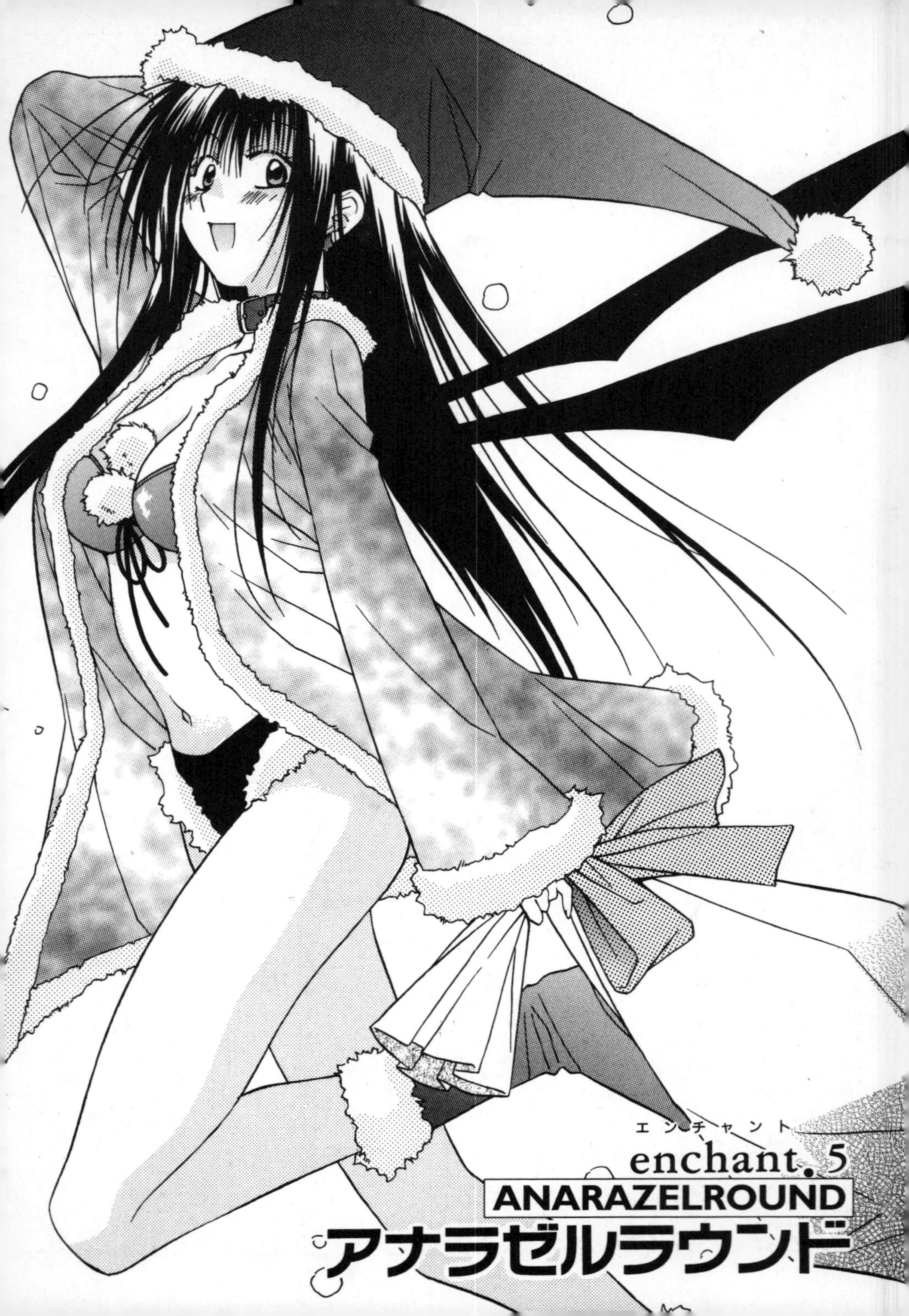
エンチャント
enchant.5
ANARAZELROUND
アナラゼルラウンド

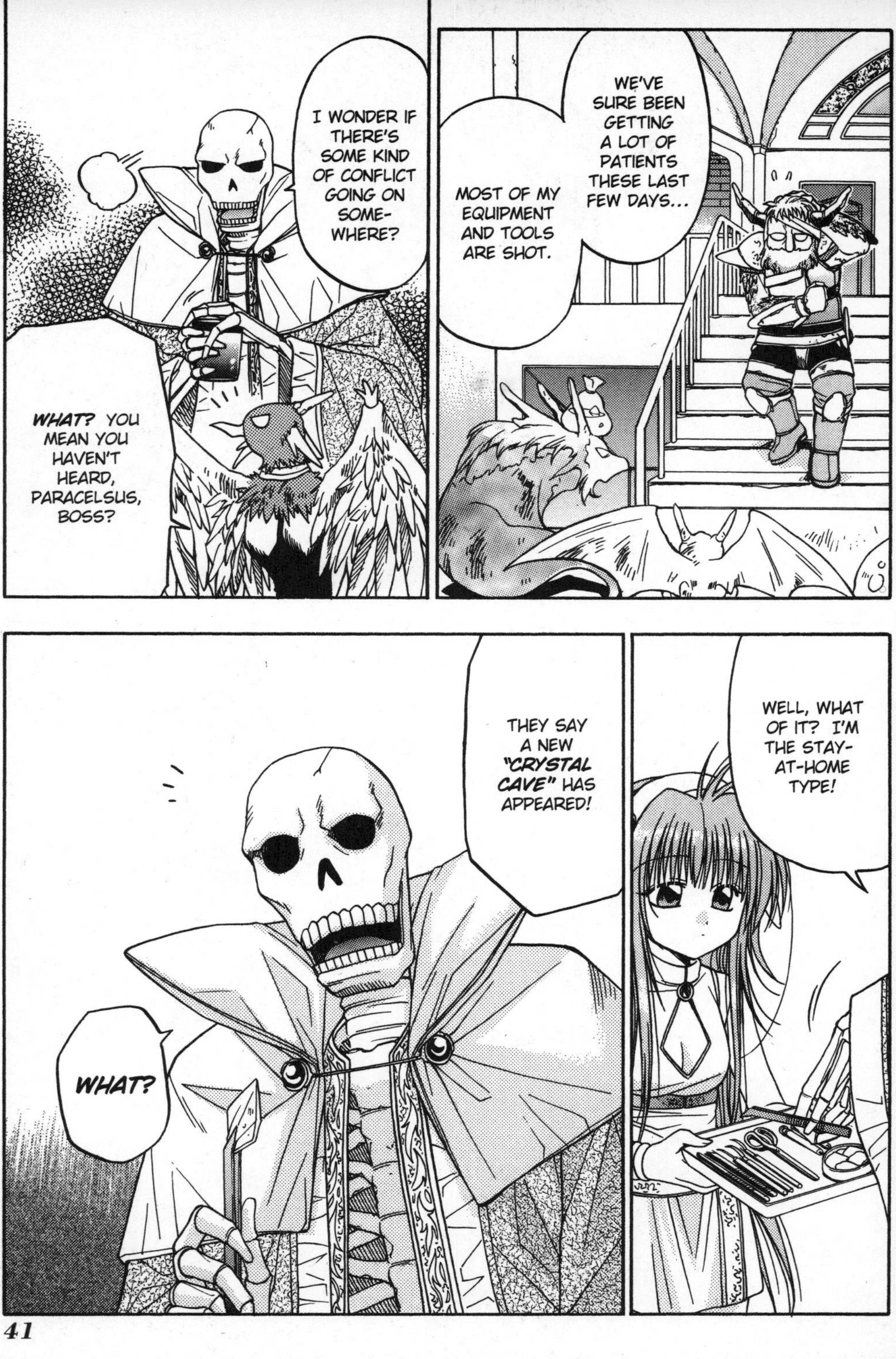
WE'VE SURE BEEN GETTING A LOT OF PATIENTS THESE LAST FEW DAYS...
MOST OF MY EQUIPMENT AND TOOLS ARE SHOT.
I WONDER IF THERE'S SOME KIND OF CONFLICT GOING ON SOME-WHERE?
WHAT? YOU MEAN YOU HAVEN'T HEARD, PARACELSUS, BOSS?
WELL, WHAT OF IT? I'M THE STAY-AT-HOME TYPE!
THEY SAY A NEW "CRYSTAL CAVE" HAS APPEARED!
WHAT?

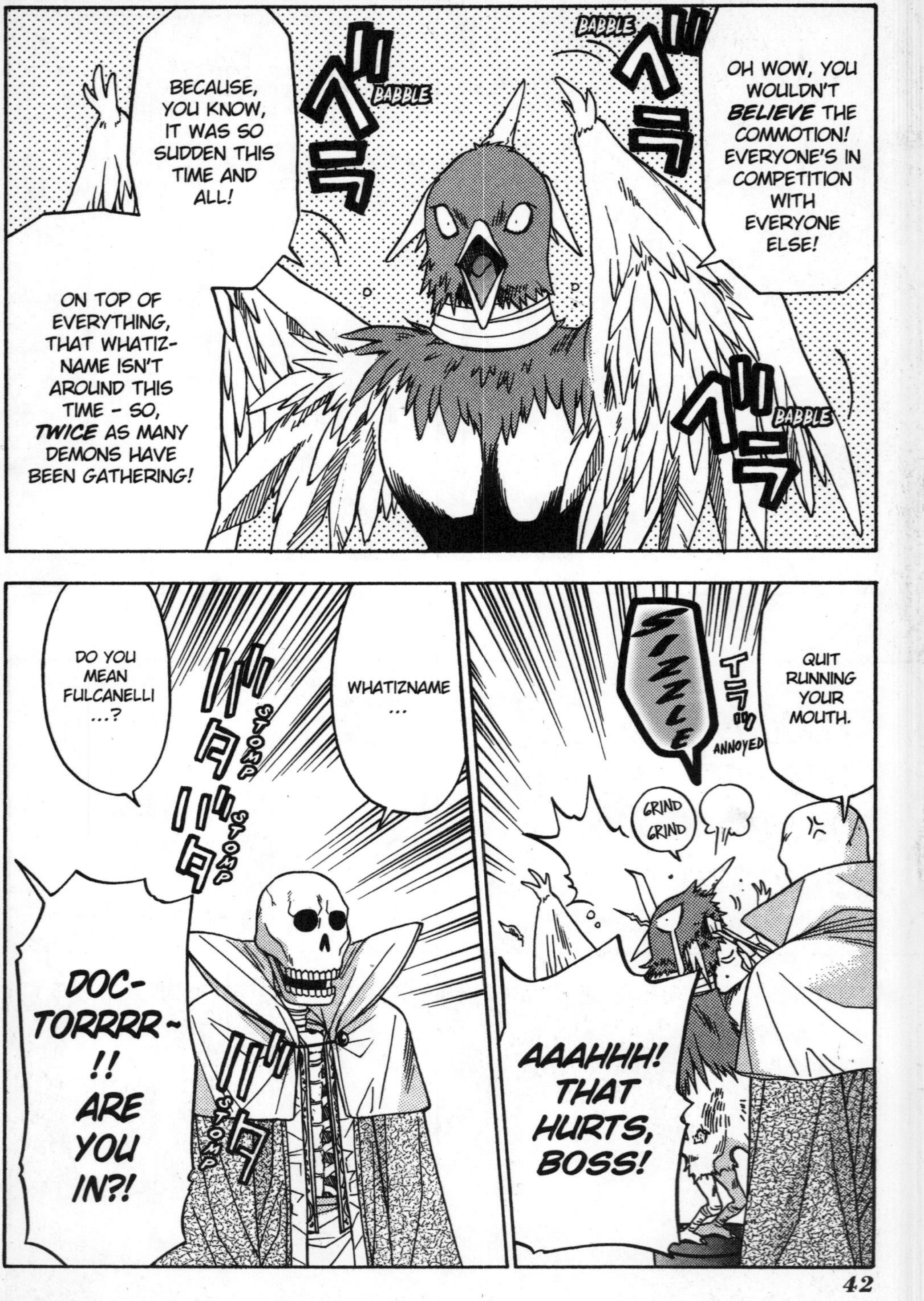
OH WOW, YOU WOULDN'T BELIEVE THE COMMOTION! EVERYONE'S IN COMPETITION WITH EVERYONE ELSE!
BABBLE
BECAUSE, YOU KNOW, IT WAS SO SUDDEN THIS TIME AND ALL!
BABBLE
BABBLE
ON TOP OF EVERYTHING, THAT WHATIZ-NAME ISN'T AROUND THIS TIME - SO, TWICE AS MANY DEMONS HAVE BEEN GATHERING!
QUIT RUNNING YOUR MOUTH.
SIZZLE
ANNOYED
GRIND GRIND
AAAHHH! THAT HURTS, BOSS!
WHATIZNAME ...
DO YOU MEAN FULCANELLI ...?
STOMP
STOMP
DOC-TORRRR~!! ARE YOU IN?!
STOMP

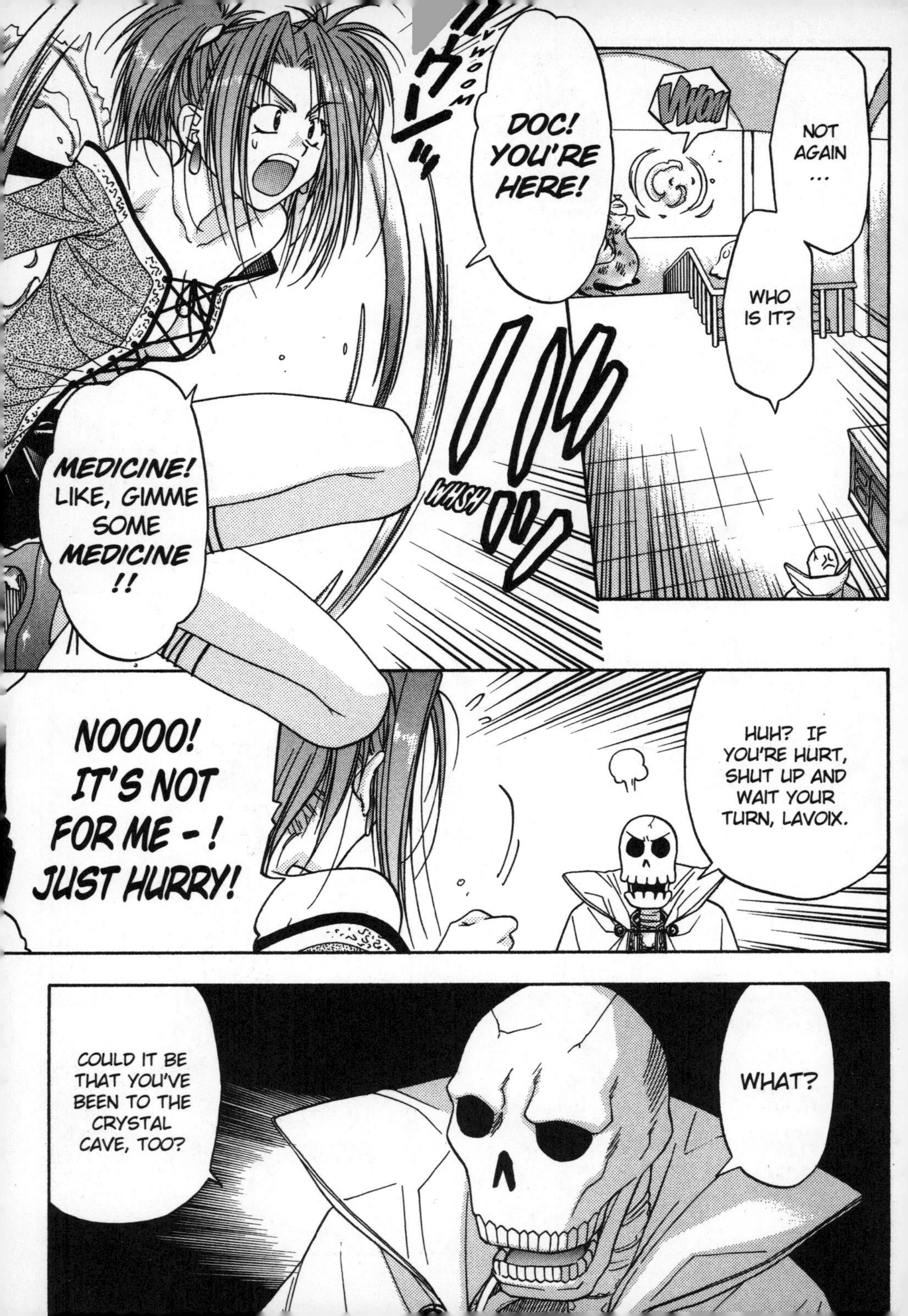
NOT AGAIN ...
WHO IS IT?
DOC! YOU'RE HERE!
MEDICINE! LIKE, GIMME SOME MEDICINE !!
WHSH
HUH? IF YOU'RE HURT, SHUT UP AND WAIT YOUR TURN, LAVOIX.
NOOOO! IT'S NOT FOR ME - ! JUST HURRY!
WHAT?
COULD IT BE THAT YOU'VE BEEN TO THE CRYSTAL CAVE, TOO?

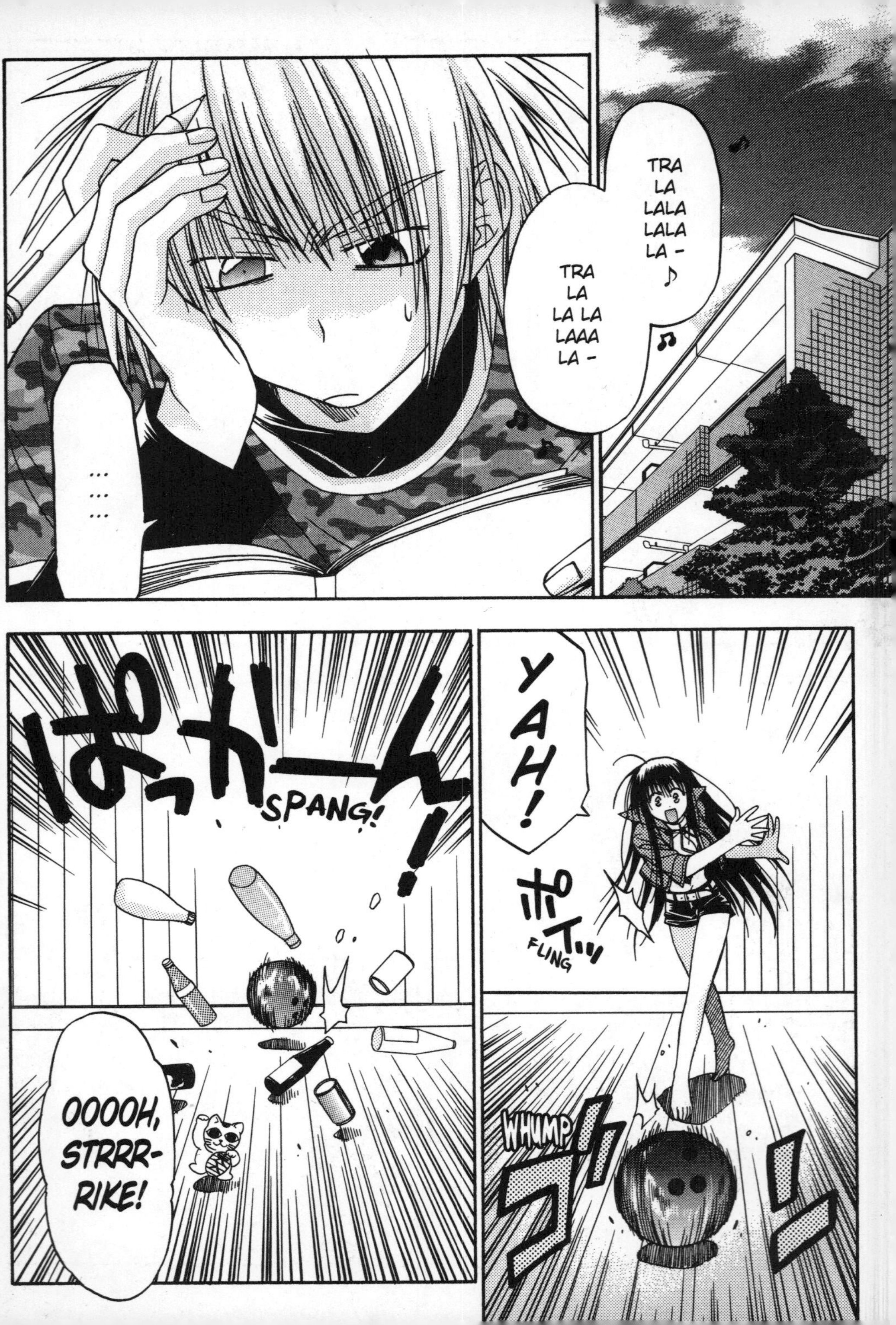
TRA LA LALA LALA LA – ♪
TRA LA LA LA LAAA LA –
…
…
…
YAH!
ポイッ
FLING
WHUMP
ゴッン
ぱっかーん!!
SPANG!
OOOOH, STRRR-RIKE!

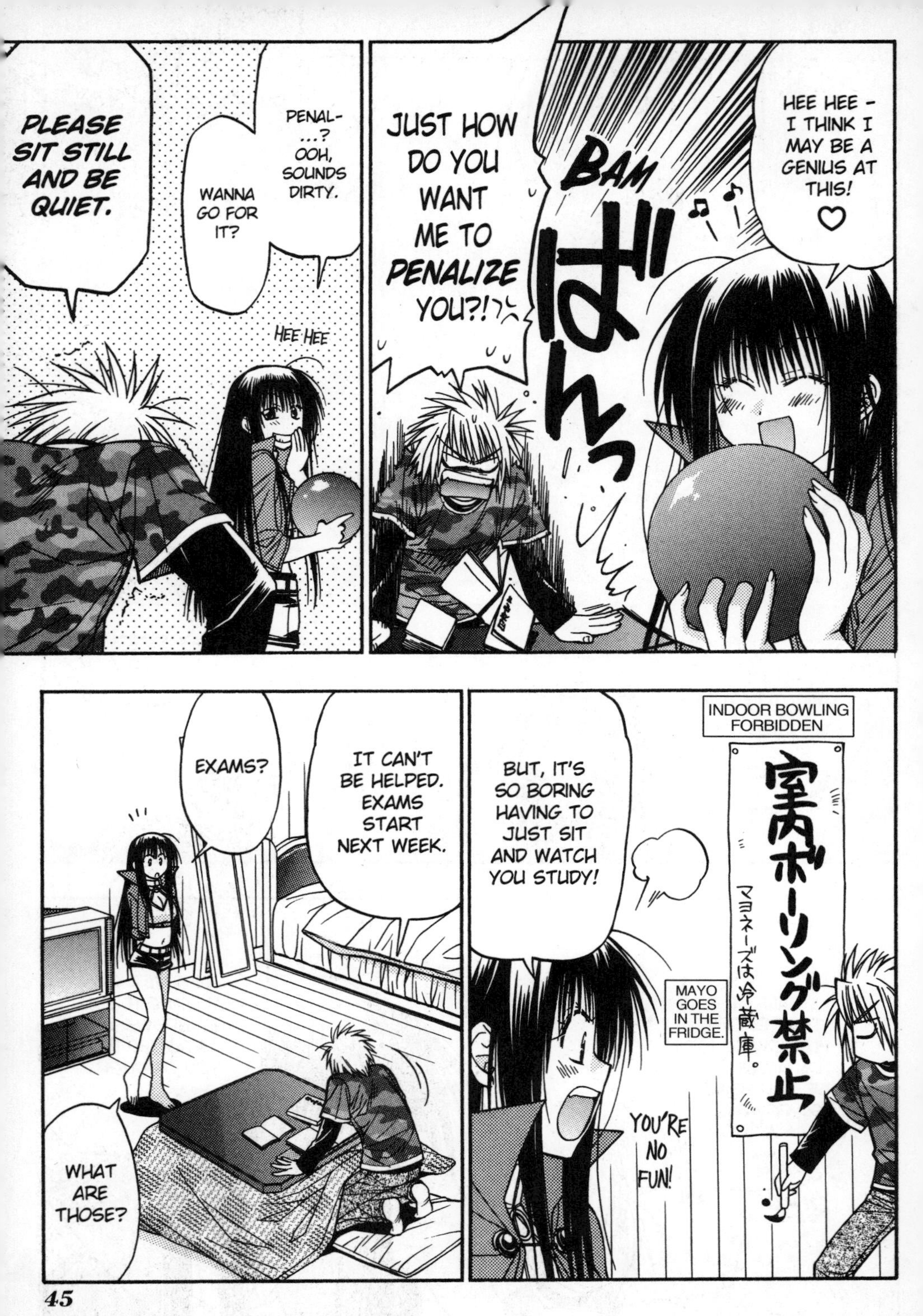
HEE HEE - I THINK I MAY BE A GENIUS AT THIS! ♡
BAM
ばんっ
JUST HOW DO YOU WANT ME TO PENALIZE YOU?!
PENAL- ...? OOH, SOUNDS DIRTY.
WANNA GO FOR IT?
PLEASE SIT STILL AND BE QUIET.
HEE HEE
INDOOR BOWLING FORBIDDEN
室内ボーリング禁止
マヨネーズは冷蔵庫。
MAYO GOES IN THE FRIDGE.
BUT, IT'S SO BORING HAVING TO JUST SIT AND WATCH YOU STUDY!
YOU'RE NO FUN!
IT CAN'T BE HELPED. EXAMS START NEXT WEEK.
EXAMS?
WHAT ARE THOSE?

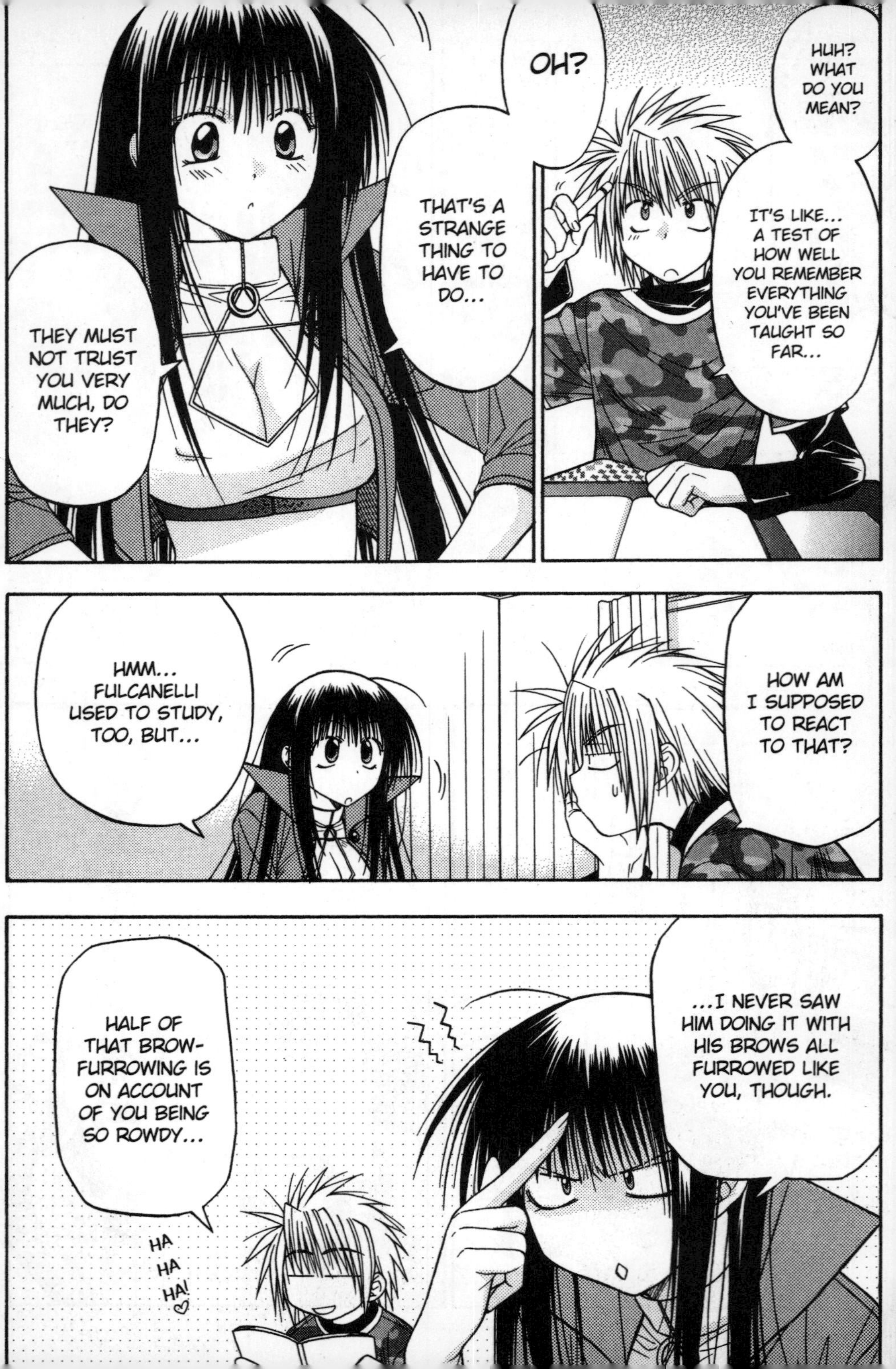
HUH? WHAT DO YOU MEAN?
IT'S LIKE... A TEST OF HOW WELL YOU REMEMBER EVERYTHING YOU'VE BEEN TAUGHT SO FAR...
OH?
THAT'S A STRANGE THING TO HAVE TO DO...
THEY MUST NOT TRUST YOU VERY MUCH, DO THEY?
HOW AM I SUPPOSED TO REACT TO THAT?
HMM... FULCANELLI USED TO STUDY, TOO, BUT...
...I NEVER SAW HIM DOING IT WITH HIS BROWS ALL FURROWED LIKE YOU, THOUGH.
HALF OF THAT BROW-FURROWING IS ON ACCOUNT OF YOU BEING SO ROWDY...
HA HA HA! ♡

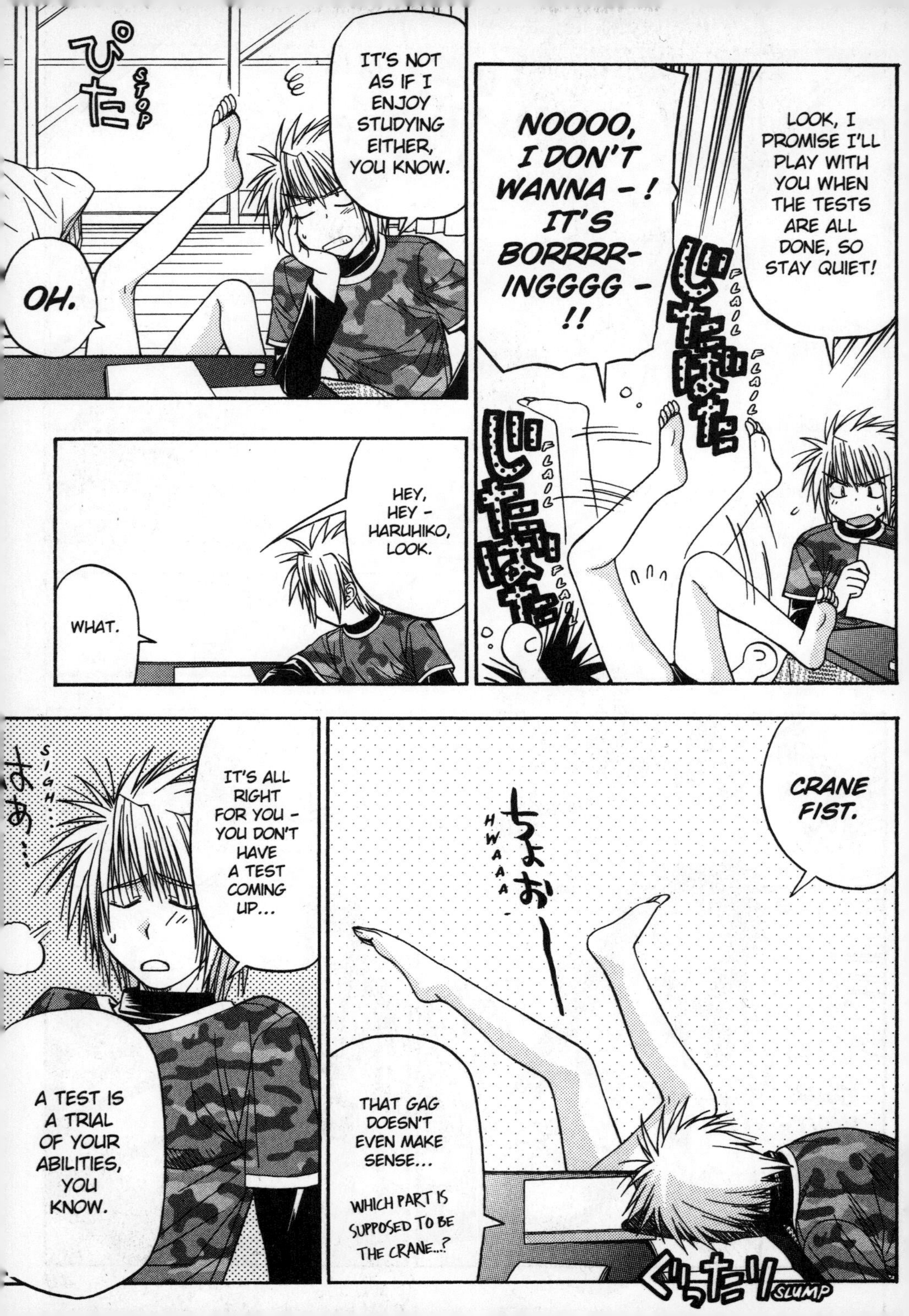
LOOK, I PROMISE I'LL PLAY WITH YOU WHEN THE TESTS ARE ALL DONE, SO STAY QUIET!
NOOOO, I DON'T WANNA -! IT'S BORRRR-INGGGG -!!
FLAIL FLAIL
FLAIL FLAIL
IT'S NOT AS IF I ENJOY STUDYING EITHER, YOU KNOW.
STOP
OH.
HEY, HEY - HARUHIKO, LOOK.
WHAT.
CRANE FIST.
HWAAAA-
THAT GAG DOESN'T EVEN MAKE SENSE...
WHICH PART IS SUPPOSED TO BE THE CRANE...?
SLUMP
IT'S ALL RIGHT FOR YOU - YOU DON'T HAVE A TEST COMING UP...
SIGH...
A TEST IS A TRIAL OF YOUR ABILITIES, YOU KNOW.

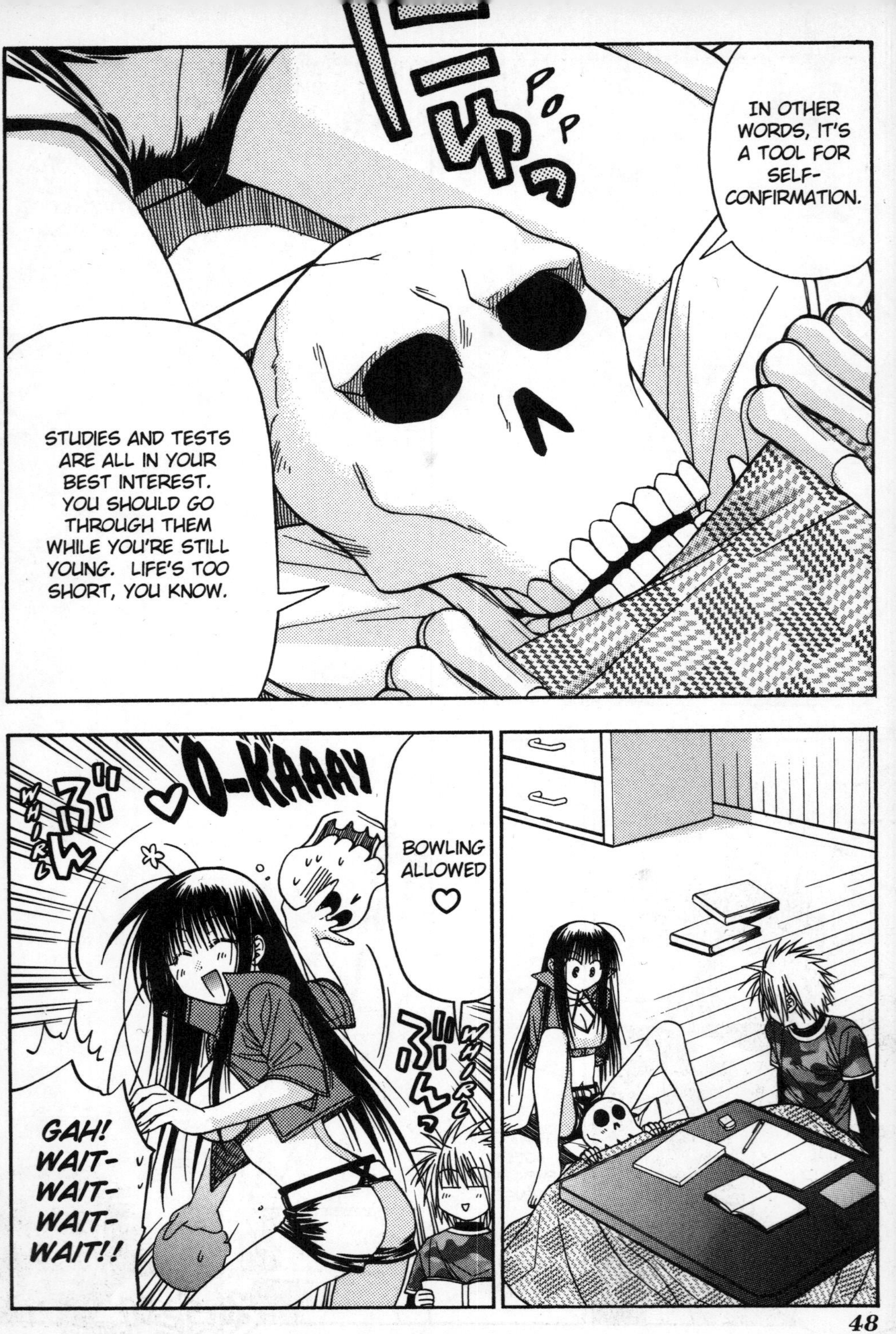
POP
IN OTHER WORDS, IT'S A TOOL FOR SELF-CONFIRMATION.
STUDIES AND TESTS ARE ALL IN YOUR BEST INTEREST. YOU SHOULD GO THROUGH THEM WHILE YOU'RE STILL YOUNG. LIFE'S TOO SHORT, YOU KNOW.
♡ O-KAAAY
BOWLING ALLOWED ♡
WHIRL
WHIRL
GAH! WAIT-WAIT-WAIT-WAIT!!

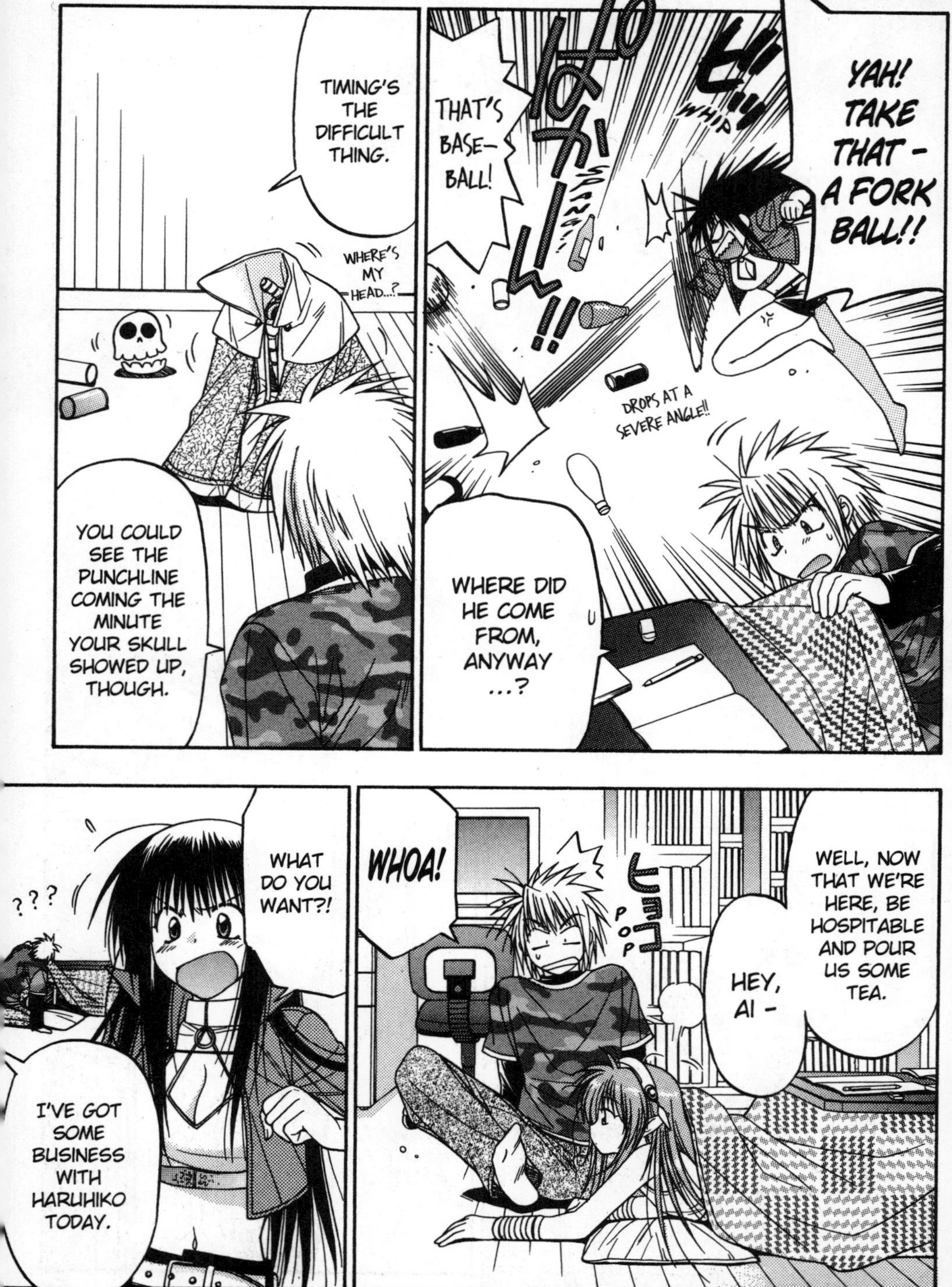
YAH! TAKE THAT - A FORK BALL!!
WHIP
THAT'S BASE-BALL!
DROPS AT A SEVERE ANGLE!!
WHERE DID HE COME FROM, ANYWAY ...?
TIMING'S THE DIFFICULT THING.
WHERE'S MY HEAD...?
YOU COULD SEE THE PUNCHLINE COMING THE MINUTE YOUR SKULL SHOWED UP, THOUGH.
WELL, NOW THAT WE'RE HERE, BE HOSPITABLE AND POUR US SOME TEA.
HEY, AI -
POP
WHOA!
WHAT DO YOU WANT?!
???
I'VE GOT SOME BUSINESS WITH HARUHIKO TODAY.

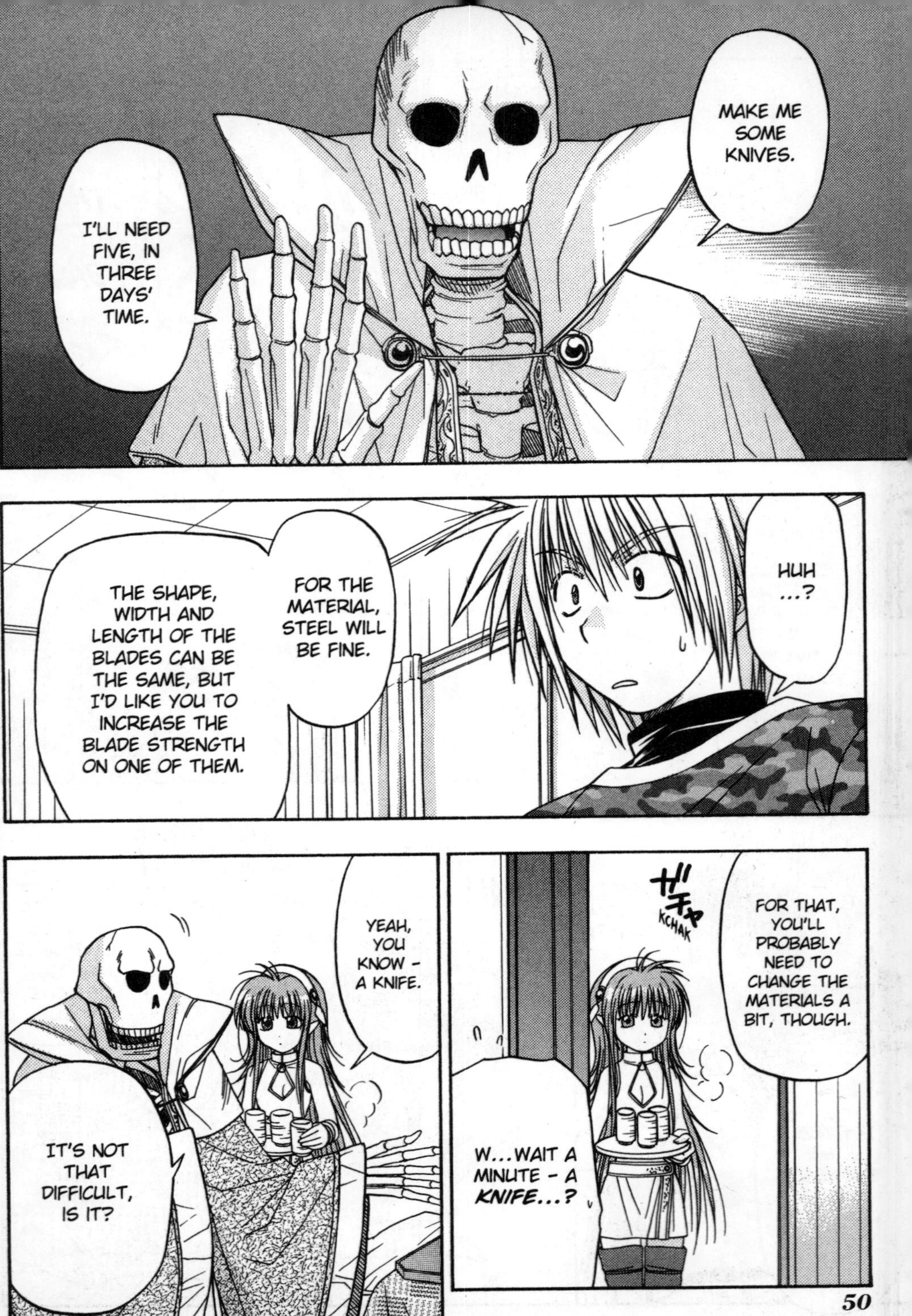
MAKE ME SOME KNIVES.
I'LL NEED FIVE, IN THREE DAYS' TIME.
HUH ...?
FOR THE MATERIAL, STEEL WILL BE FINE.
THE SHAPE, WIDTH AND LENGTH OF THE BLADES CAN BE THE SAME, BUT I'D LIKE YOU TO INCREASE THE BLADE STRENGTH ON ONE OF THEM.
FOR THAT, YOU'LL PROBABLY NEED TO CHANGE THE MATERIALS A BIT, THOUGH.
ガチャ
KCHAK
W...WAIT A MINUTE - A *KNIFE*...?
YEAH, YOU KNOW - A KNIFE.
IT'S NOT THAT DIFFICULT, IS IT?

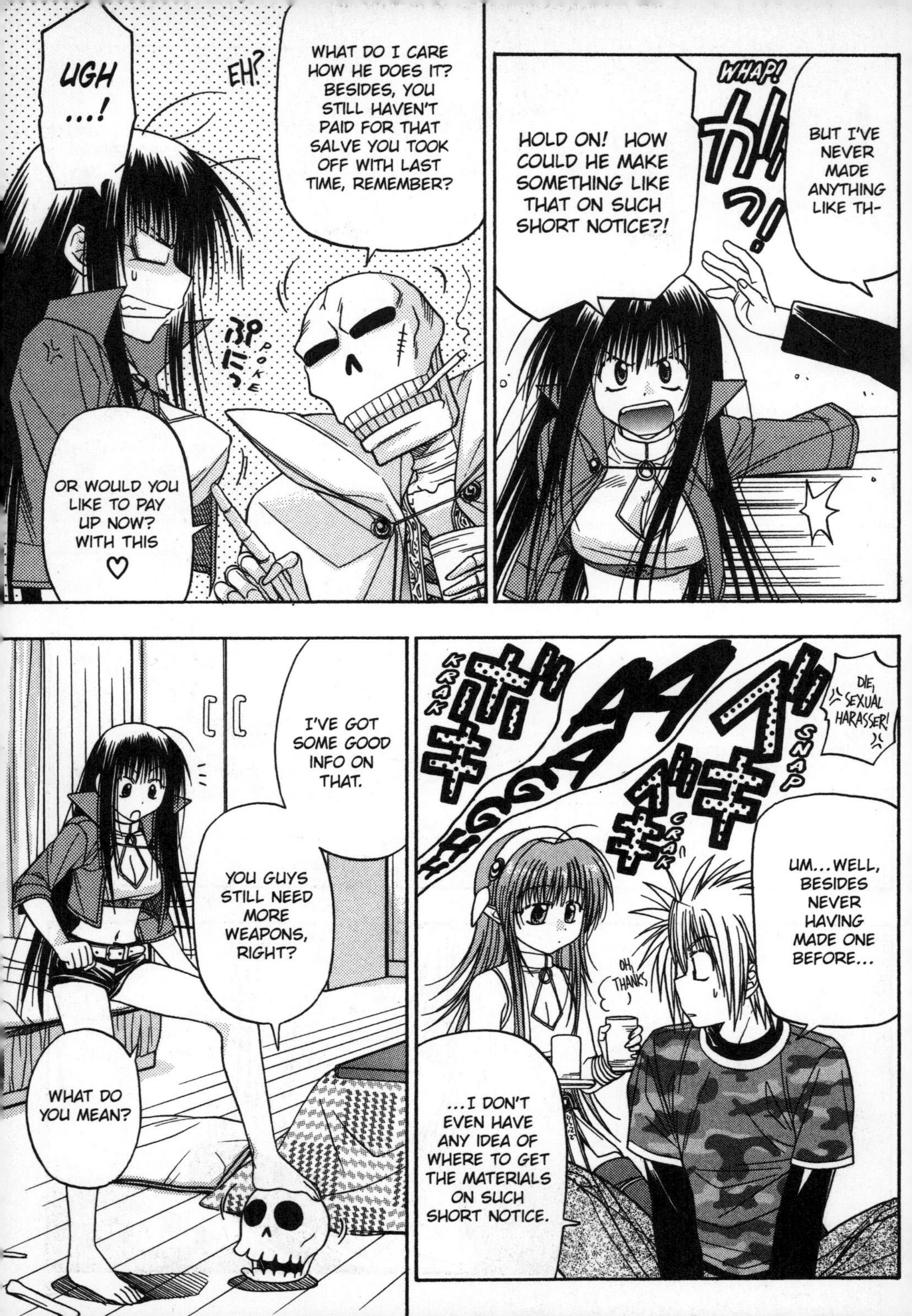
BUT I'VE NEVER MADE ANYTHING LIKE TH-
WHAP!
HOLD ON! HOW COULD HE MAKE SOMETHING LIKE THAT ON SUCH SHORT NOTICE?!
WHAT DO I CARE HOW HE DOES IT? BESIDES, YOU STILL HAVEN'T PAID FOR THAT SALVE YOU TOOK OFF WITH LAST TIME, REMEMBER?
EH?
UGH ...!
POKE
OR WOULD YOU LIKE TO PAY UP NOW? WITH THIS ♡
DIE, SEXUAL HARASSER!
SNAP
KRAK
CRAK
UM...WELL, BESIDES NEVER HAVING MADE ONE BEFORE...
OH, THANKS
...I DON'T EVEN HAVE ANY IDEA OF WHERE TO GET THE MATERIALS ON SUCH SHORT NOTICE.
I'VE GOT SOME GOOD INFO ON THAT.
YOU GUYS STILL NEED MORE WEAPONS, RIGHT?
WHAT DO YOU MEAN?

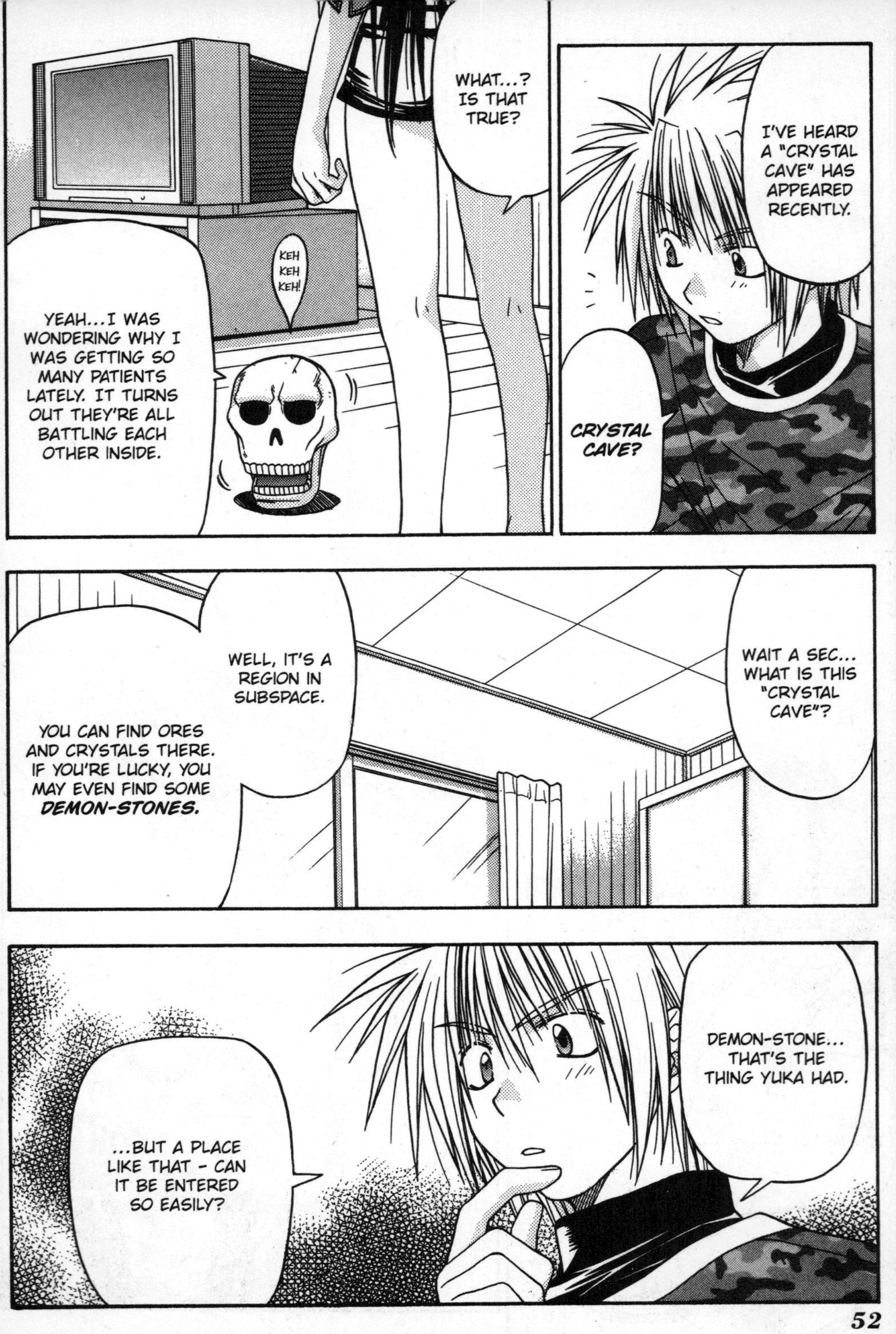
I'VE HEARD A "CRYSTAL CAVE" HAS APPEARED RECENTLY.
CRYSTAL CAVE?
WHAT...? IS THAT TRUE?
KEH KEH KEH!
YEAH...I WAS WONDERING WHY I WAS GETTING SO MANY PATIENTS LATELY. IT TURNS OUT THEY'RE ALL BATTLING EACH OTHER INSIDE.
WAIT A SEC... WHAT IS THIS "CRYSTAL CAVE"?
WELL, IT'S A REGION IN SUBSPACE.
YOU CAN FIND ORES AND CRYSTALS THERE. IF YOU'RE LUCKY, YOU MAY EVEN FIND SOME DEMON-STONES.
DEMON-STONE... THAT'S THE THING YUKA HAD.
...BUT A PLACE LIKE THAT - CAN IT BE ENTERED SO EASILY?

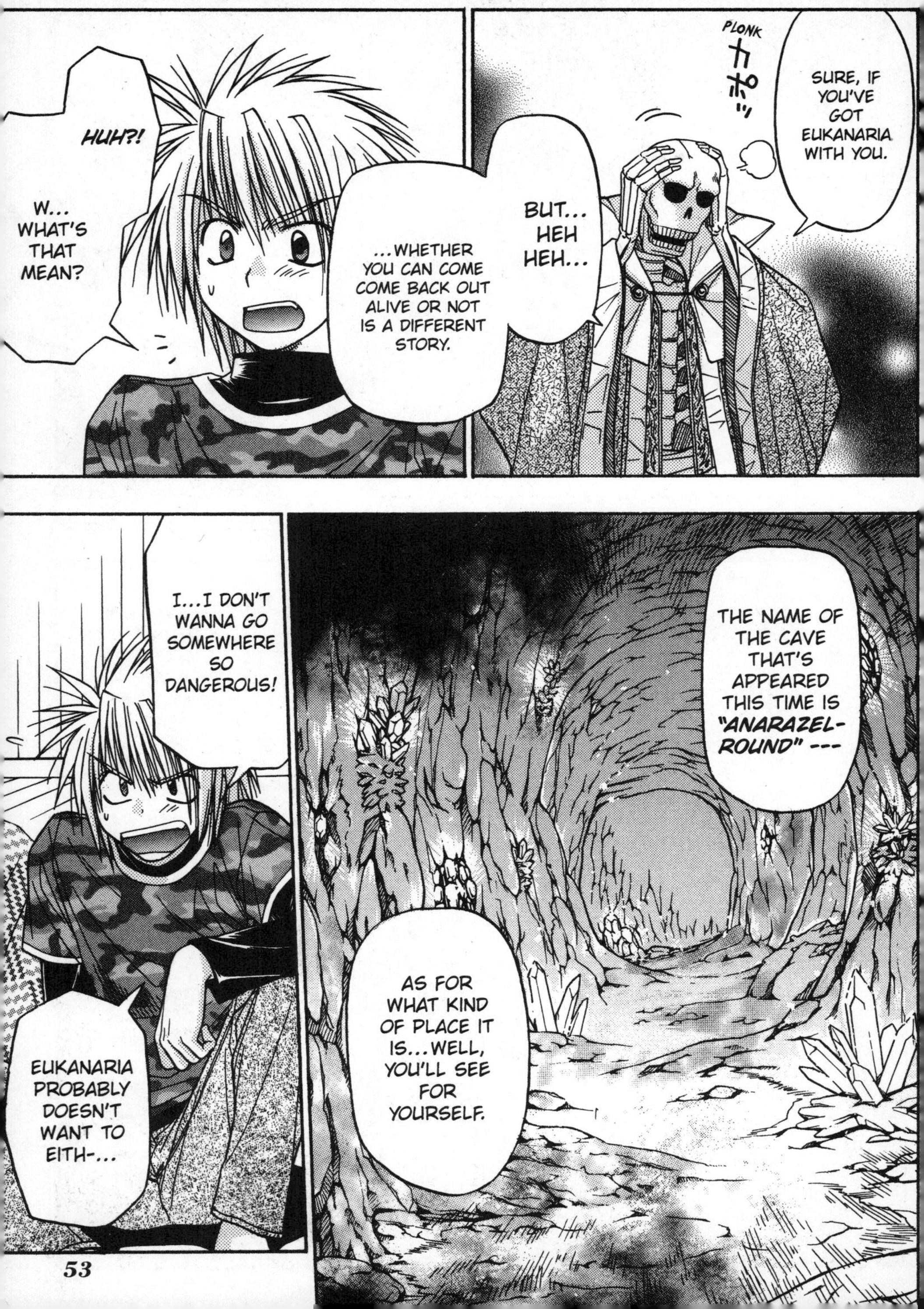
PLONK
カポッ
SURE, IF YOU'VE GOT EUKANARIA WITH YOU.
BUT... HEH HEH...
...WHETHER YOU CAN COME COME BACK OUT ALIVE OR NOT IS A DIFFERENT STORY.
HUH?!
W... WHAT'S THAT MEAN?
THE NAME OF THE CAVE THAT'S APPEARED THIS TIME IS "ANARAZEL-ROUND" ---
AS FOR WHAT KIND OF PLACE IT IS...WELL, YOU'LL SEE FOR YOURSELF.
I...I DON'T WANNA GO SOMEWHERE SO DANGEROUS!
EUKANARIA PROBABLY DOESN'T WANT TO EITH-...

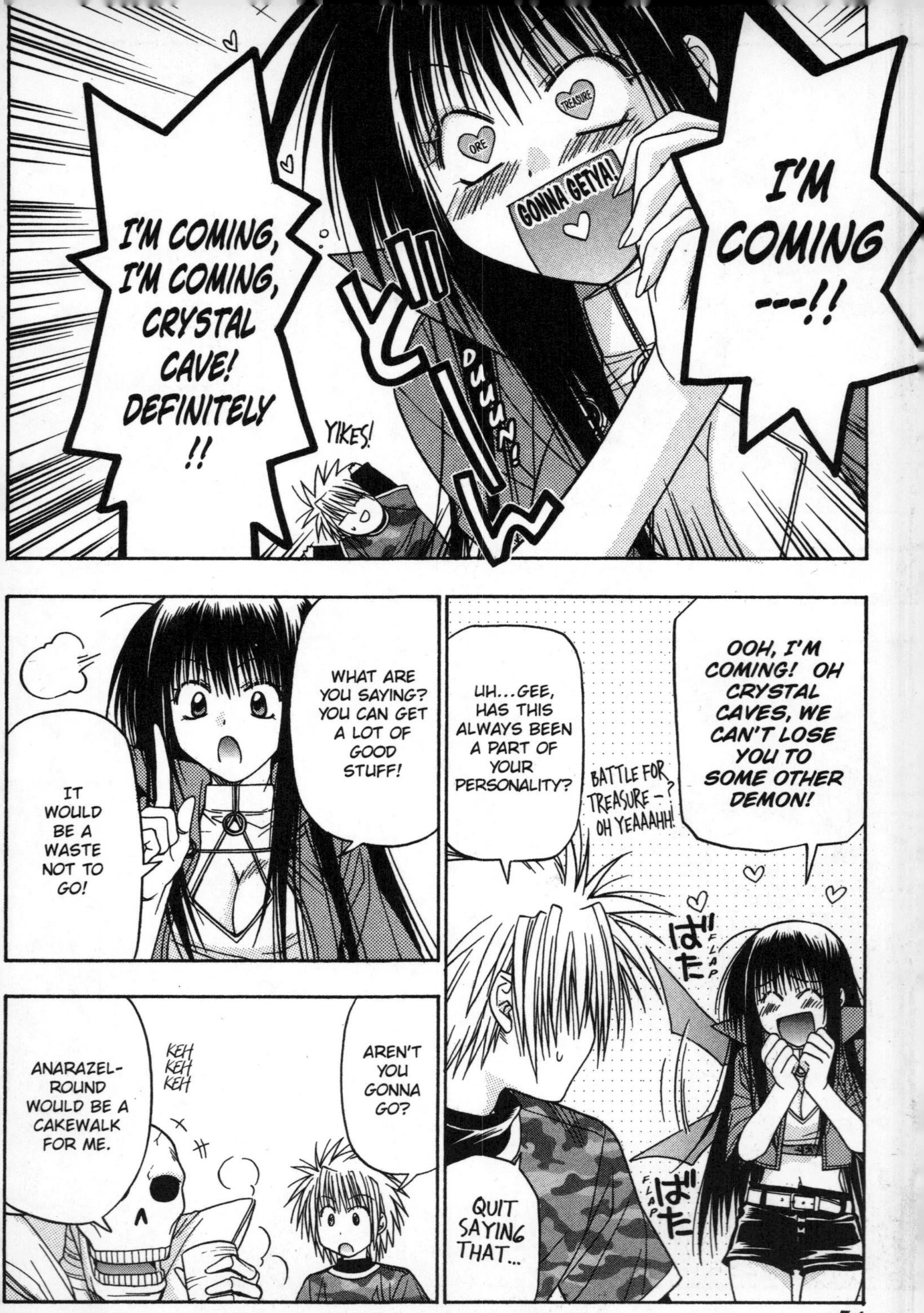
I'M COMING ---!!
TREASURE
ORE
GONNA GETYA!
DUUUN!
YIKES!
I'M COMING, I'M COMING, CRYSTAL CAVE! DEFINITELY!!
OOH, I'M COMING! OH CRYSTAL CAVES, WE CAN'T LOSE YOU TO SOME OTHER DEMON!
BATTLE FOR TREASURE-? OH YEAAAHH!
UH...GEE, HAS THIS ALWAYS BEEN A PART OF YOUR PERSONALITY?
ぱた FLAP
ぱた FLAP
QUIT SAYING THAT...
WHAT ARE YOU SAYING? YOU CAN GET A LOT OF GOOD STUFF!
IT WOULD BE A WASTE NOT TO GO!
AREN'T YOU GONNA GO?
KEH KEH KEH
ANARAZEL-ROUND WOULD BE A CAKEWALK FOR ME.

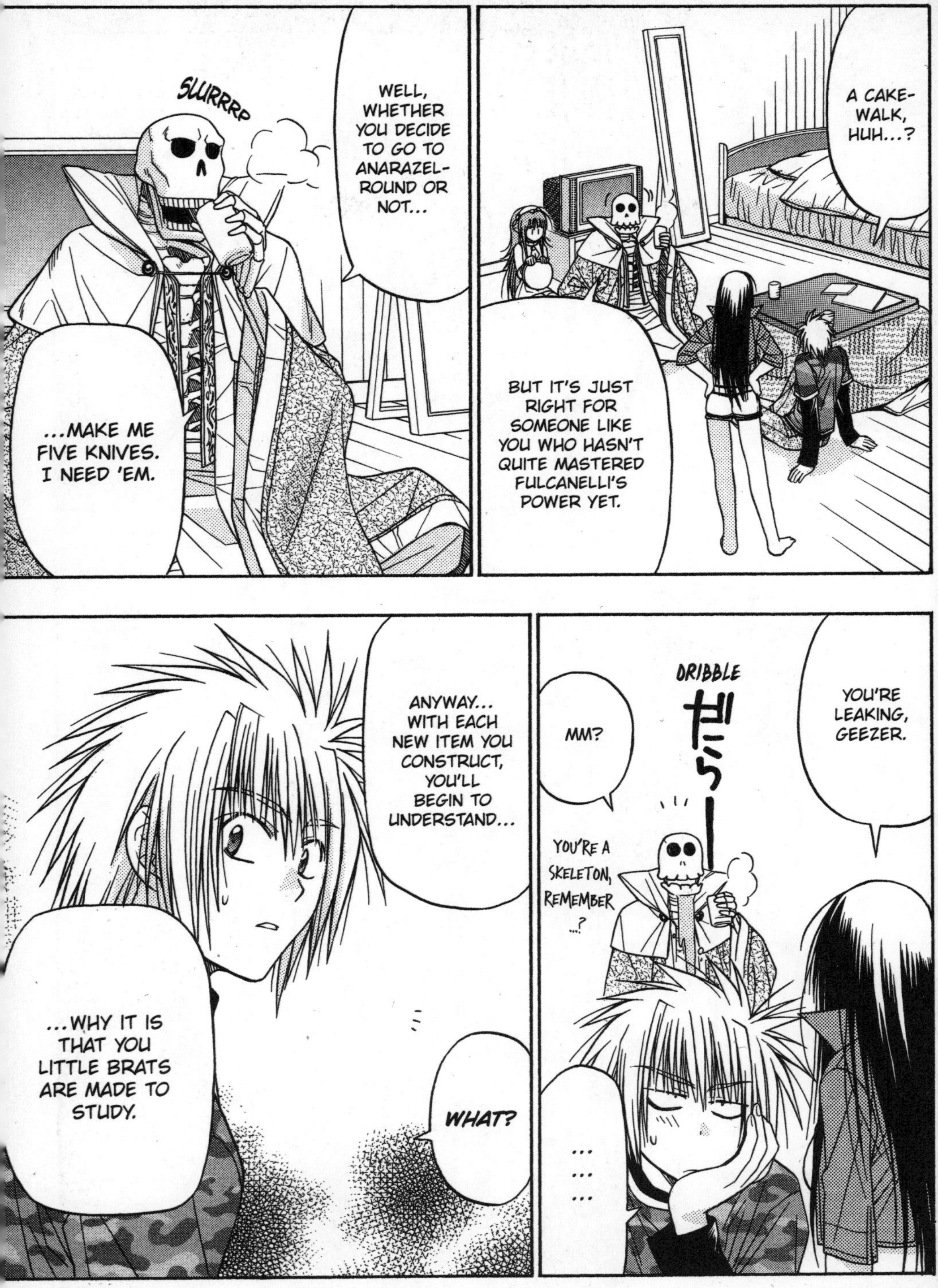
A CAKE-WALK, HUH...?
BUT IT'S JUST RIGHT FOR SOMEONE LIKE YOU WHO HASN'T QUITE MASTERED FULCANELLI'S POWER YET.
SLURRRP
WELL, WHETHER YOU DECIDE TO GO TO ANARAZEL-ROUND OR NOT...
...MAKE ME FIVE KNIVES. I NEED 'EM.
YOU'RE LEAKING, GEEZER.
DRIBBLE
MM?
YOU'RE A SKELETON, REMEMBER ...?
...
...
...
ANYWAY... WITH EACH NEW ITEM YOU CONSTRUCT, YOU'LL BEGIN TO UNDERSTAND...
...WHY IT IS THAT YOU LITTLE BRATS ARE MADE TO STUDY.
WHAT?

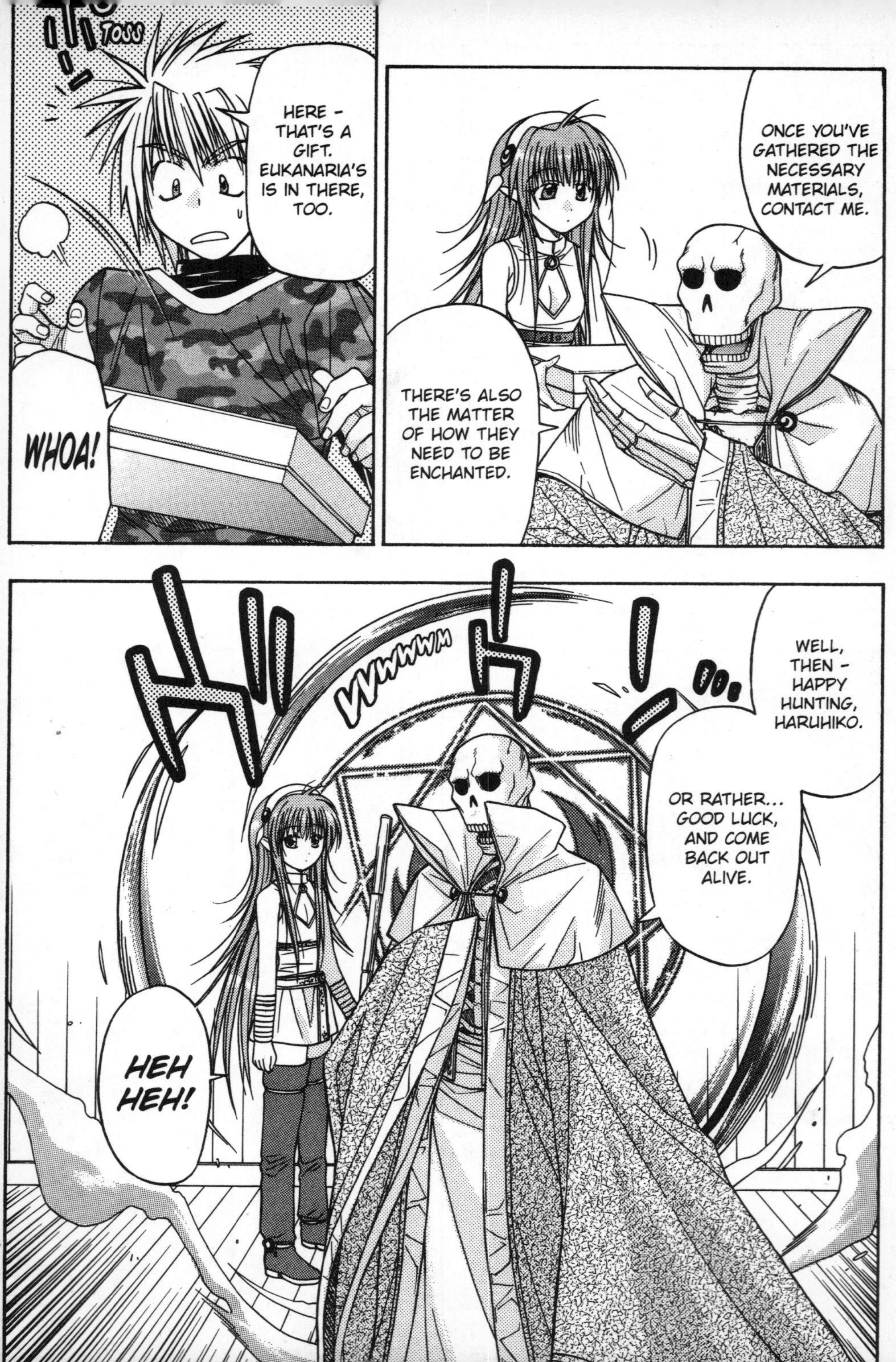
ONCE YOU'VE GATHERED THE NECESSARY MATERIALS, CONTACT ME.
THERE'S ALSO THE MATTER OF HOW THEY NEED TO BE ENCHANTED.
TOSS
HERE - THAT'S A GIFT. EUKANARIA'S IS IN THERE, TOO.
WHOA!
WELL, THEN - HAPPY HUNTING, HARUHIKO.
OR RATHER... GOOD LUCK, AND COME BACK OUT ALIVE.
VVWWWWM
HEH HEH!

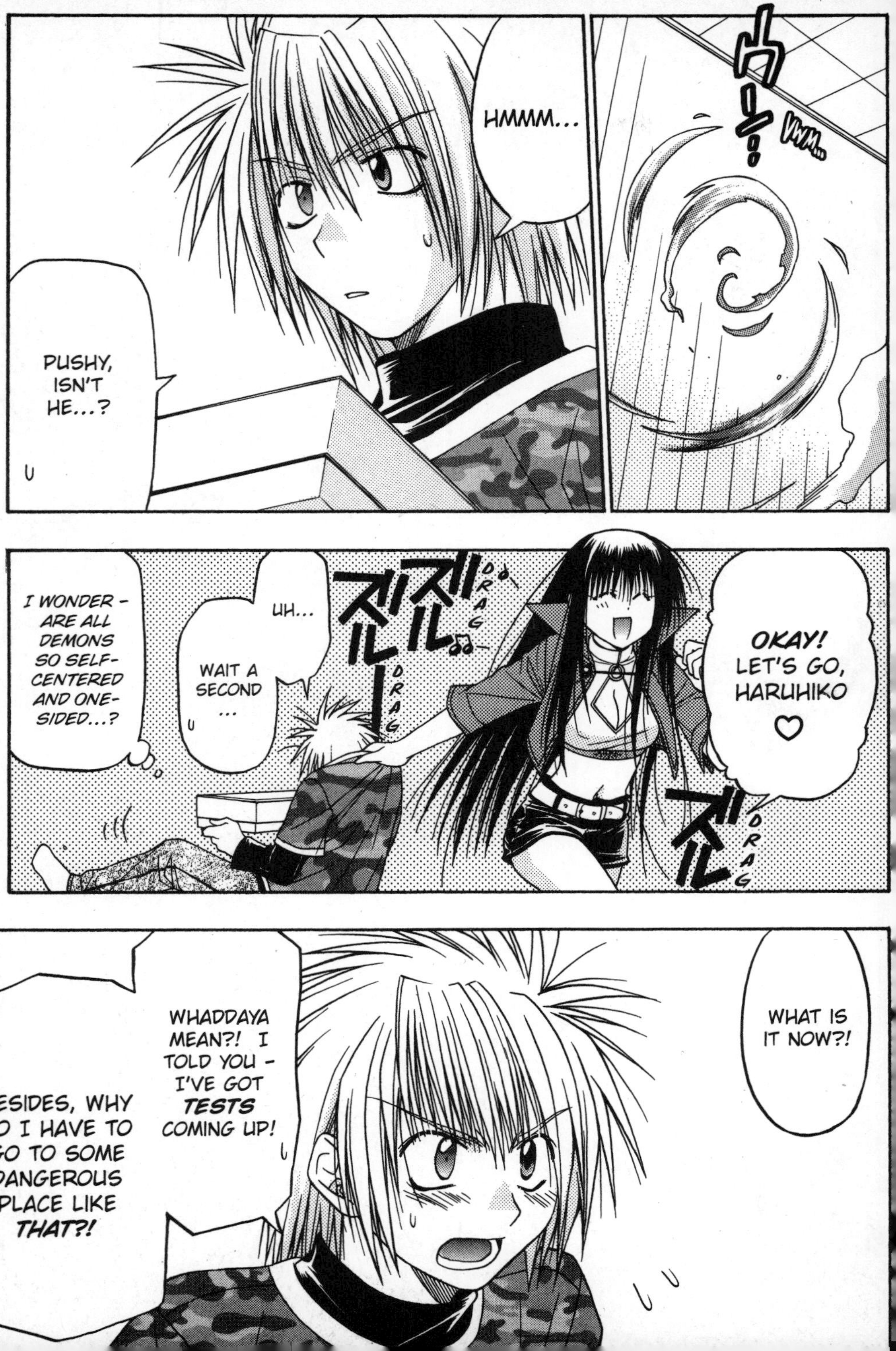
VWM...
HMMM...
PUSHY, ISN'T HE...?
OKAY! LET'S GO, HARUHIKO ♡
DRAG
DRAG
DRAG
UH...
WAIT A SECOND ...
I WONDER - ARE ALL DEMONS SO SELF-CENTERED AND ONE-SIDED...?
WHAT IS IT NOW?!
WHADDAYA MEAN?! I TOLD YOU - I'VE GOT TESTS COMING UP!
BESIDES, WHY DO I HAVE TO GO TO SOME DANGEROUS PLACE LIKE THAT?!

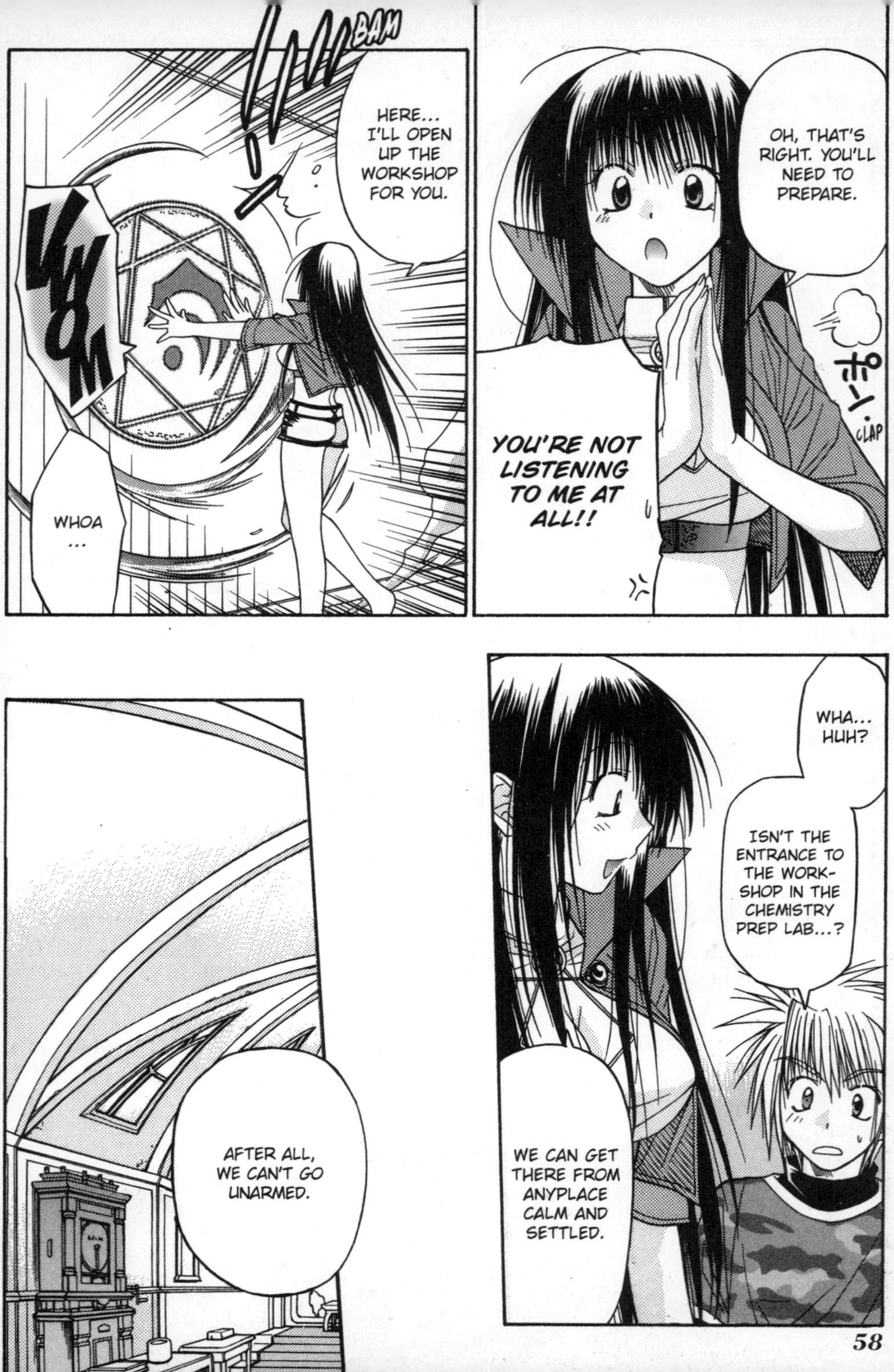
OH, THAT'S RIGHT. YOU'LL NEED TO PREPARE.
ポン
CLAP
YOU'RE NOT LISTENING TO ME AT ALL!!
BAM
HERE... I'LL OPEN UP THE WORKSHOP FOR YOU.
WHOA ...
WHA... HUH?
ISN'T THE ENTRANCE TO THE WORK-SHOP IN THE CHEMISTRY PREP LAB...?
WE CAN GET THERE FROM ANYPLACE CALM AND SETTLED.
AFTER ALL, WE CAN'T GO UNARMED.

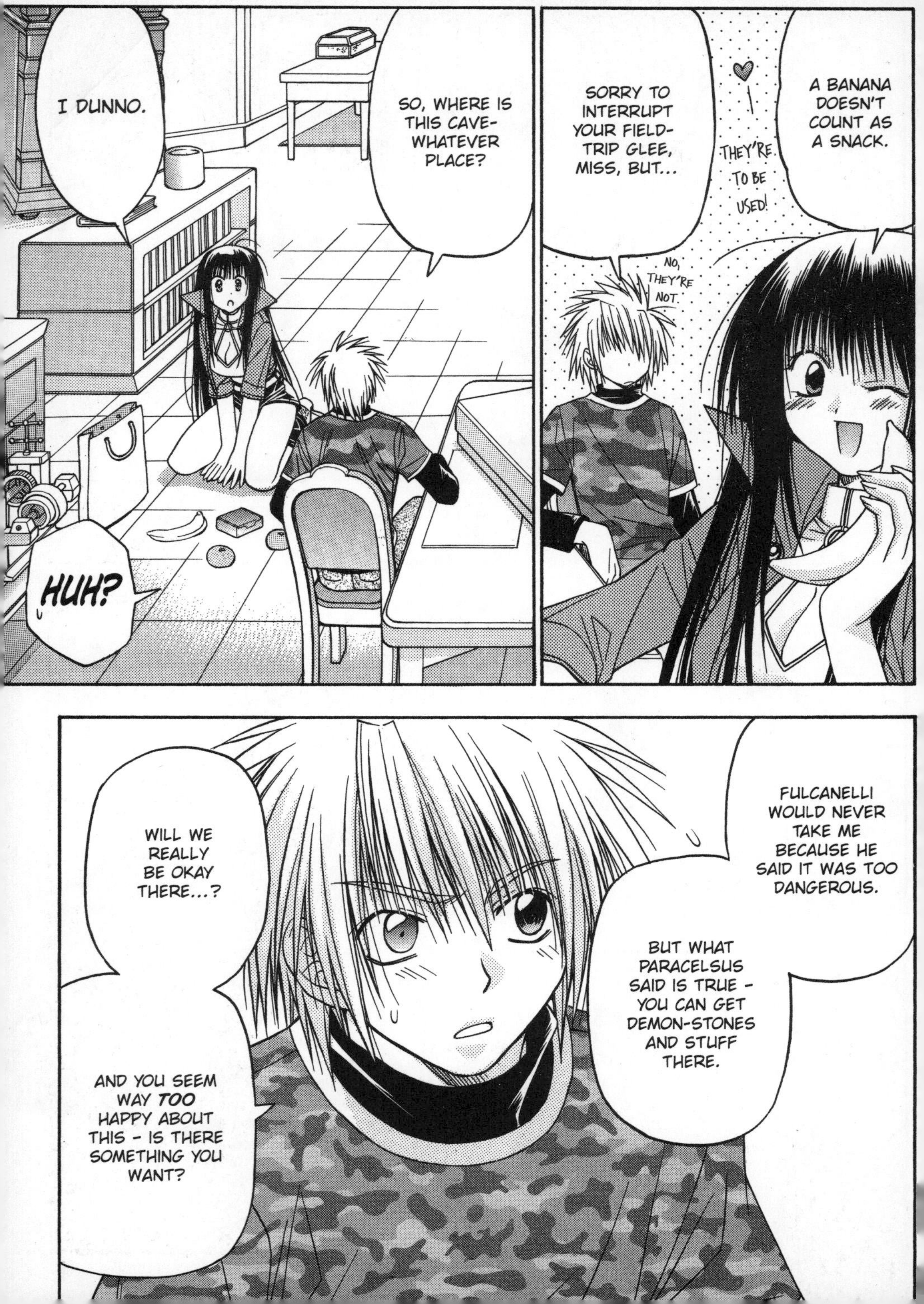
A BANANA DOESN'T COUNT AS A SNACK.
THEY'RE TO BE USED!
SORRY TO INTERRUPT YOUR FIELD-TRIP GLEE, MISS, BUT...
NO, THEY'RE NOT.
SO, WHERE IS THIS CAVE-WHATEVER PLACE?
I DUNNO.
HUH?
FULCANELLI WOULD NEVER TAKE ME BECAUSE HE SAID IT WAS TOO DANGEROUS.
BUT WHAT PARACELSUS SAID IS TRUE - YOU CAN GET DEMON-STONES AND STUFF THERE.
WILL WE REALLY BE OKAY THERE...?
AND YOU SEEM WAY *TOO* HAPPY ABOUT THIS - IS THERE SOMETHING YOU WANT?

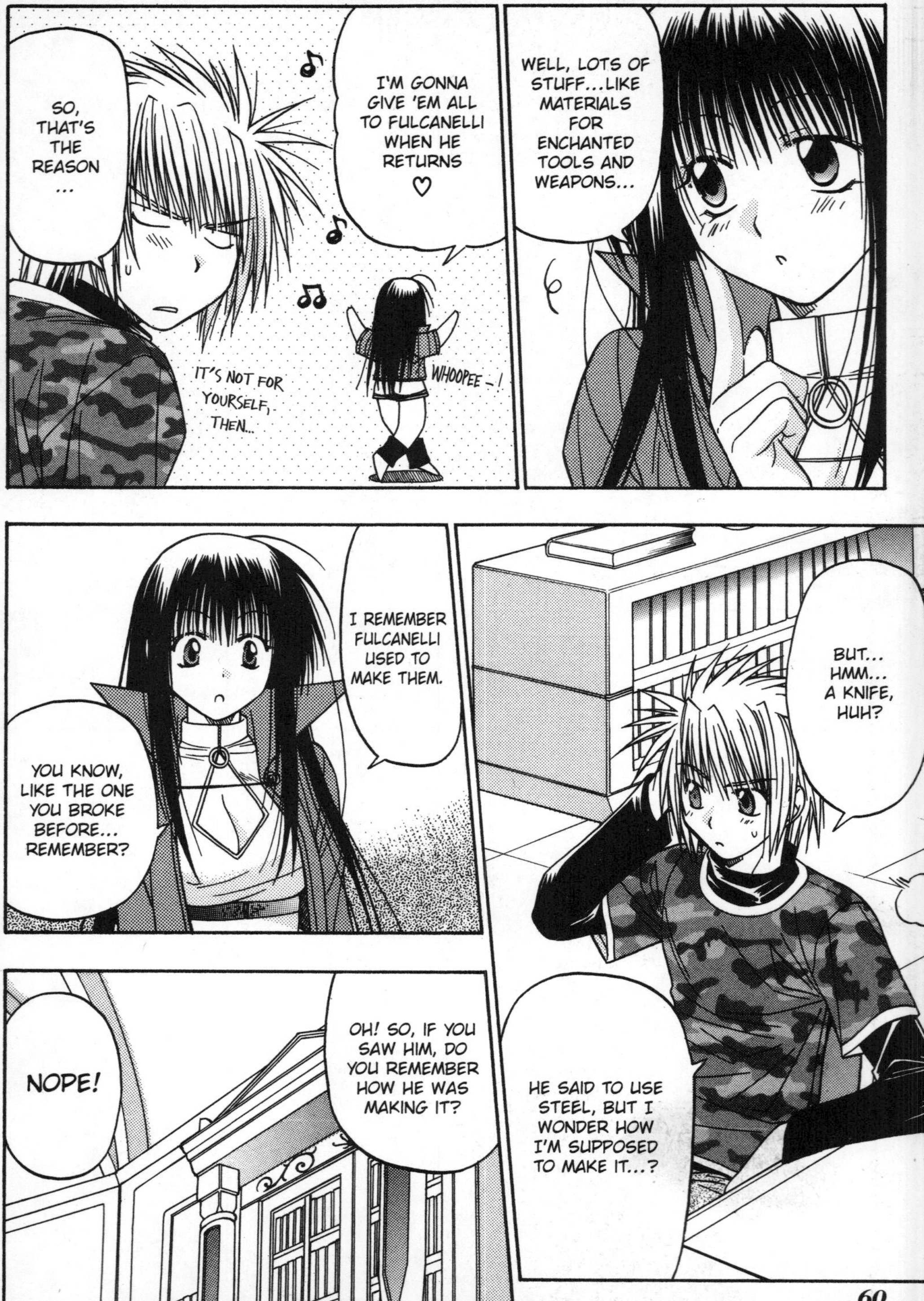
WELL, LOTS OF STUFF...LIKE MATERIALS FOR ENCHANTED TOOLS AND WEAPONS...
I'M GONNA GIVE 'EM ALL TO FULCANELLI WHEN HE RETURNS ♡
WHOOPEE~!
SO, THAT'S THE REASON ...
IT'S NOT FOR YOURSELF, THEN...
BUT... HMM... A KNIFE, HUH?
I REMEMBER FULCANELLI USED TO MAKE THEM.
YOU KNOW, LIKE THE ONE YOU BROKE BEFORE... REMEMBER?
HE SAID TO USE STEEL, BUT I WONDER HOW I'M SUPPOSED TO MAKE IT...?
OH! SO, IF YOU SAW HIM, DO YOU REMEMBER HOW HE WAS MAKING IT?
NOPE!

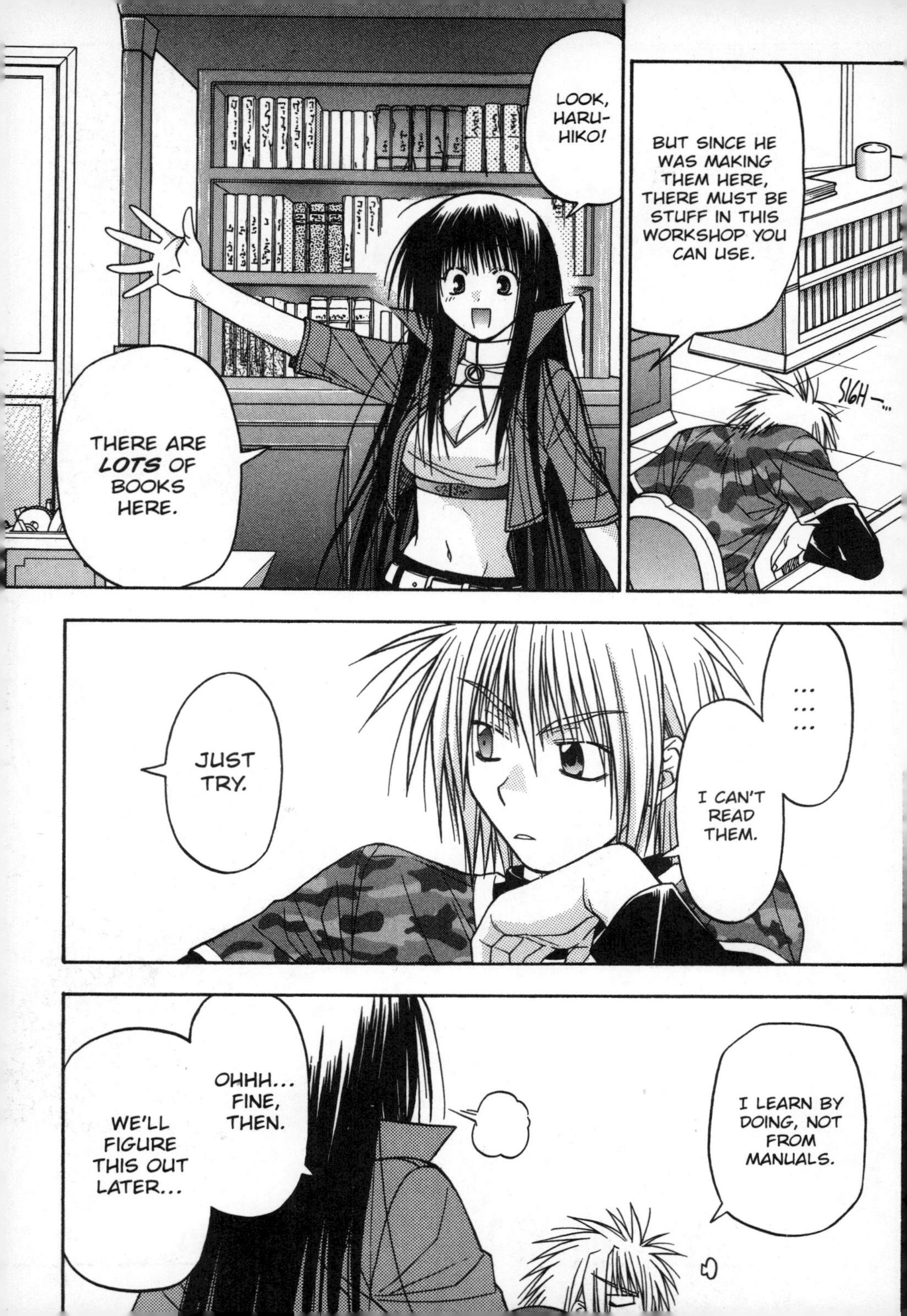
BUT SINCE HE WAS MAKING THEM HERE, THERE MUST BE STUFF IN THIS WORKSHOP YOU CAN USE.
SIGH–...
LOOK, HARU-HIKO!
THERE ARE LOTS OF BOOKS HERE.
....
I CAN'T READ THEM.
JUST TRY.
I LEARN BY DOING, NOT FROM MANUALS.
OHHH... FINE, THEN.
WE'LL FIGURE THIS OUT LATER...

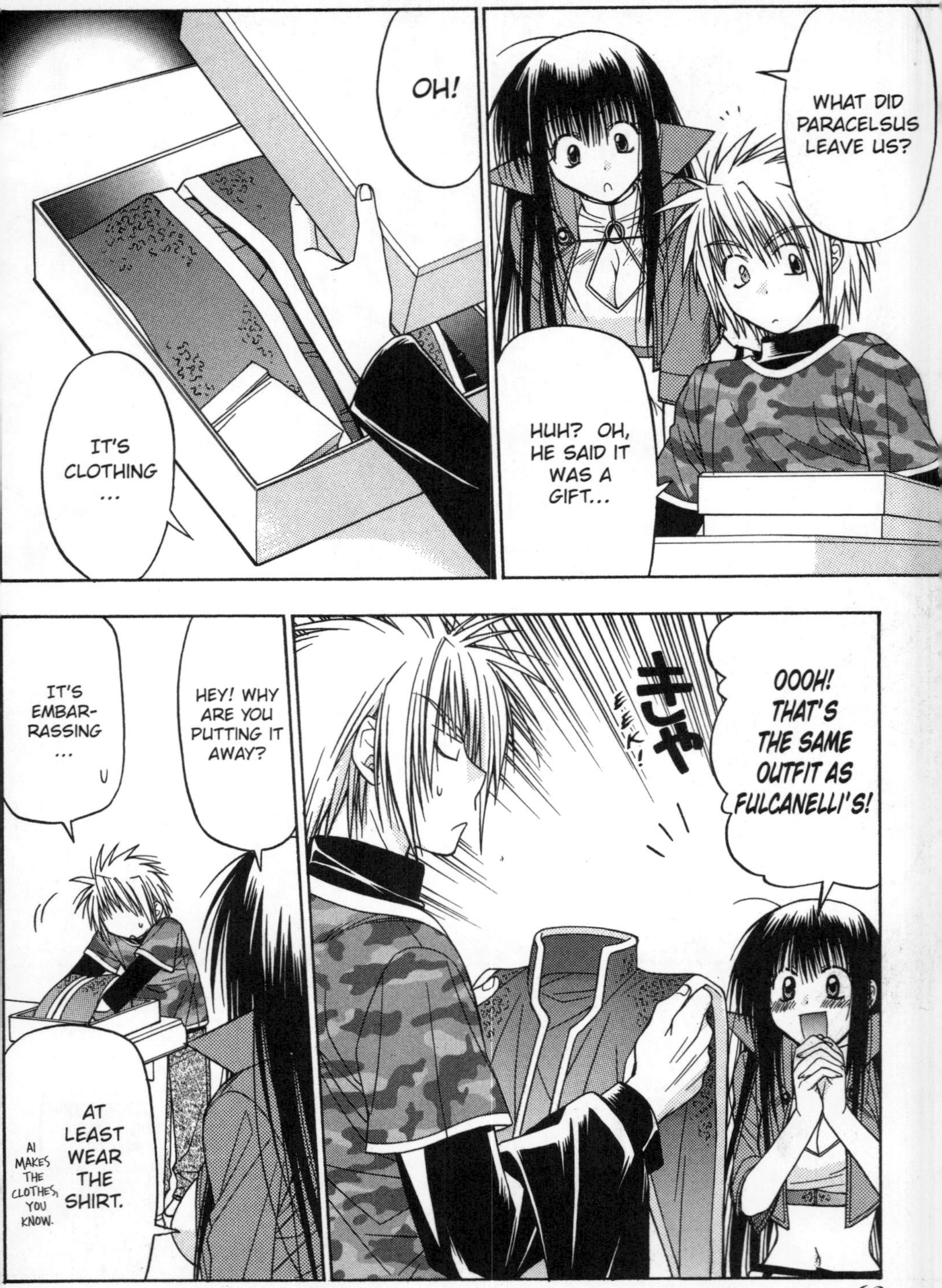
WHAT DID PARACELSUS LEAVE US?
HUH? OH, HE SAID IT WAS A GIFT...
OH!
IT'S CLOTHING ...
OOOH! THAT'S THE SAME OUTFIT AS FULCANELLI'S!
きゃ
EEEK!
HEY! WHY ARE YOU PUTTING IT AWAY?
IT'S EMBARRASSING ...
AT LEAST WEAR THE SHIRT.
AI MAKES THE CLOTHES, YOU KNOW.

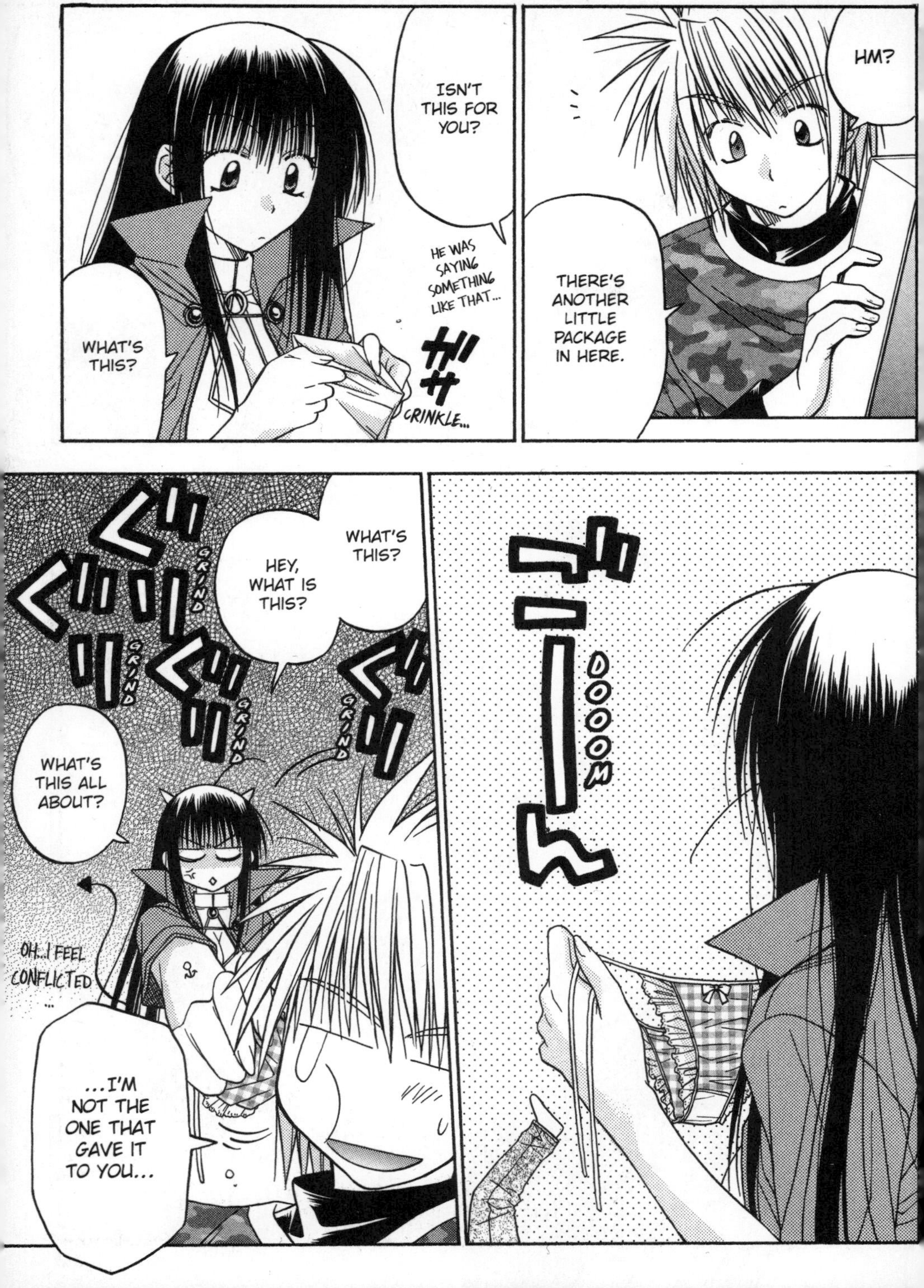
HM?
THERE'S ANOTHER LITTLE PACKAGE IN HERE.
ISN'T THIS FOR YOU?
HE WAS SAYING SOMETHING LIKE THAT...
ガサ
CRINKLE...
WHAT'S THIS?
どーん
DOOOOM
WHAT'S THIS?
HEY, WHAT IS THIS?
GRIND
GRIND
GRIND
GRIND
WHAT'S THIS ALL ABOUT?
OH...I FEEL CONFLICTED...
...I'M NOT THE ONE THAT GAVE IT TO YOU...

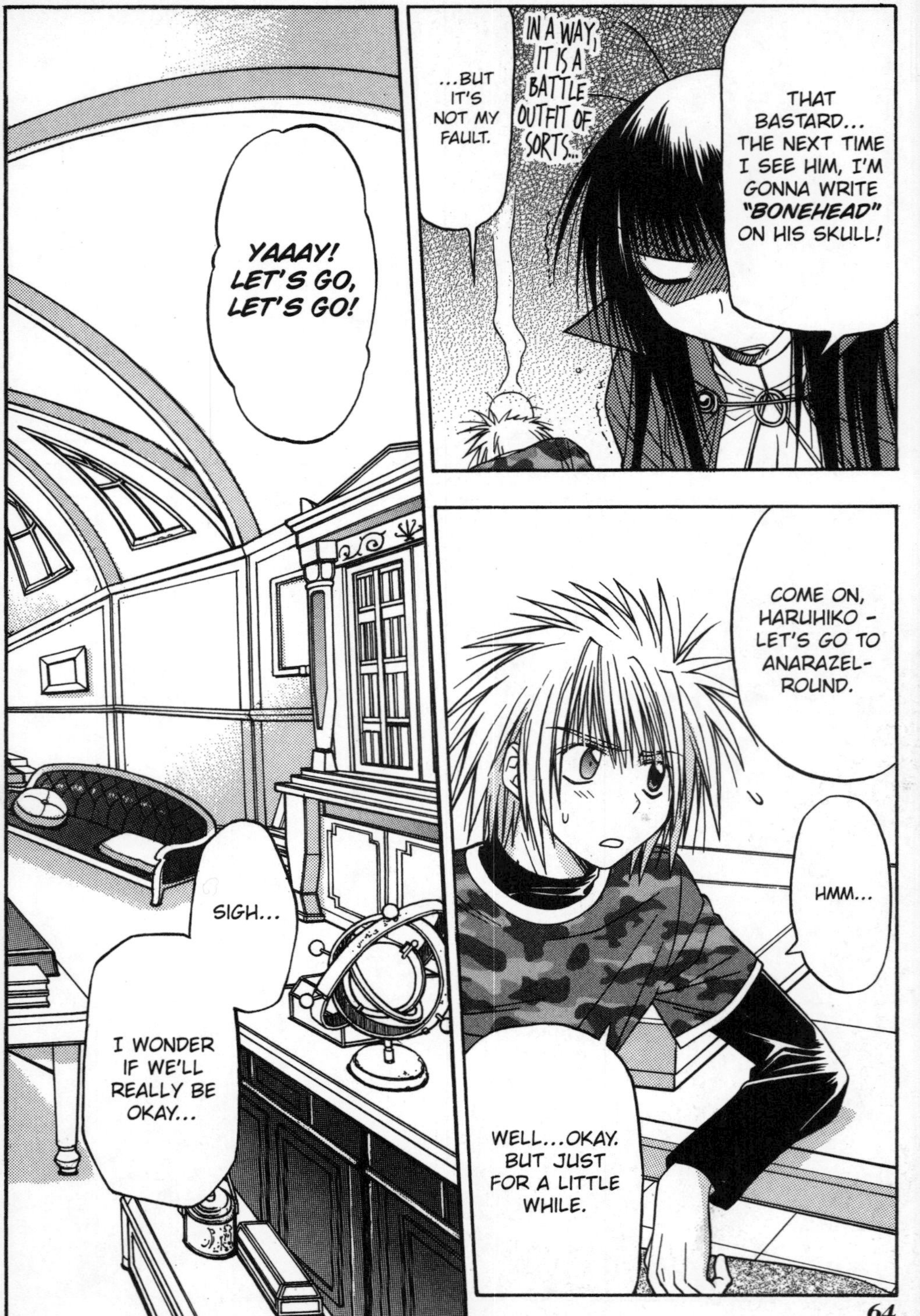
THAT BASTARD... THE NEXT TIME I SEE HIM, I'M GONNA WRITE "BONEHEAD" ON HIS SKULL!
IN A WAY, IT IS A BATTLE OUTFIT OF SORTS...
...BUT IT'S NOT MY FAULT.
COME ON, HARUHIKO - LET'S GO TO ANARAZEL-ROUND.
HMM...
WELL...OKAY. BUT JUST FOR A LITTLE WHILE.
YAAAY! LET'S GO, LET'S GO!
SIGH...
I WONDER IF WE'LL REALLY BE OKAY...

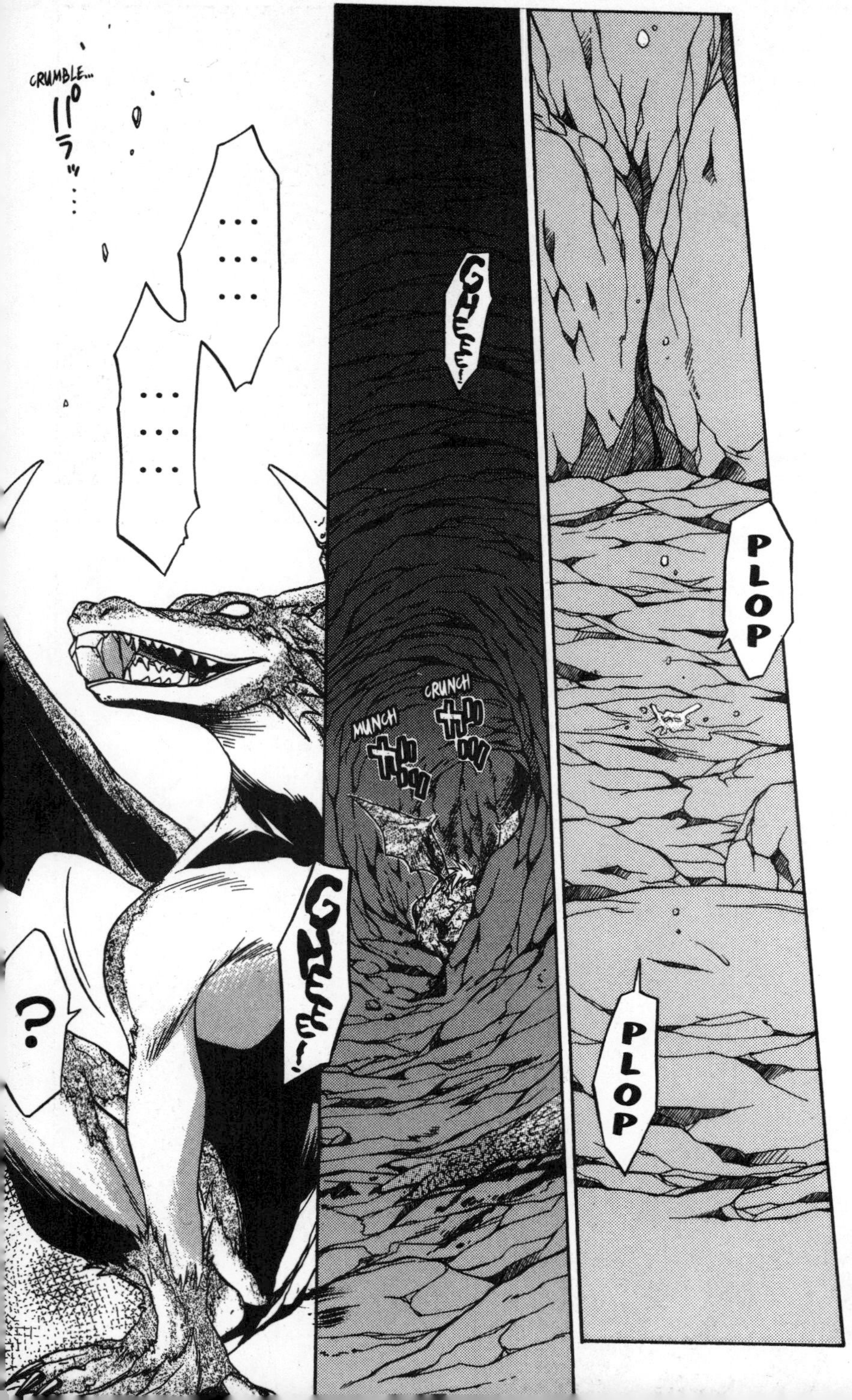
PLOP
PLOP
GHEEE...!
CRUNCH
MUNCH
GHEEE...!
CRUMBLE...
......
......
?

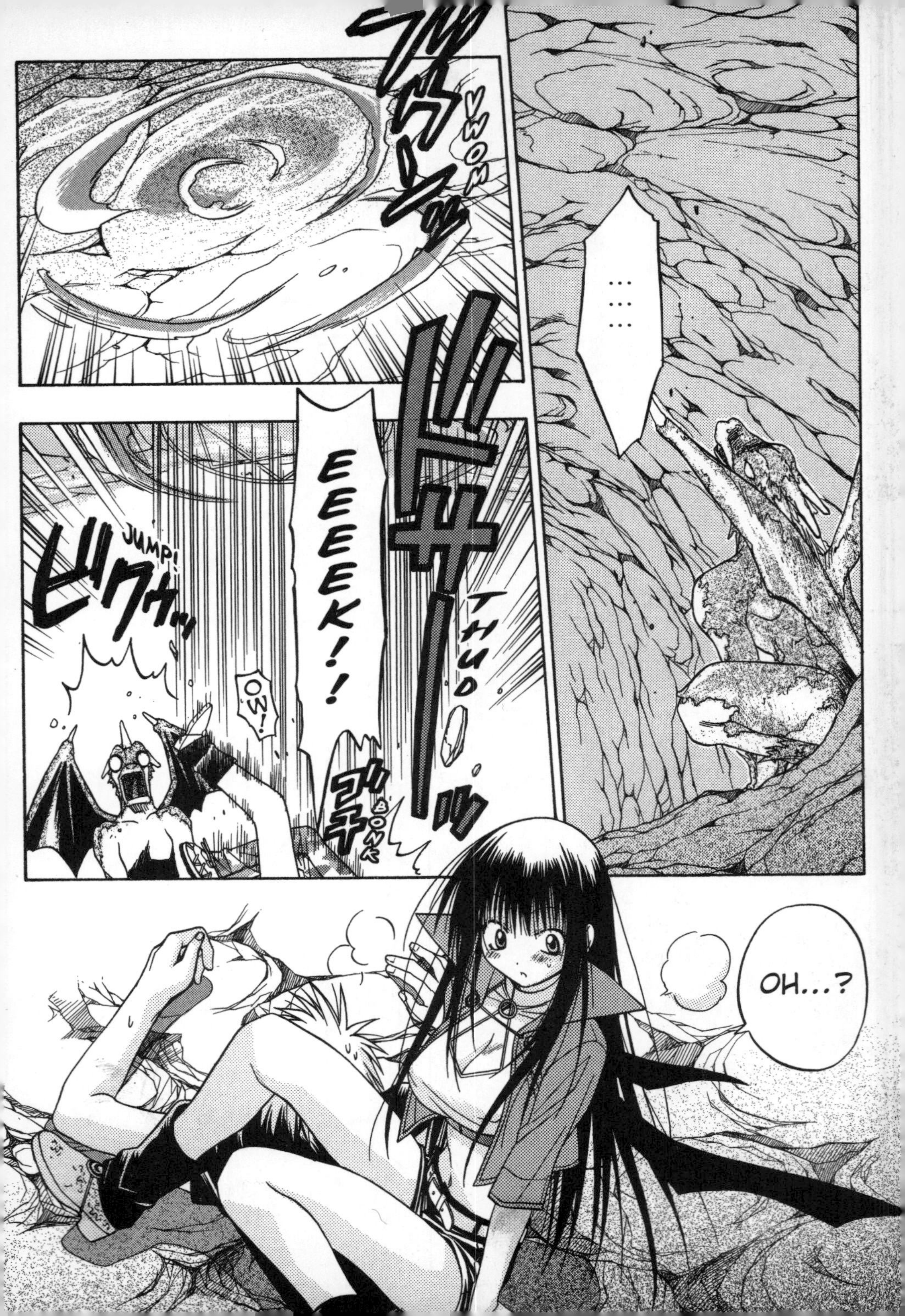
....
VWOM
EEEEEK!!
THUD
JUMP!
OW!
BONK
OH...?

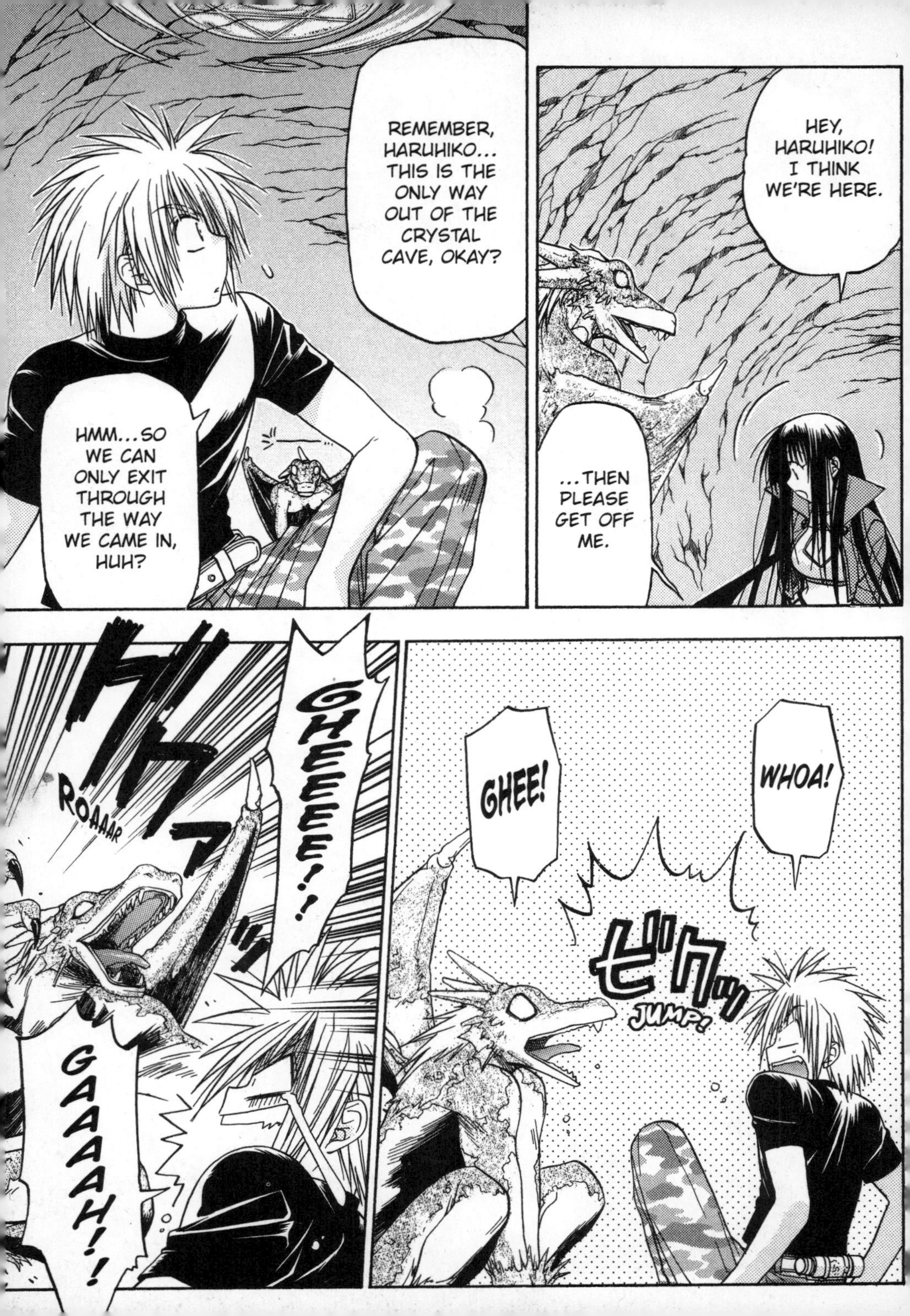
HEY, HARUHIKO! I THINK WE'RE HERE.
...THEN PLEASE GET OFF ME.
REMEMBER, HARUHIKO... THIS IS THE ONLY WAY OUT OF THE CRYSTAL CAVE, OKAY?
HMM...SO WE CAN ONLY EXIT THROUGH THE WAY WE CAME IN, HUH?
WHOA!
GHEE!
JUMP!
GHEEEEE!!
ROAAAR
GAAAAAH!!

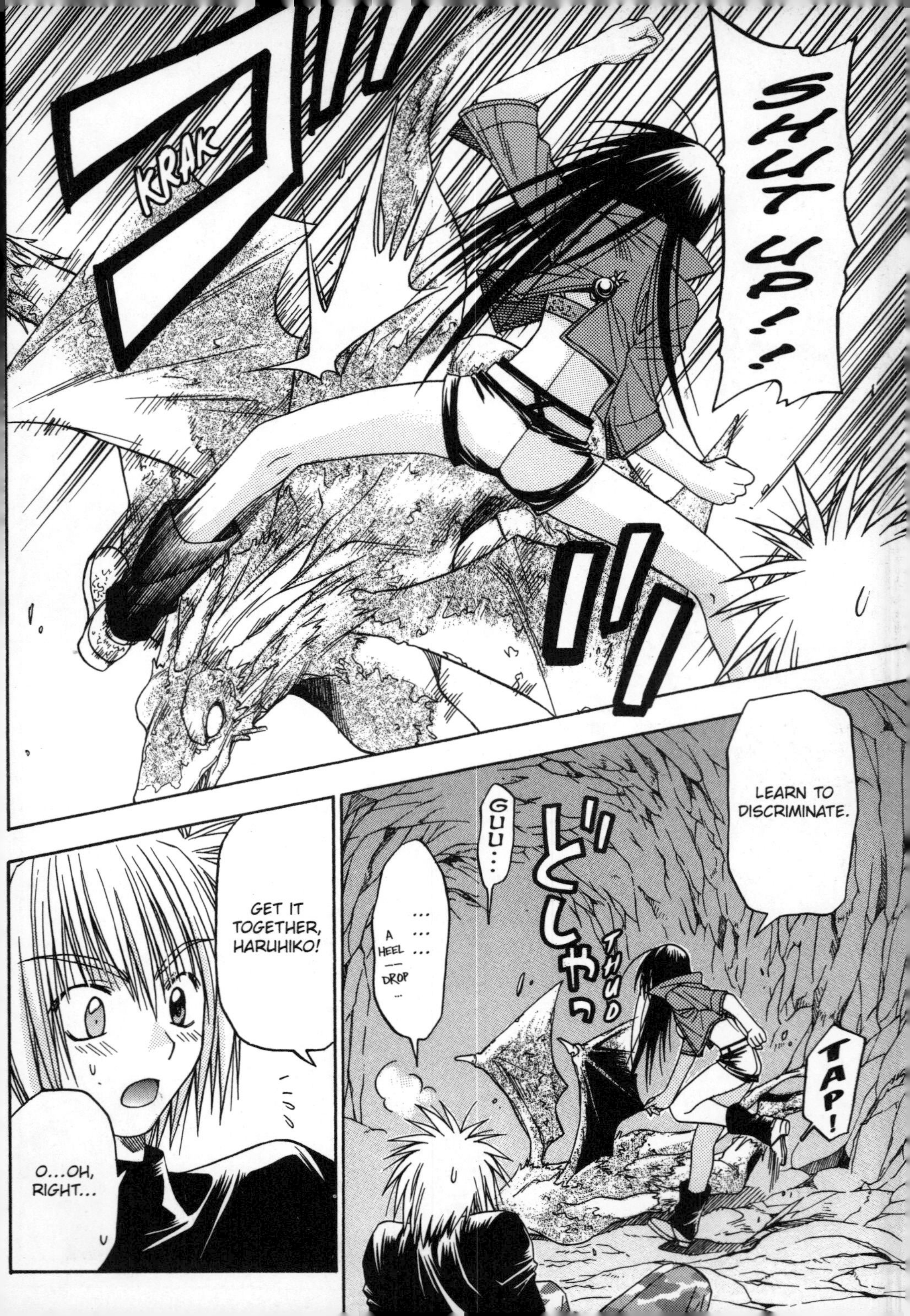
SHUT UP!!!
KRAK
LEARN TO DISCRIMINATE.
GUU...
どしゃっ
THUD
... ... A HEEL — DROP ...
TAP!
GET IT TOGETHER, HARUHIKO!
O...OH, RIGHT...

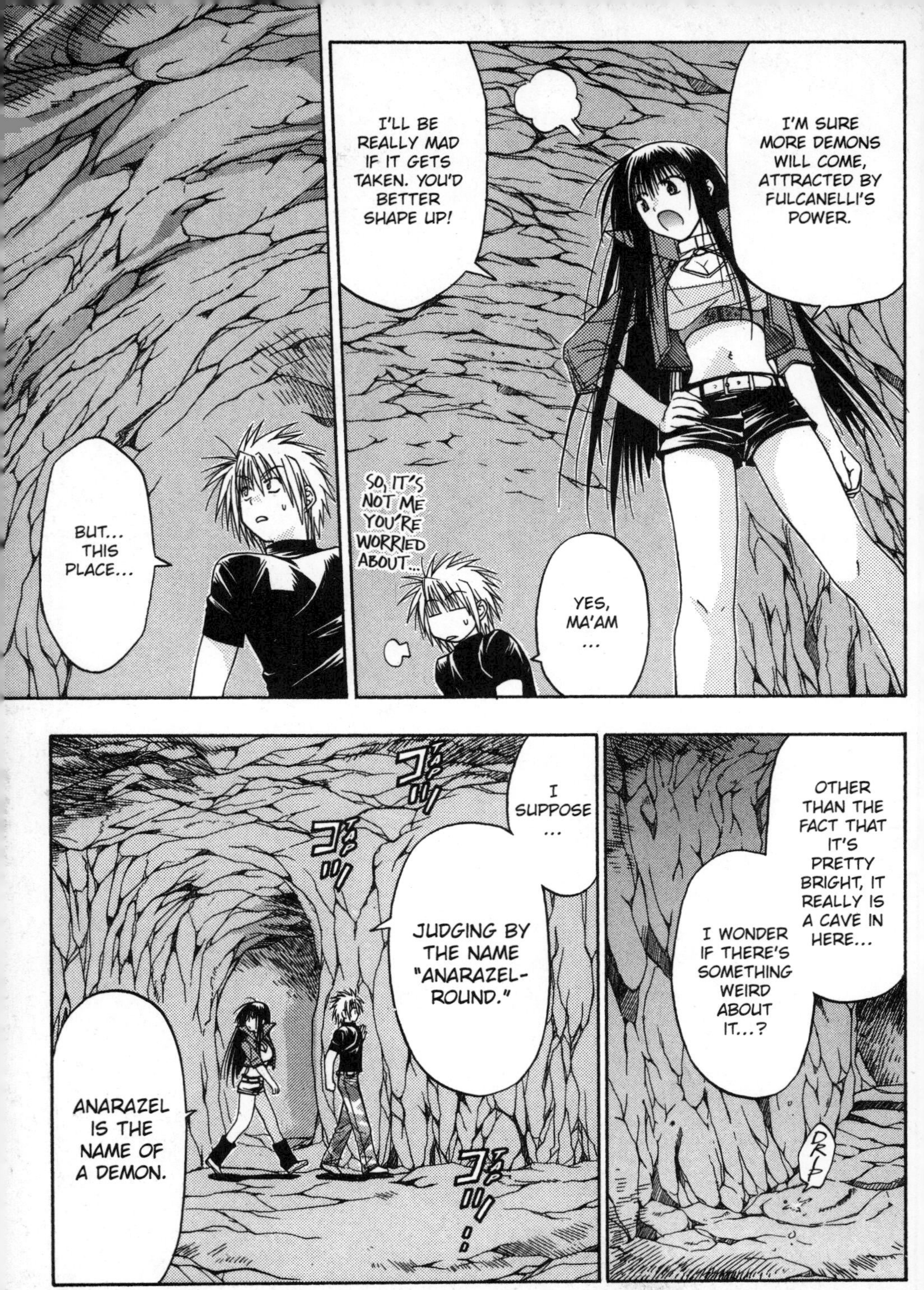

I'M SURE MORE DEMONS WILL COME, ATTRACTED BY FULCANELLI'S POWER.
I'LL BE REALLY MAD IF IT GETS TAKEN. YOU'D BETTER SHAPE UP!
YES, MA'AM ...
SO, IT'S NOT ME YOU'RE WORRIED ABOUT...
BUT... THIS PLACE...
OTHER THAN THE FACT THAT IT'S PRETTY BRIGHT, IT REALLY IS A CAVE IN HERE...
I WONDER IF THERE'S SOMETHING WEIRD ABOUT IT...?
DRIP
I SUPPOSE ...
JUDGING BY THE NAME "ANARAZEL-ROUND."
ANARAZEL IS THE NAME OF A DEMON.

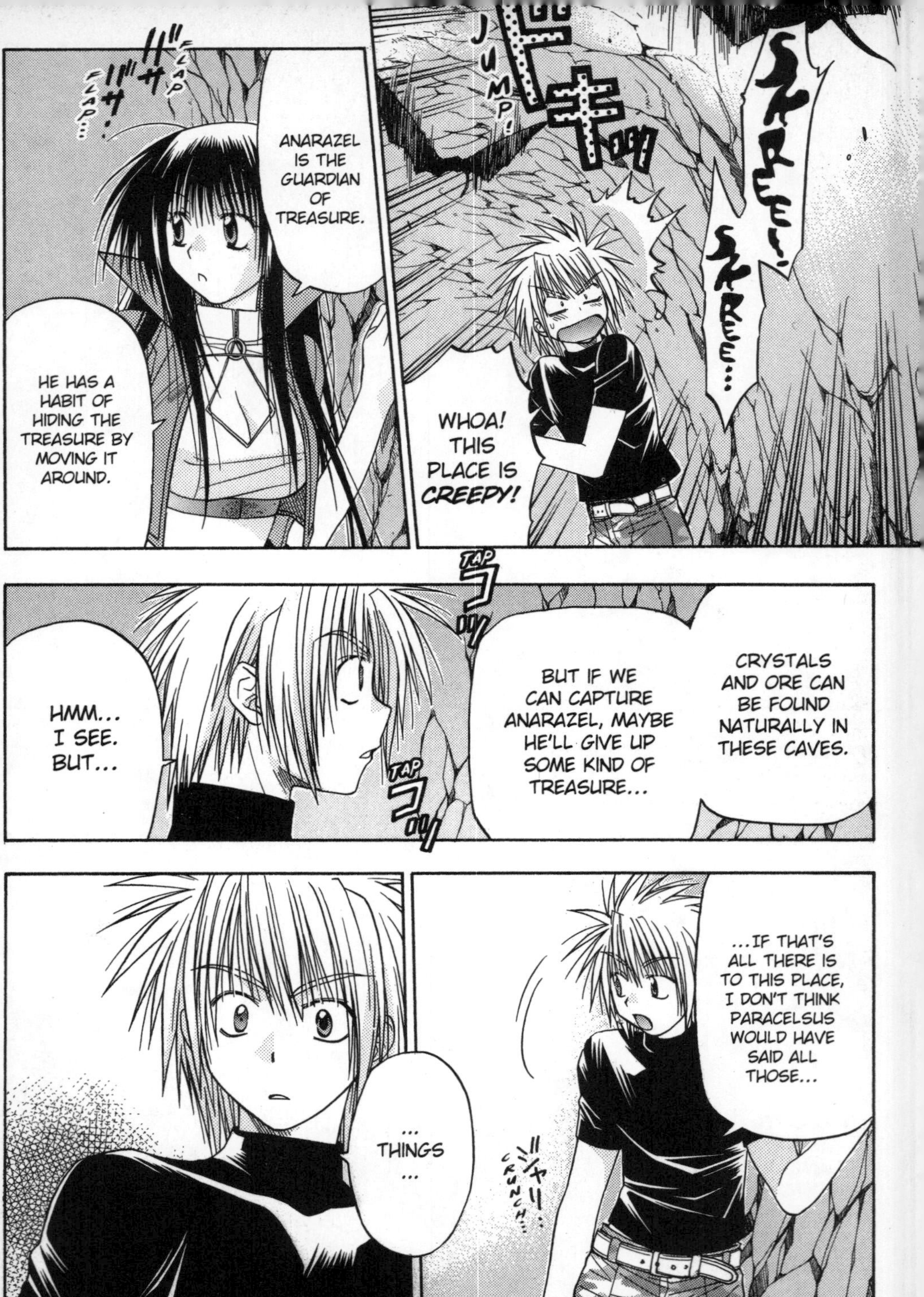
SKREE!
SKREE...
JUMP!
WHOA! THIS PLACE IS CREEPY!
FLAP FLAP...
ANARAZEL IS THE GUARDIAN OF TREASURE.
HE HAS A HABIT OF HIDING THE TREASURE BY MOVING IT AROUND.
CRYSTALS AND ORE CAN BE FOUND NATURALLY IN THESE CAVES.
BUT IF WE CAN CAPTURE ANARAZEL, MAYBE HE'LL GIVE UP SOME KIND OF TREASURE...
TAP
TAP
HMM... I SEE. BUT...
...IF THAT'S ALL THERE IS TO THIS PLACE, I DON'T THINK PARACELSUS WOULD HAVE SAID ALL THOSE...
CRUNCH...
... THINGS ...

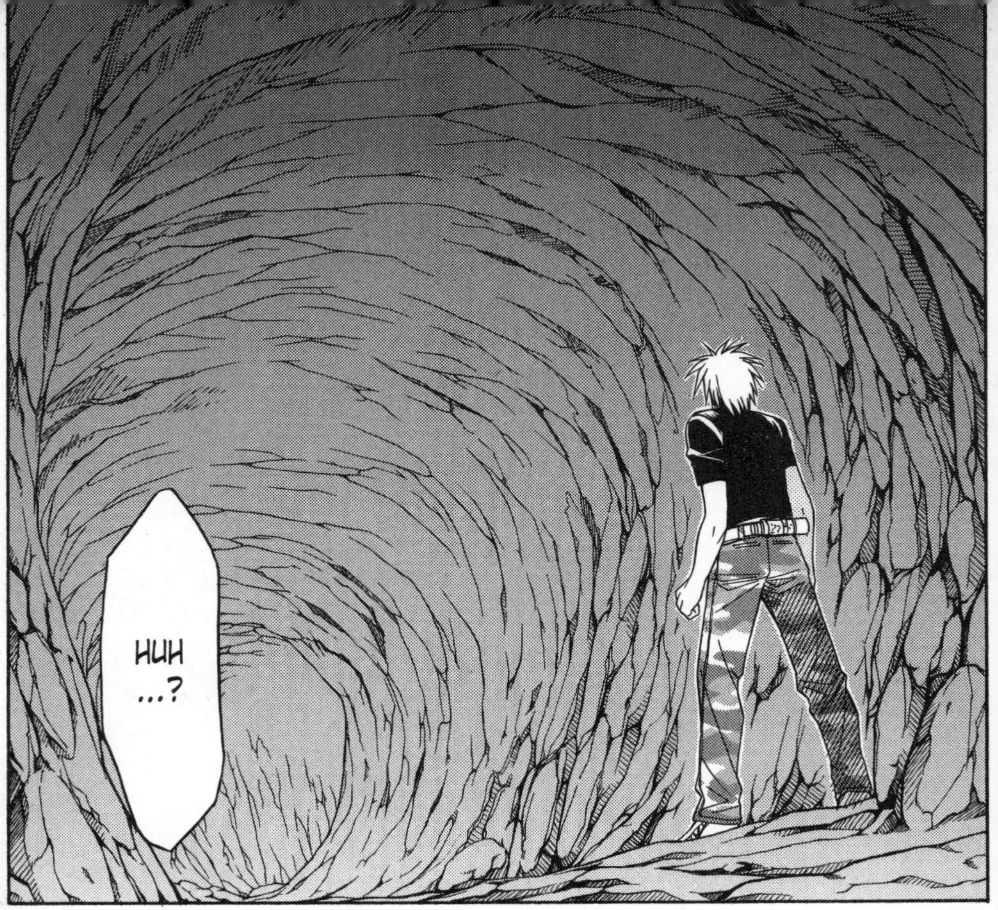
HUH ...?

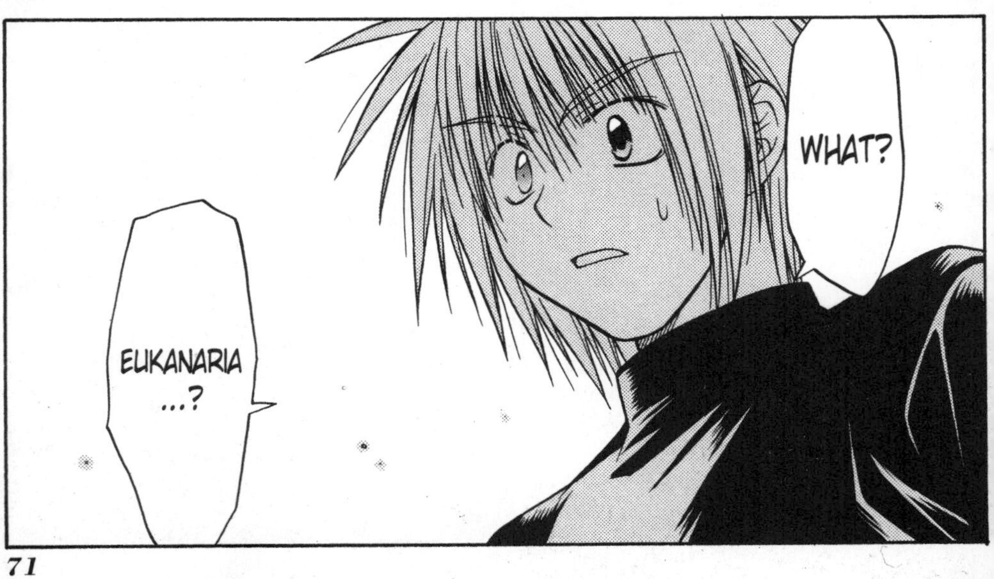
WHAT?
EUKANARIA ...?

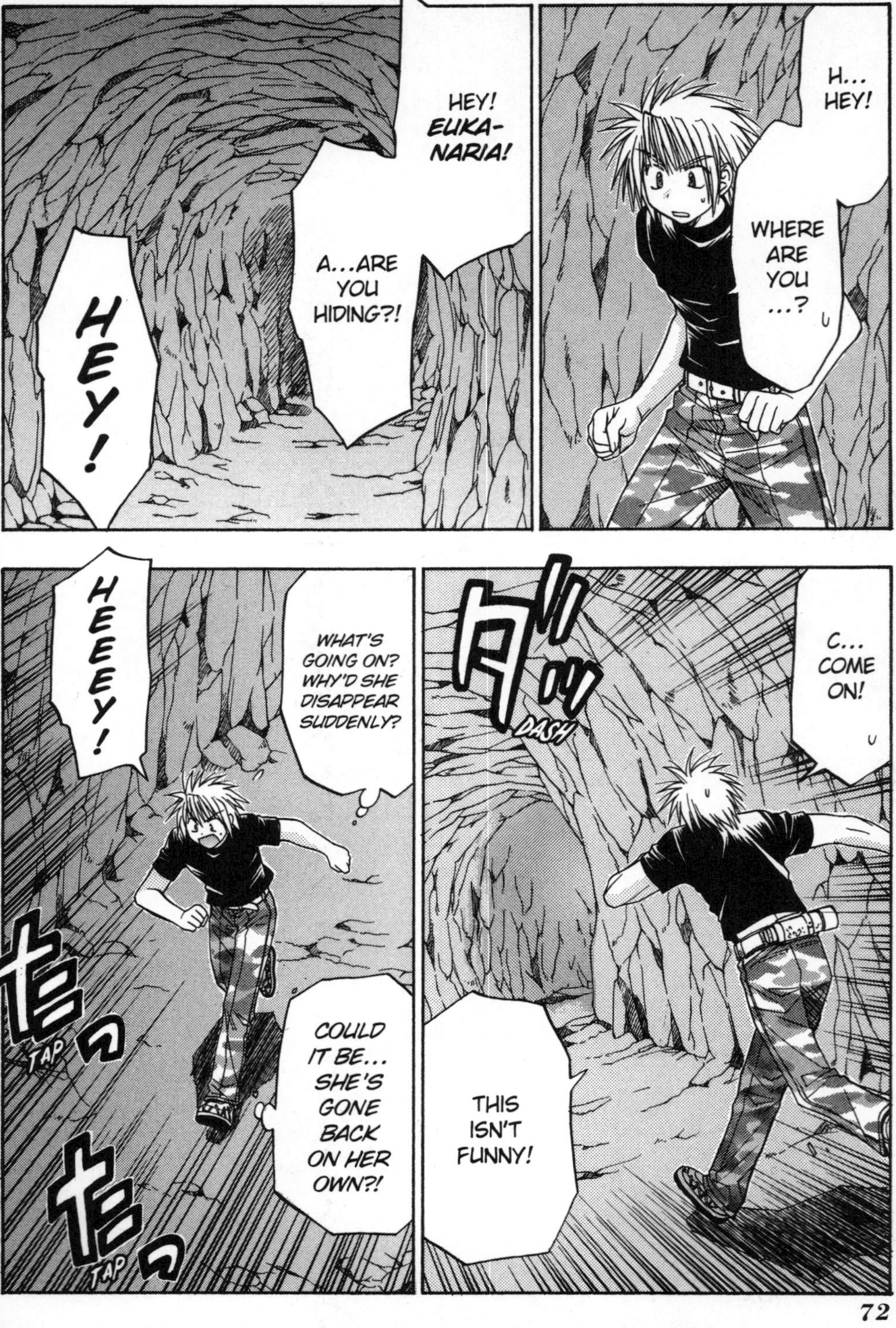
H... HEY!
WHERE ARE YOU ...?
HEY! EUKA-NARIA!
A...ARE YOU HIDING?!
HEY!
C... COME ON!
DASH
THIS ISN'T FUNNY!
WHAT'S GOING ON? WHY'D SHE DISAPPEAR SUDDENLY?
HEEEEY!
COULD IT BE... SHE'S GONE BACK ON HER OWN?!
TAP
TAP

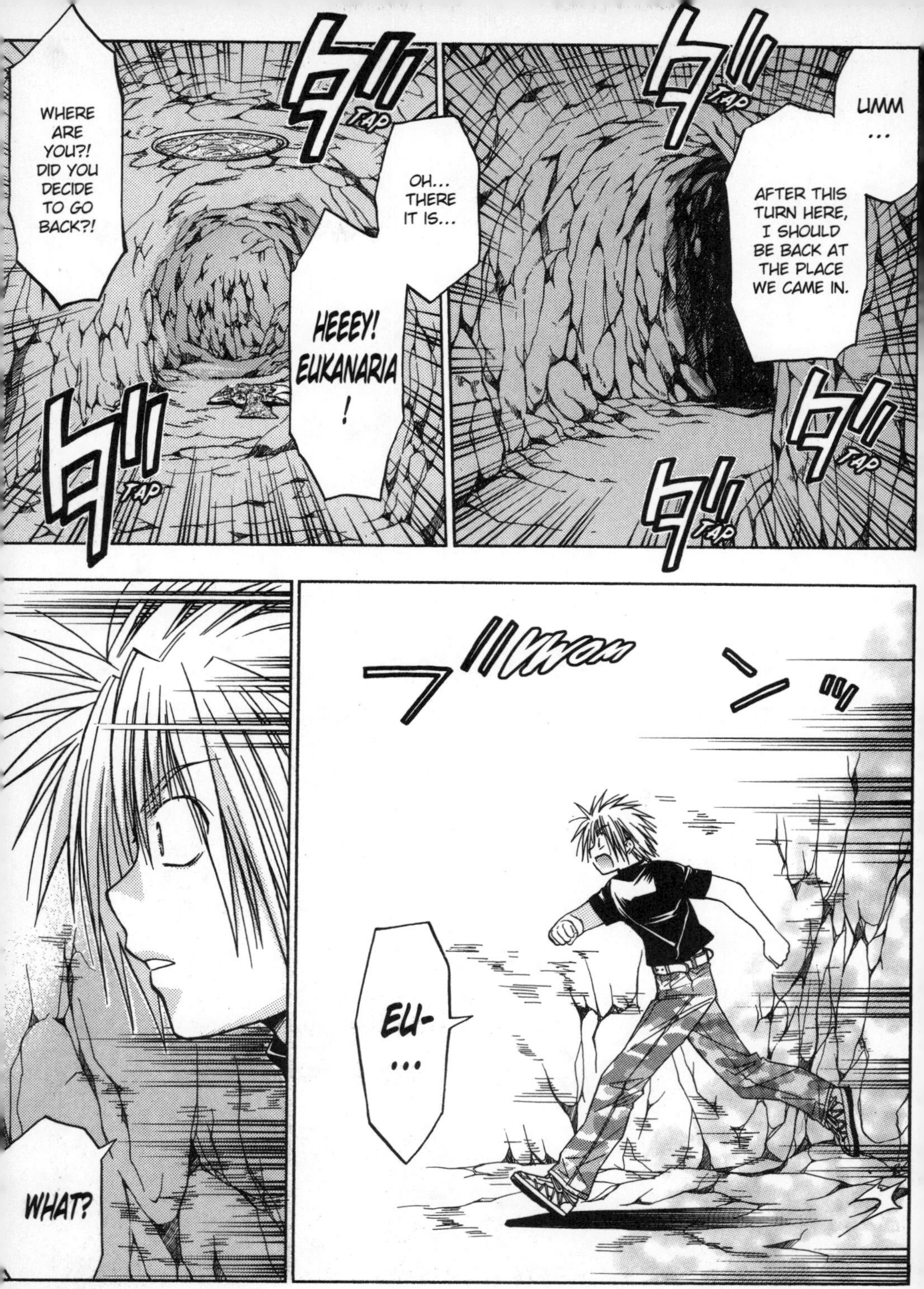
TAP
UMM ...
AFTER THIS TURN HERE, I SHOULD BE BACK AT THE PLACE WE CAME IN.
TAP
TAP
TAP
OH... THERE IT IS...
HEEEY! EUKANARIA!
WHERE ARE YOU?! DID YOU DECIDE TO GO BACK?!
TAP
WWOM
EU-...
WHAT?

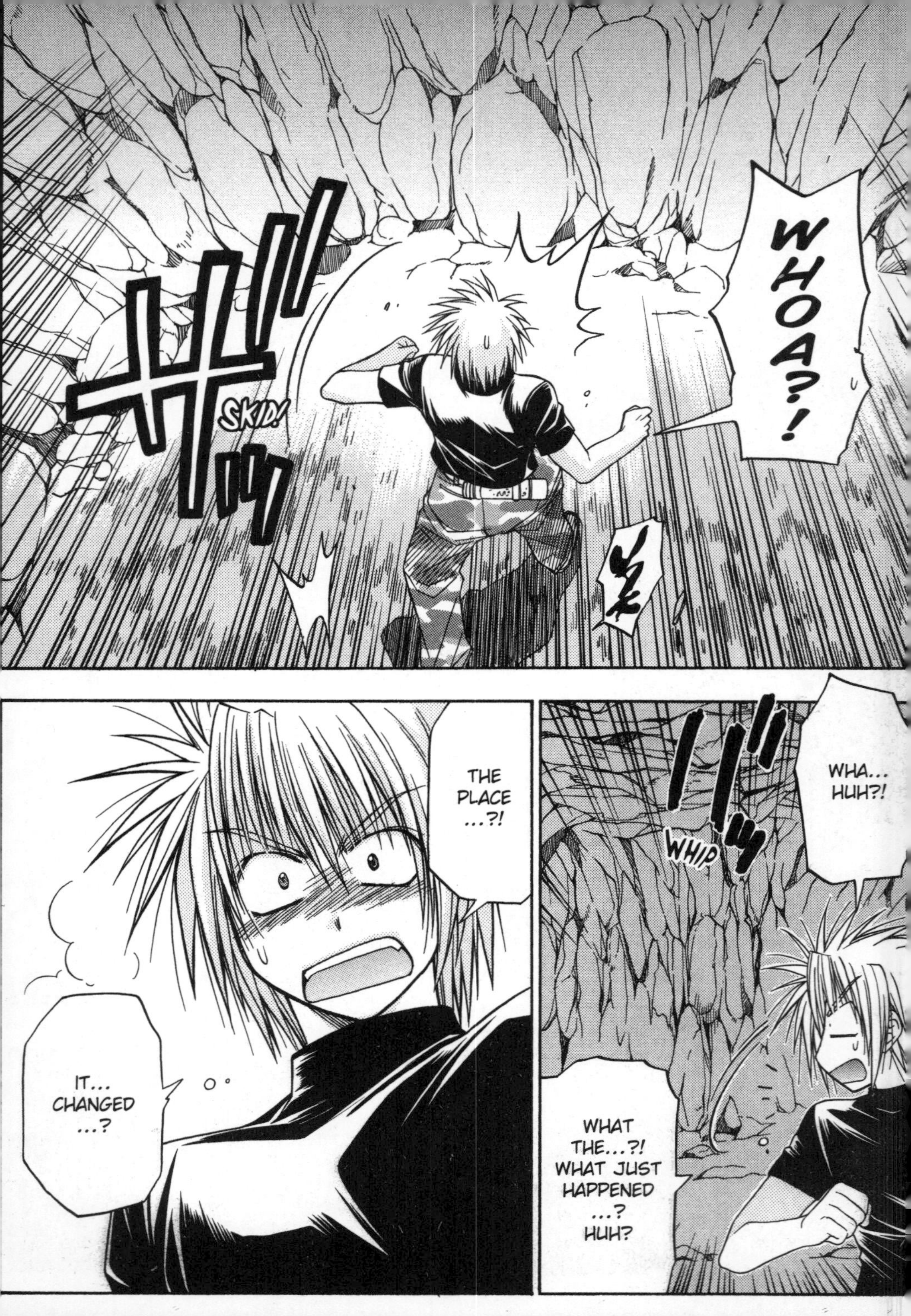
WHOA?!
SKID!
WHA... HUH?!
WHIP
WHAT THE...?! WHAT JUST HAPPENED ...? HUH?
THE PLACE ...?!
IT... CHANGED ...?

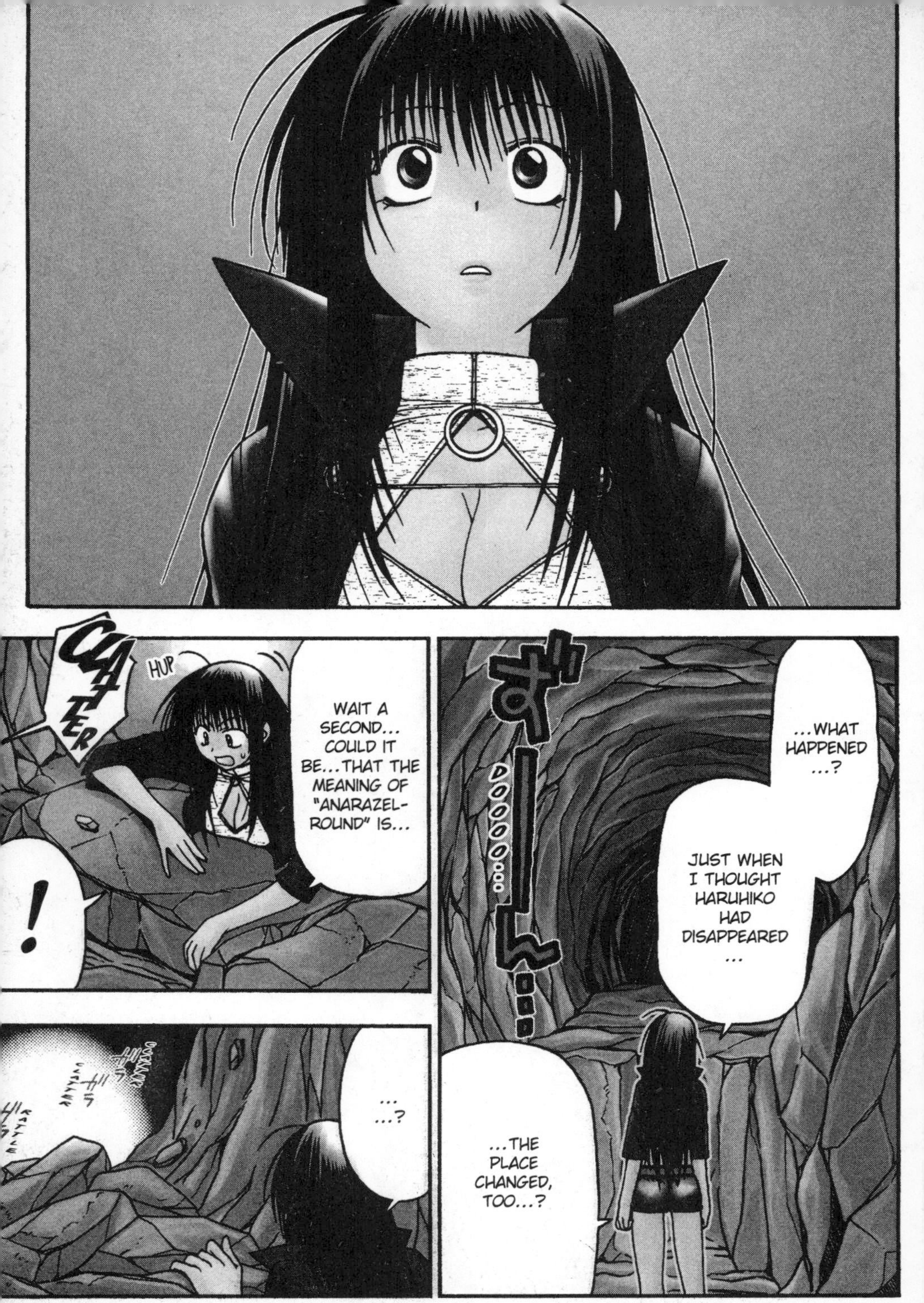
ずーん…
DOOOOOO...
...WHAT HAPPENED ...?
JUST WHEN I THOUGHT HARUHIKO HAD DISAPPEARED ...
CLATTER
HUP
WAIT A SECOND... COULD IT BE...THAT THE MEANING OF "ANARAZEL-ROUND" IS...
!
...THE PLACE CHANGED, TOO...?
... ...?

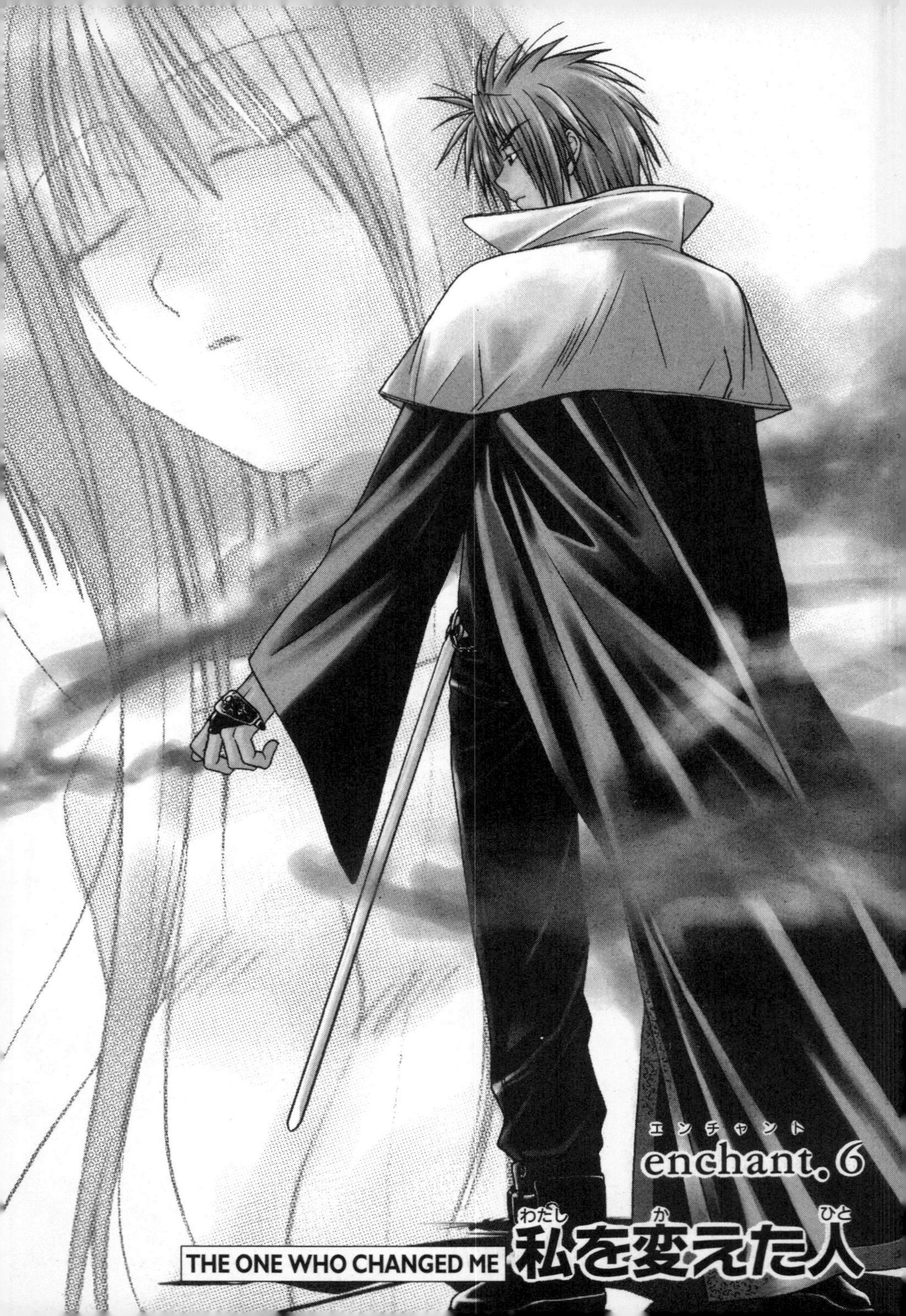
エンチャント
enchant. 6
THE ONE WHO CHANGED ME
私を変えた人

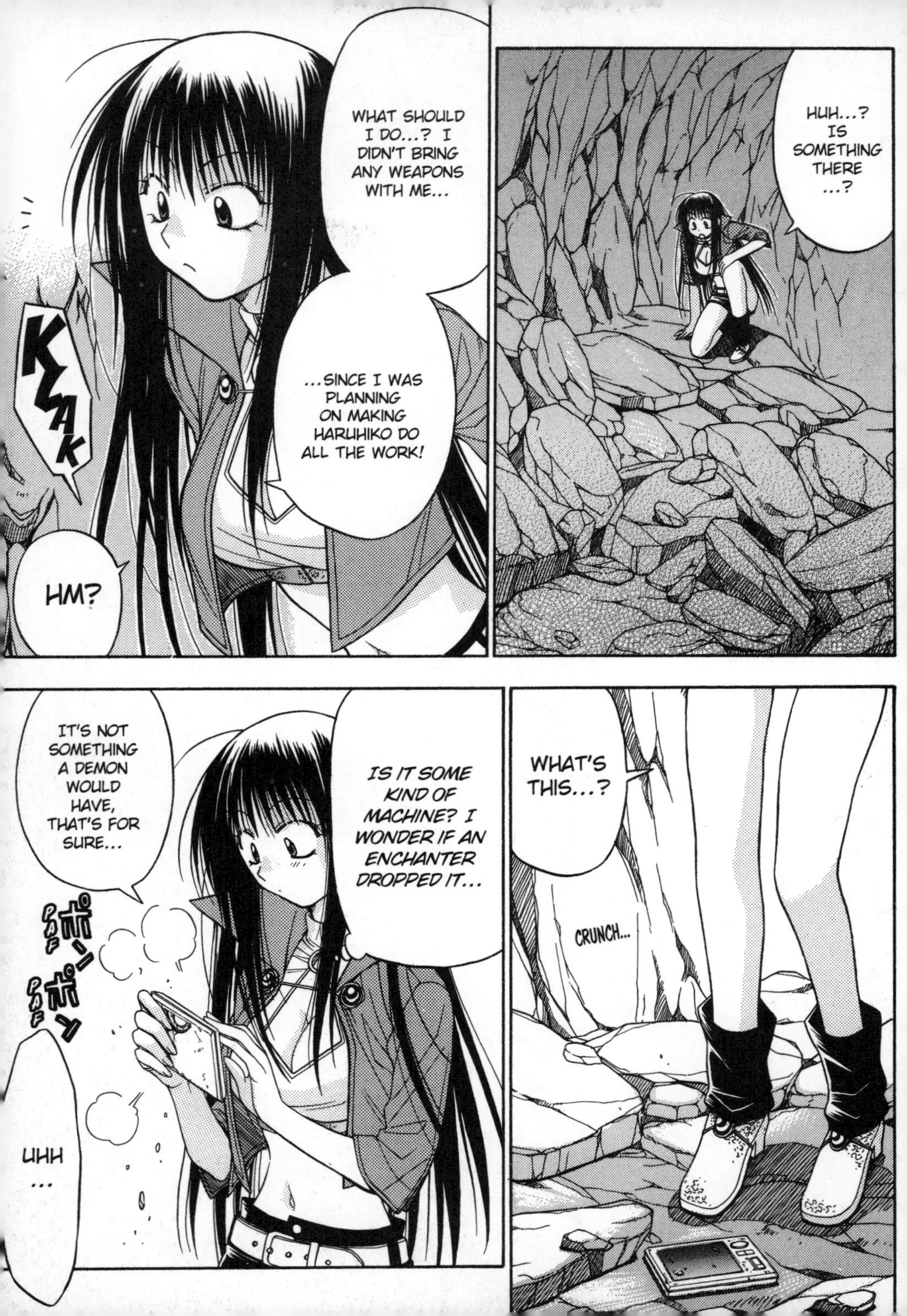
HUH...? IS SOMETHING THERE ...?
WHAT SHOULD I DO...? I DIDN'T BRING ANY WEAPONS WITH ME...
...SINCE I WAS PLANNING ON MAKING HARUHIKO DO ALL THE WORK!
KSAK
HM?
WHAT'S THIS...?
CRUNCH...
IS IT SOME KIND OF MACHINE? I WONDER IF AN ENCHANTER DROPPED IT...
IT'S NOT SOMETHING A DEMON WOULD HAVE, THAT'S FOR SURE...
PAF
PAF
UHH ...

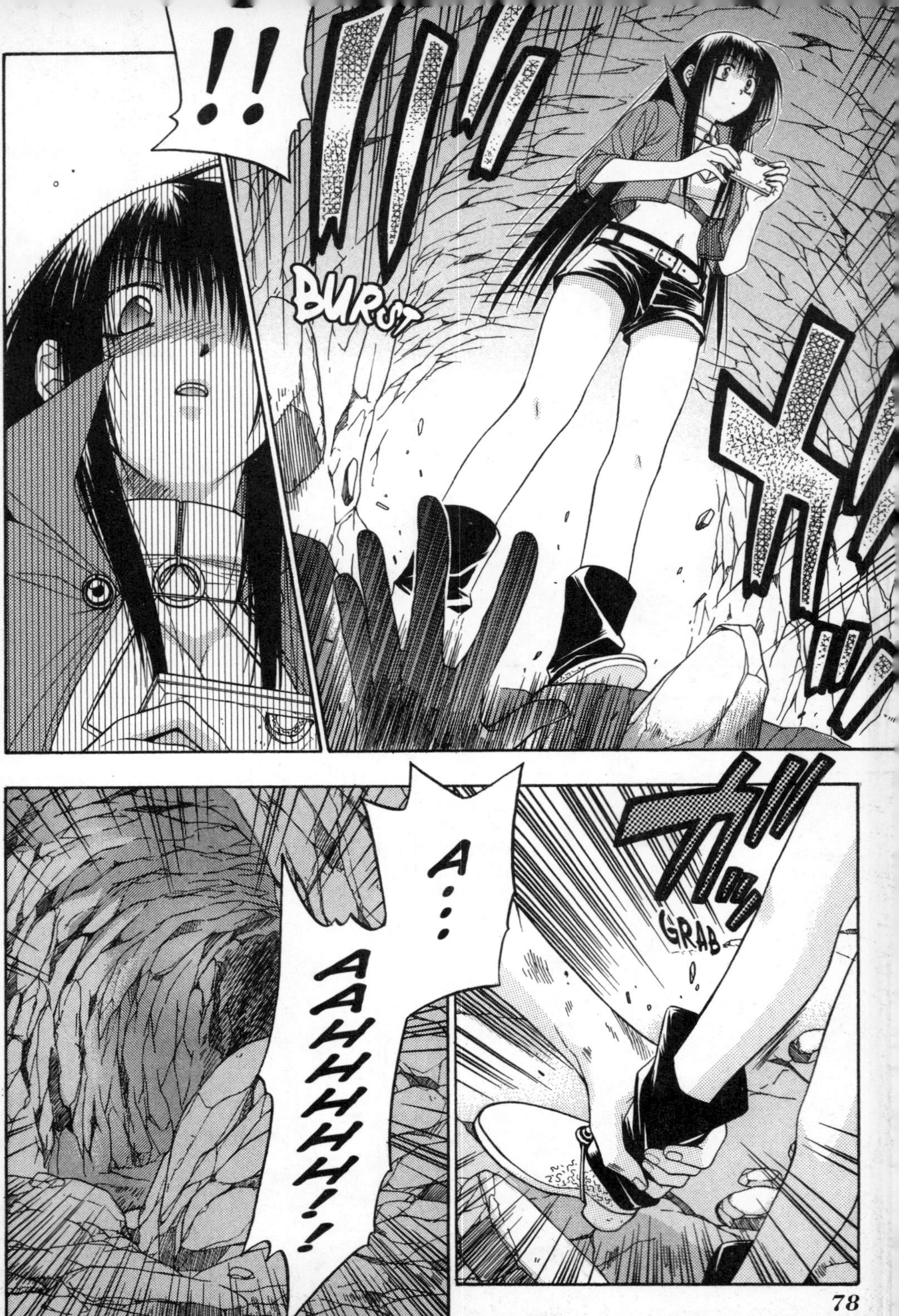
BURST
!!
GRAB
A...
AAHHHHHH!!

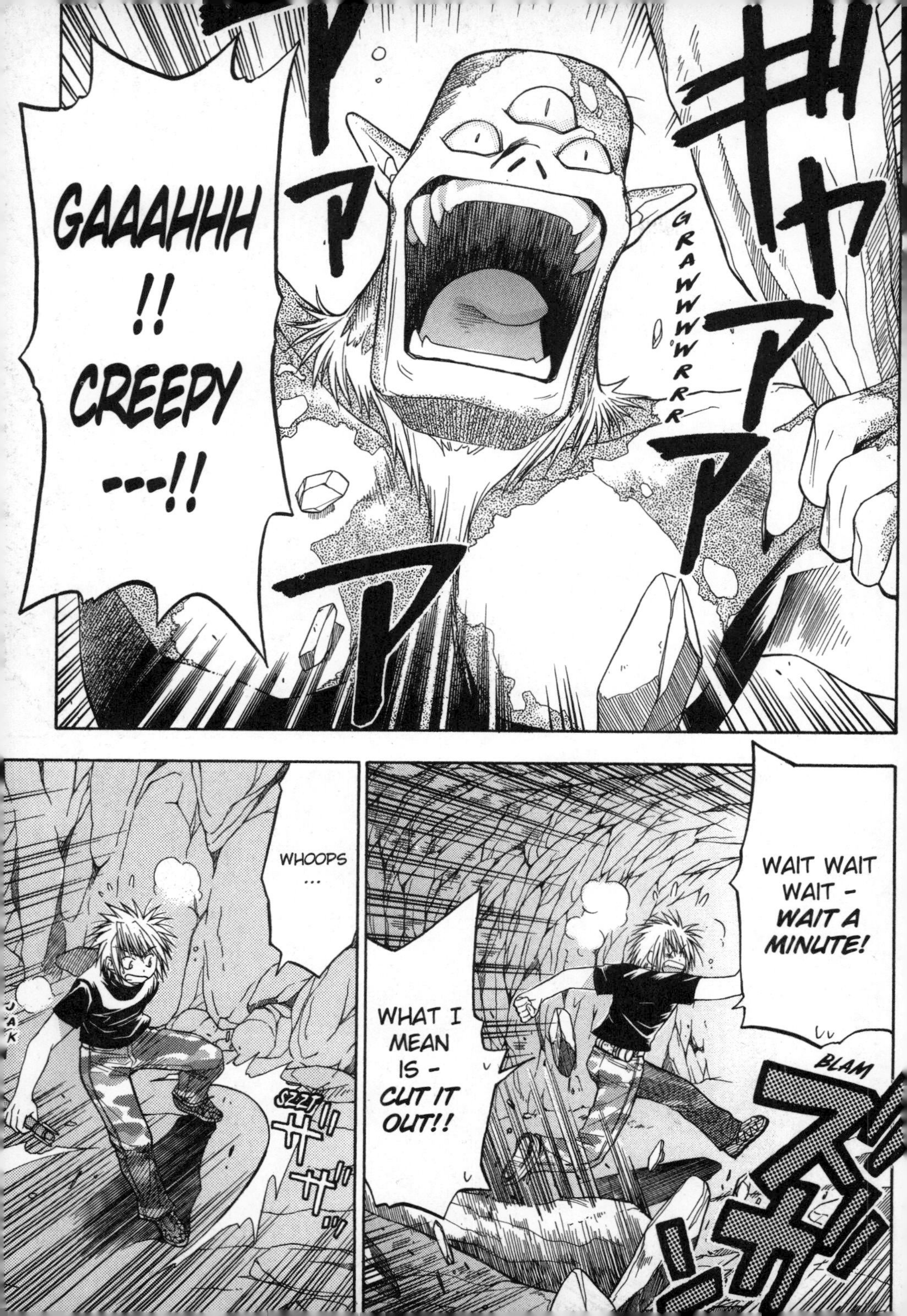
GAAAHHH!! CREEPY---!!
GRAWWWWRRR
WAIT WAIT WAIT - WAIT A MINUTE!
WHAT I MEAN IS - CUT IT OUT!!
BLAM
WHOOPS ...
JAK
SZZT

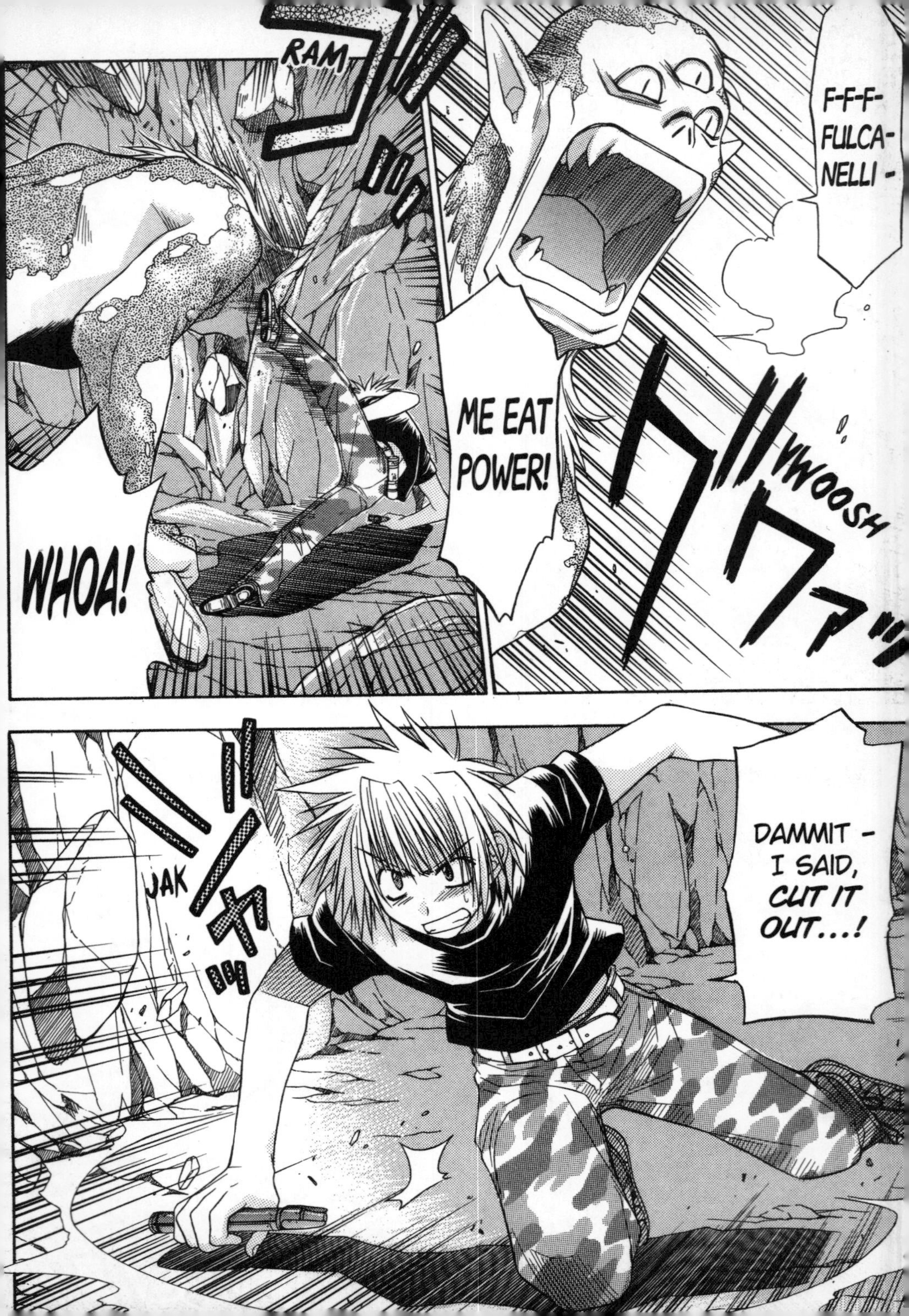
F-F-F-FULCANELLI -
ME EAT POWER!
WHOOSH
RAM
WHOA!
DAMMIT - I SAID, CUT IT OUT...!
JAK

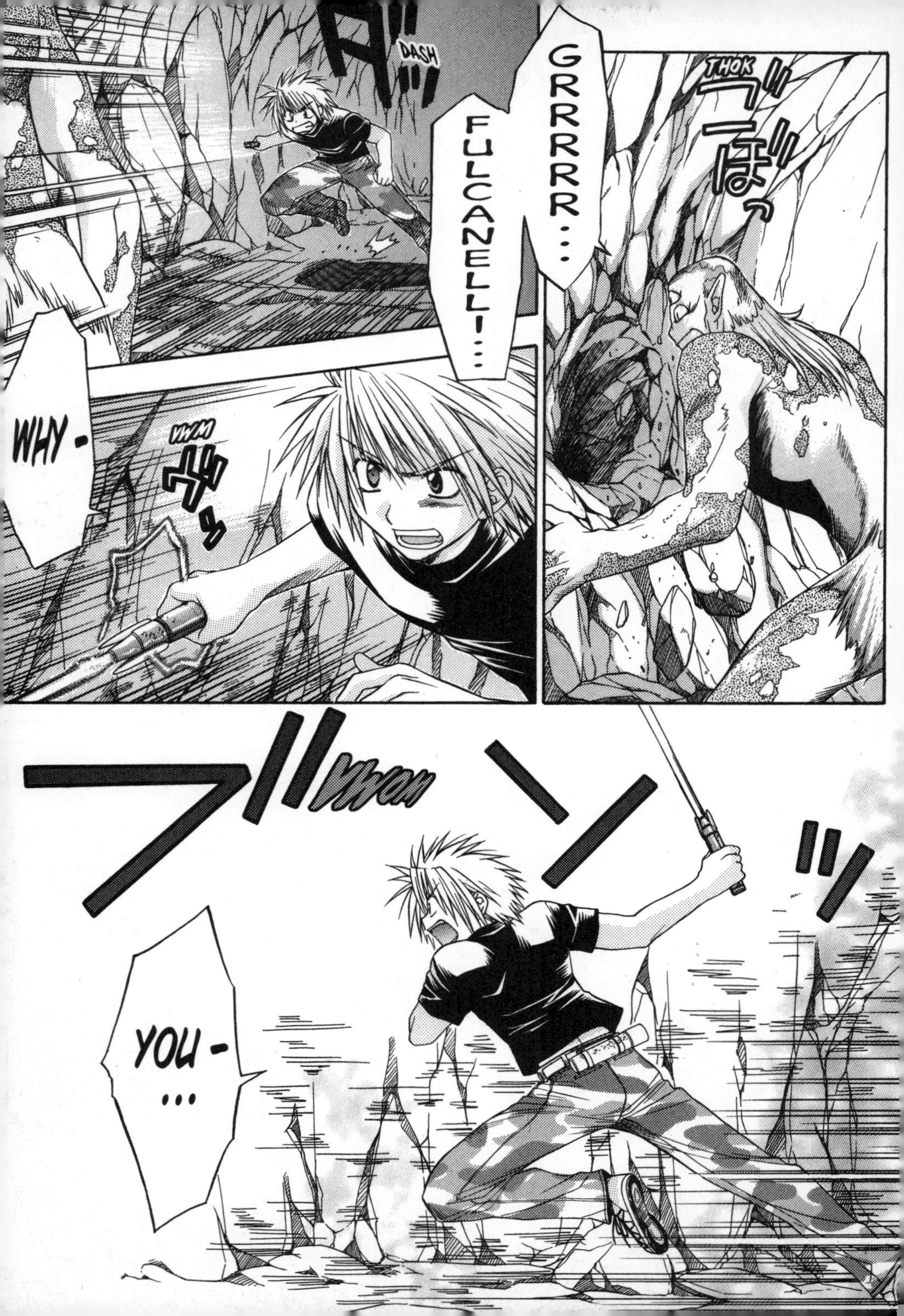
THOK
GRRRRR...
DASH
FULLCANELLI...
VWM
WHY -
YOU - ...

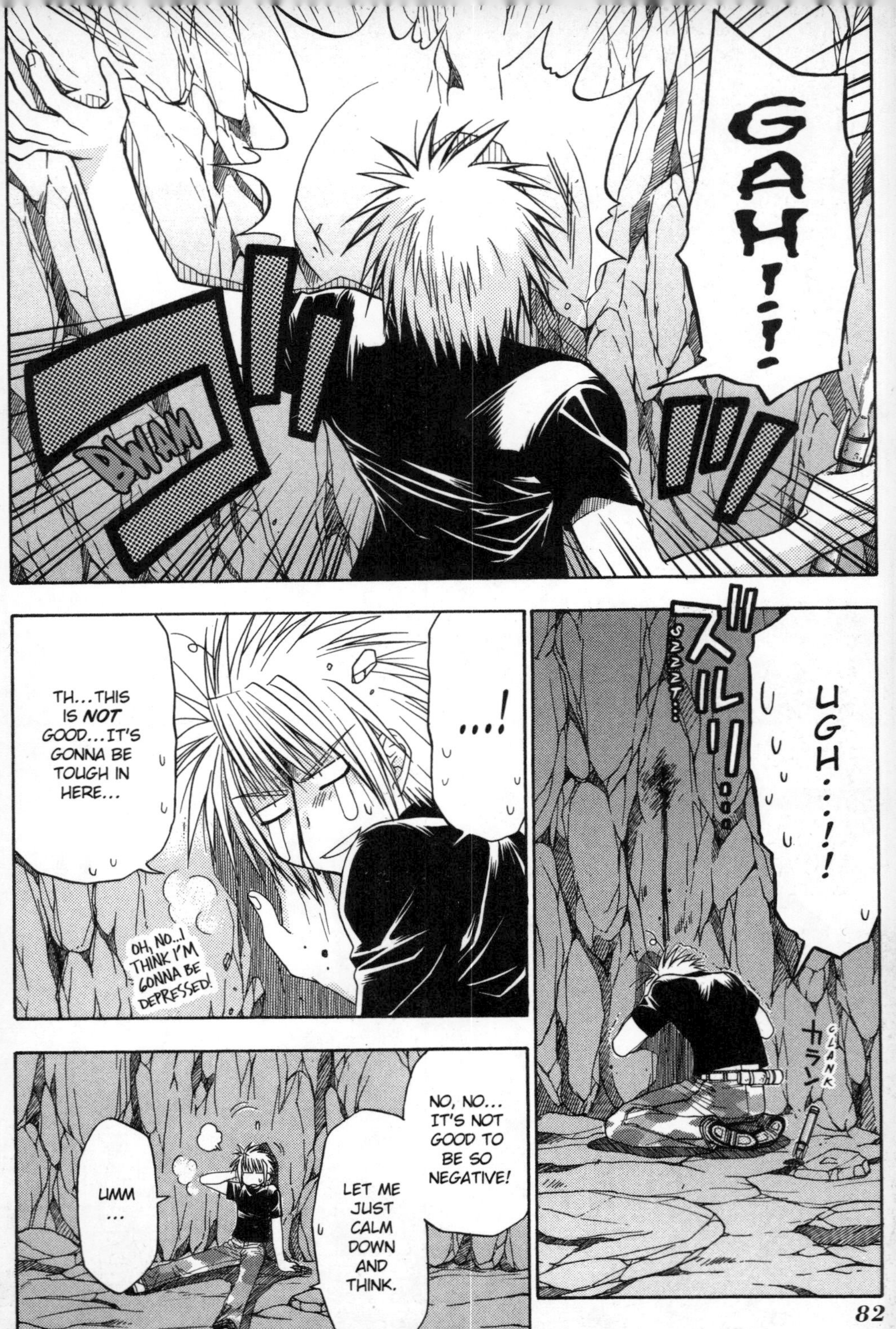
GAH!!!
DWAM
ズルー…
SZZZT…
UGH…!!
カラン
CLANK
…!
TH…THIS IS *NOT* GOOD…IT'S GONNA BE TOUGH IN HERE…
OH, NO…I THINK I'M GONNA BE DEPRESSED!
NO, NO… IT'S NOT GOOD TO BE SO NEGATIVE!
LET ME JUST CALM DOWN AND THINK.
UMM …

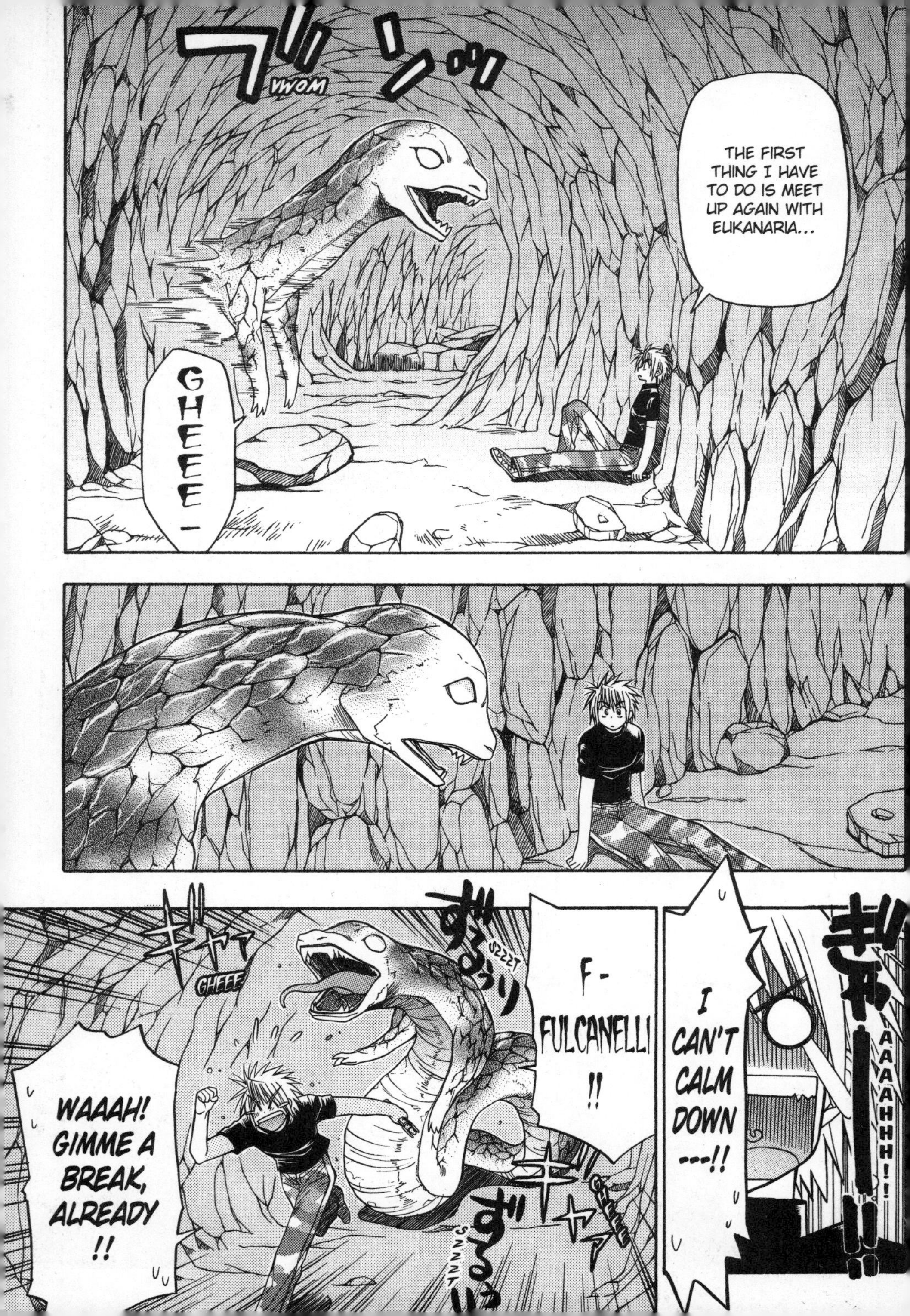
THE FIRST THING I HAVE TO DO IS MEET UP AGAIN WITH EUKANARIA...
VWOM
GHEEEE-
AAAAAHHH!!!
I CAN'T CALM DOWN---!!
F-FULCANELLI!!
SZZZT
GHEEE
WAAAH! GIMME A BREAK, ALREADY!!
SNZZT

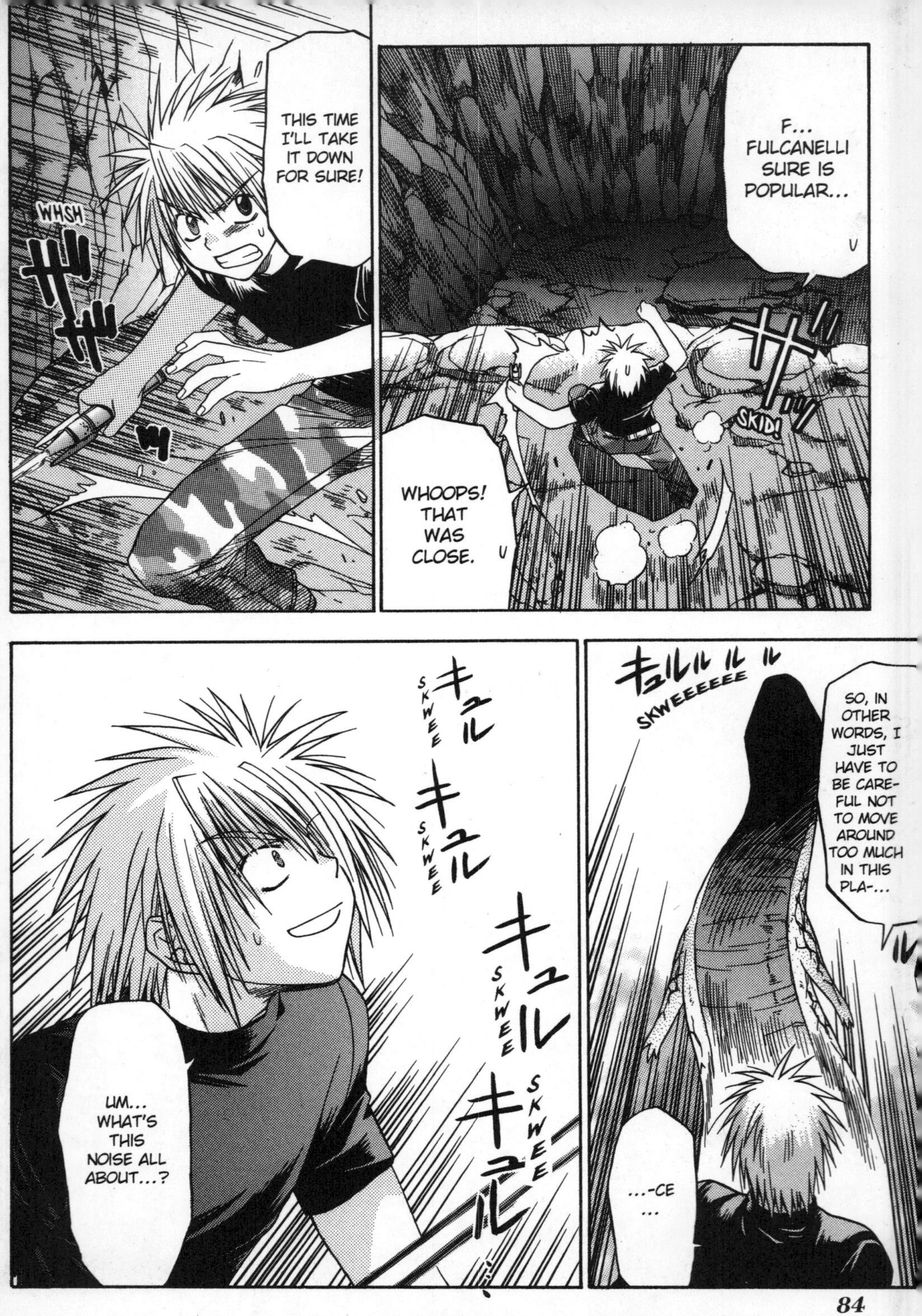
F... FULCANELLI SURE IS POPULAR...
SKID!
WHOOPS! THAT WAS CLOSE.
THIS TIME I'LL TAKE IT DOWN FOR SURE!
WHSH
キュルルルル
SKWEEEEEE
SO, IN OTHER WORDS, I JUST HAVE TO BE CARE-FUL NOT TO MOVE AROUND TOO MUCH IN THIS PLA-...
...-CE ...
キュル
SKWEE
キュル
SKWEE
キュル
SKWEE
キュル
SKWEE
UM... WHAT'S THIS NOISE ALL ABOUT...?

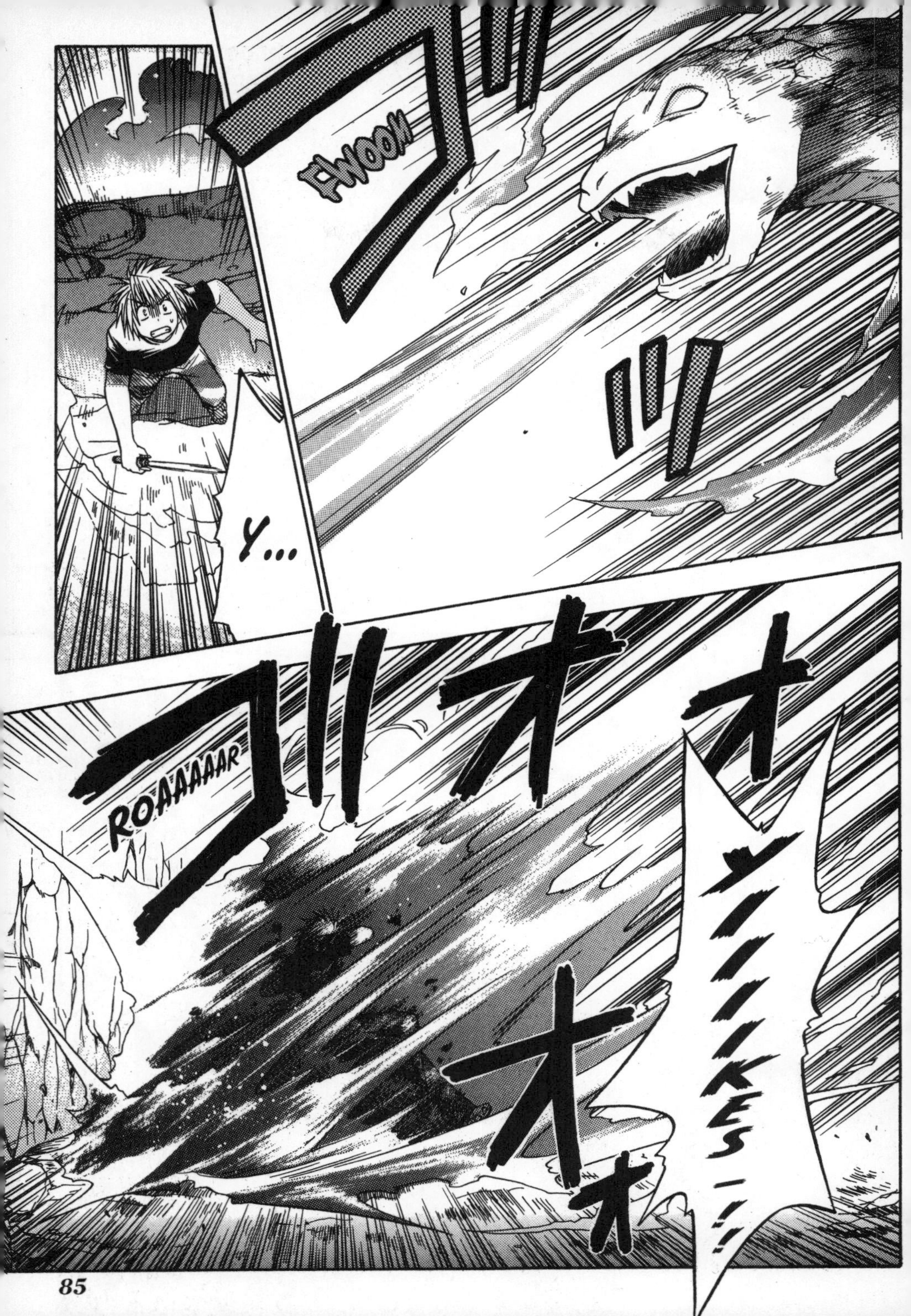
ゴッ
FWOOM
Y...
ゴオオオォ
ROAAAAAR
YIIIIIKES—!!

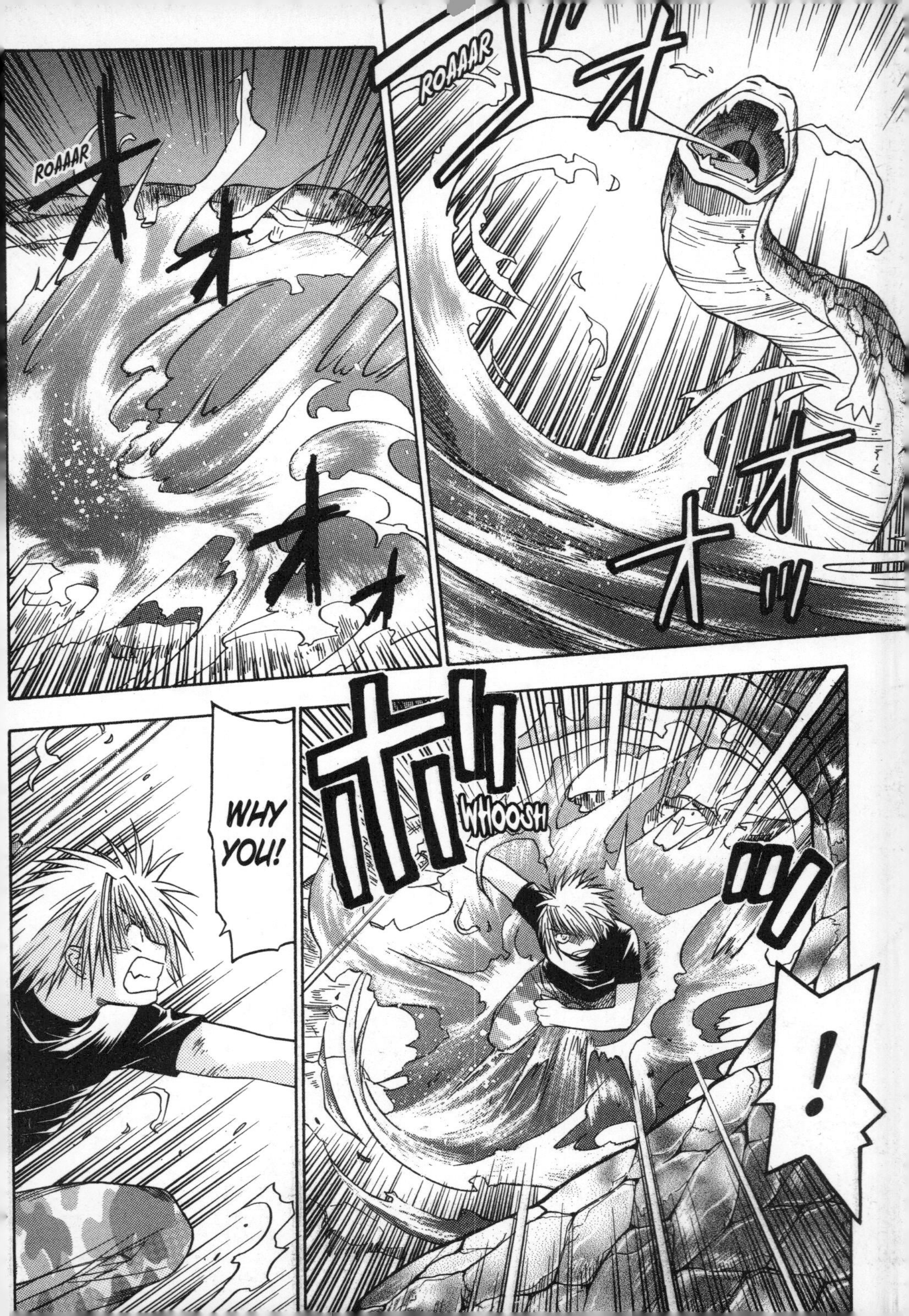
ROAAAR
ROAAAR
WHOOSH
!
WHY YOU!

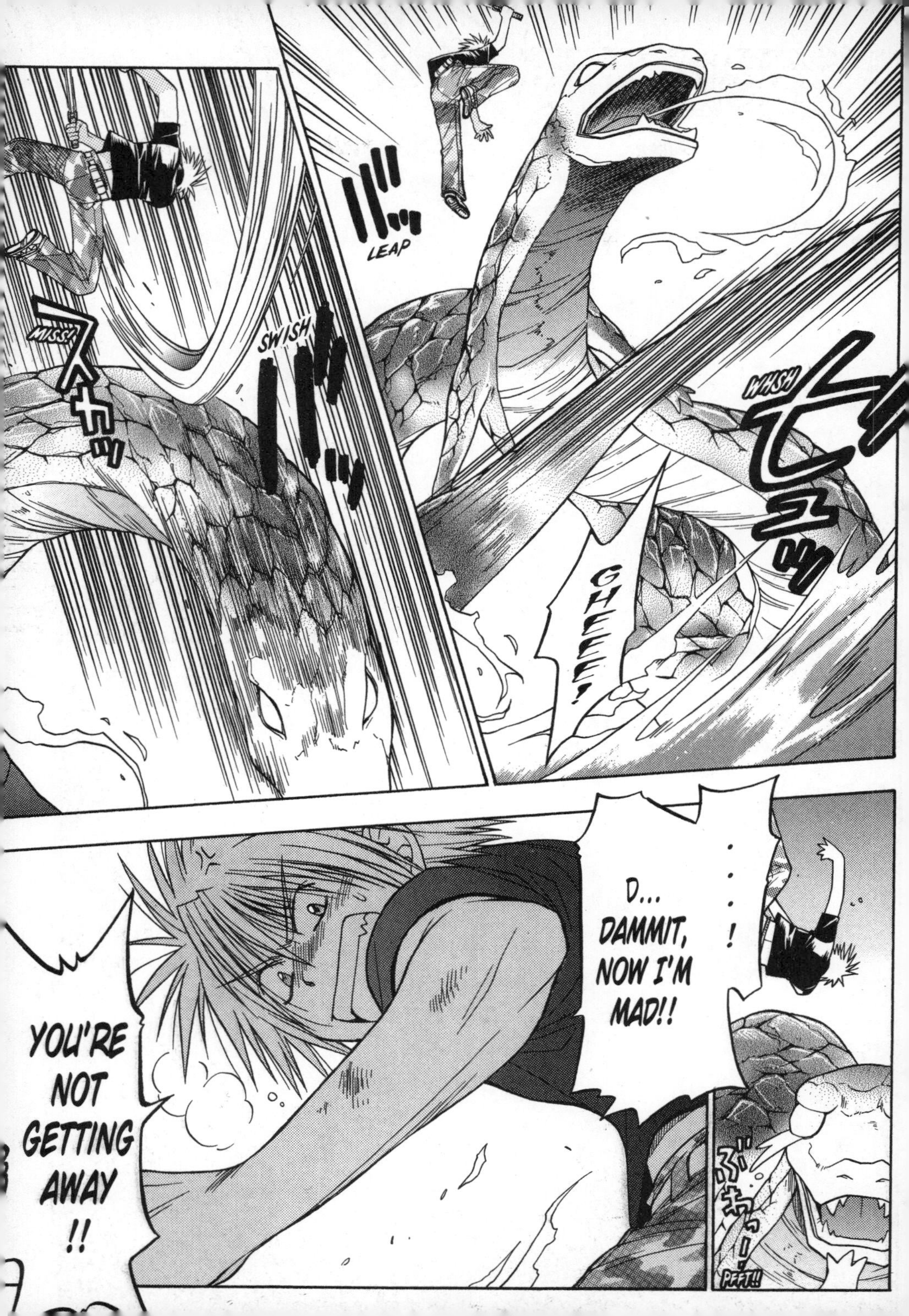
WHSH
GHEEEE!?
LEAP
SWISH
MISS!
...!
PFFT!!
D... DAMMIT, NOW I'M MAD!!
YOU'RE NOT GETTING AWAY !!

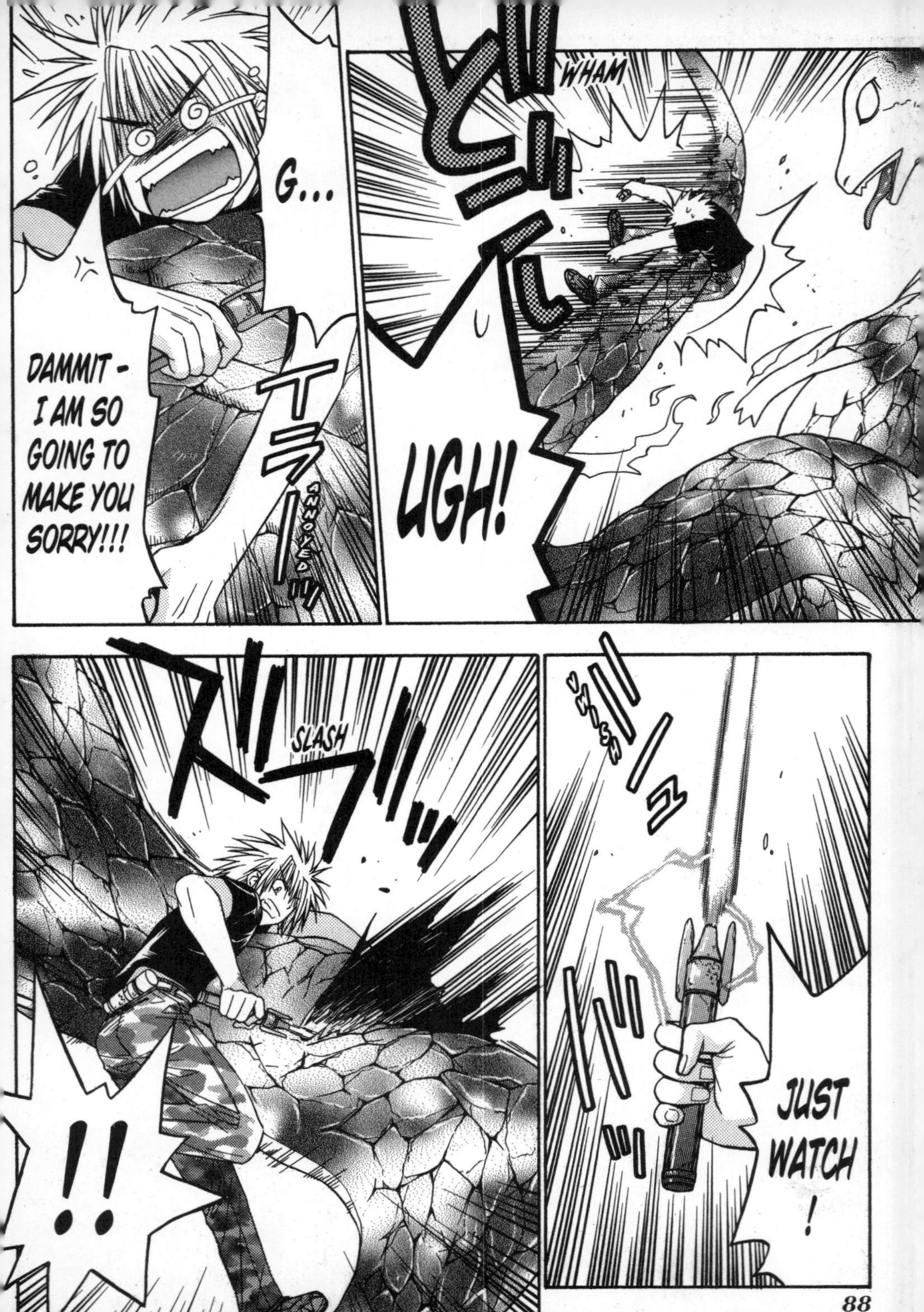
WHAM
UGH!
G...
DAMMIT - I AM SO GOING TO MAKE YOU SORRY!!!
ANNOYED
WHISH
JUST WATCH!
SLASH
!!

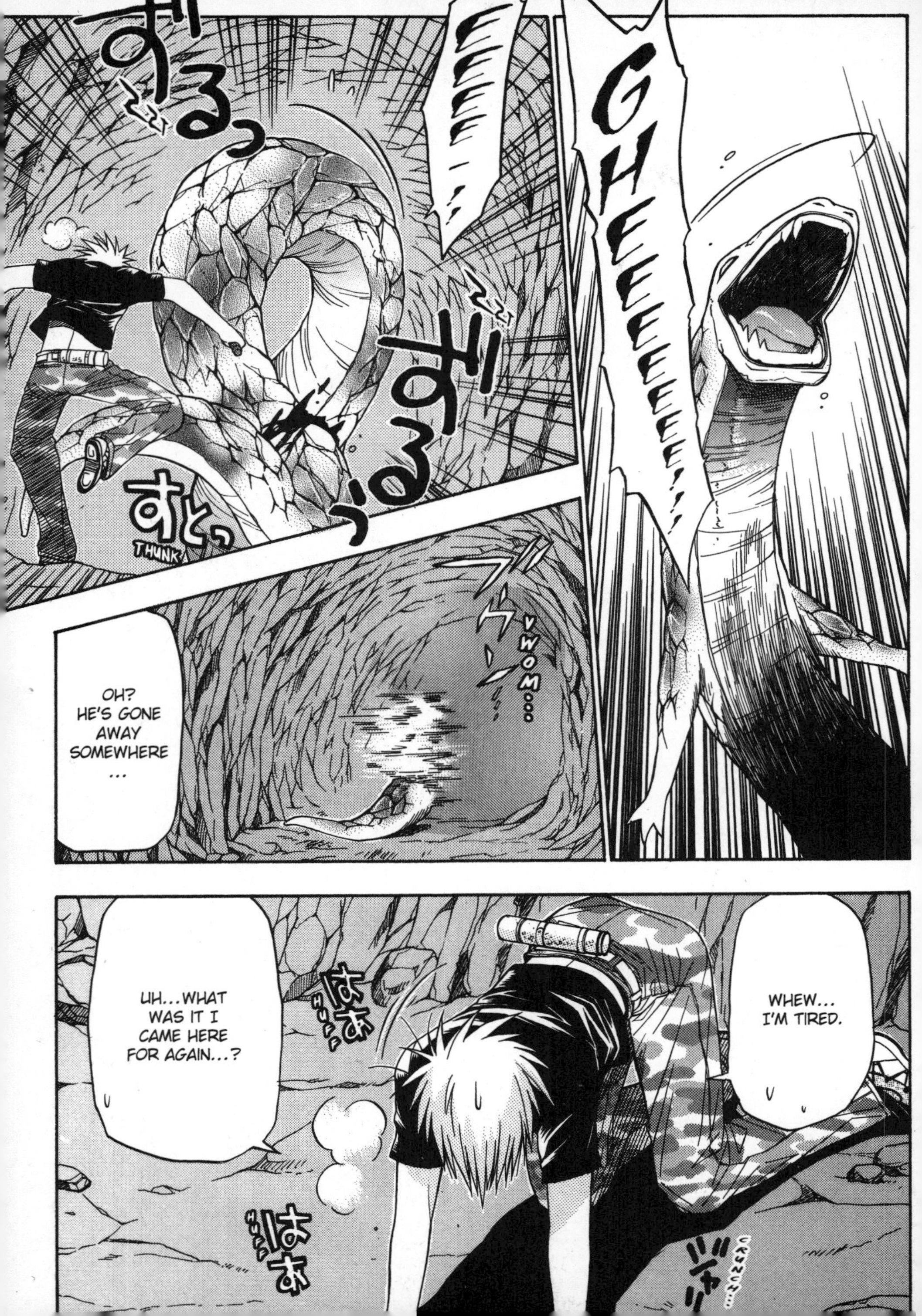
GHEEEEEEEE!!!
EEEEE!!
ずるっ
ずるっ
すとっ
THUNK
OH? HE'S GONE AWAY SOMEWHERE...
VWOM...
WHEW... I'M TIRED.
UH...WHAT WAS IT I CAME HERE FOR AGAIN...?
はぁ
はぁ
CRUNCH...

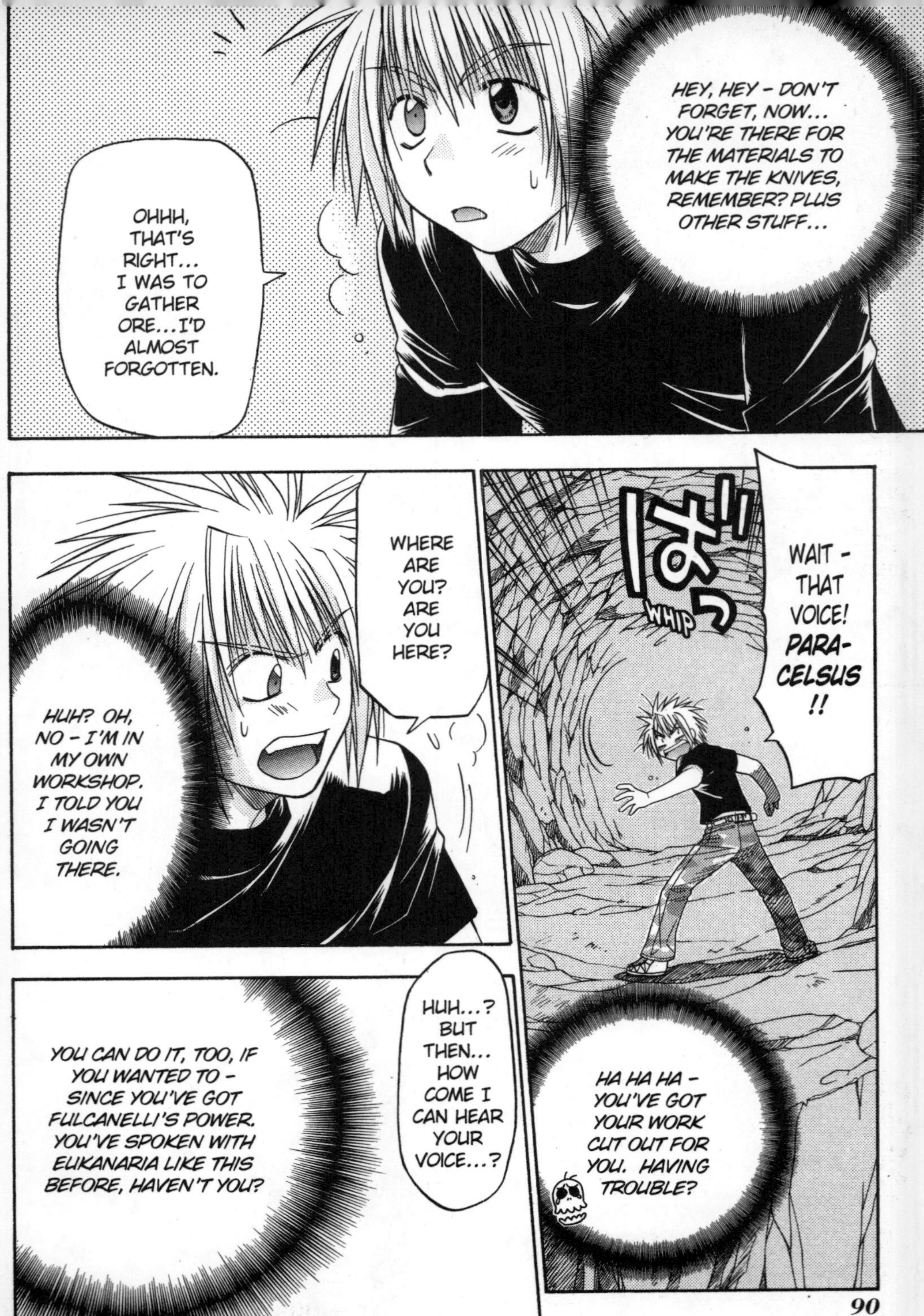
HEY, HEY - DON'T FORGET, NOW... YOU'RE THERE FOR THE MATERIALS TO MAKE THE KNIVES, REMEMBER? PLUS OTHER STUFF...
OHHH, THAT'S RIGHT... I WAS TO GATHER ORE...I'D ALMOST FORGOTTEN.
WAIT - THAT VOICE! PARA-CELSUS !!
ぱっ
WHIP
HA HA HA - YOU'VE GOT YOUR WORK CUT OUT FOR YOU. HAVING TROUBLE?
WHERE ARE YOU? ARE YOU HERE?
HUH? OH, NO - I'M IN MY OWN WORKSHOP. I TOLD YOU I WASN'T GOING THERE.
HUH...? BUT THEN... HOW COME I CAN HEAR YOUR VOICE...?
YOU CAN DO IT, TOO, IF YOU WANTED TO - SINCE YOU'VE GOT FULCANELLI'S POWER. YOU'VE SPOKEN WITH EUKANARIA LIKE THIS BEFORE, HAVEN'T YOU?

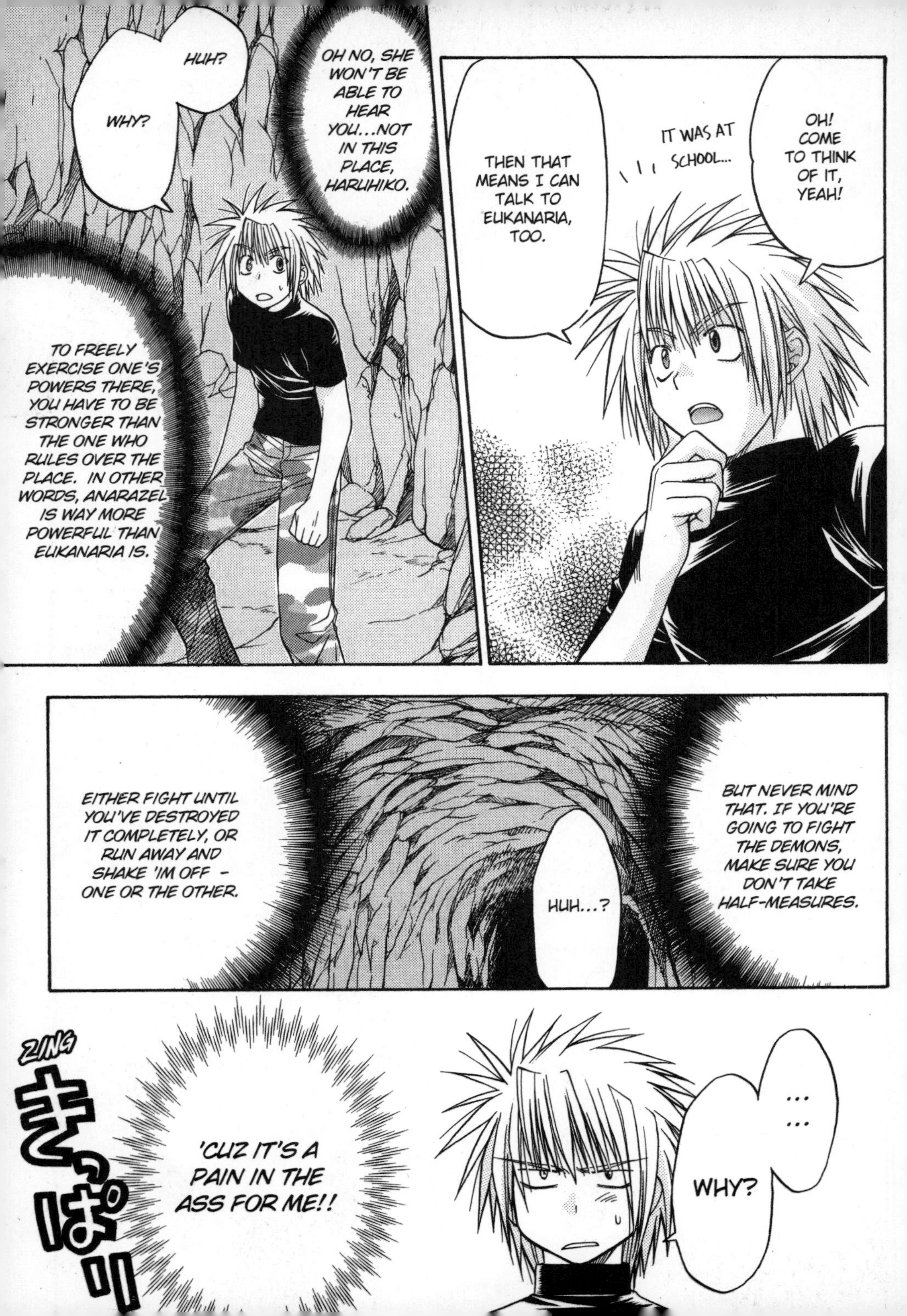
OH! COME TO THINK OF IT, YEAH!
IT WAS AT SCHOOL...
THEN THAT MEANS I CAN TALK TO EUKANARIA, TOO.
OH NO, SHE WON'T BE ABLE TO HEAR YOU...NOT IN THIS PLACE, HARUHIKO.
HUH?
WHY?
TO FREELY EXERCISE ONE'S POWERS THERE, YOU HAVE TO BE STRONGER THAN THE ONE WHO RULES OVER THE PLACE. IN OTHER WORDS, ANARAZEL IS WAY MORE POWERFUL THAN EUKANARIA IS.
BUT NEVER MIND THAT. IF YOU'RE GOING TO FIGHT THE DEMONS, MAKE SURE YOU DON'T TAKE HALF-MEASURES.
HUH...?
EITHER FIGHT UNTIL YOU'VE DESTROYED IT COMPLETELY, OR RUN AWAY AND SHAKE 'IM OFF - ONE OR THE OTHER.
......
WHY?
'CUZ IT'S A PAIN IN THE ASS FOR ME!!
ZING

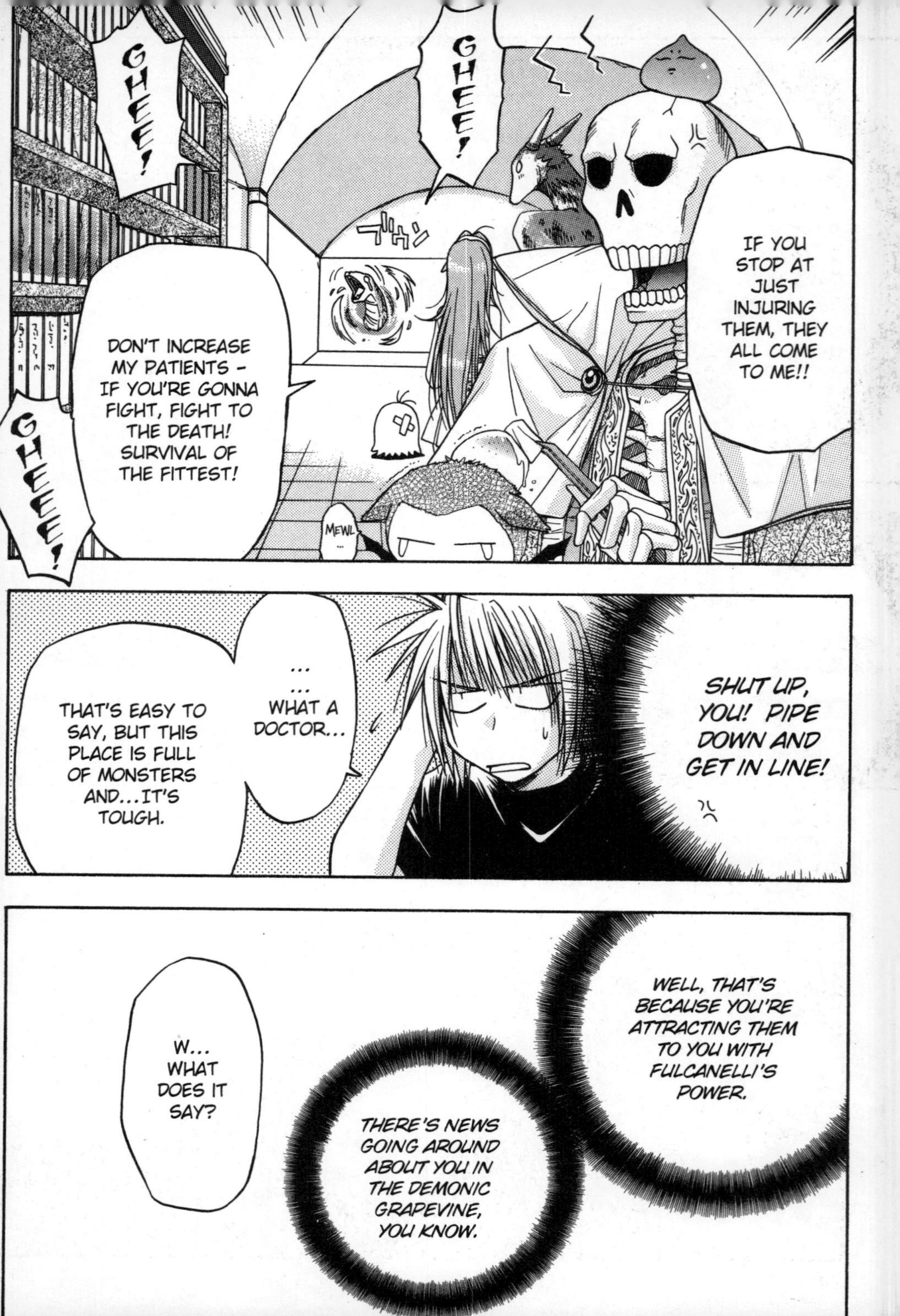
GHEE!
GHEE!
IF YOU STOP AT JUST INJURING THEM, THEY ALL COME TO ME!!
DON'T INCREASE MY PATIENTS - IF YOU'RE GONNA FIGHT, FIGHT TO THE DEATH! SURVIVAL OF THE FITTEST!
MEWL...
GHEEE!
SHUT UP, YOU! PIPE DOWN AND GET IN LINE!
... ... WHAT A DOCTOR...
THAT'S EASY TO SAY, BUT THIS PLACE IS FULL OF MONSTERS AND...IT'S TOUGH.
WELL, THAT'S BECAUSE YOU'RE ATTRACTING THEM TO YOU WITH FULCANELLI'S POWER.
THERE'S NEWS GOING AROUND ABOUT YOU IN THE DEMONIC GRAPEVINE, YOU KNOW.
W... WHAT DOES IT SAY?

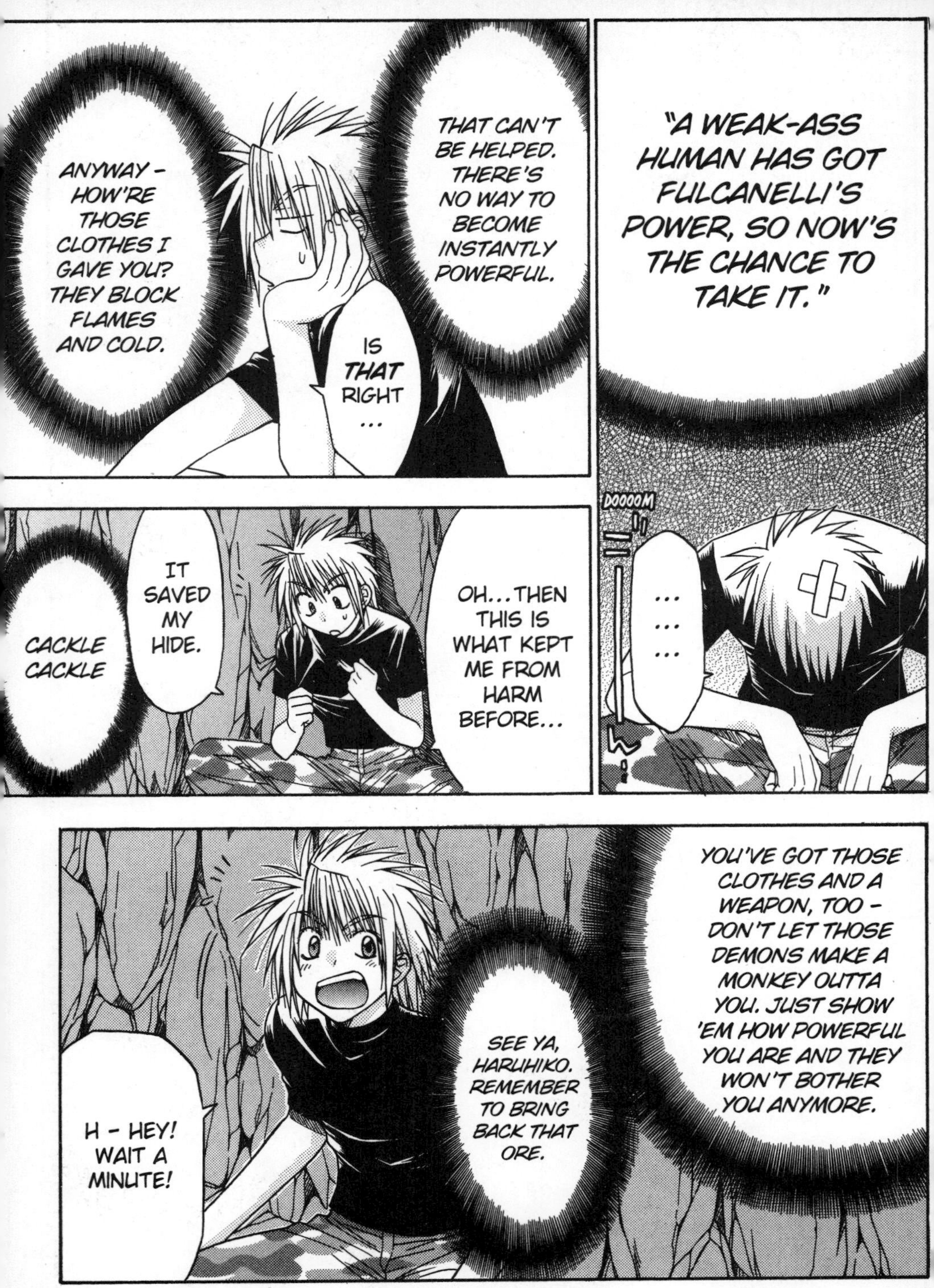
"A WEAK-ASS HUMAN HAS GOT FULCANELLI'S POWER, SO NOW'S THE CHANCE TO TAKE IT."
DOOOOM
... ...
THAT CAN'T BE HELPED. THERE'S NO WAY TO BECOME INSTANTLY POWERFUL.
ANYWAY - HOW'RE THOSE CLOTHES I GAVE YOU? THEY BLOCK FLAMES AND COLD.
IS THAT RIGHT ...
OH... THEN THIS IS WHAT KEPT ME FROM HARM BEFORE...
IT SAVED MY HIDE.
CACKLE CACKLE
YOU'VE GOT THOSE CLOTHES AND A WEAPON, TOO - DON'T LET THOSE DEMONS MAKE A MONKEY OUTTA YOU. JUST SHOW 'EM HOW POWERFUL YOU ARE AND THEY WON'T BOTHER YOU ANYMORE.
SEE YA, HARUHIKO. REMEMBER TO BRING BACK THAT ORE.
H - HEY! WAIT A MINUTE!

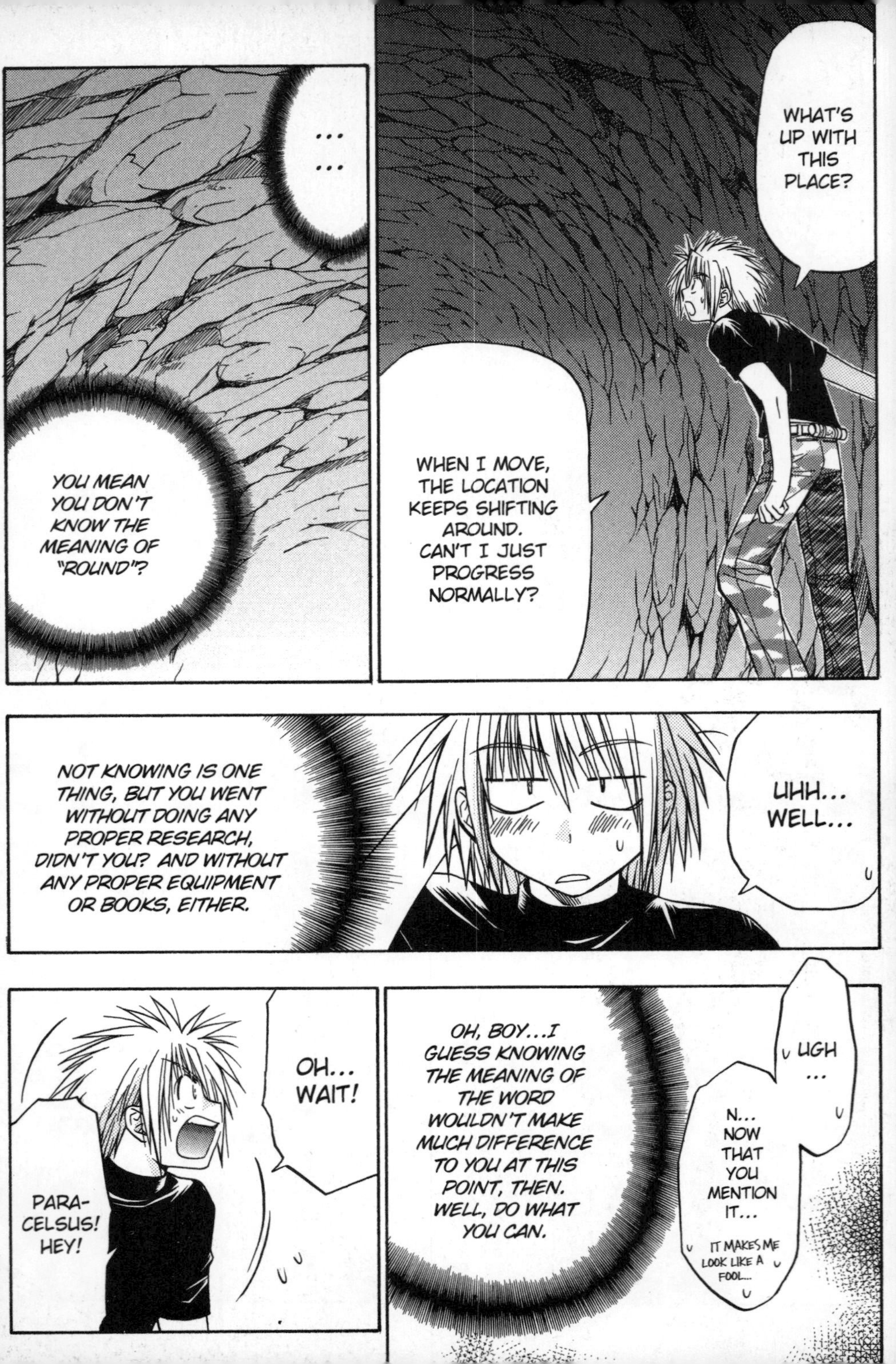
WHAT'S UP WITH THIS PLACE?
WHEN I MOVE, THE LOCATION KEEPS SHIFTING AROUND. CAN'T I JUST PROGRESS NORMALLY?
... ...
YOU MEAN YOU DON'T KNOW THE MEANING OF "ROUND"?
UHH... WELL...
NOT KNOWING IS ONE THING, BUT YOU WENT WITHOUT DOING ANY PROPER RESEARCH, DIDN'T YOU? AND WITHOUT ANY PROPER EQUIPMENT OR BOOKS, EITHER.
UGH ...
N... NOW THAT YOU MENTION IT...
IT MAKES ME LOOK LIKE A FOOL...
OH, BOY...I GUESS KNOWING THE MEANING OF THE WORD WOULDN'T MAKE MUCH DIFFERENCE TO YOU AT THIS POINT, THEN. WELL, DO WHAT YOU CAN.
OH... WAIT!
PARA-CELSUS! HEY!

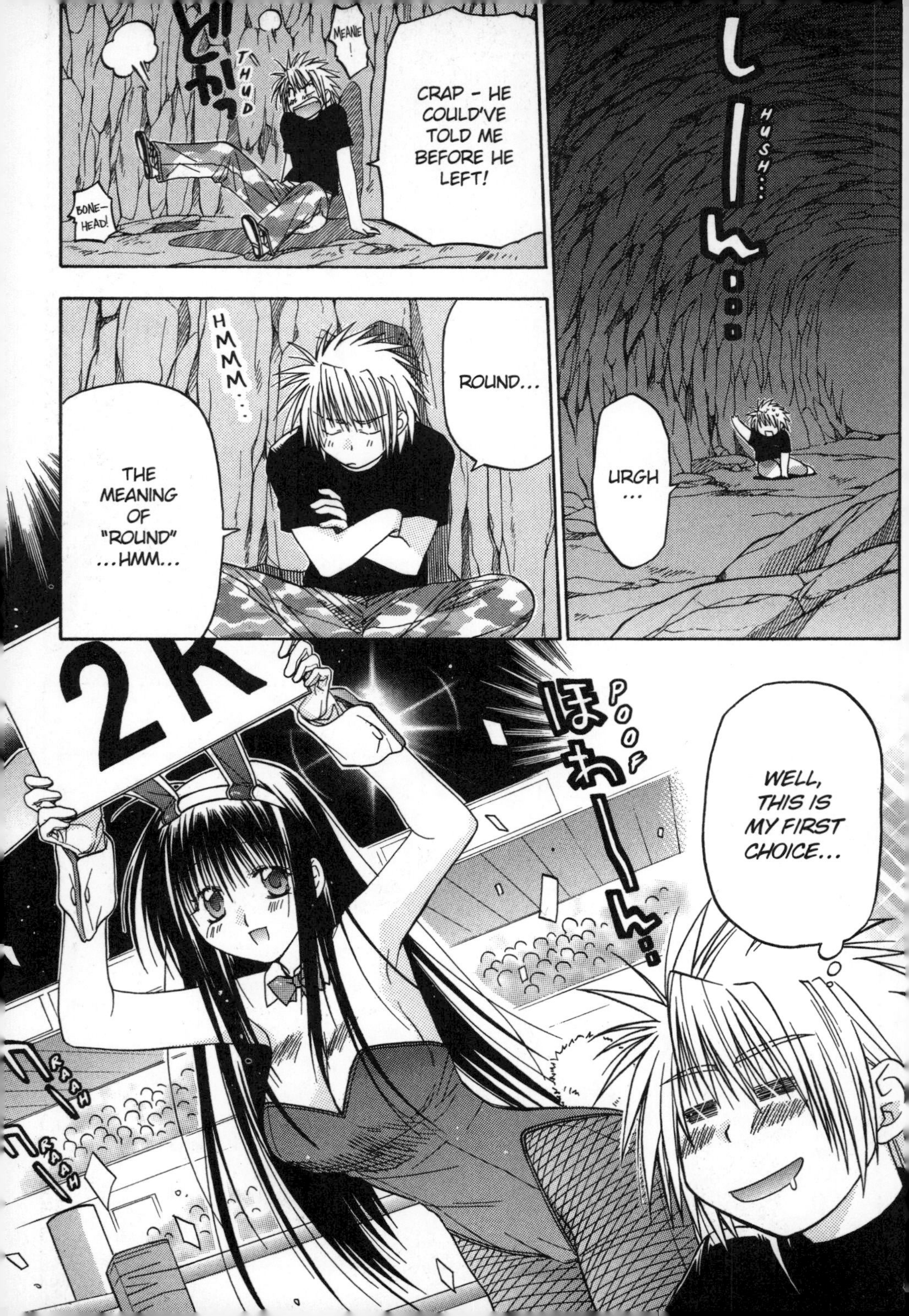
しーん…
HUSH…
URGH…
どかっ
THUD
MEANIE!
CRAP – HE COULD'VE TOLD ME BEFORE HE LEFT!
BONE-HEAD!
HMMM…
ROUND…
THE MEANING OF "ROUND" …HMM…
WELL, THIS IS MY FIRST CHOICE…
ほわーん..
POOF
2K
RAAAH
RAAAH

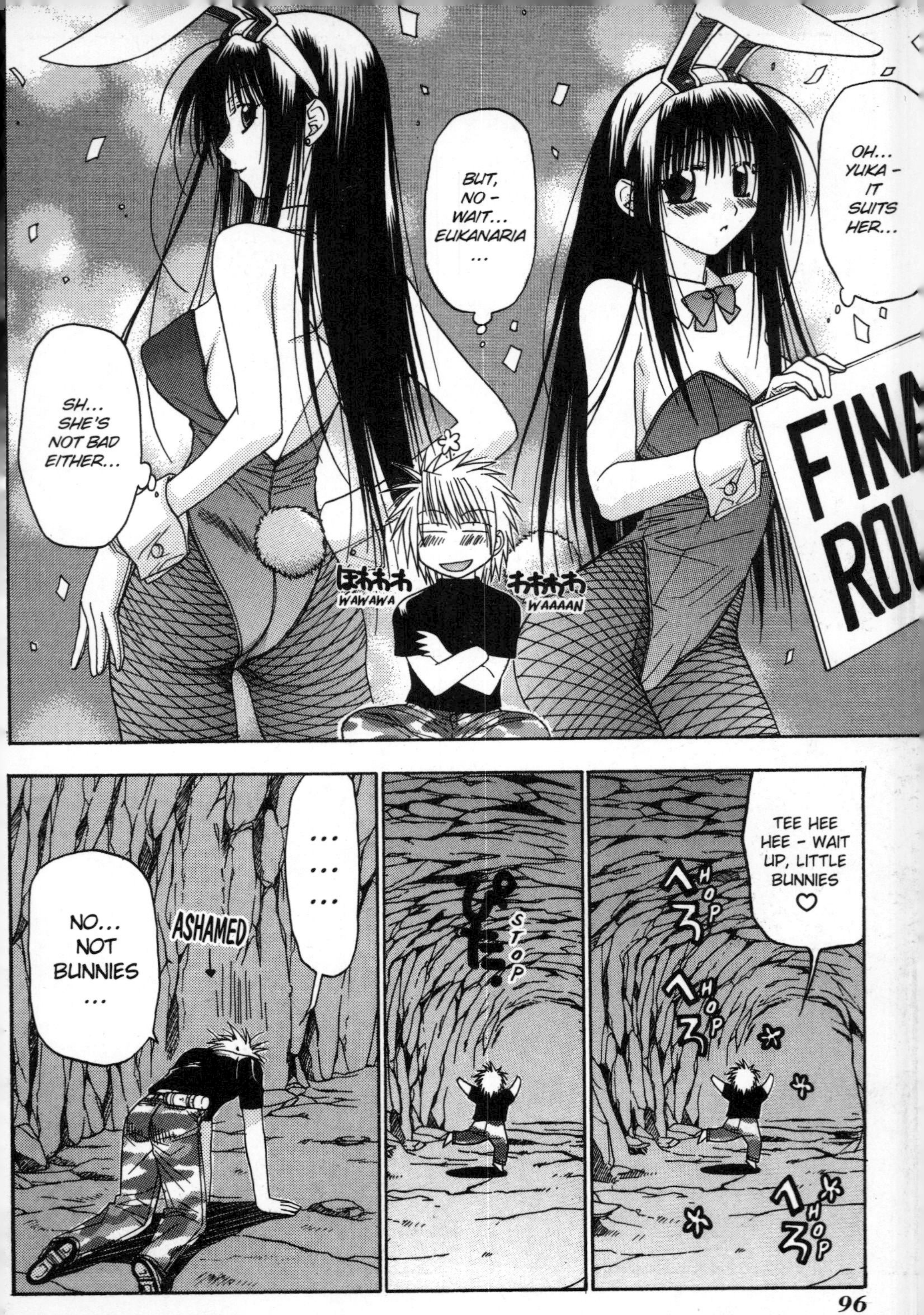
OH... YUKA - IT SUITS HER...
BUT, NO - WAIT... EUKANARIA ...
SH... SHE'S NOT BAD EITHER...
FINA
ROU
WAAAAN
WAWAWA
TEE HEE HEE - WAIT UP, LITTLE BUNNIES ♡
HOP
HOP
HOP
STOP
... ...
ASHAMED
NO... NOT BUNNIES ...

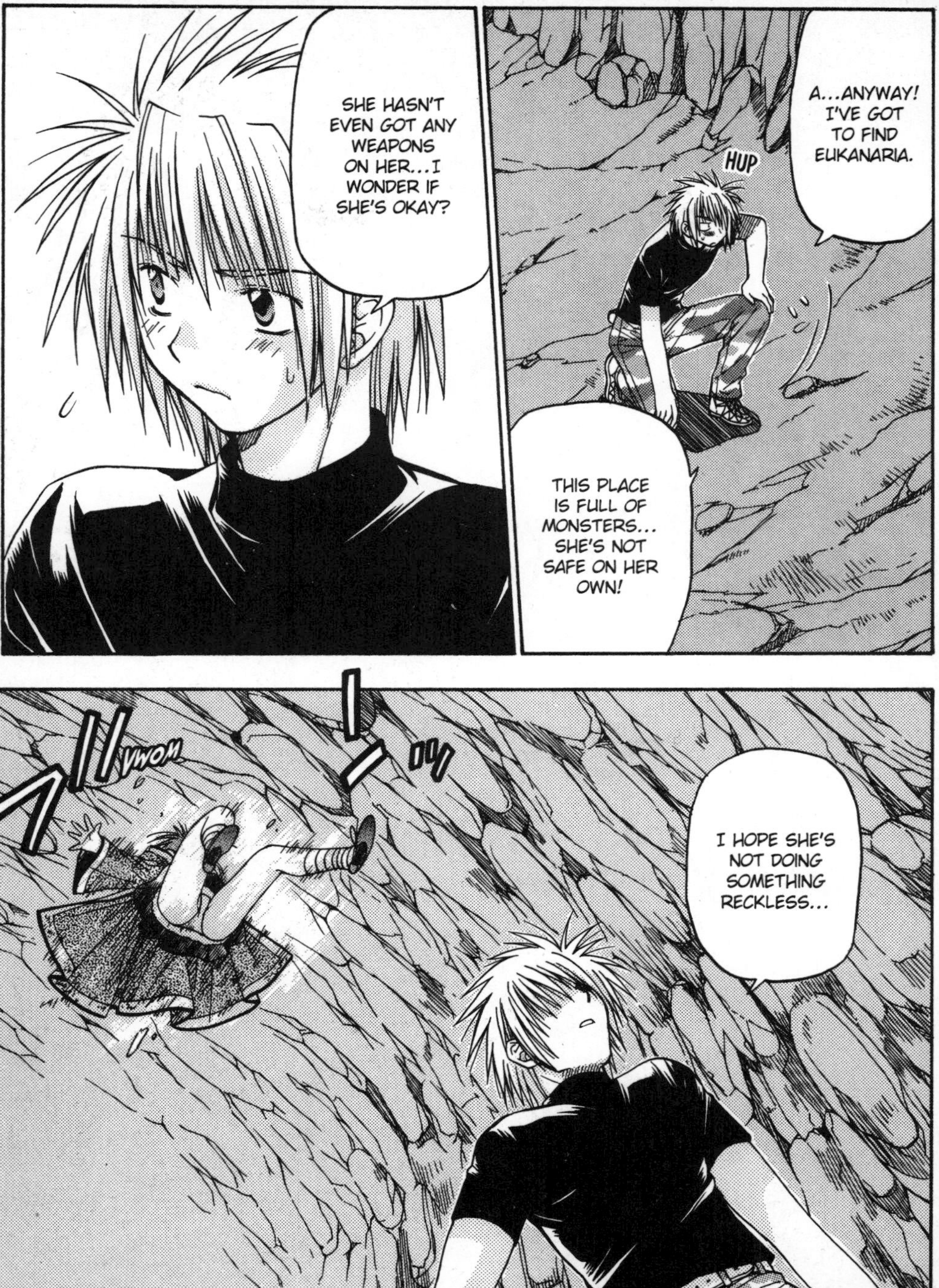
HUP
A...ANYWAY! I'VE GOT TO FIND EUKANARIA.
THIS PLACE IS FULL OF MONSTERS... SHE'S NOT SAFE ON HER OWN!
SHE HASN'T EVEN GOT ANY WEAPONS ON HER...I WONDER IF SHE'S OKAY?
VWON
I HOPE SHE'S NOT DOING SOMETHING RECKLESS...

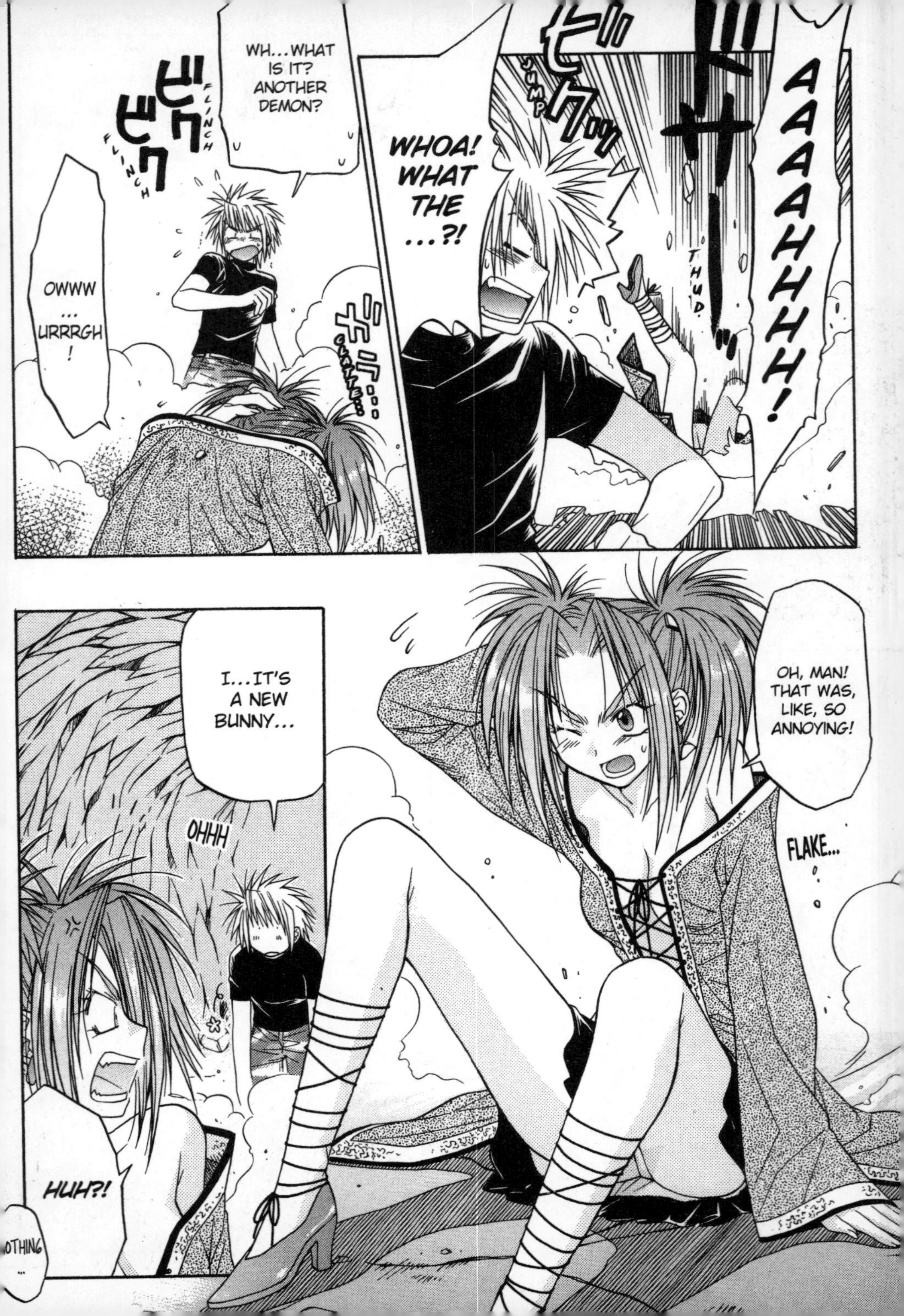
AAAAAHHHHH!
THUD
JUMP
WHOA! WHAT THE ...?!
WH...WHAT IS IT? ANOTHER DEMON?
FLINCH
FLINCH
OWWW ... URRRGH !
CLATTE...
OH, MAN! THAT WAS, LIKE, SO ANNOYING!
FLAKE...
I...IT'S A NEW BUNNY...
OHHH
HUH?!
OTHING ...

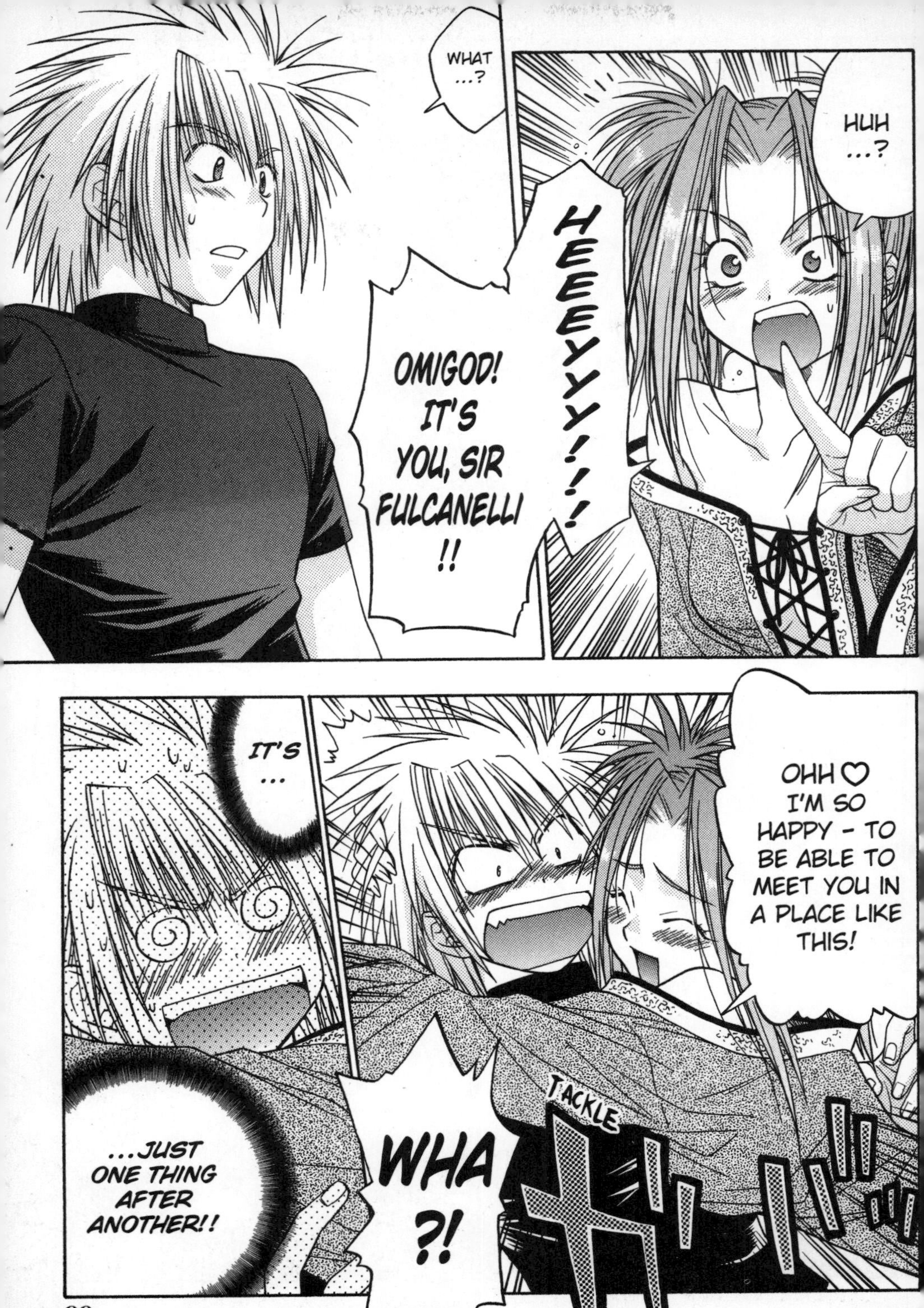
HUH ...?
HEEEYYY!!!
OMIGOD! IT'S YOU, SIR FULCANELLI !!
WHAT ...?
OHH♡ I'M SO HAPPY - TO BE ABLE TO MEET YOU IN A PLACE LIKE THIS!
TACKLE
WHA ?!
IT'S ...
...JUST ONE THING AFTER ANOTHER!!

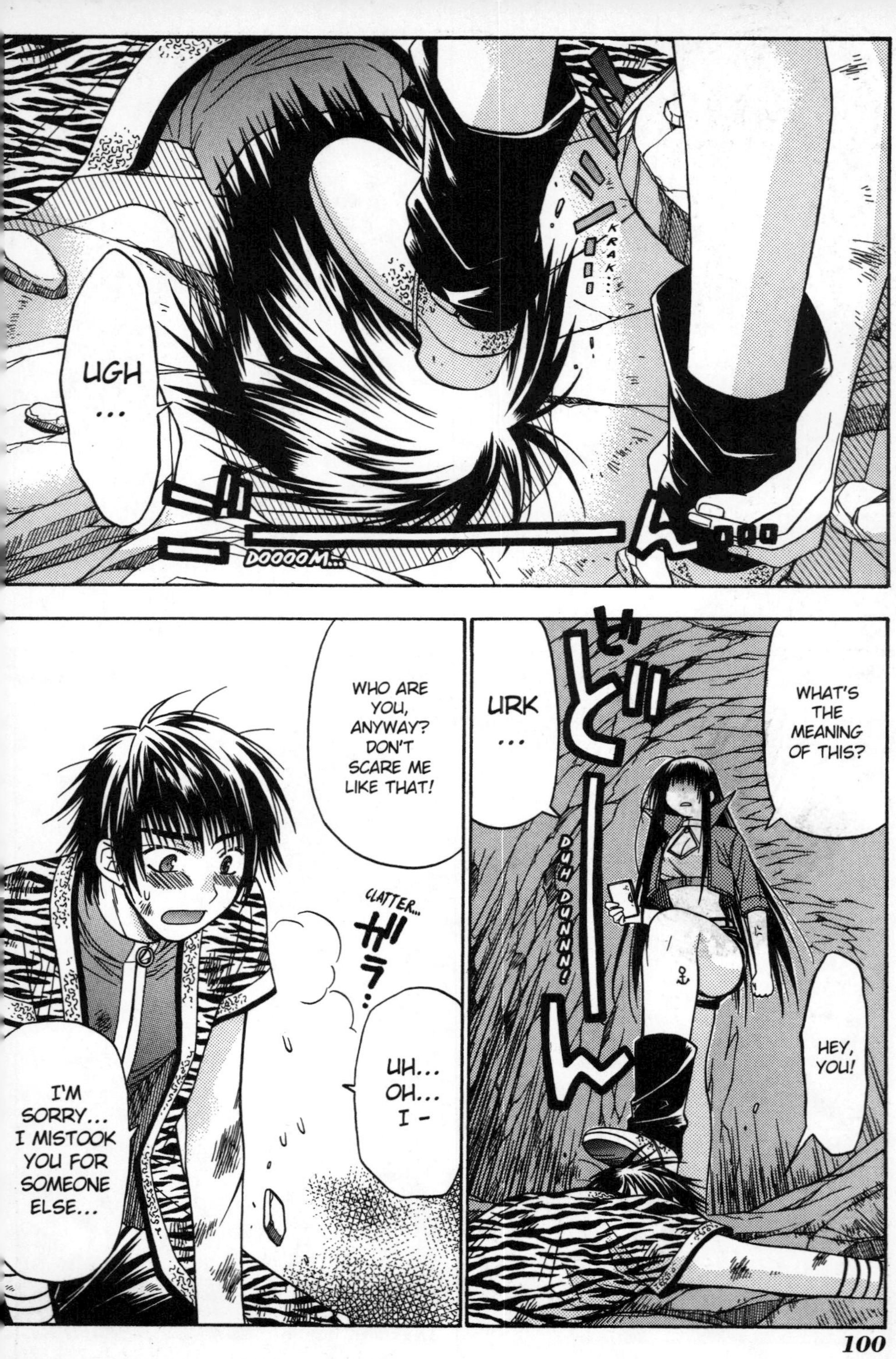
KRAK...
UGH...
DOOOOM...
WHAT'S THE MEANING OF THIS?
URK...
DUH DUNN!
HEY, YOU!
WHO ARE YOU, ANYWAY? DON'T SCARE ME LIKE THAT!
CLATTER...
UH... OH... I -
I'M SORRY... I MISTOOK YOU FOR SOMEONE ELSE...

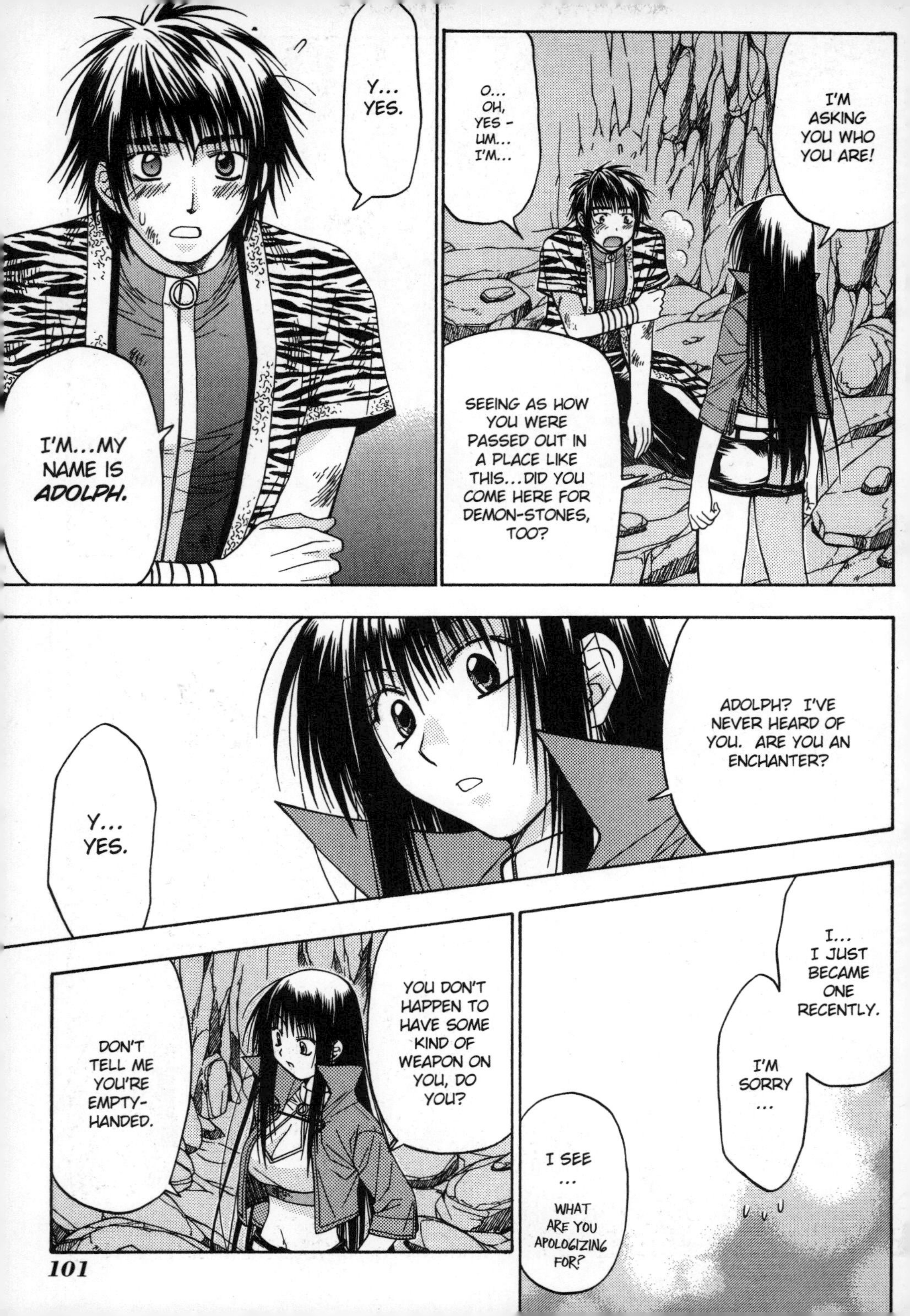
I'M ASKING YOU WHO YOU ARE!
O... OH, YES - UM... I'M...
SEEING AS HOW YOU WERE PASSED OUT IN A PLACE LIKE THIS...DID YOU COME HERE FOR DEMON-STONES, TOO?
Y... YES.
I'M...MY NAME IS *ADOLPH.*
ADOLPH? I'VE NEVER HEARD OF YOU. ARE YOU AN ENCHANTER?
Y... YES.
I... I JUST BECAME ONE RECENTLY.
I'M SORRY ...
I SEE ...
WHAT ARE YOU APOLOGIZING FOR?
YOU DON'T HAPPEN TO HAVE SOME KIND OF WEAPON ON YOU, DO YOU?
DON'T TELL ME YOU'RE EMPTY-HANDED.

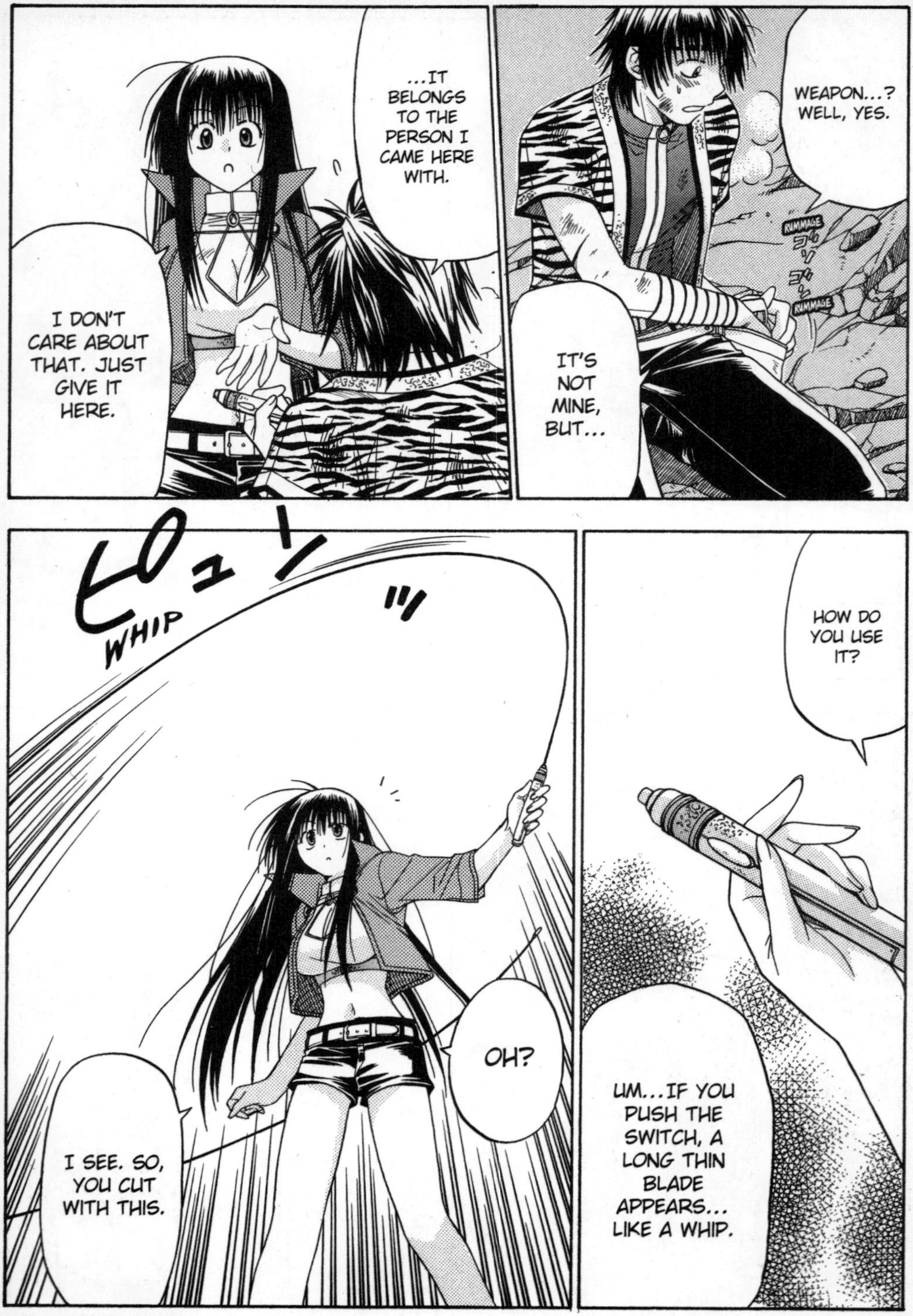
WEAPON...? WELL, YES.
RUMMAGE
RUMMAGE
IT'S NOT MINE, BUT...
...IT BELONGS TO THE PERSON I CAME HERE WITH.
I DON'T CARE ABOUT THAT. JUST GIVE IT HERE.
HOW DO YOU USE IT?
UM...IF YOU PUSH THE SWITCH, A LONG THIN BLADE APPEARS... LIKE A WHIP.
WHIP
OH?
I SEE. SO, YOU CUT WITH THIS.

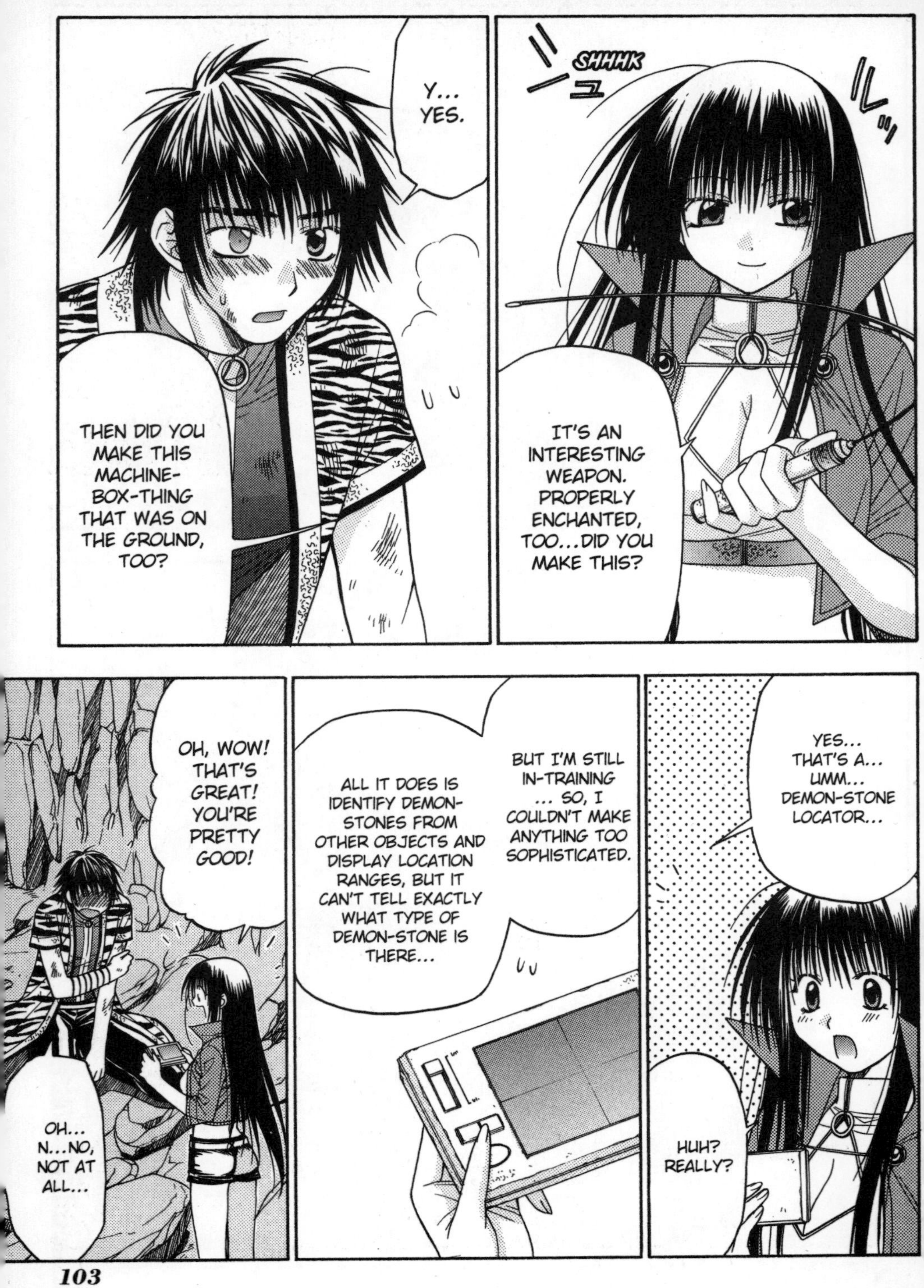
SHHHK
IT'S AN INTERESTING WEAPON. PROPERLY ENCHANTED, TOO...DID YOU MAKE THIS?
Y... YES.
THEN DID YOU MAKE THIS MACHINE-BOX-THING THAT WAS ON THE GROUND, TOO?
YES... THAT'S A... UMM... DEMON-STONE LOCATOR...
HUH? REALLY?
BUT I'M STILL IN-TRAINING ... SO, I COULDN'T MAKE ANYTHING TOO SOPHISTICATED.
ALL IT DOES IS IDENTIFY DEMON-STONES FROM OTHER OBJECTS AND DISPLAY LOCATION RANGES, BUT IT CAN'T TELL EXACTLY WHAT TYPE OF DEMON-STONE IS THERE...
OH, WOW! THAT'S GREAT! YOU'RE PRETTY GOOD!
OH... N...NO, NOT AT ALL...

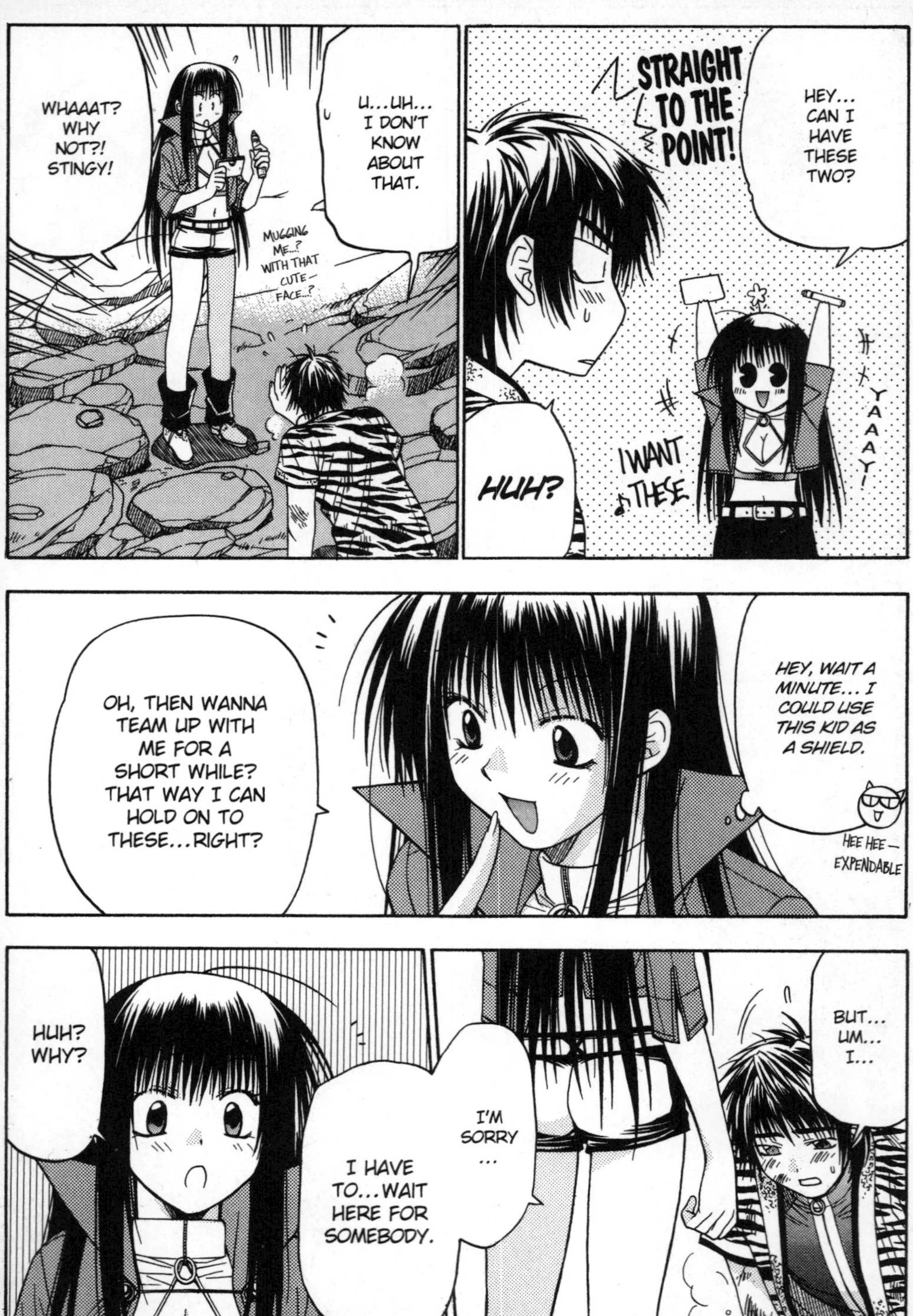
HEY... CAN I HAVE THESE TWO?
STRAIGHT TO THE POINT!
YAAAAY!
I WANT THESE
HUH?
U...UH... I DON'T KNOW ABOUT THAT.
WHAAAT? WHY NOT?! STINGY!
MUGGING ME..? WITH THAT CUTE-FACE..?
HEY, WAIT A MINUTE... I COULD USE THIS KID AS A SHIELD.
HEE HEE— EXPENDABLE
OH, THEN WANNA TEAM UP WITH ME FOR A SHORT WHILE? THAT WAY I CAN HOLD ON TO THESE...RIGHT?
BUT... UM... I...
I'M SORRY...
I HAVE TO...WAIT HERE FOR SOMEBODY.
HUH? WHY?

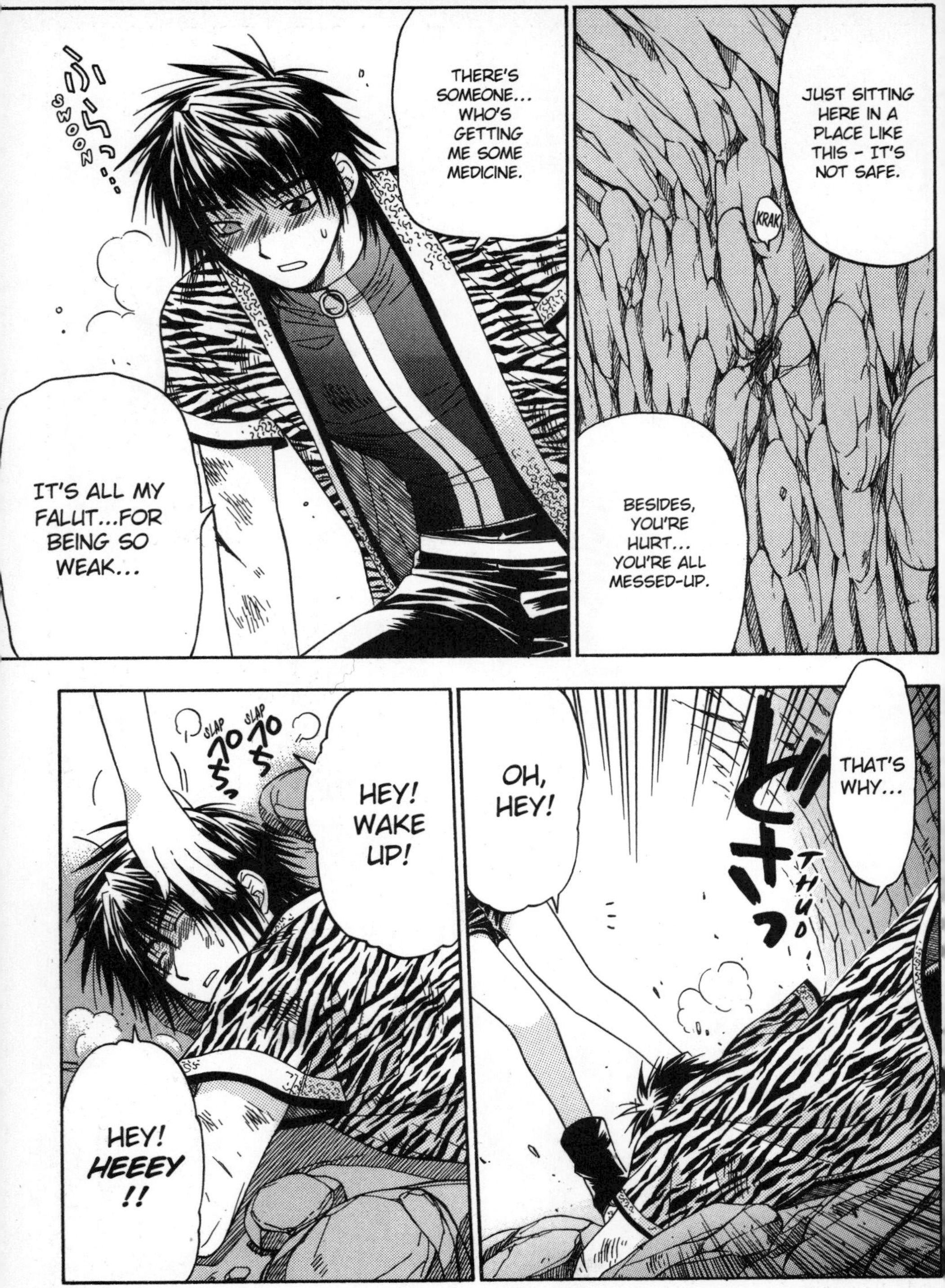
JUST SITTING HERE IN A PLACE LIKE THIS - IT'S NOT SAFE.
KRAK
BESIDES, YOU'RE HURT... YOU'RE ALL MESSED-UP.
SWOON
THERE'S SOMEONE... WHO'S GETTING ME SOME MEDICINE.
IT'S ALL MY FALUT...FOR BEING SO WEAK...
THAT'S WHY...
THUD
OH, HEY!
SLAP SLAP
HEY! WAKE UP!
HEY! HEEEY !!

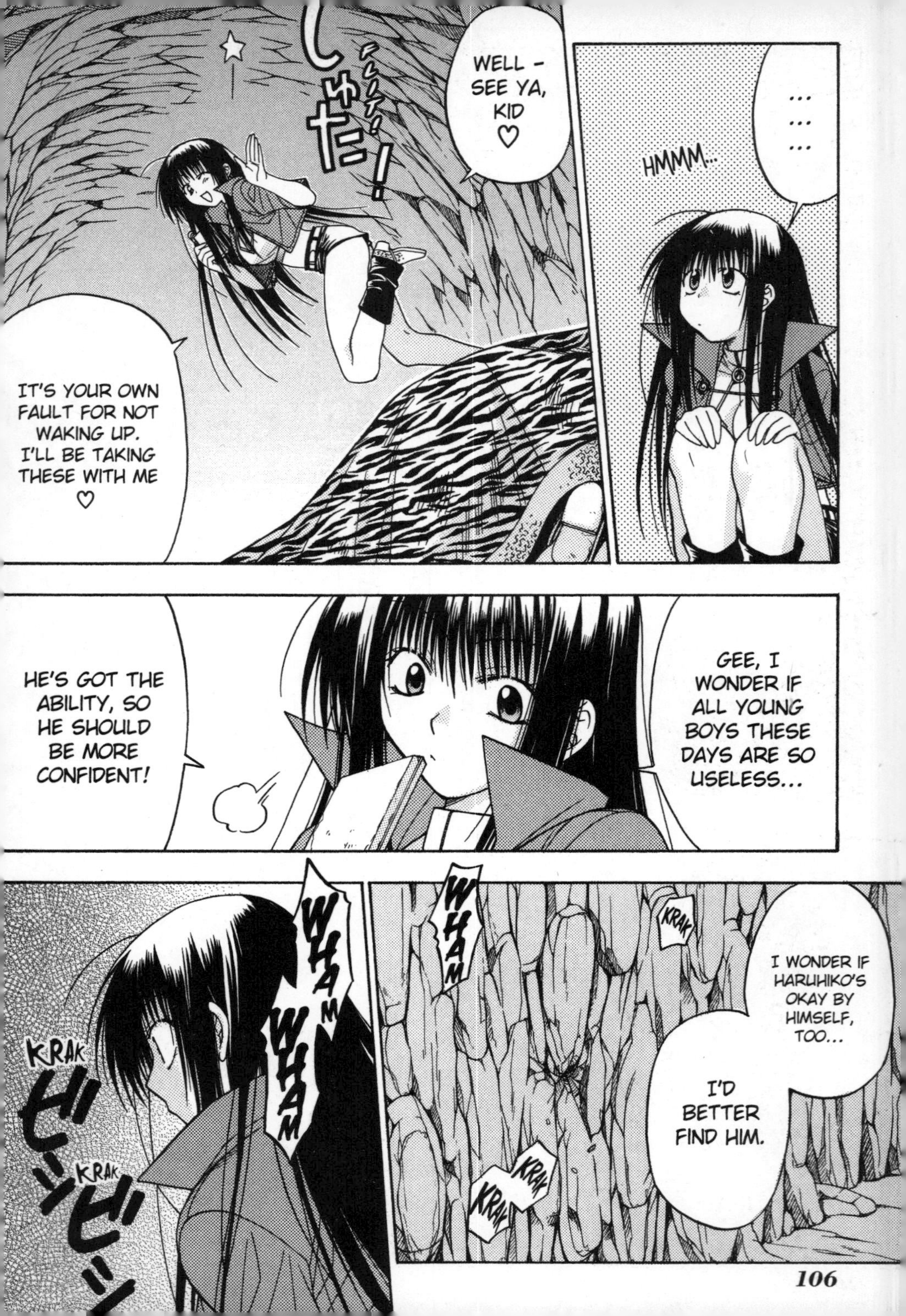
……
……
……
HMMM…
WELL - SEE YA, KID ♡
しゅたっ!
IT'S YOUR OWN FAULT FOR NOT WAKING UP. I'LL BE TAKING THESE WITH ME ♡
GEE, I WONDER IF ALL YOUNG BOYS THESE DAYS ARE SO USELESS…
HE'S GOT THE ABILITY, SO HE SHOULD BE MORE CONFIDENT!
KRAK
I WONDER IF HARUHIKO'S OKAY BY HIMSELF, TOO…
I'D BETTER FIND HIM.
KRAK
KRAK
WHAM
WHAM
WHAM
KRAK
KRAK
ビシビシッ

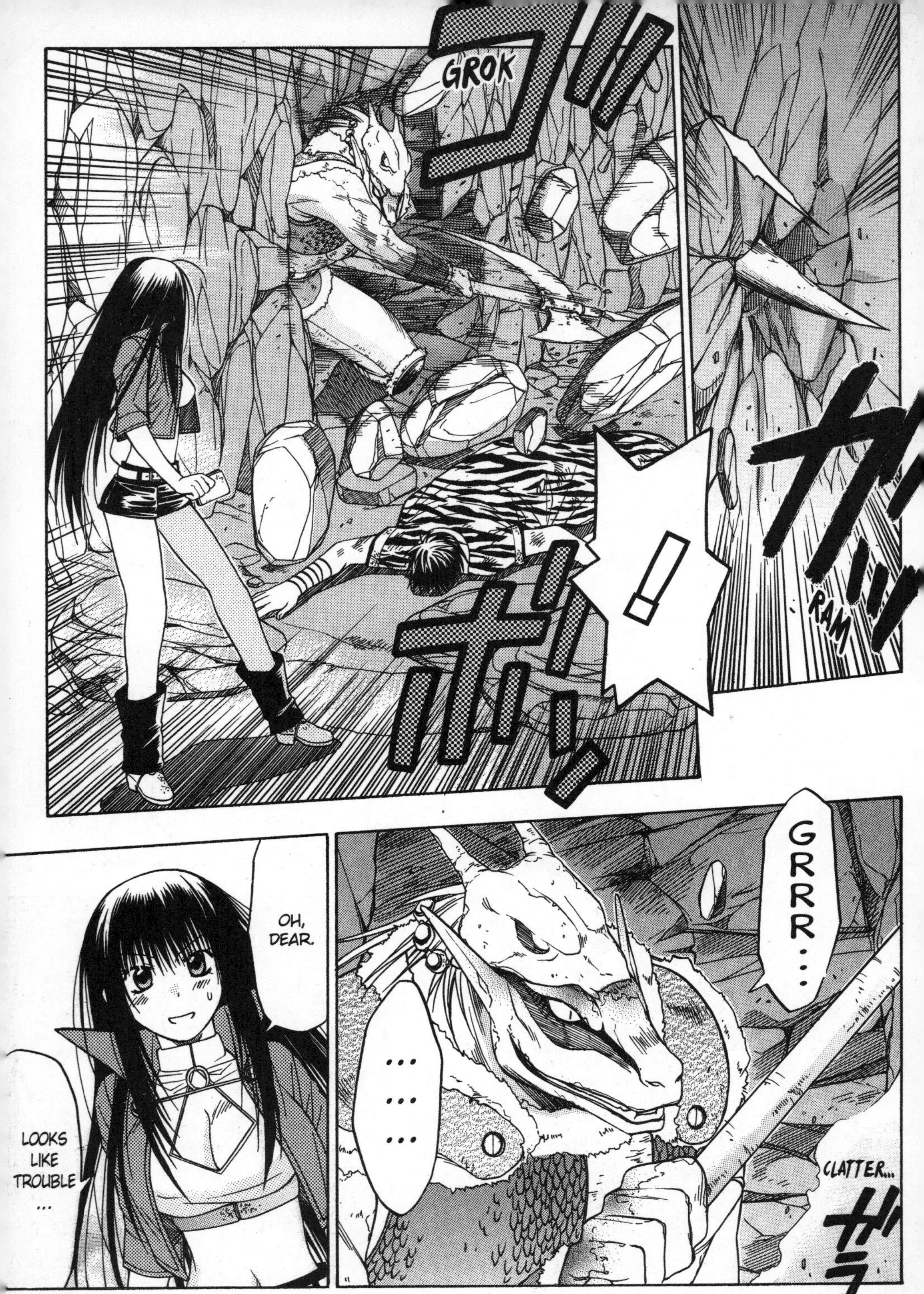
GROK
!
RAM
GRRR...
...
...
...
CLATTER...
OH, DEAR.
LOOKS LIKE TROUBLE ...

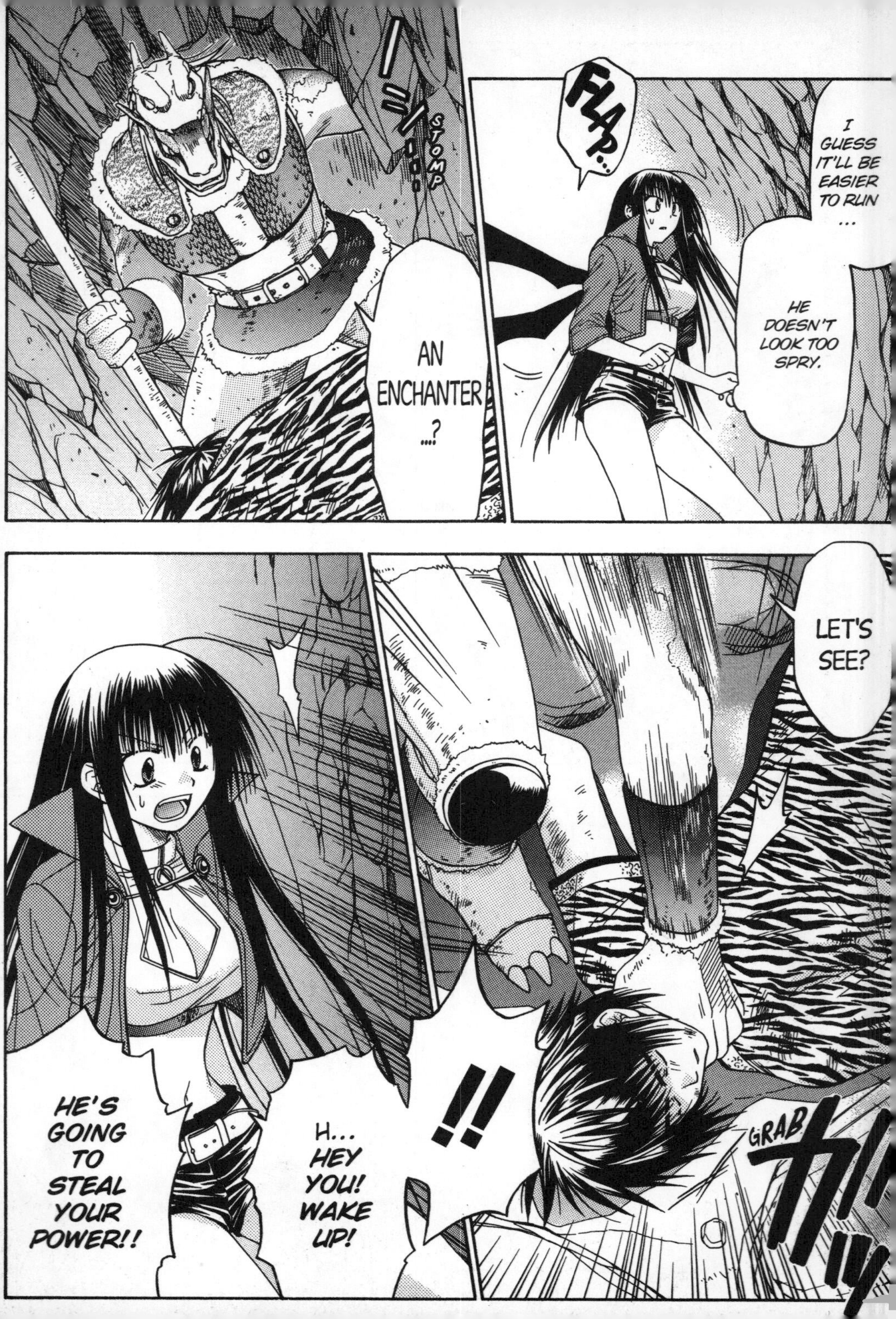
FLAP...
I GUESS IT'LL BE EASIER TO RUN ...
HE DOESN'T LOOK TOO SPRY.
STOMP
AN ENCHANTER ...?
LET'S SEE?
GRAB
!!
H... HEY YOU! WAKE UP!
HE'S GOING TO STEAL YOUR POWER!!

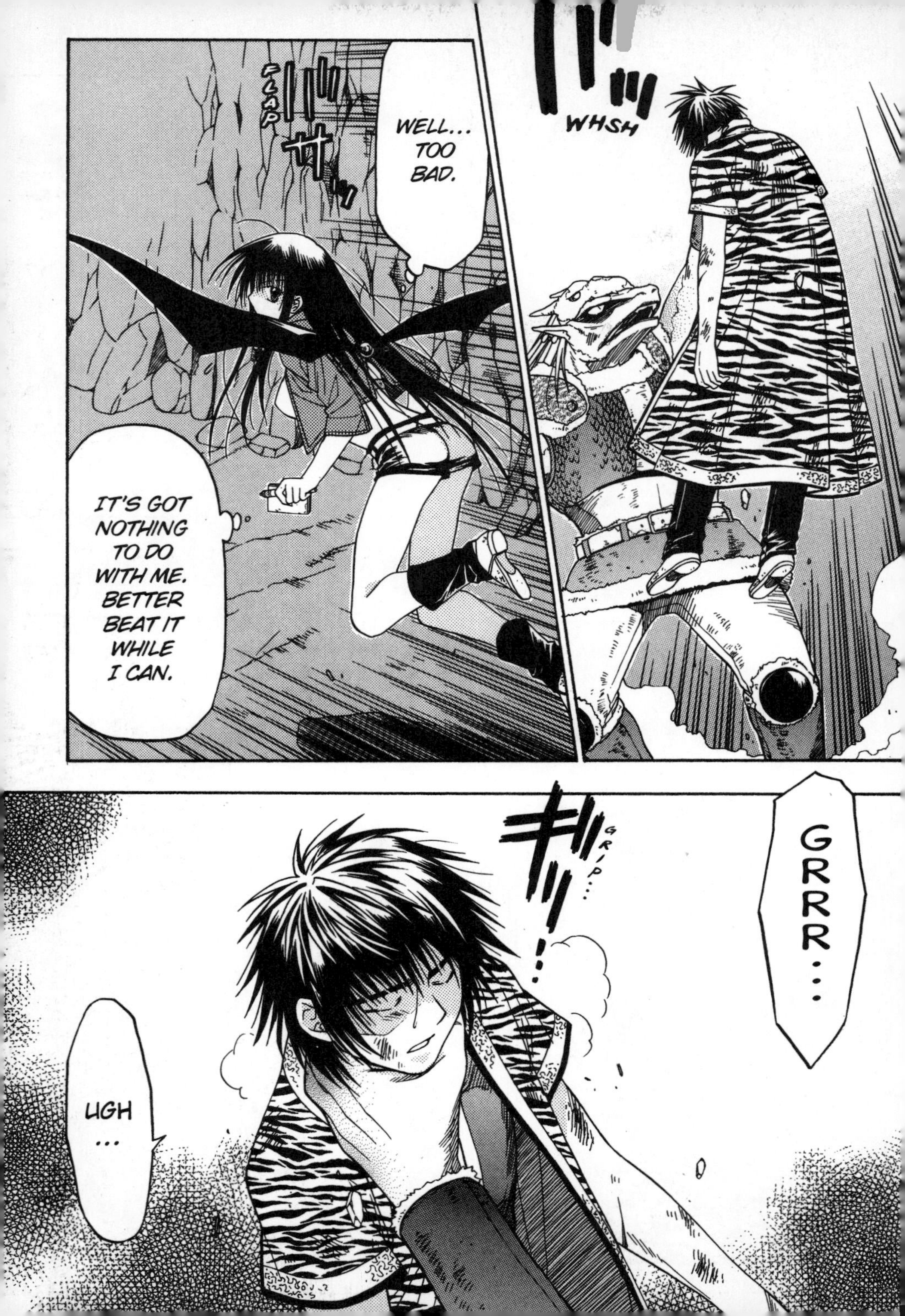
WHSH
FLAP
WELL... TOO BAD.
IT'S GOT NOTHING TO DO WITH ME. BETTER BEAT IT WHILE I CAN.
GRRR...
GRIP...
UGH ...

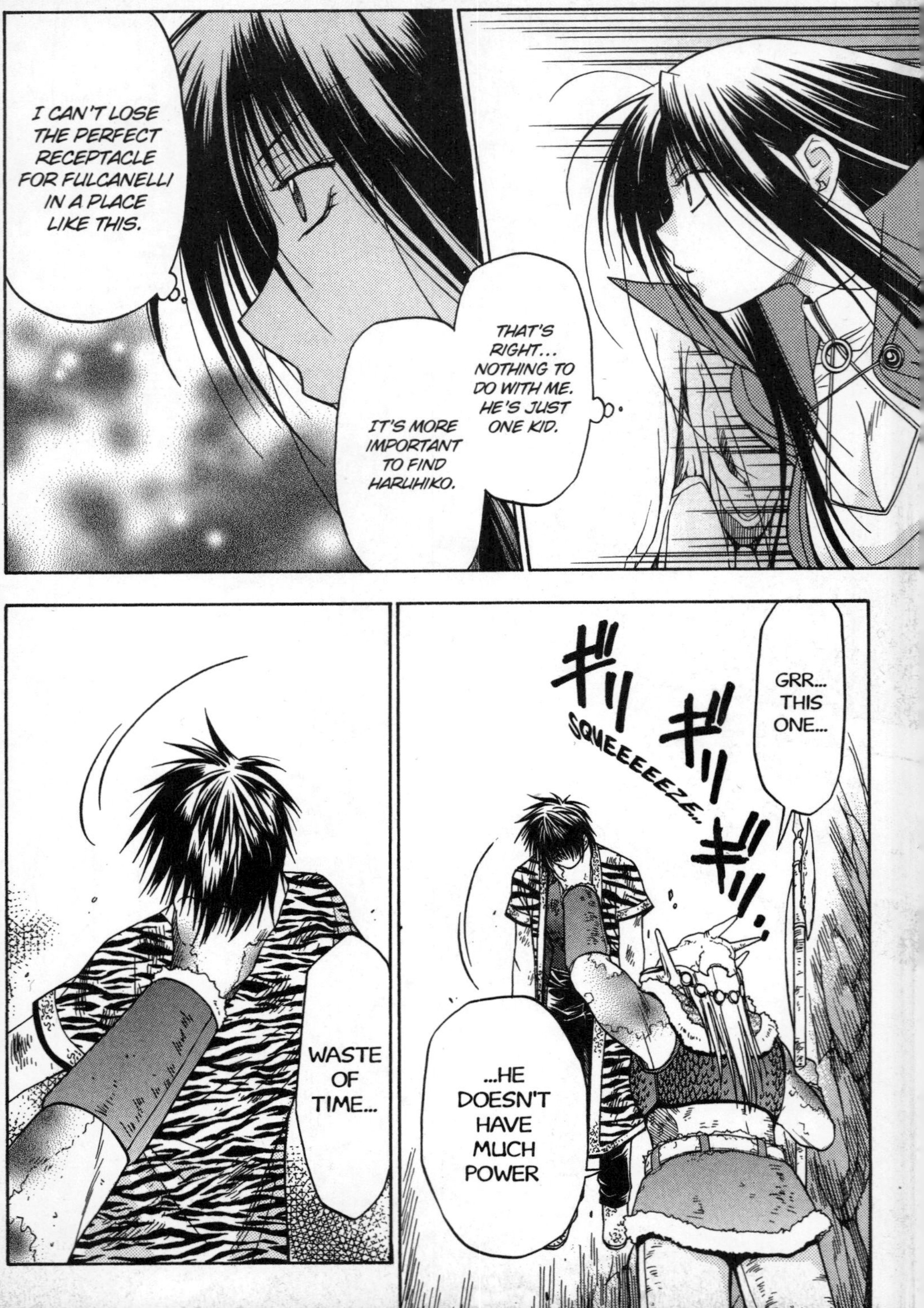
THAT'S RIGHT... NOTHING TO DO WITH ME. HE'S JUST ONE KID.
IT'S MORE IMPORTANT TO FIND HARUHIKO.
I CAN'T LOSE THE PERFECT RECEPTACLE FOR FULCANELLI IN A PLACE LIKE THIS.
GRR... THIS ONE...
ギリ ギリ ギリ
SQUEEEEEEEZE...
...HE DOESN'T HAVE MUCH POWER
WASTE OF TIME...

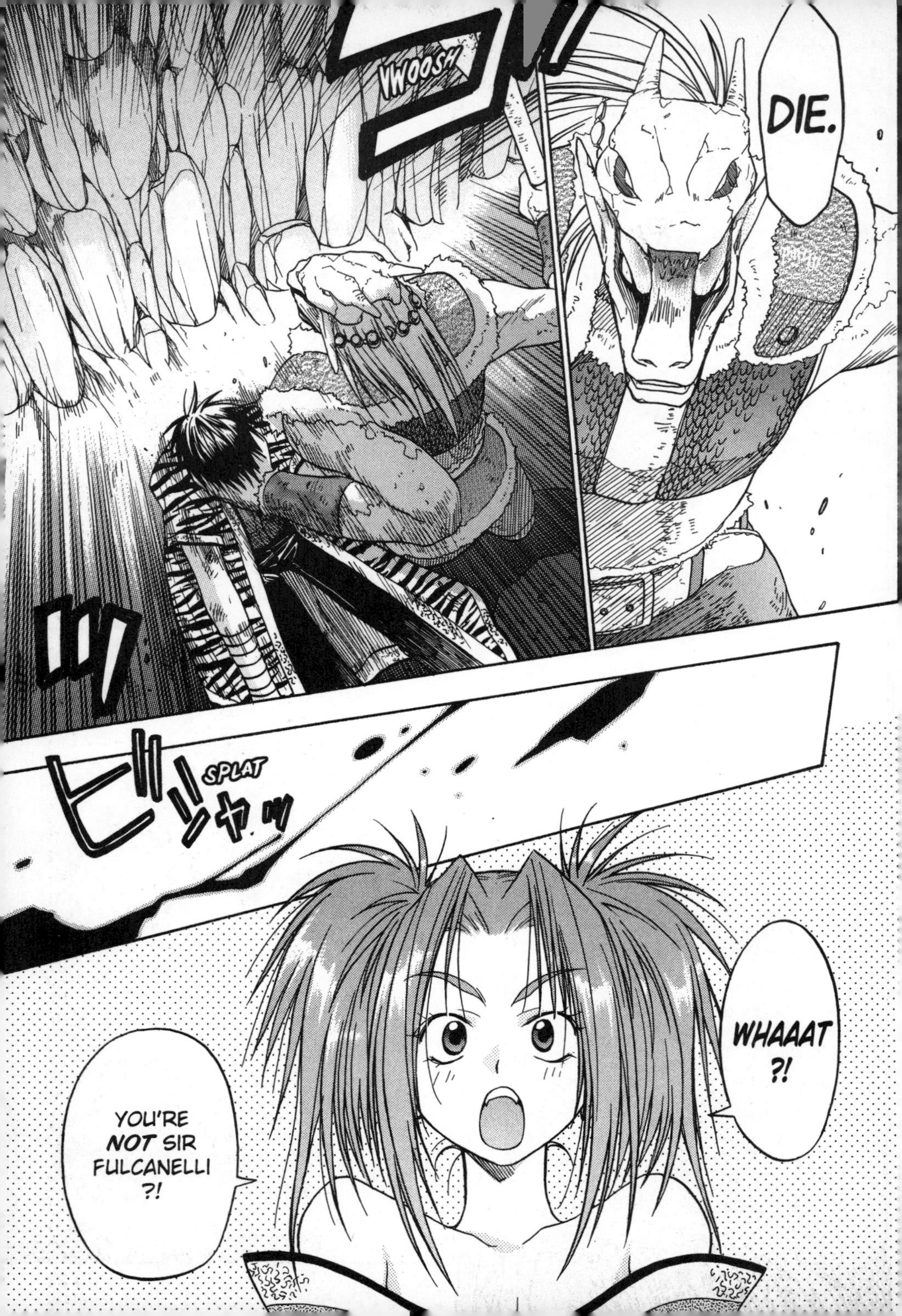
VWOOSH
DIE.
SPLAT
WHAAAT ?!
YOU'RE NOT SIR FULCANELLI ?!

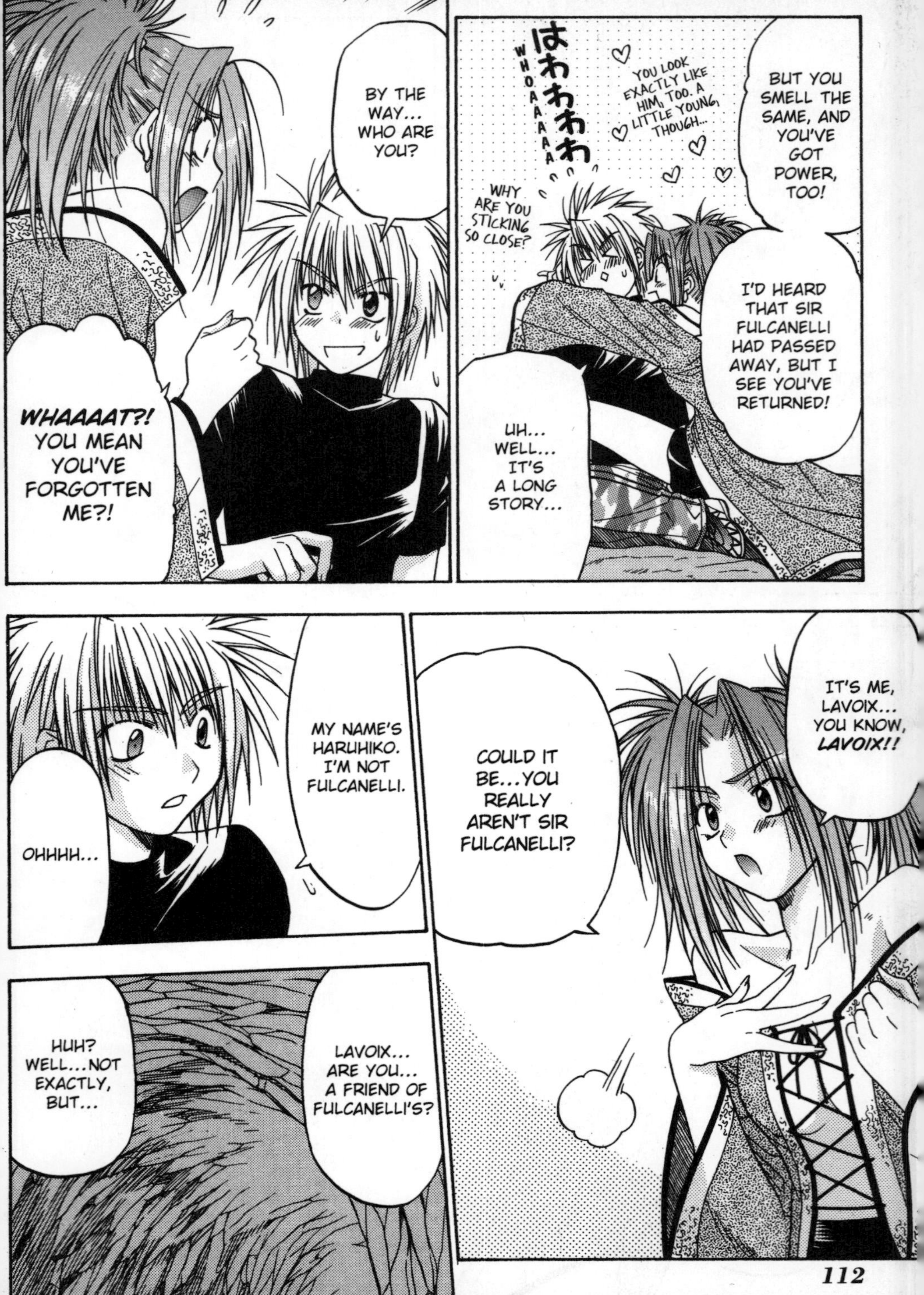

BUT YOU SMELL THE SAME, AND YOU'VE GOT POWER, TOO!
はわわわわ
WHOAAAAA
YOU LOOK EXACTLY LIKE HIM, TOO. A LITTLE YOUNG, THOUGH...
WHY ARE YOU STICKING SO CLOSE?
I'D HEARD THAT SIR FULCANELLI HAD PASSED AWAY, BUT I SEE YOU'VE RETURNED!
UH... WELL... IT'S A LONG STORY...
BY THE WAY... WHO ARE YOU?
WHAAAAT?! YOU MEAN YOU'VE FORGOTTEN ME?!
IT'S ME, LAVOIX... YOU KNOW, LAVOIX!!
COULD IT BE...YOU REALLY AREN'T SIR FULCANELLI?
MY NAME'S HARUHIKO. I'M NOT FULCANELLI.
OHHHH...
LAVOIX... ARE YOU... A FRIEND OF FULCANELLI'S?
HUH? WELL...NOT EXACTLY, BUT...

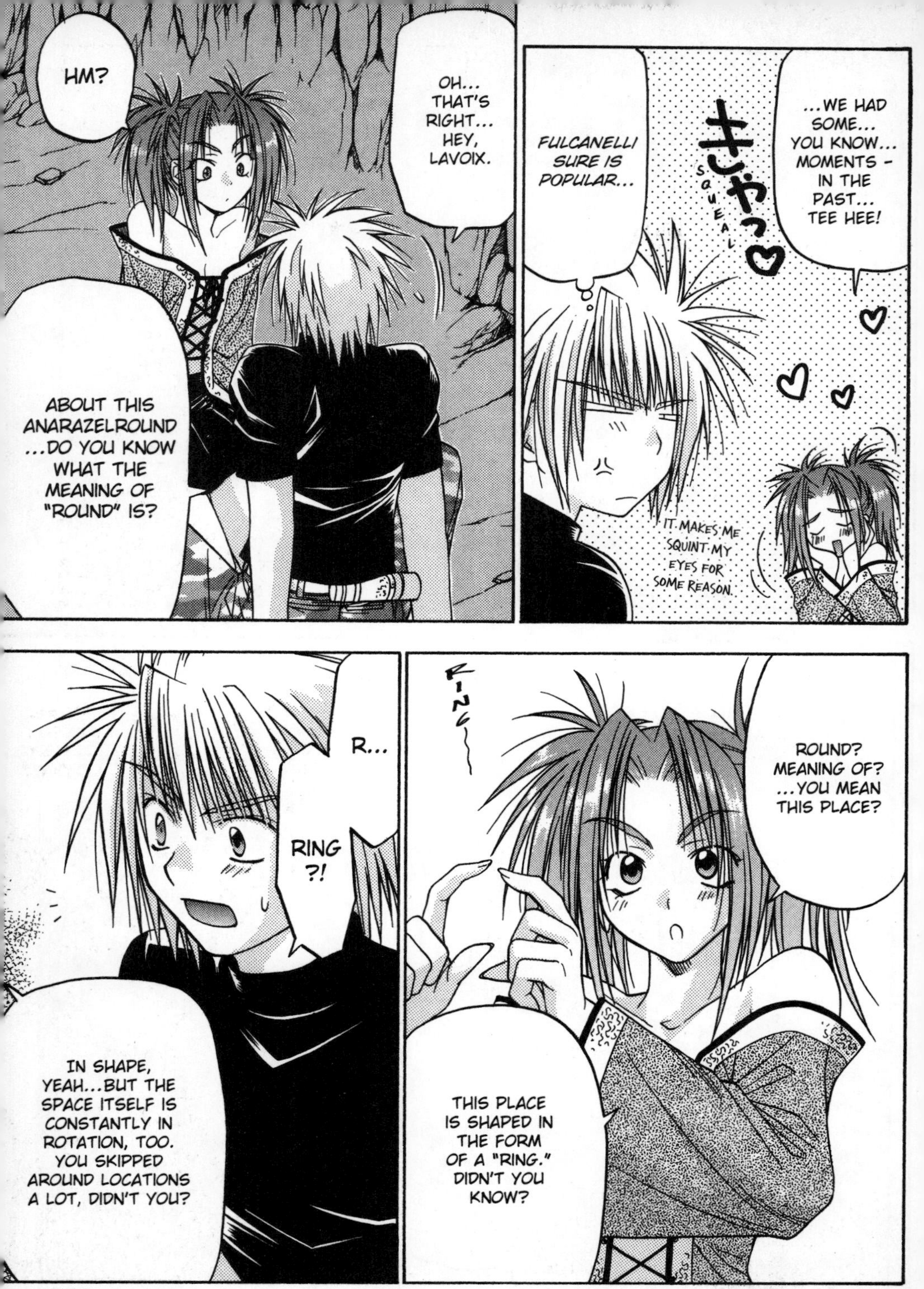
...WE HAD SOME... YOU KNOW... MOMENTS - IN THE PAST... TEE HEE!
きゃっ♡
SQUEAL
FULCANELLI SURE IS POPULAR...
IT MAKES ME SQUINT MY EYES FOR SOME REASON.
OH... THAT'S RIGHT... HEY, LAVOIX.
HM?
ABOUT THIS ANARAZELROUND ...DO YOU KNOW WHAT THE MEANING OF "ROUND" IS?
ROUND? MEANING OF? ...YOU MEAN THIS PLACE?
RING~
THIS PLACE IS SHAPED IN THE FORM OF A "RING." DIDN'T YOU KNOW?
R...
RING ?!
IN SHAPE, YEAH...BUT THE SPACE ITSELF IS CONSTANTLY IN ROTATION, TOO. YOU SKIPPED AROUND LOCATIONS A LOT, DIDN'T YOU?

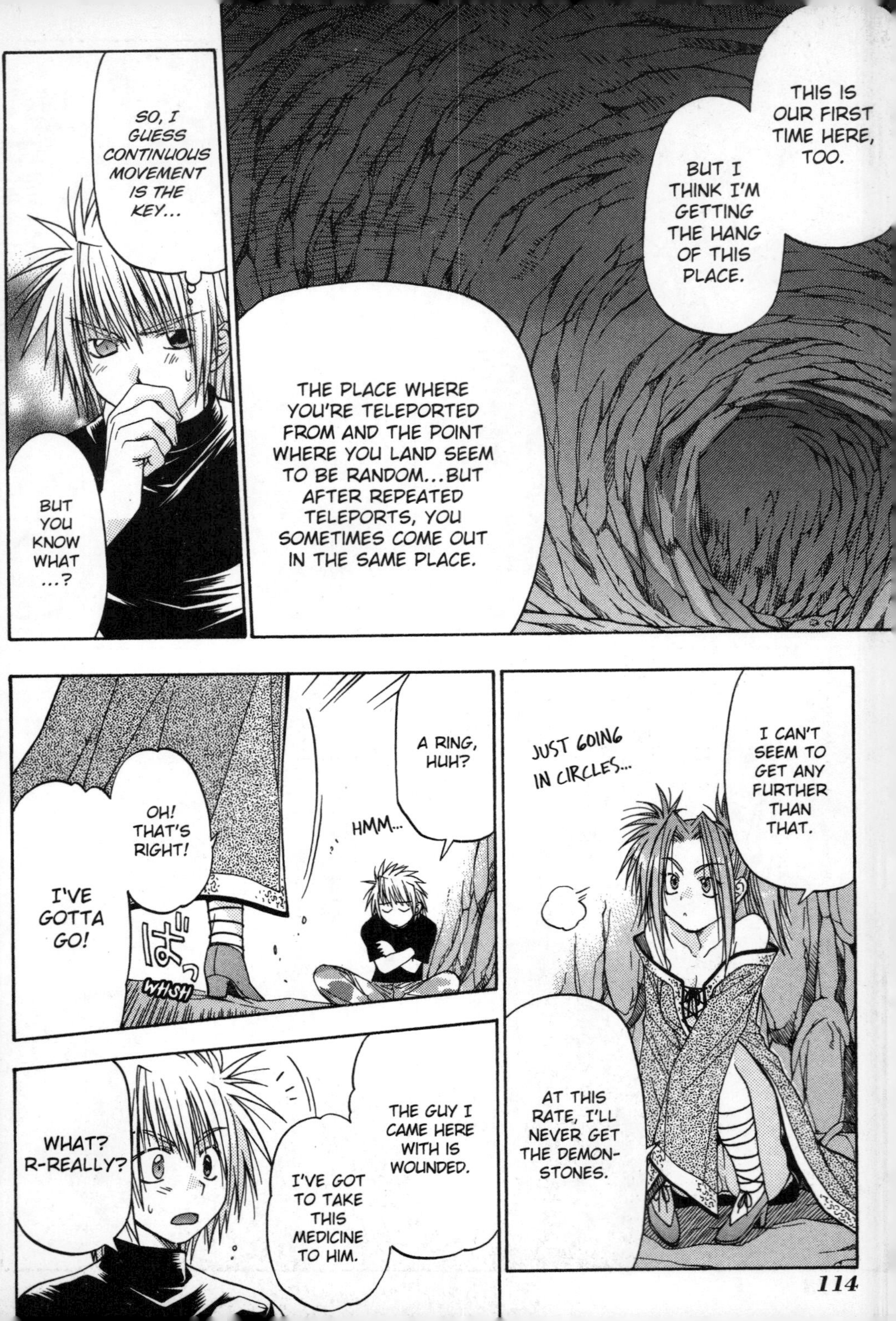
THIS IS OUR FIRST TIME HERE, TOO.
BUT I THINK I'M GETTING THE HANG OF THIS PLACE.
THE PLACE WHERE YOU'RE TELEPORTED FROM AND THE POINT WHERE YOU LAND SEEM TO BE RANDOM...BUT AFTER REPEATED TELEPORTS, YOU SOMETIMES COME OUT IN THE SAME PLACE.
SO, I GUESS CONTINUOUS MOVEMENT IS THE KEY...
BUT YOU KNOW WHAT ...?
I CAN'T SEEM TO GET ANY FURTHER THAN THAT.
JUST GOING IN CIRCLES...
AT THIS RATE, I'LL NEVER GET THE DEMON-STONES.
A RING, HUH?
HMM...
OH! THAT'S RIGHT!
I'VE GOTTA GO!
ばっ
WHSH
THE GUY I CAME HERE WITH IS WOUNDED.
I'VE GOT TO TAKE THIS MEDICINE TO HIM.
WHAT? R-REALLY?

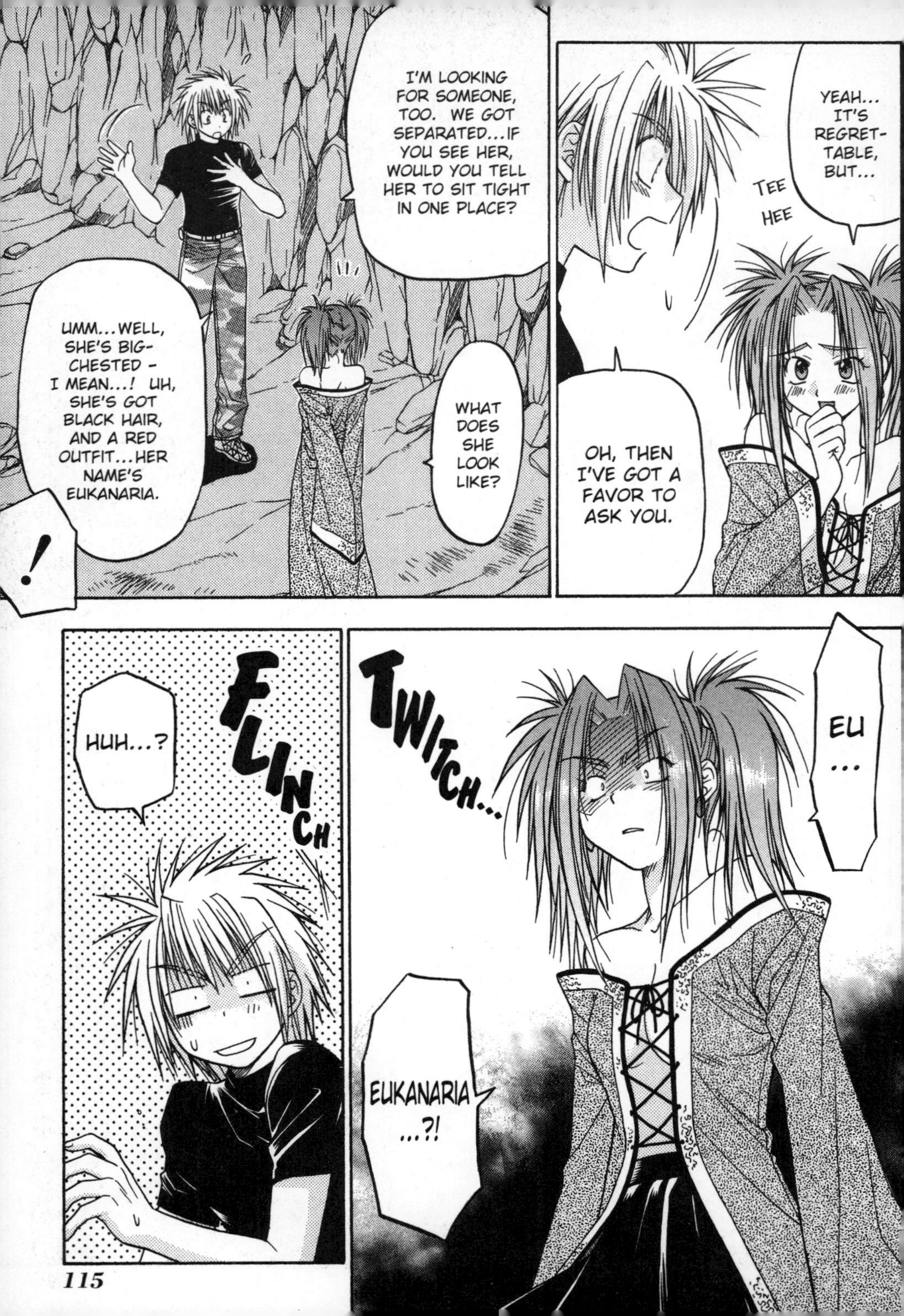
YEAH... IT'S REGRET-TABLE, BUT...
TEE HEE
OH, THEN I'VE GOT A FAVOR TO ASK YOU.
I'M LOOKING FOR SOMEONE, TOO. WE GOT SEPARATED...IF YOU SEE HER, WOULD YOU TELL HER TO SIT TIGHT IN ONE PLACE?
WHAT DOES SHE LOOK LIKE?
UMM...WELL, SHE'S BIG-CHESTED - I MEAN...! UH, SHE'S GOT BLACK HAIR, AND A RED OUTFIT...HER NAME'S EUKANARIA.
!
EU...
TWITCH...
EUKANARIA...?!
FLINCH
HUH...?

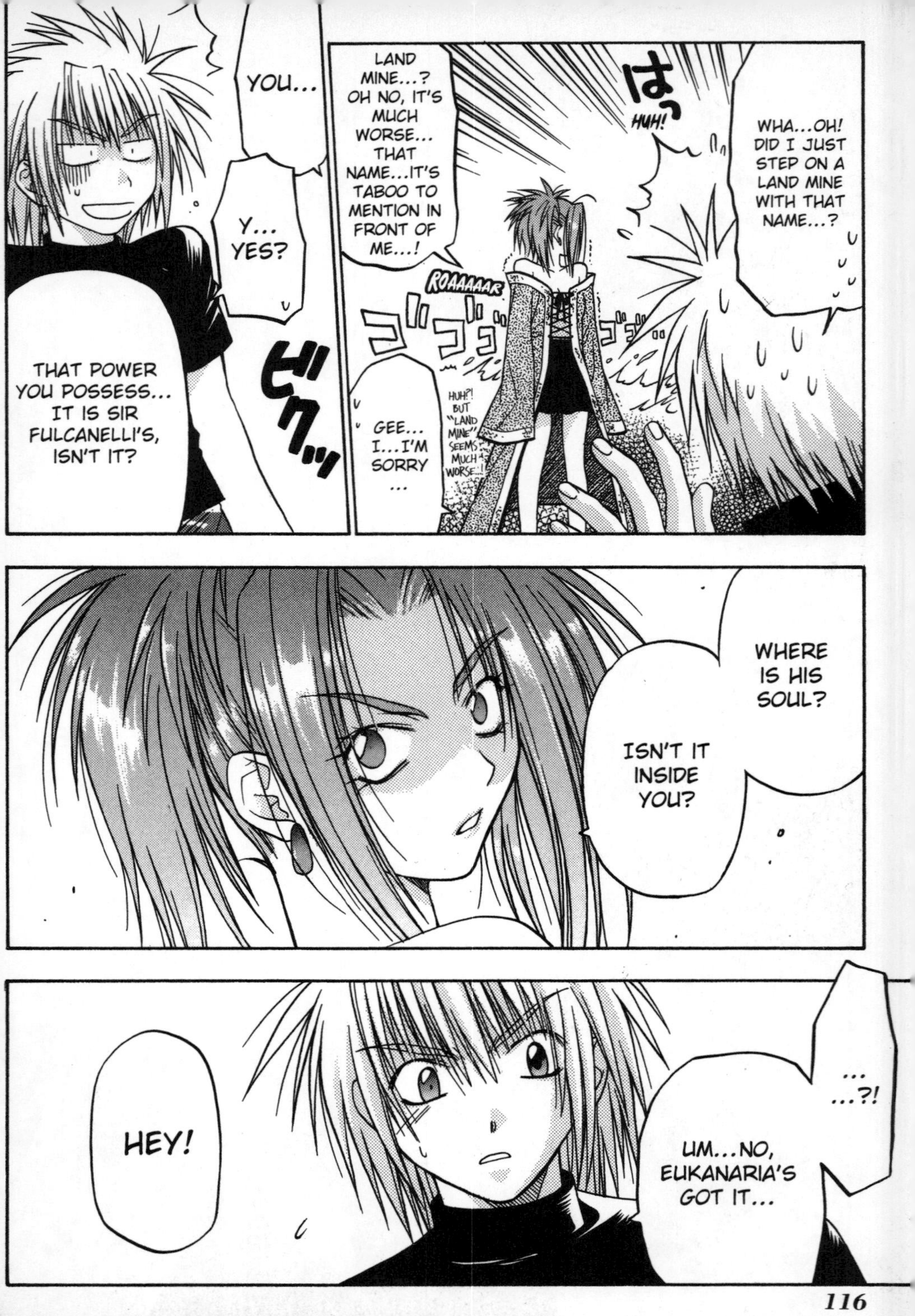
は
HUH!
WHA...OH! DID I JUST STEP ON A LAND MINE WITH THAT NAME...?
LAND MINE...? OH NO, IT'S MUCH WORSE... THAT NAME...IT'S TABOO TO MENTION IN FRONT OF ME...!
ROAAAAAR
GEE... I...I'M SORRY ...
HUH?! BUT "LAND MINE" SEEMS MUCH WORSE...!
YOU...
Y... YES?
THAT POWER YOU POSSESS... IT IS SIR FULCANELLI'S, ISN'T IT?
WHERE IS HIS SOUL?
ISN'T IT INSIDE YOU?
... ...?!
UM...NO, EUKANARIA'S GOT IT...
HEY!

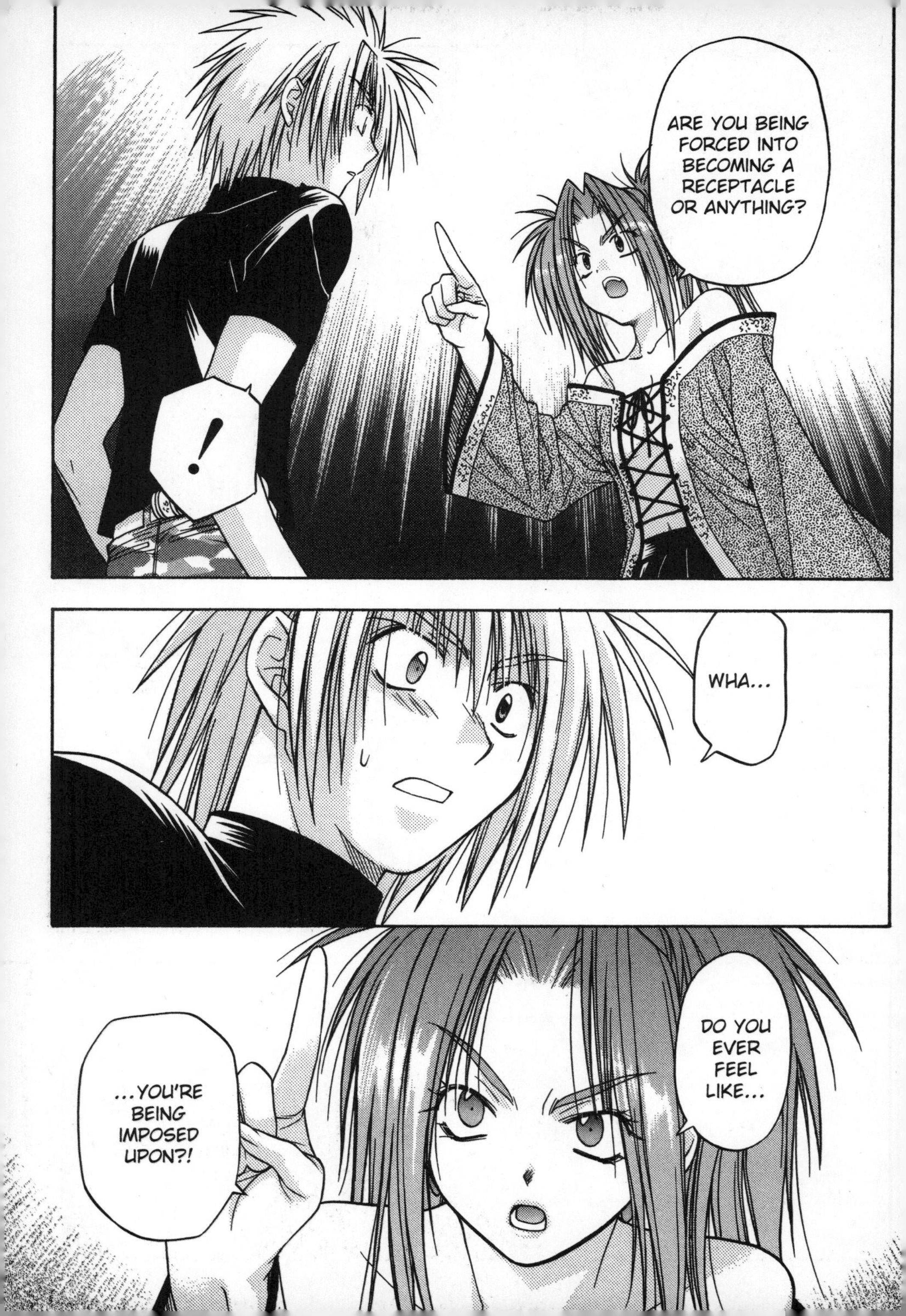
ARE YOU BEING FORCED INTO BECOMING A RECEPTACLE OR ANYTHING?
!
WHA...
DO YOU EVER FEEL LIKE...
...YOU'RE BEING IMPOSED UPON?!

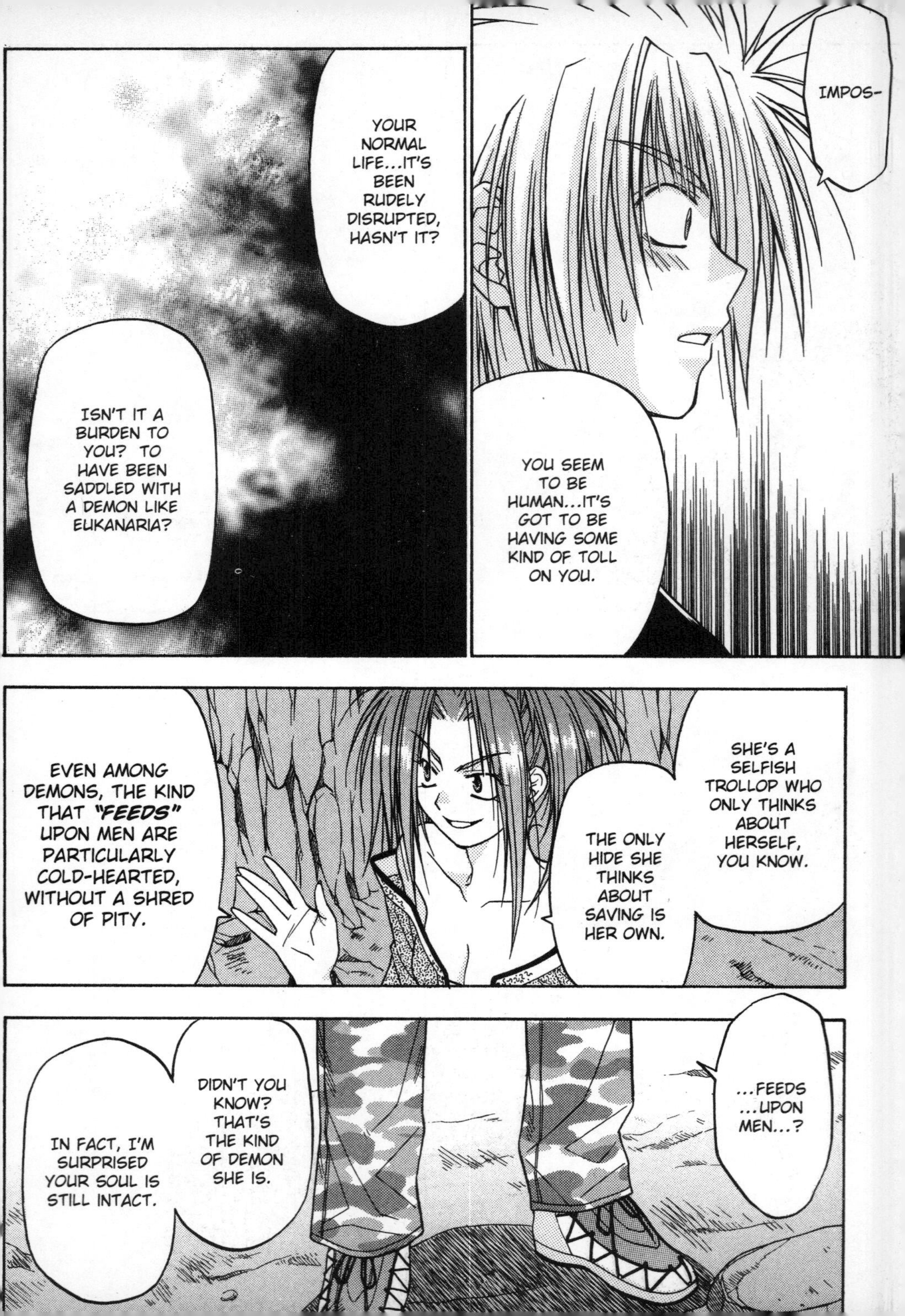
IMPOS-
YOU SEEM TO BE HUMAN...IT'S GOT TO BE HAVING SOME KIND OF TOLL ON YOU.
YOUR NORMAL LIFE...IT'S BEEN RUDELY DISRUPTED, HASN'T IT?
ISN'T IT A BURDEN TO YOU? TO HAVE BEEN SADDLED WITH A DEMON LIKE EUKANARIA?
SHE'S A SELFISH TROLLOP WHO ONLY THINKS ABOUT HERSELF, YOU KNOW.
THE ONLY HIDE SHE THINKS ABOUT SAVING IS HER OWN.
EVEN AMONG DEMONS, THE KIND THAT "FEEDS" UPON MEN ARE PARTICULARLY COLD-HEARTED, WITHOUT A SHRED OF PITY.
...FEEDS ...UPON MEN...?
DIDN'T YOU KNOW? THAT'S THE KIND OF DEMON SHE IS.
IN FACT, I'M SURPRISED YOUR SOUL IS STILL INTACT.

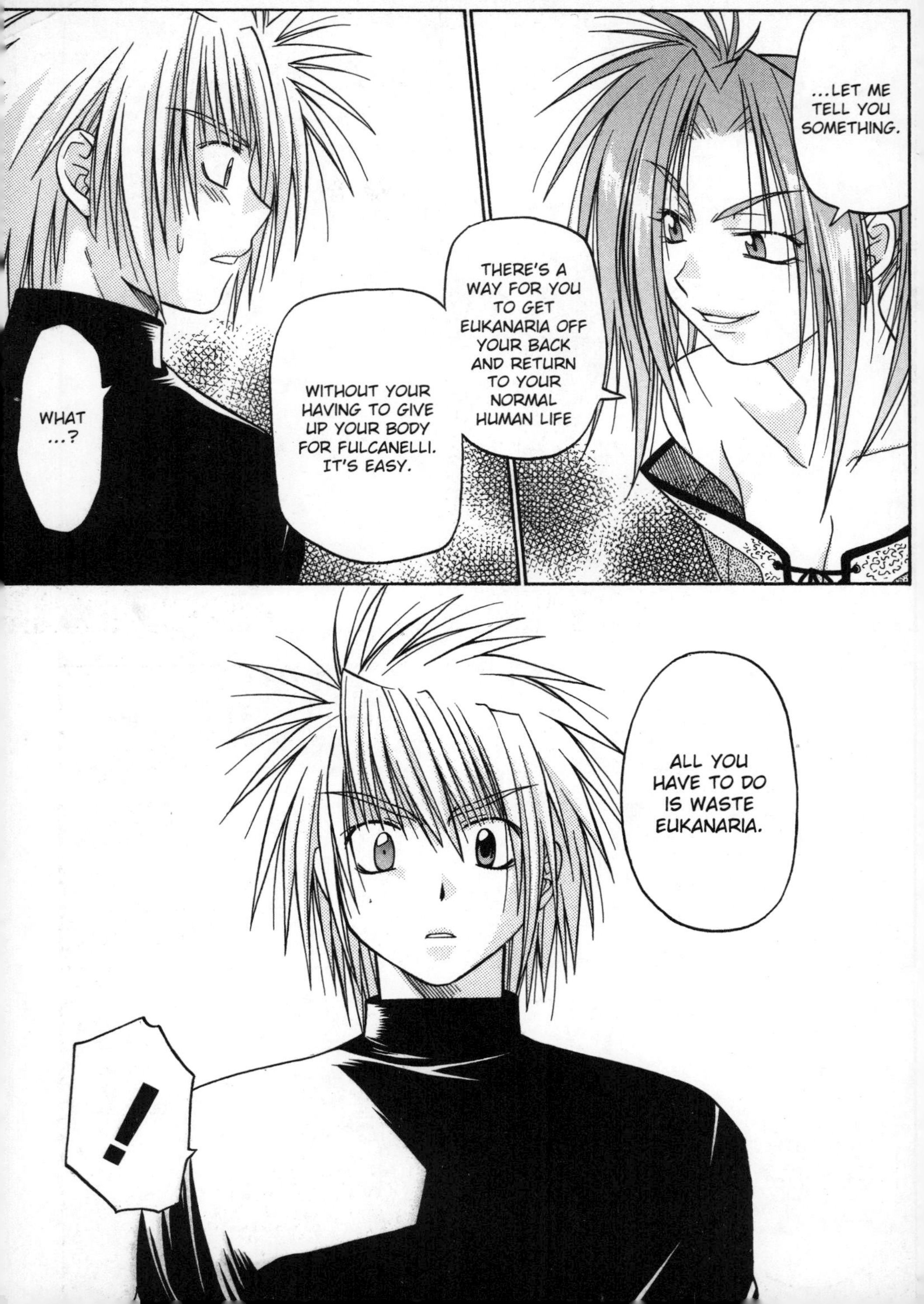
...LET ME TELL YOU SOMETHING.
THERE'S A WAY FOR YOU TO GET EUKANARIA OFF YOUR BACK AND RETURN TO YOUR NORMAL HUMAN LIFE
WITHOUT YOUR HAVING TO GIVE UP YOUR BODY FOR FULCANELLI. IT'S EASY.
WHAT ...?
ALL YOU HAVE TO DO IS WASTE EUKANARIA.
!

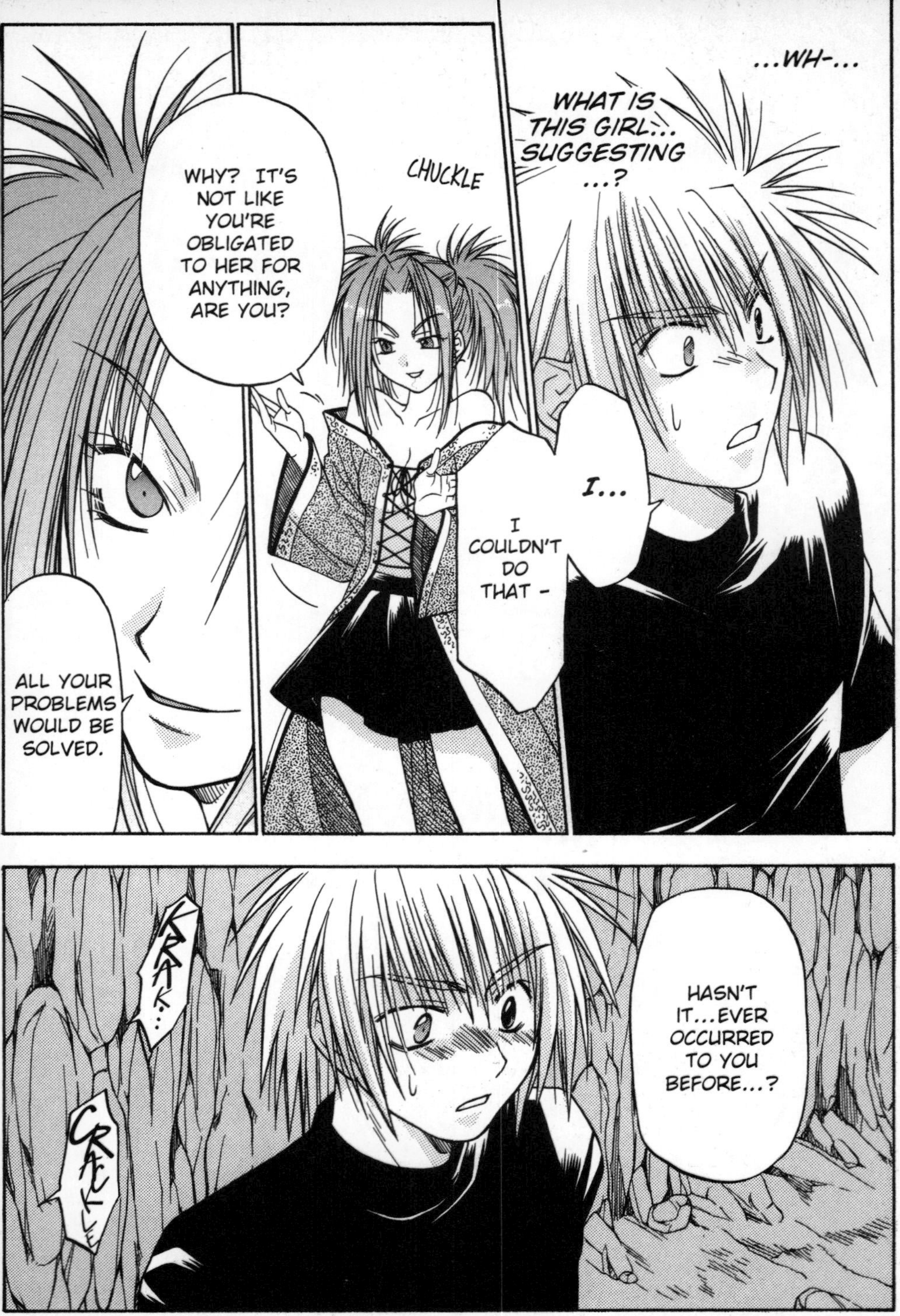
...WH-...
WHAT IS THIS GIRL... SUGGESTING ...?
I...
I COULDN'T DO THAT -
CHUCKLE
WHY? IT'S NOT LIKE YOU'RE OBLIGATED TO HER FOR ANYTHING, ARE YOU?
ALL YOUR PROBLEMS WOULD BE SOLVED.
HASN'T IT...EVER OCCURRED TO YOU BEFORE...?
KRAK...
CRACKLE

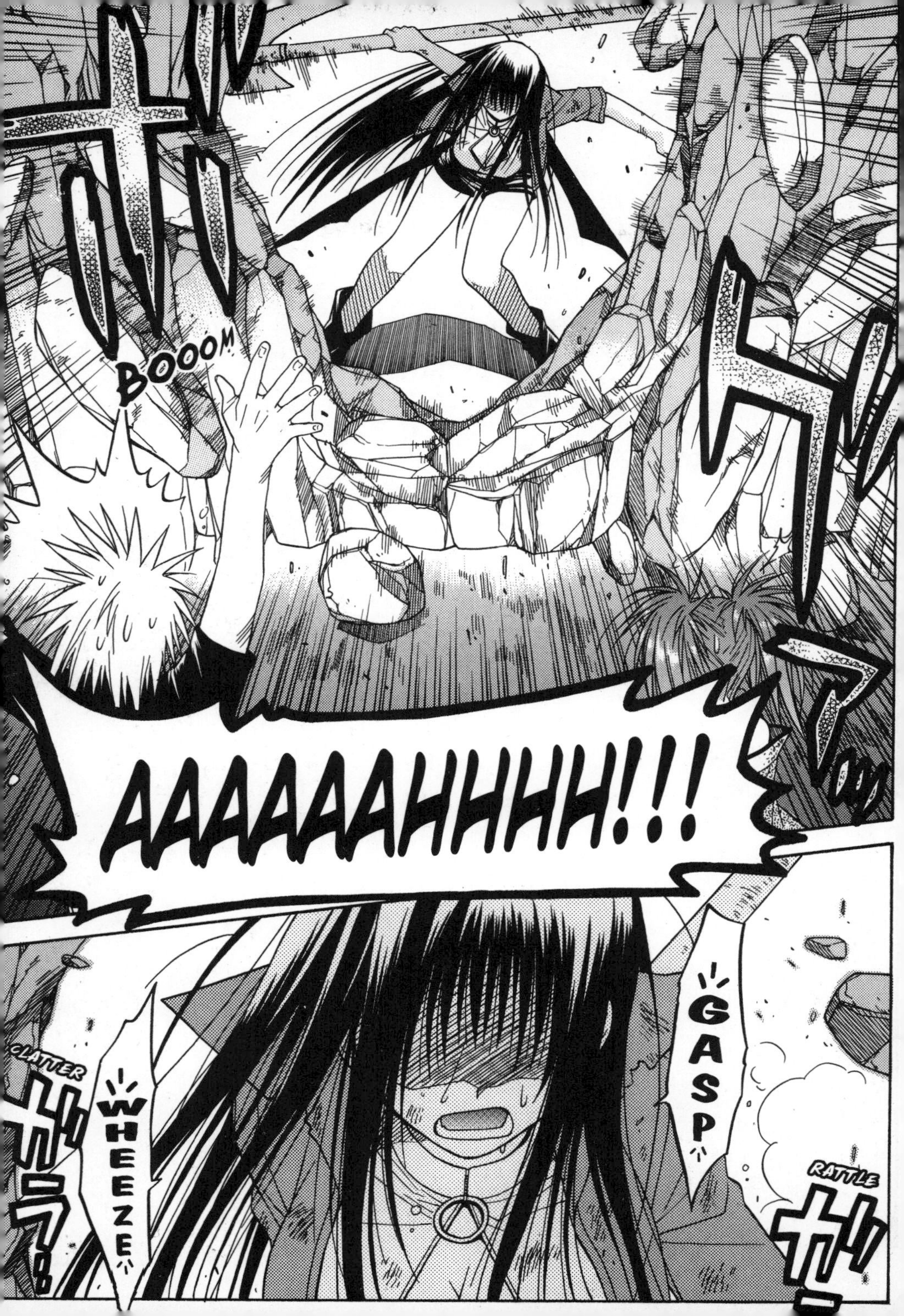
BOOOM
AAAAAAHHHHH!!!
GASP
CLATTER
WHEEZE
RATTLE

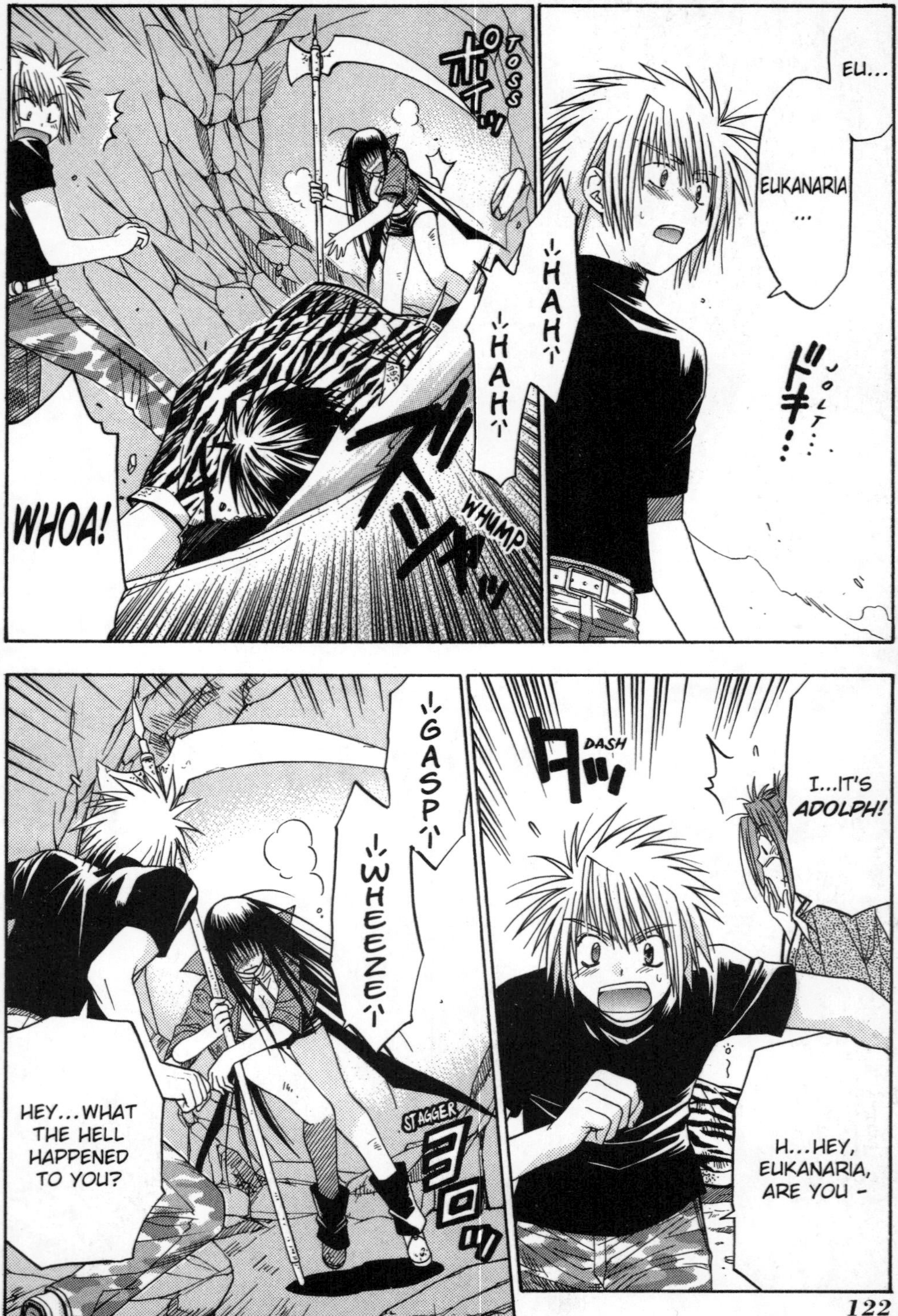
EU...
EUKANARIA ...
JOLT...
HAH HAH
TOSS
WHUMP
WHOA!
I...IT'S ADOLPH!
DASH
H...HEY, EUKANARIA, ARE YOU -
GASP
WHEEZE
STAGGER
HEY...WHAT THE HELL HAPPENED TO YOU?

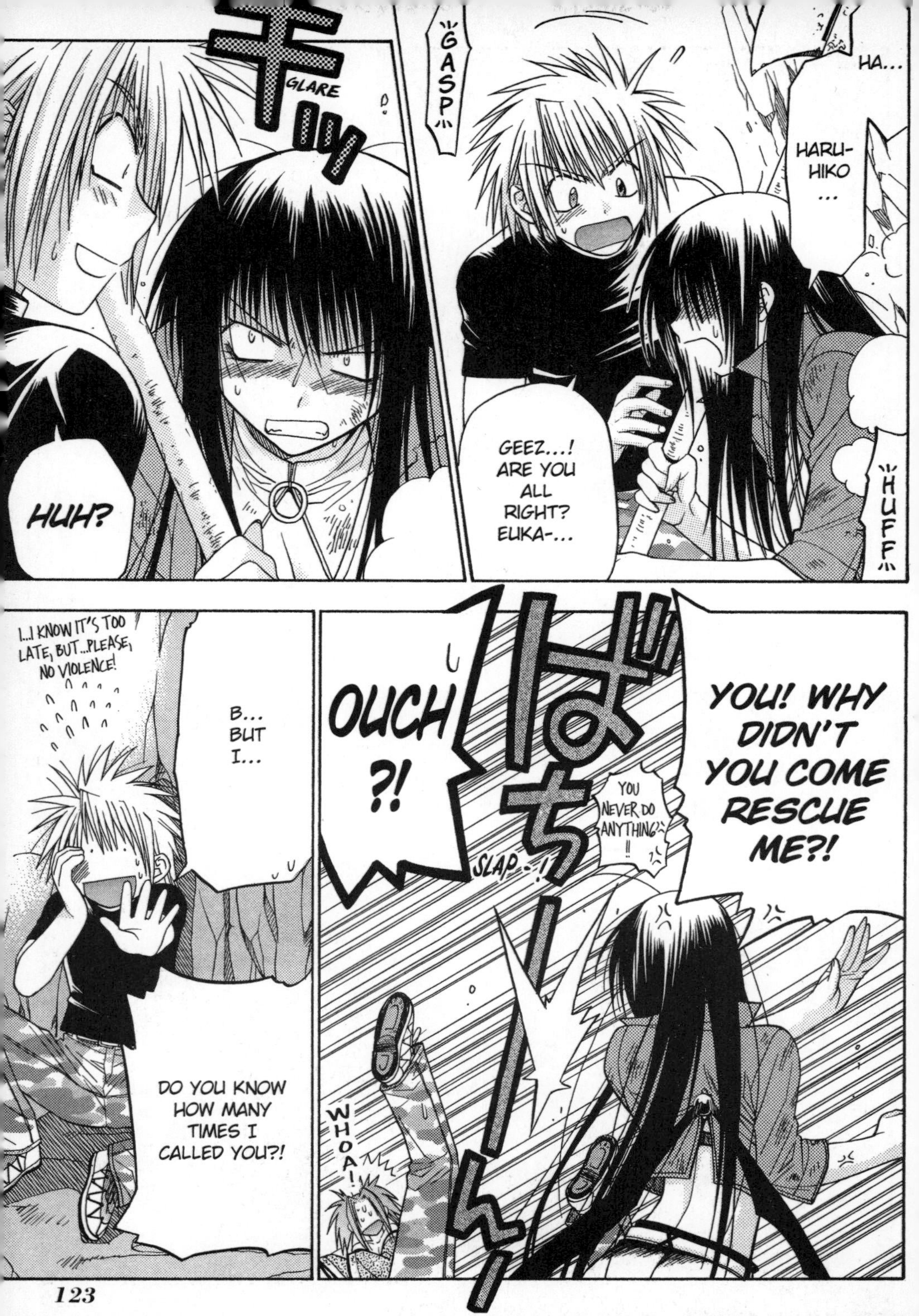
HA...
HARUHIKO ...
HUFF
GASP
GEEZ...! ARE YOU ALL RIGHT? EUKA-...
GLARE
HUH?
YOU! WHY DIDN'T YOU COME RESCUE ME?!
YOU NEVER DO ANYTHING!!
SLAP
OUCH ?!
WHOA!
B... BUT I...
DO YOU KNOW HOW MANY TIMES I CALLED YOU?!
I...I KNOW IT'S TOO LATE, BUT...PLEASE, NO VIOLENCE!

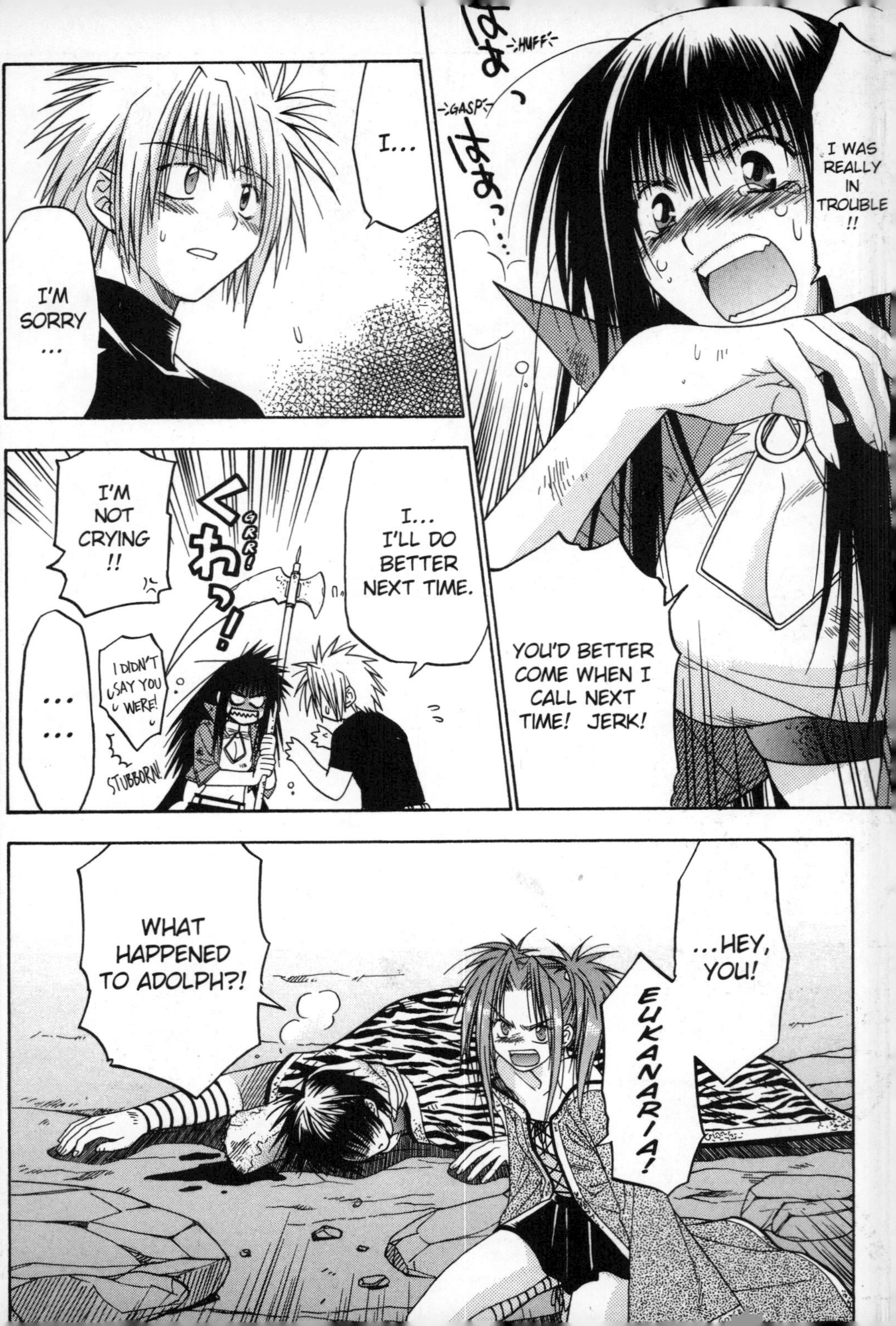
はぁ
HUFF
GASP
はぁっ…
I WAS REALLY IN TROUBLE !!
YOU'D BETTER COME WHEN I CALL NEXT TIME! JERK!
I...
I'M SORRY ...
I... I'LL DO BETTER NEXT TIME.
くわっ!
GRR!
I'M NOT CRYING !!
I DIDN'T SAY YOU WERE!
... ...
STUBBORN!
...HEY, YOU!
EUKANARIA!
WHAT HAPPENED TO ADOLPH?!

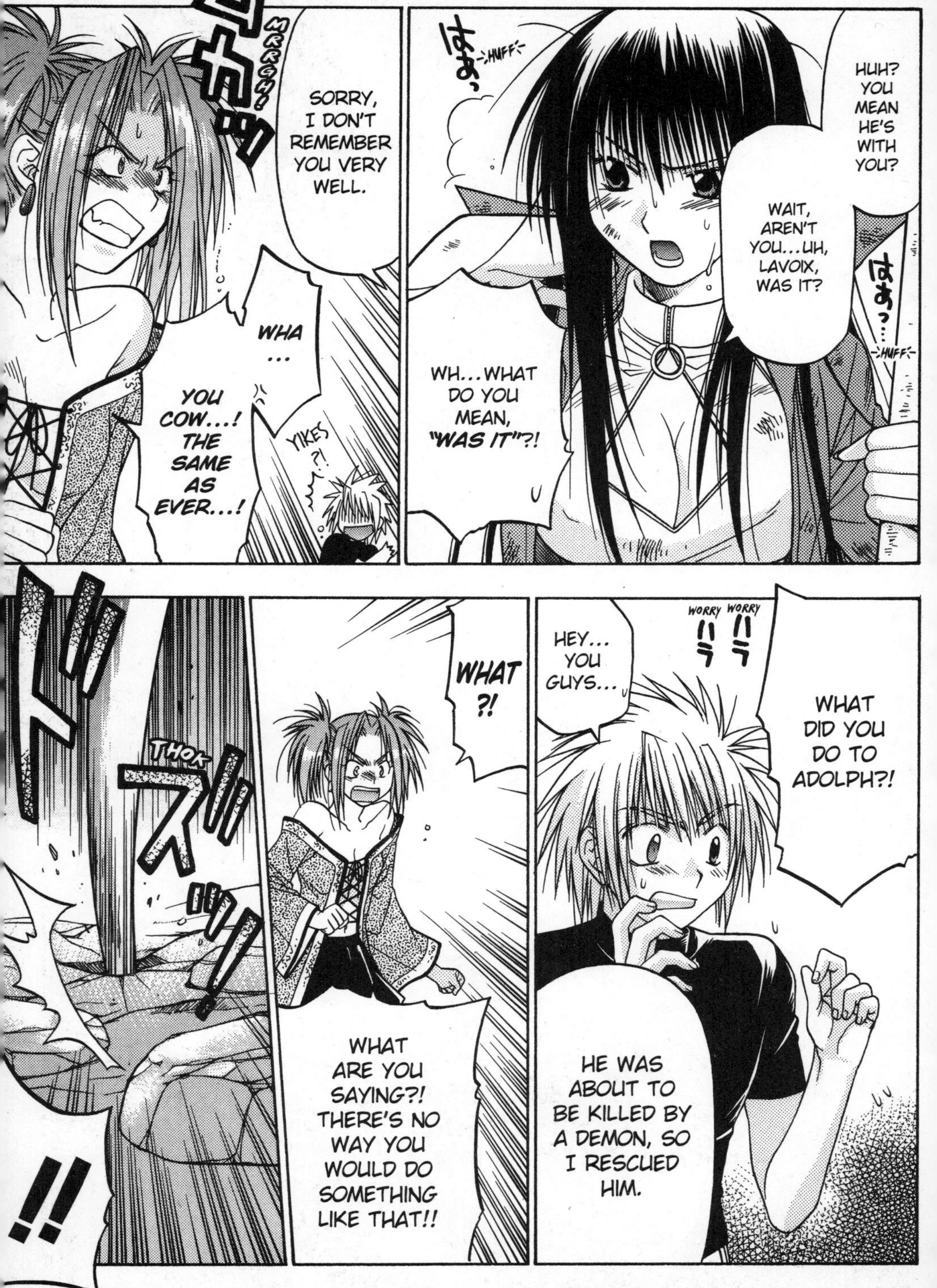
はぁっ
HUFF
HUH? YOU MEAN HE'S WITH YOU?
WAIT, AREN'T YOU...UH, LAVOIX, WAS IT?
はあっ…
HUFF
WH...WHAT DO YOU MEAN, "WAS IT"?!
ムカッ
MRRGH!
SORRY, I DON'T REMEMBER YOU VERY WELL.
WHA...
YOU COW...! THE SAME AS EVER...!
YIKES?!
WORRY WORRY
ハラハラ
HEY... YOU GUYS...
WHAT DID YOU DO TO ADOLPH?!
HE WAS ABOUT TO BE KILLED BY A DEMON, SO I RESCUED HIM.
WHAT?!
WHAT ARE YOU SAYING?! THERE'S NO WAY YOU WOULD DO SOMETHING LIKE THAT!!
THOK
!!

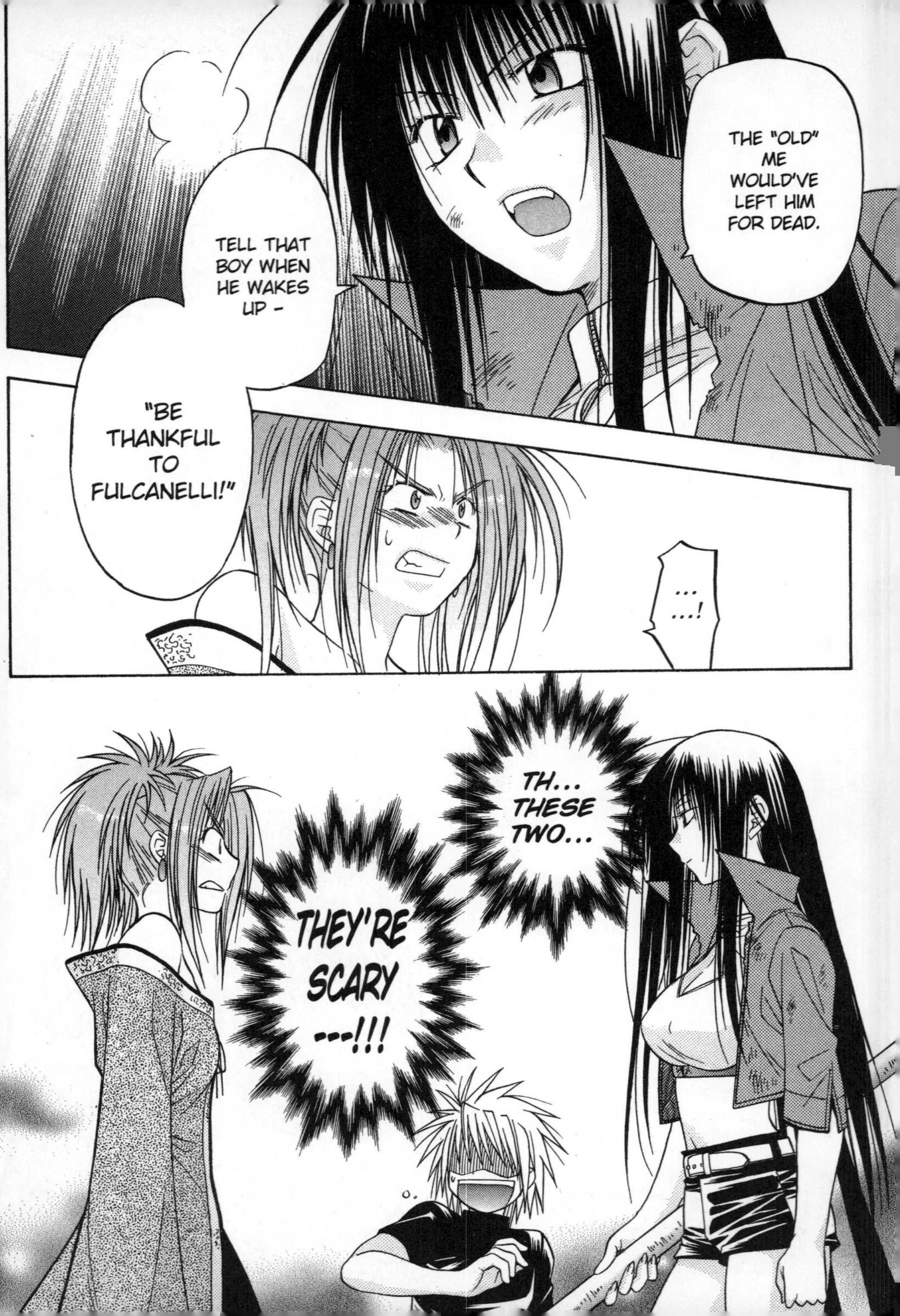
THE "OLD" ME WOULD'VE LEFT HIM FOR DEAD.
TELL THAT BOY WHEN HE WAKES UP -
"BE THANKFUL TO FULCANELLI!"
... ...!
TH... THESE TWO...
THEY'RE SCARY ---!!!

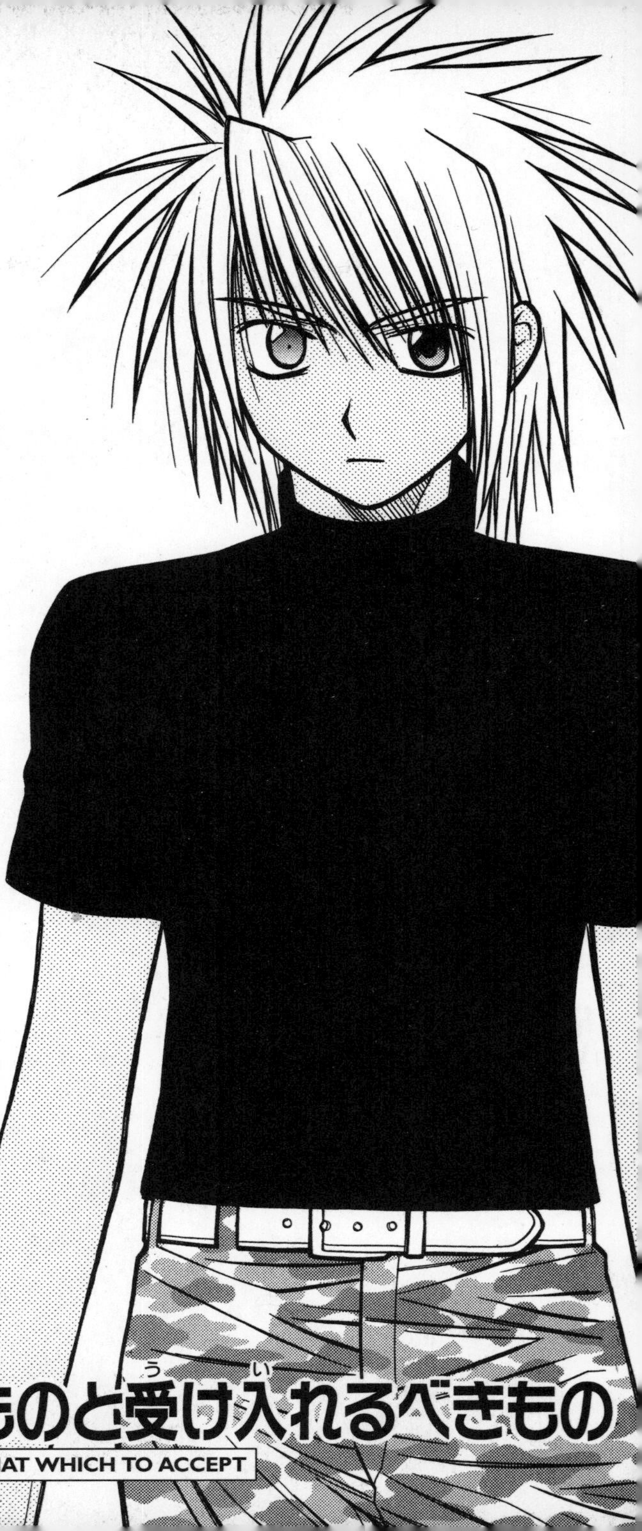

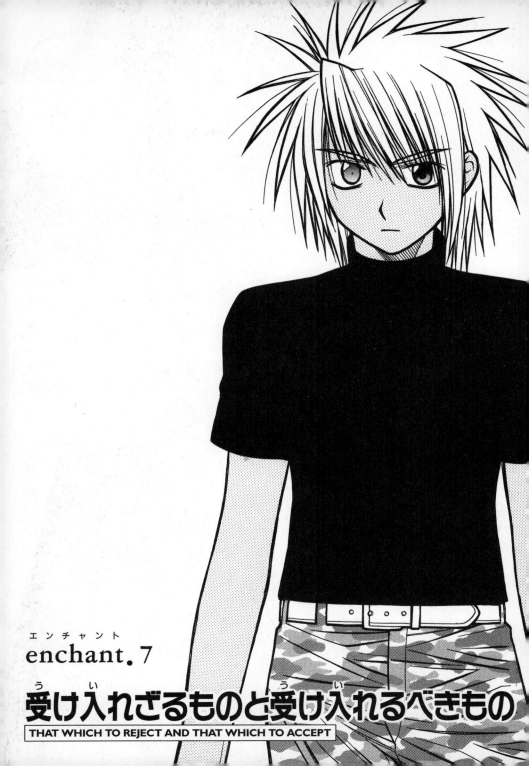

エンチャント

enchant. 7

受け入れざるものと受け入れるべきもの

THAT WHICH TO REJECT AND THAT WHICH TO ACCEPT

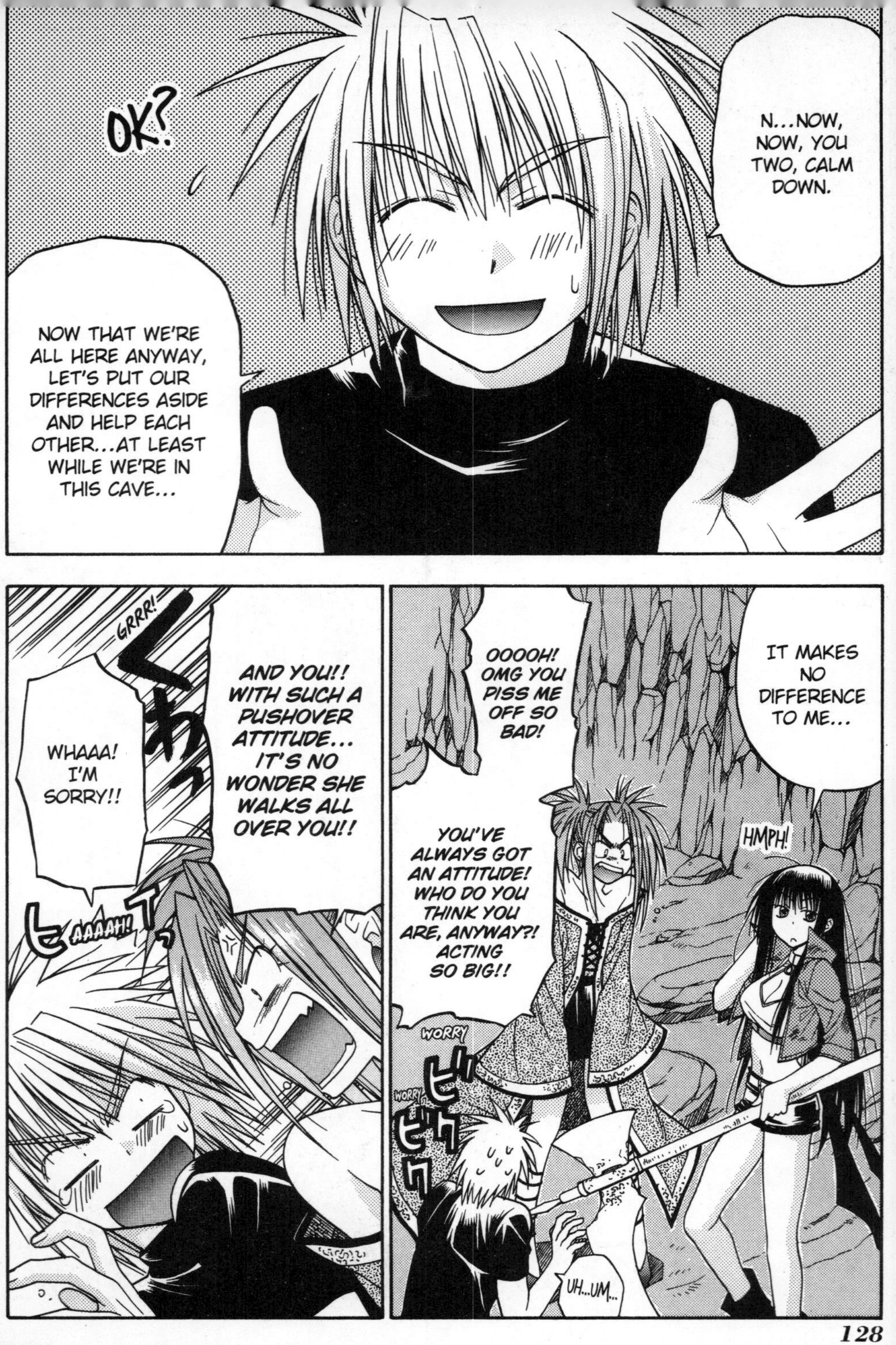
N...NOW, NOW, YOU TWO, CALM DOWN.
OK?
NOW THAT WE'RE ALL HERE ANYWAY, LET'S PUT OUR DIFFERENCES ASIDE AND HELP EACH OTHER...AT LEAST WHILE WE'RE IN THIS CAVE...
IT MAKES NO DIFFERENCE TO ME...
HMPH!
OOOOH! OMG YOU PISS ME OFF SO BAD!
YOU'VE ALWAYS GOT AN ATTITUDE! WHO DO YOU THINK YOU ARE, ANYWAY?! ACTING SO BIG!!
WORRY
WORRY
UH...UM...
AND YOU!! WITH SUCH A PUSHOVER ATTITUDE... IT'S NO WONDER SHE WALKS ALL OVER YOU!!
GRRR!
WHAAA! I'M SORRY!!
AAAAH!

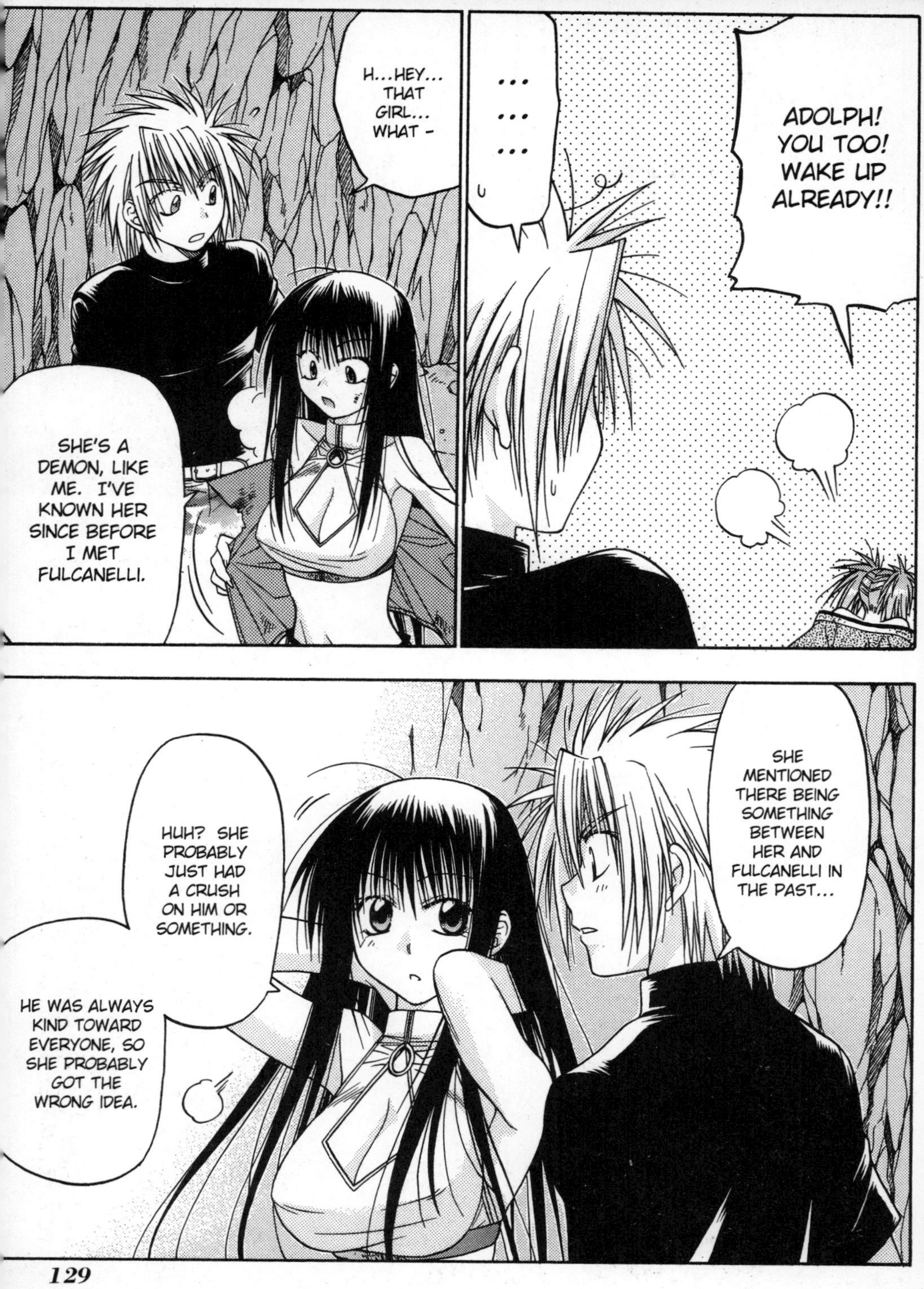
ADOLPH! YOU TOO! WAKE UP ALREADY!!
... ...
H...HEY... THAT GIRL... WHAT -
SHE'S A DEMON, LIKE ME. I'VE KNOWN HER SINCE BEFORE I MET FULCANELLI.
SHE MENTIONED THERE BEING SOMETHING BETWEEN HER AND FULCANELLI IN THE PAST...
HUH? SHE PROBABLY JUST HAD A CRUSH ON HIM OR SOMETHING.
HE WAS ALWAYS KIND TOWARD EVERYONE, SO SHE PROBABLY GOT THE WRONG IDEA.

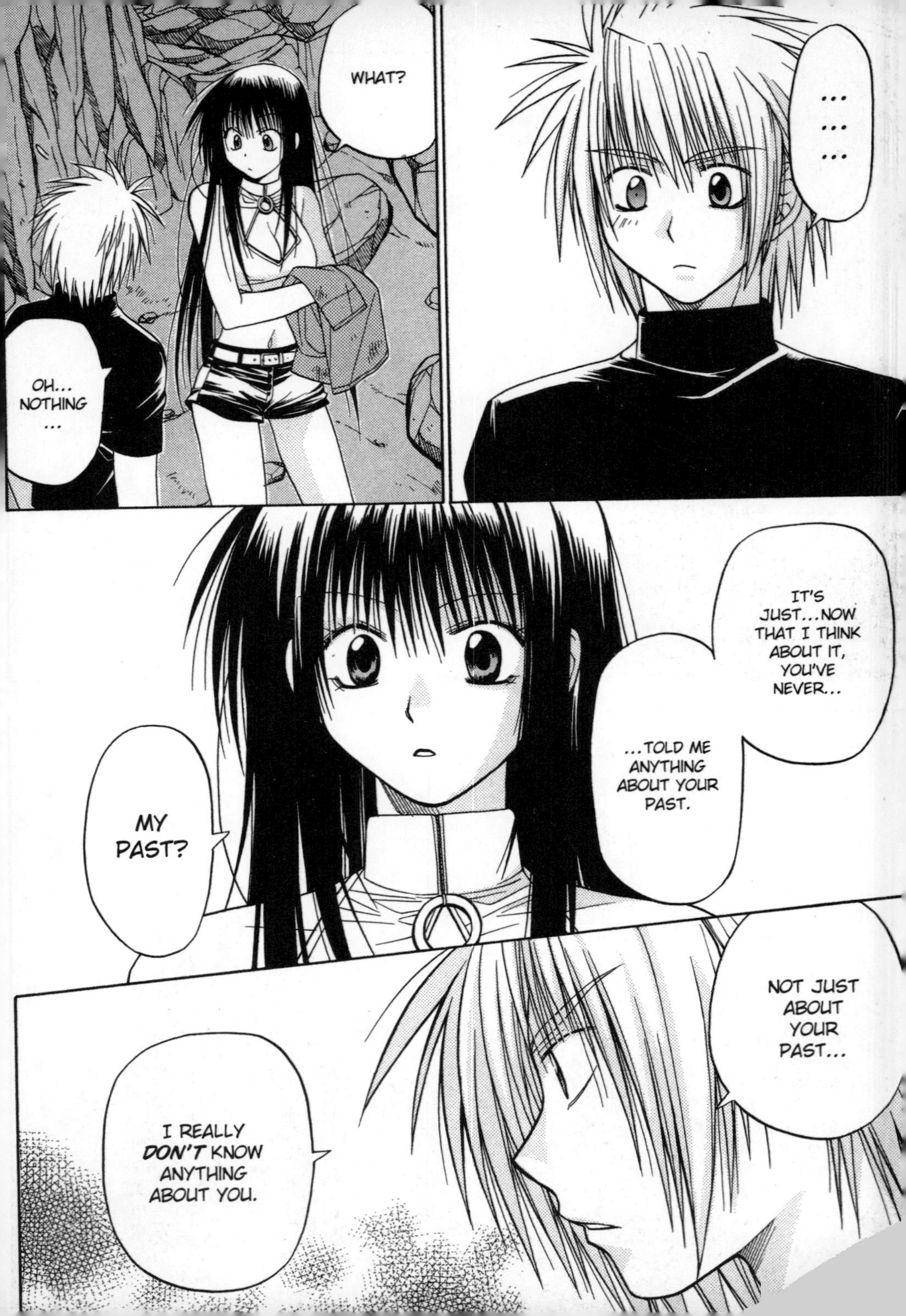
...
...
...
WHAT?
OH... NOTHING ...
IT'S JUST...NOW THAT I THINK ABOUT IT, YOU'VE NEVER...
...TOLD ME ANYTHING ABOUT YOUR PAST.
MY PAST?
NOT JUST ABOUT YOUR PAST...
I REALLY ***DON'T*** KNOW ANYTHING ABOUT YOU.

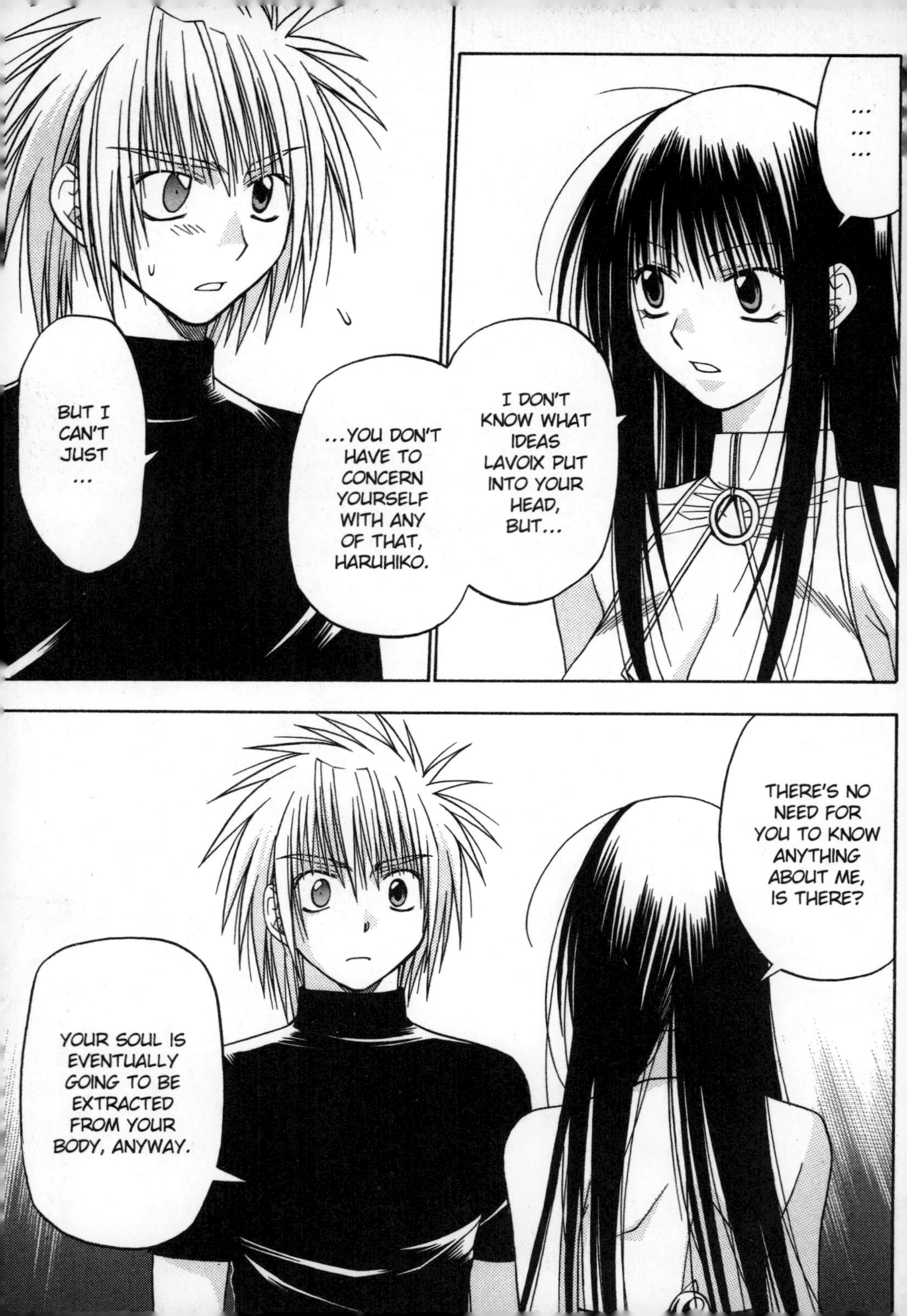
... ...
I DON'T KNOW WHAT IDEAS LAVOIX PUT INTO YOUR HEAD, BUT...
...YOU DON'T HAVE TO CONCERN YOURSELF WITH ANY OF THAT, HARUHIKO.
BUT I CAN'T JUST ...
THERE'S NO NEED FOR YOU TO KNOW ANYTHING ABOUT ME, IS THERE?
YOUR SOUL IS EVENTUALLY GOING TO BE EXTRACTED FROM YOUR BODY, ANYWAY.

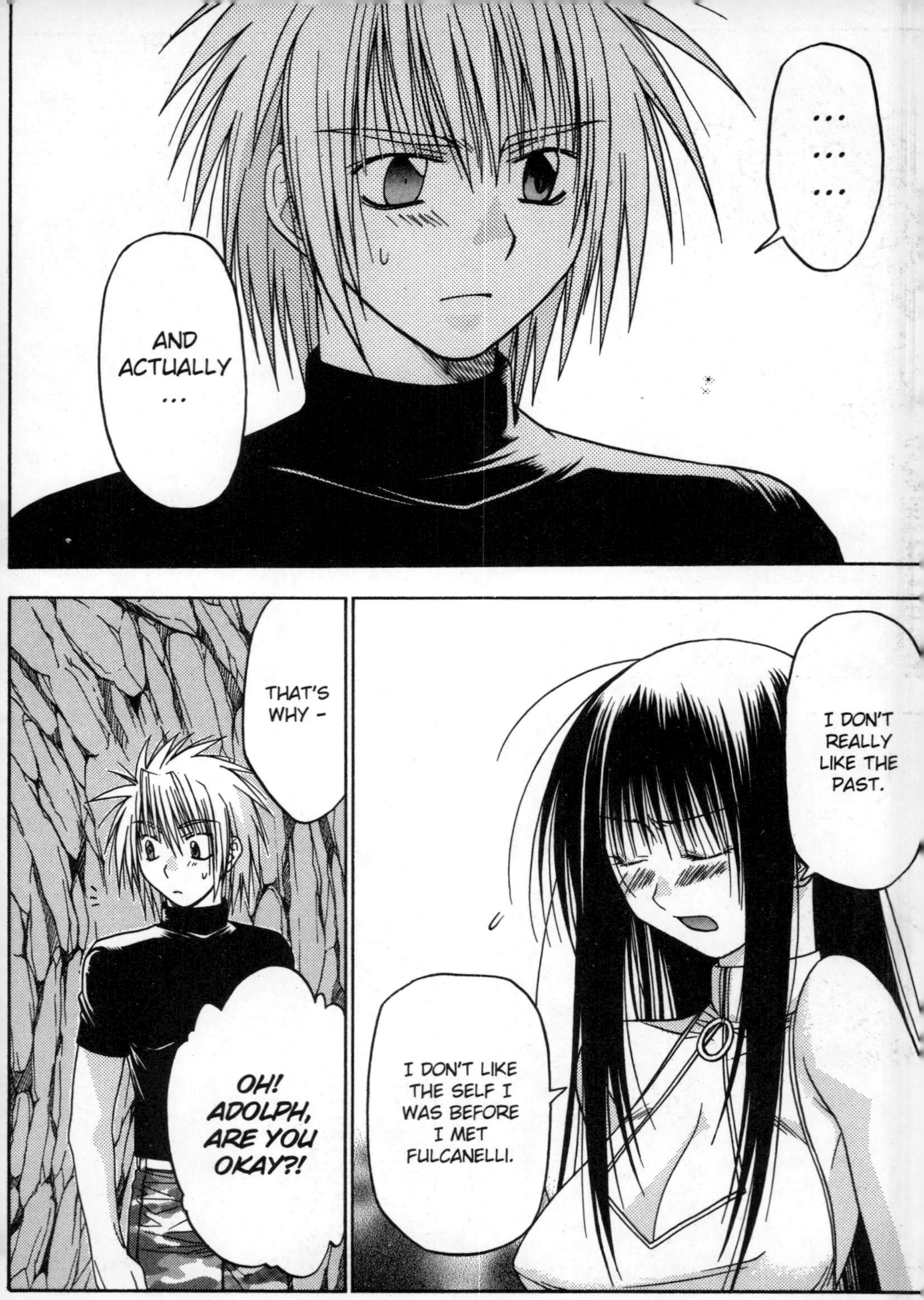
... ...
AND ACTUALLY ...
I DON'T REALLY LIKE THE PAST.
I DON'T LIKE THE SELF I WAS BEFORE I MET FULCANELLI.
THAT'S WHY -
OH! ADOLPH, ARE YOU OKAY?!

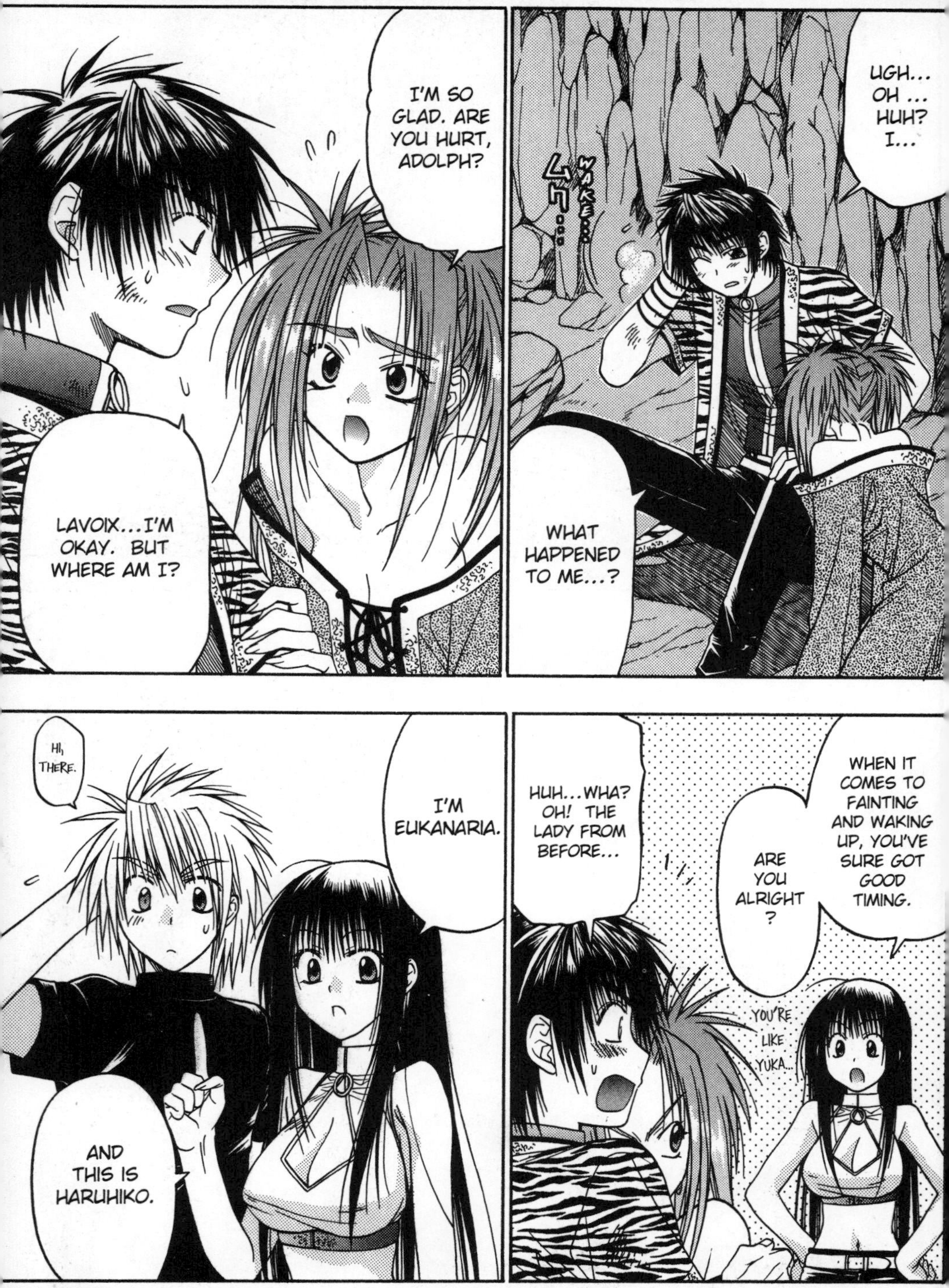
UGH... OH ... HUH? I...
ムク...
WAKE...
WHAT HAPPENED TO ME...?
I'M SO GLAD. ARE YOU HURT, ADOLPH?
LAVOIX...I'M OKAY. BUT WHERE AM I?
WHEN IT COMES TO FAINTING AND WAKING UP, YOU'VE SURE GOT GOOD TIMING.
ARE YOU ALRIGHT?
HUH...WHA? OH! THE LADY FROM BEFORE...
YOU'RE LIKE YUKA...
I'M EUKANARIA.
HI, THERE.
AND THIS IS HARUHIKO.

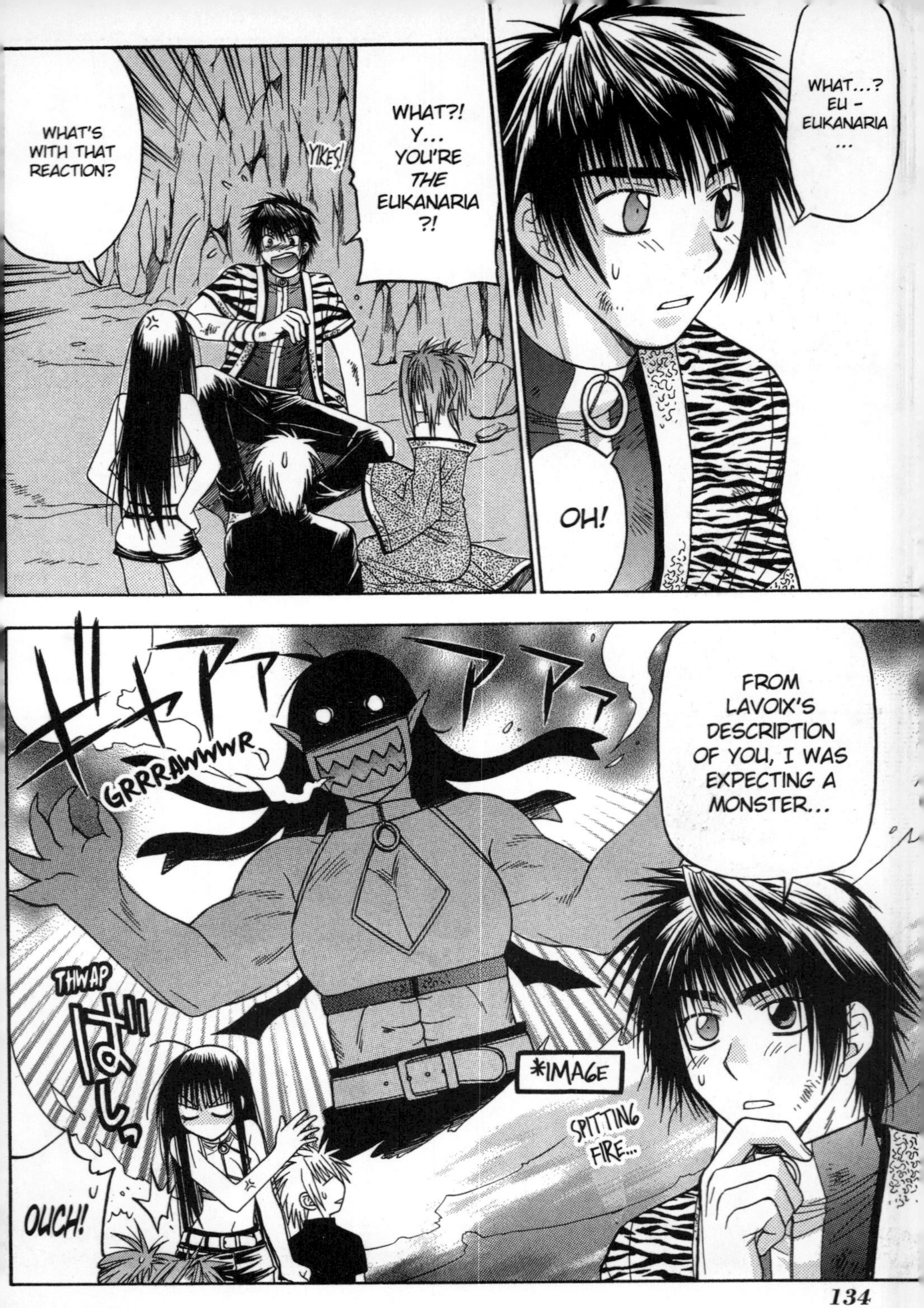
WHAT...? EU - EUKANARIA ...
OH!
WHAT?! Y... YOU'RE *THE* EUKANARIA ?!
YIKES!
WHAT'S WITH THAT REACTION?
FROM LAVOIX'S DESCRIPTION OF YOU, I WAS EXPECTING A MONSTER...
*IMAGE
SPITTING FIRE...
GRRRAWWWR
THWAP
OUCH!

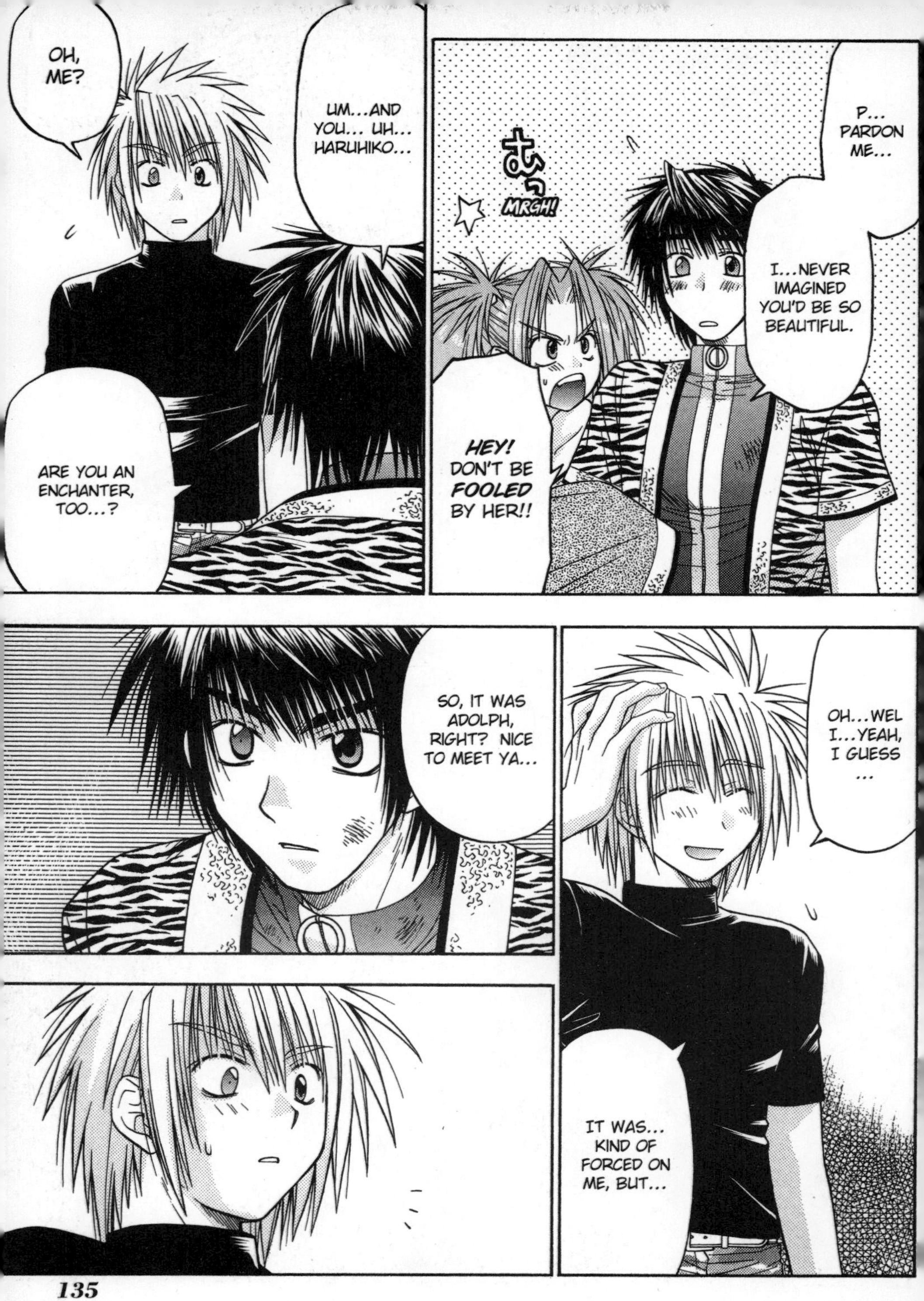
P... PARDON ME...
I...NEVER IMAGINED YOU'D BE SO BEAUTIFUL.
むっ
MRGH!
HEY! DON'T BE FOOLED BY HER!!
UM...AND YOU... UH... HARUHIKO...
OH, ME?
ARE YOU AN ENCHANTER, TOO...?
OH...WEL I...YEAH, I GUESS ...
IT WAS... KIND OF FORCED ON ME, BUT...
SO, IT WAS ADOLPH, RIGHT? NICE TO MEET YA...

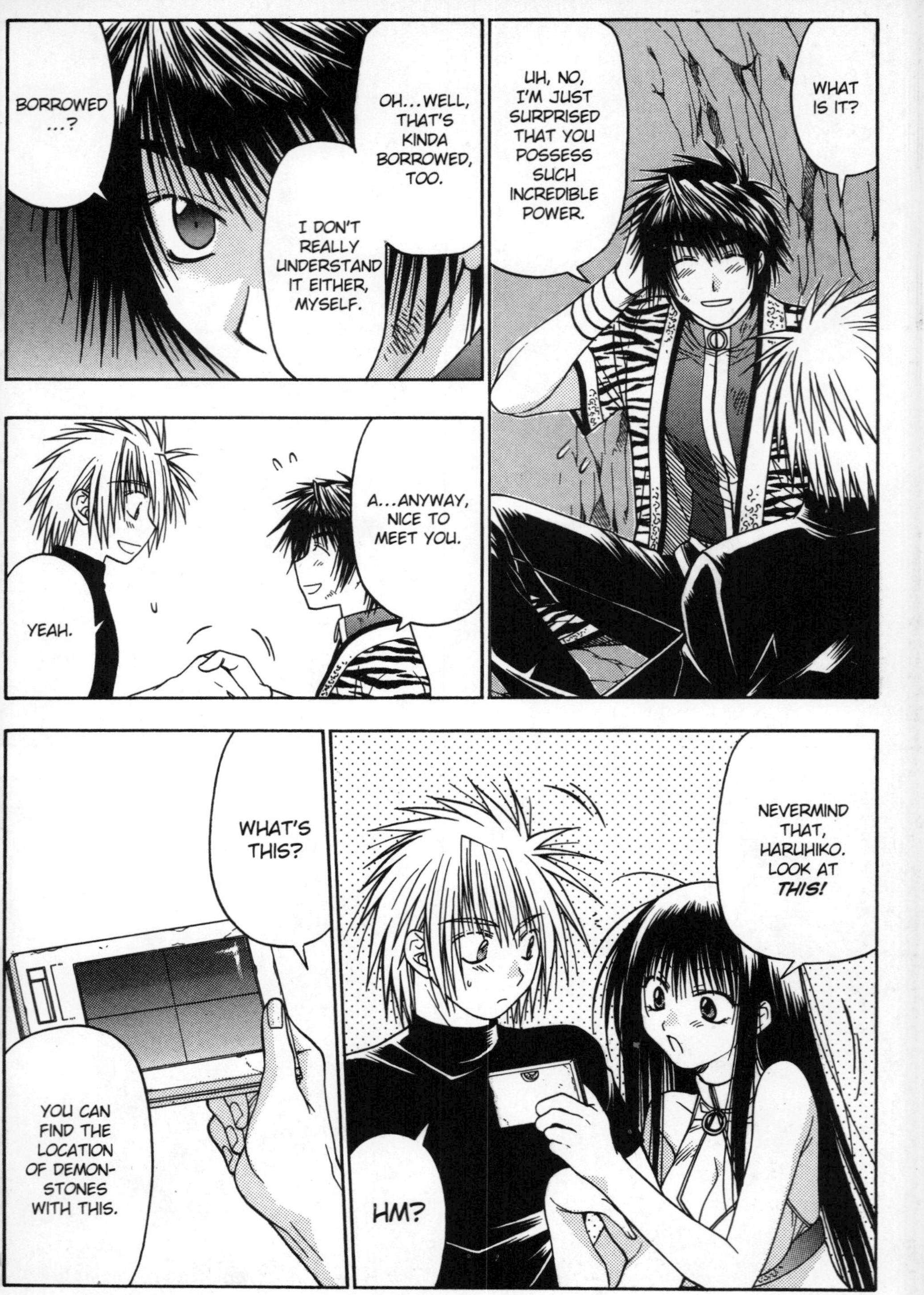
WHAT IS IT?
UH, NO, I'M JUST SURPRISED THAT YOU POSSESS SUCH INCREDIBLE POWER.
BORROWED ...?
OH...WELL, THAT'S KINDA BORROWED, TOO.
I DON'T REALLY UNDERSTAND IT EITHER, MYSELF.
A...ANYWAY, NICE TO MEET YOU.
YEAH.
NEVERMIND THAT, HARUHIKO. LOOK AT *THIS!*
HM?
WHAT'S THIS?
YOU CAN FIND THE LOCATION OF DEMON-STONES WITH THIS.

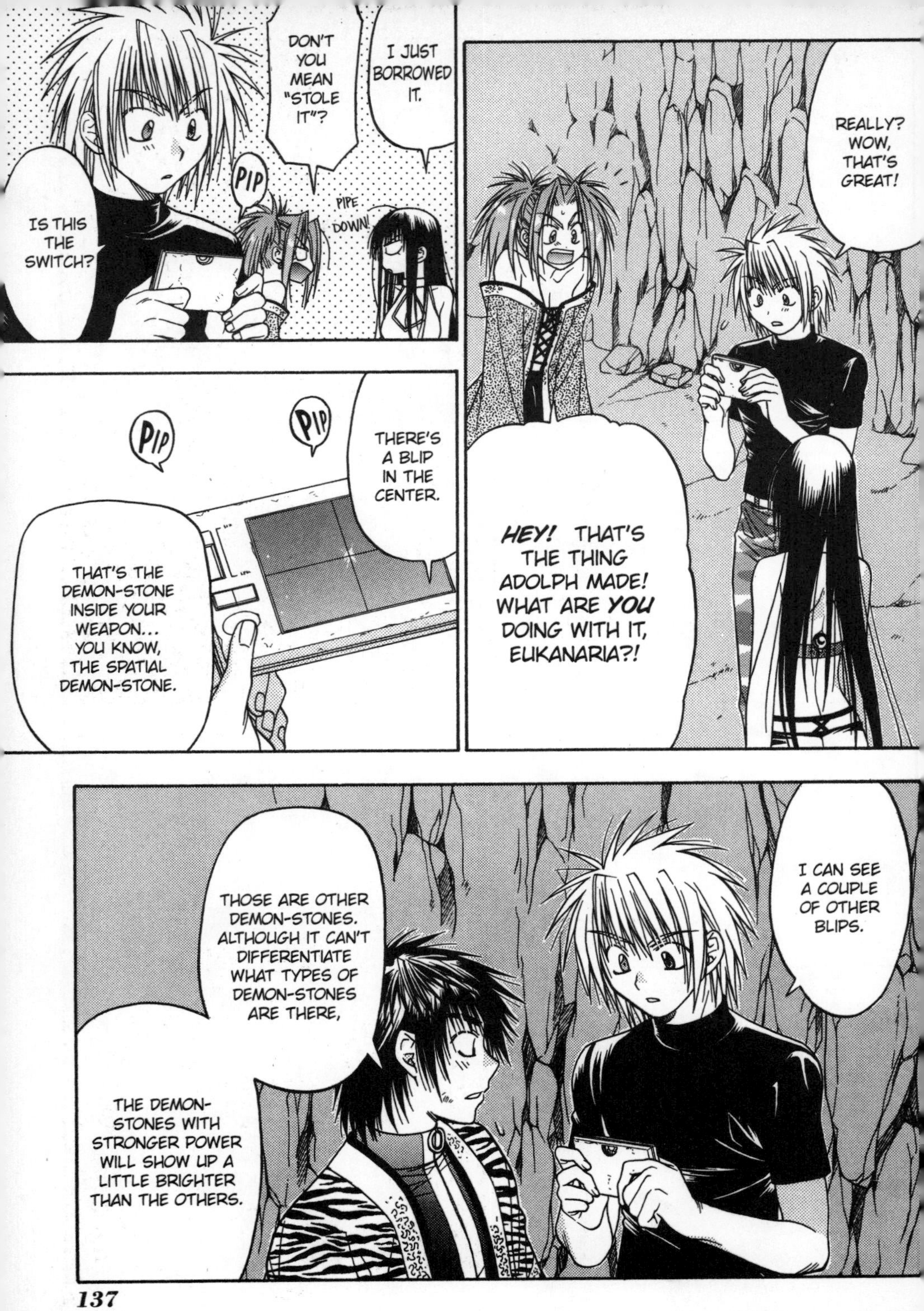
REALLY? WOW, THAT'S GREAT!
HEY! THAT'S THE THING ADOLPH MADE! WHAT ARE **YOU** DOING WITH IT, EUKANARIA?!
I JUST BORROWED IT.
DON'T YOU MEAN "STOLE IT"?
PIP
PIPE DOWN!
IS THIS THE SWITCH?
PIP
PIP
THERE'S A BLIP IN THE CENTER.
THAT'S THE DEMON-STONE INSIDE YOUR WEAPON... YOU KNOW, THE SPATIAL DEMON-STONE.
I CAN SEE A COUPLE OF OTHER BLIPS.
THOSE ARE OTHER DEMON-STONES. ALTHOUGH IT CAN'T DIFFERENTIATE WHAT TYPES OF DEMON-STONES ARE THERE,
THE DEMON-STONES WITH STRONGER POWER WILL SHOW UP A LITTLE BRIGHTER THAN THE OTHERS.

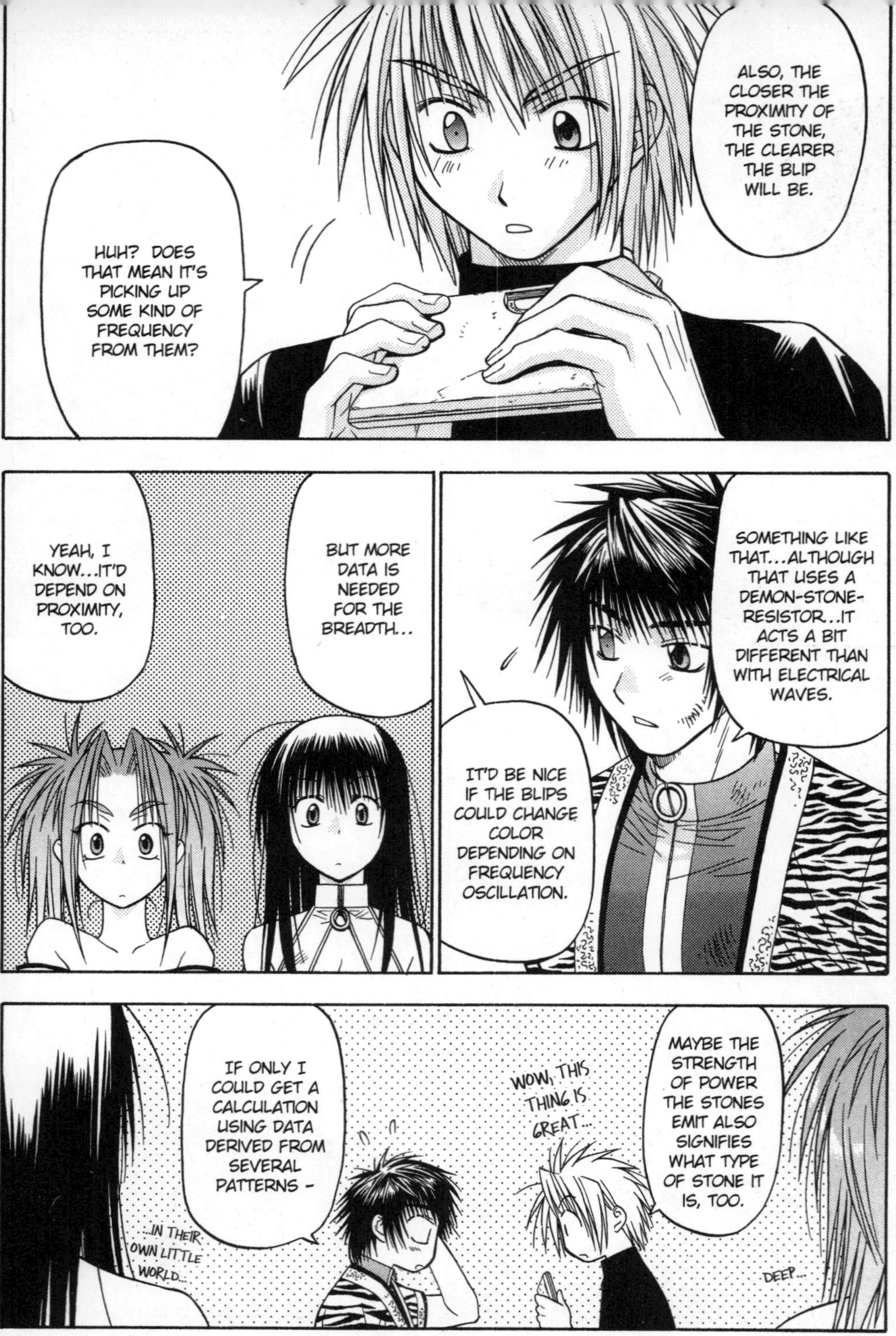
ALSO, THE CLOSER THE PROXIMITY OF THE STONE, THE CLEARER THE BLIP WILL BE.
HUH? DOES THAT MEAN IT'S PICKING UP SOME KIND OF FREQUENCY FROM THEM?
SOMETHING LIKE THAT...ALTHOUGH THAT USES A DEMON-STONE-RESISTOR...IT ACTS A BIT DIFFERENT THAN WITH ELECTRICAL WAVES.
IT'D BE NICE IF THE BLIPS COULD CHANGE COLOR DEPENDING ON FREQUENCY OSCILLATION.
BUT MORE DATA IS NEEDED FOR THE BREADTH...
YEAH, I KNOW...IT'D DEPEND ON PROXIMITY, TOO.
MAYBE THE STRENGTH OF POWER THE STONES EMIT ALSO SIGNIFIES WHAT TYPE OF STONE IT IS, TOO.
WOW, THIS THING IS GREAT...
DEEP...
IF ONLY I COULD GET A CALCULATION USING DATA DERIVED FROM SEVERAL PATTERNS -
...IN THEIR OWN LITTLE WORLD...

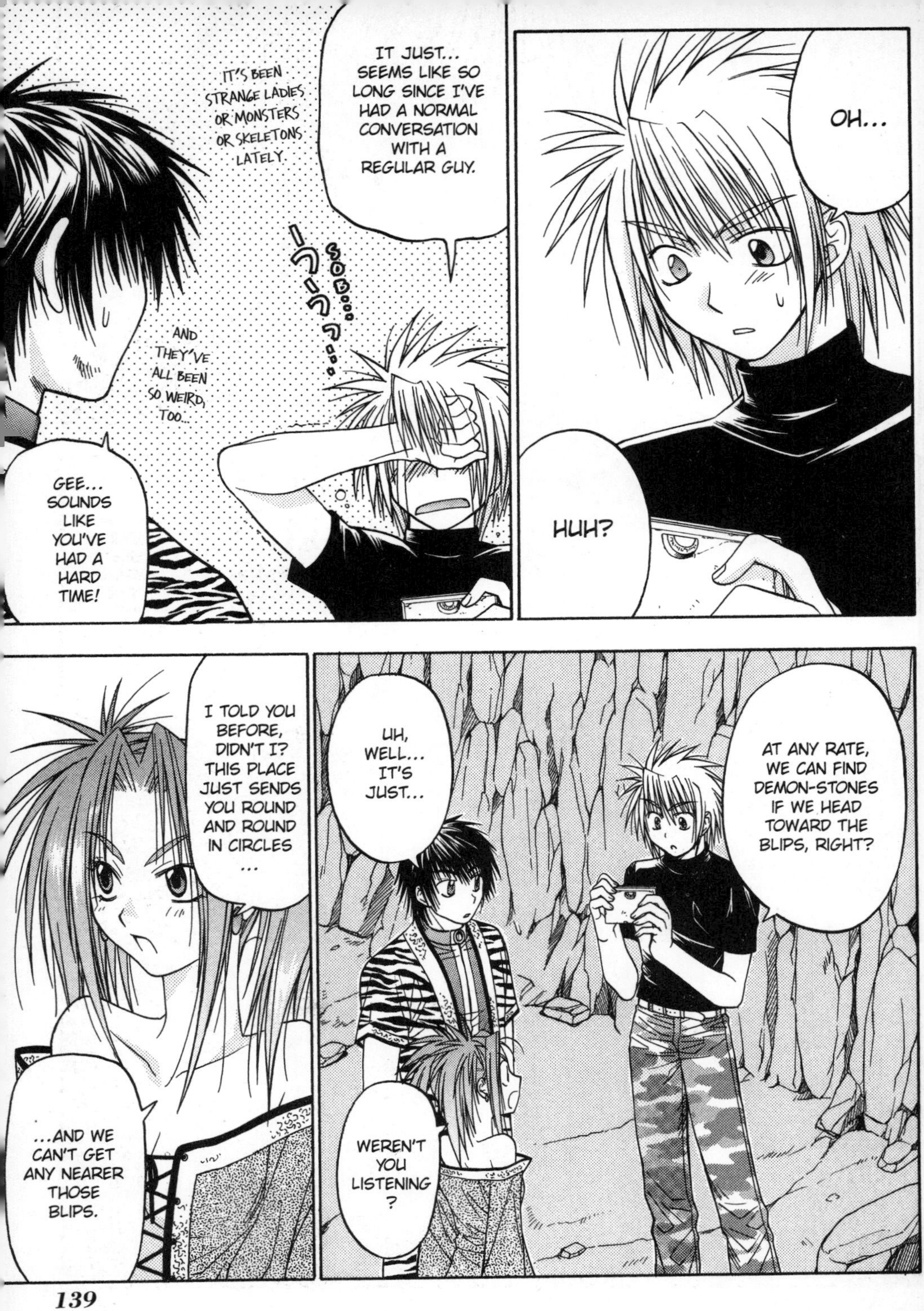
OH...
HUH?
IT JUST... SEEMS LIKE SO LONG SINCE I'VE HAD A NORMAL CONVERSATION WITH A REGULAR GUY.
IT'S BEEN STRANGE LADIES OR MONSTERS OR SKELETONS LATELY.
SOB...
AND THEY'VE ALL BEEN SO WEIRD, TOO...
GEE... SOUNDS LIKE YOU'VE HAD A HARD TIME!
AT ANY RATE, WE CAN FIND DEMON-STONES IF WE HEAD TOWARD THE BLIPS, RIGHT?
UH, WELL... IT'S JUST...
WEREN'T YOU LISTENING?
I TOLD YOU BEFORE, DIDN'T I? THIS PLACE JUST SENDS YOU ROUND AND ROUND IN CIRCLES...
...AND WE CAN'T GET ANY NEARER THOSE BLIPS.

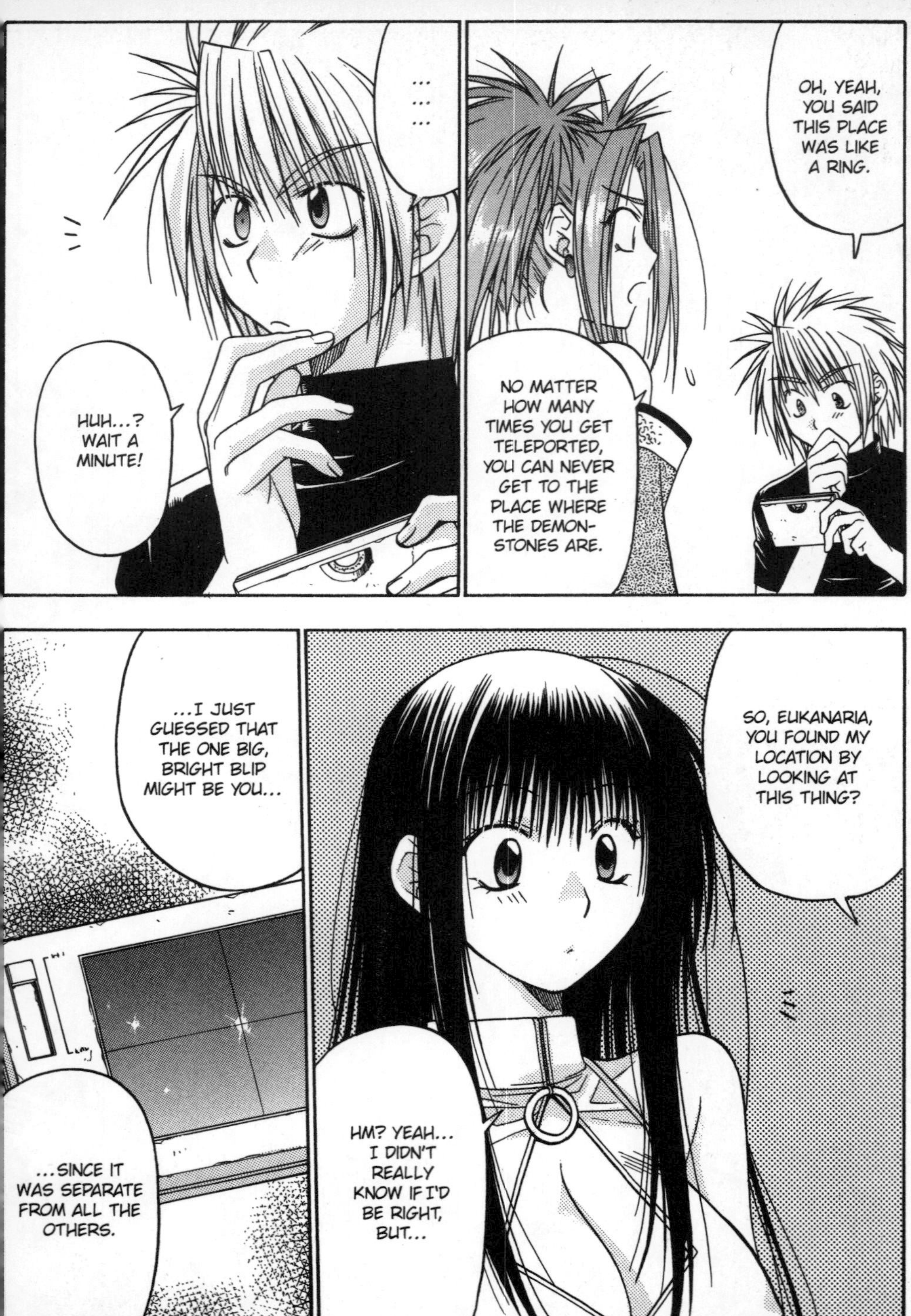
OH, YEAH, YOU SAID THIS PLACE WAS LIKE A RING.
NO MATTER HOW MANY TIMES YOU GET TELEPORTED, YOU CAN NEVER GET TO THE PLACE WHERE THE DEMON-STONES ARE.
... ...
HUH...? WAIT A MINUTE!
SO, EUKANARIA, YOU FOUND MY LOCATION BY LOOKING AT THIS THING?
HM? YEAH... I DIDN'T REALLY KNOW IF I'D BE RIGHT, BUT...
...I JUST GUESSED THAT THE ONE BIG, BRIGHT BLIP MIGHT BE YOU...
...SINCE IT WAS SEPARATE FROM ALL THE OTHERS.

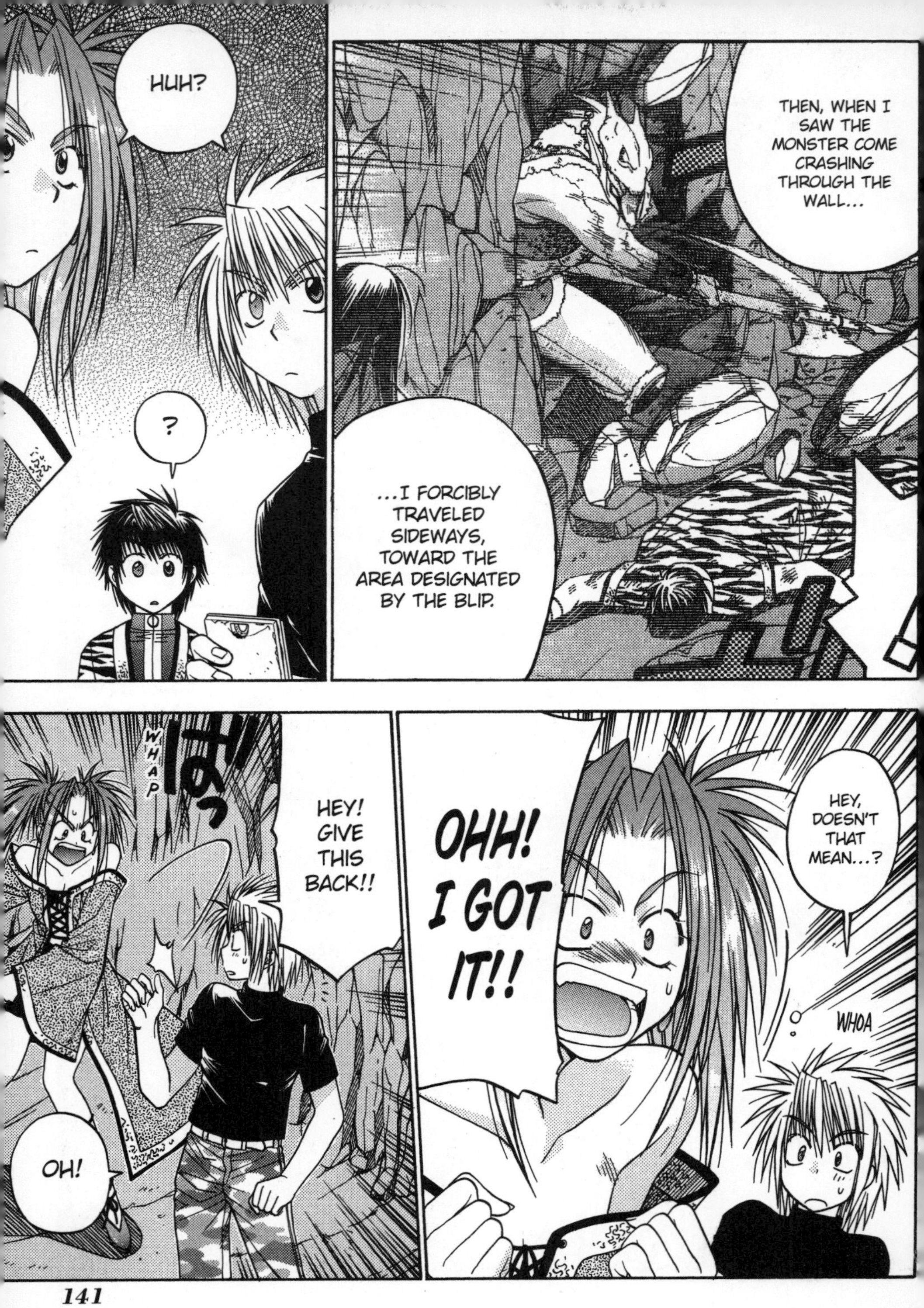
THEN, WHEN I SAW THE MONSTER COME CRASHING THROUGH THE WALL...
...I FORCIBLY TRAVELED SIDEWAYS, TOWARD THE AREA DESIGNATED BY THE BLIP.
HUH?
?
HEY, DOESN'T THAT MEAN...?
OHH! I GOT IT!!
WHOA
ばっ
WHAP
HEY! GIVE THIS BACK!!
OH!

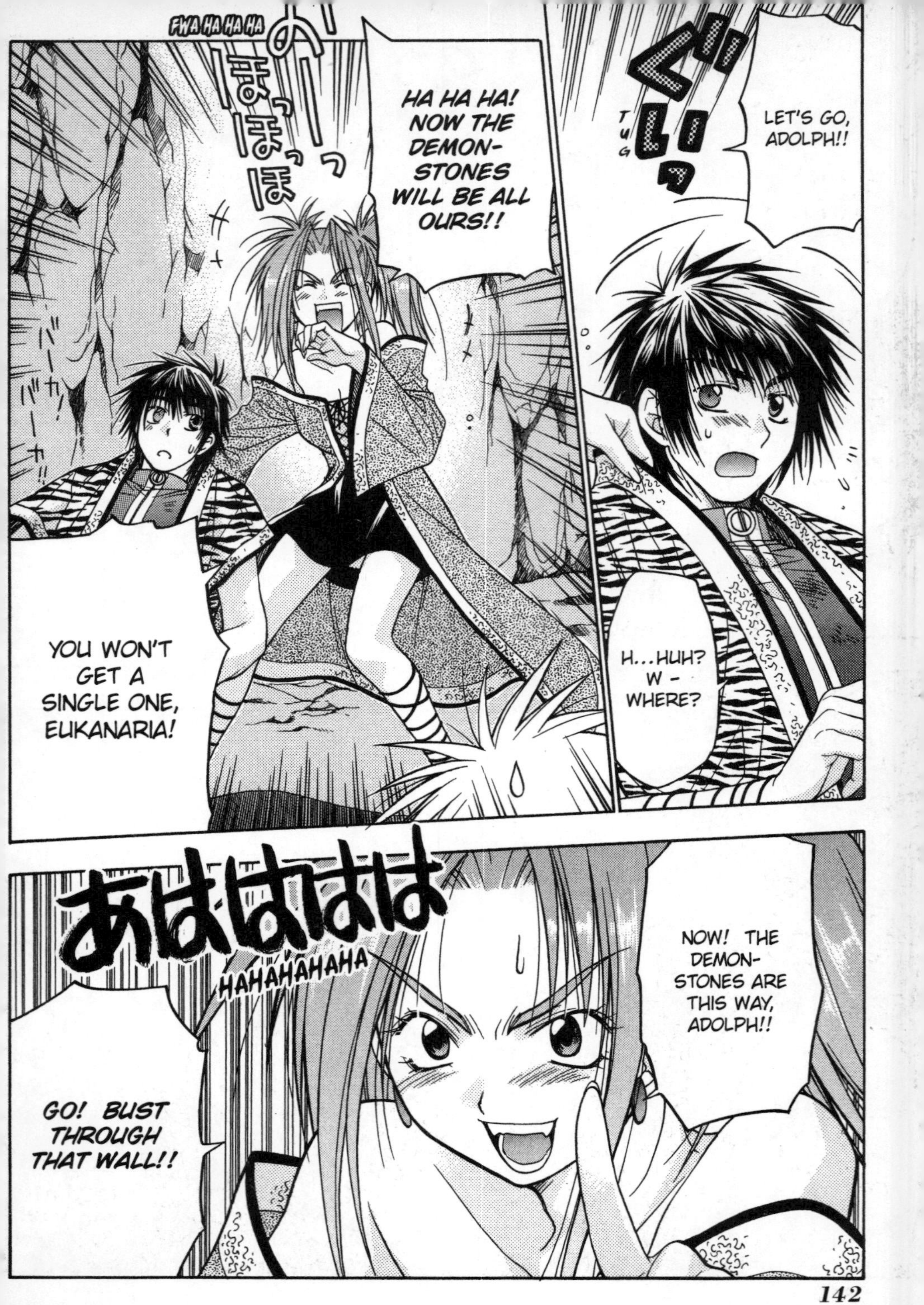
ぐいっ
TUG
LET'S GO, ADOLPH!!
H...HUH? W - WHERE?
FWA HA HA HA
ほっほっほ
HA HA HA! NOW THE DEMON-STONES WILL BE ALL OURS!!
YOU WON'T GET A SINGLE ONE, EUKANARIA!
NOW! THE DEMON-STONES ARE THIS WAY, ADOLPH!!
あはははは
HAHAHAHAHA
GO! BUST THROUGH THAT WALL!!

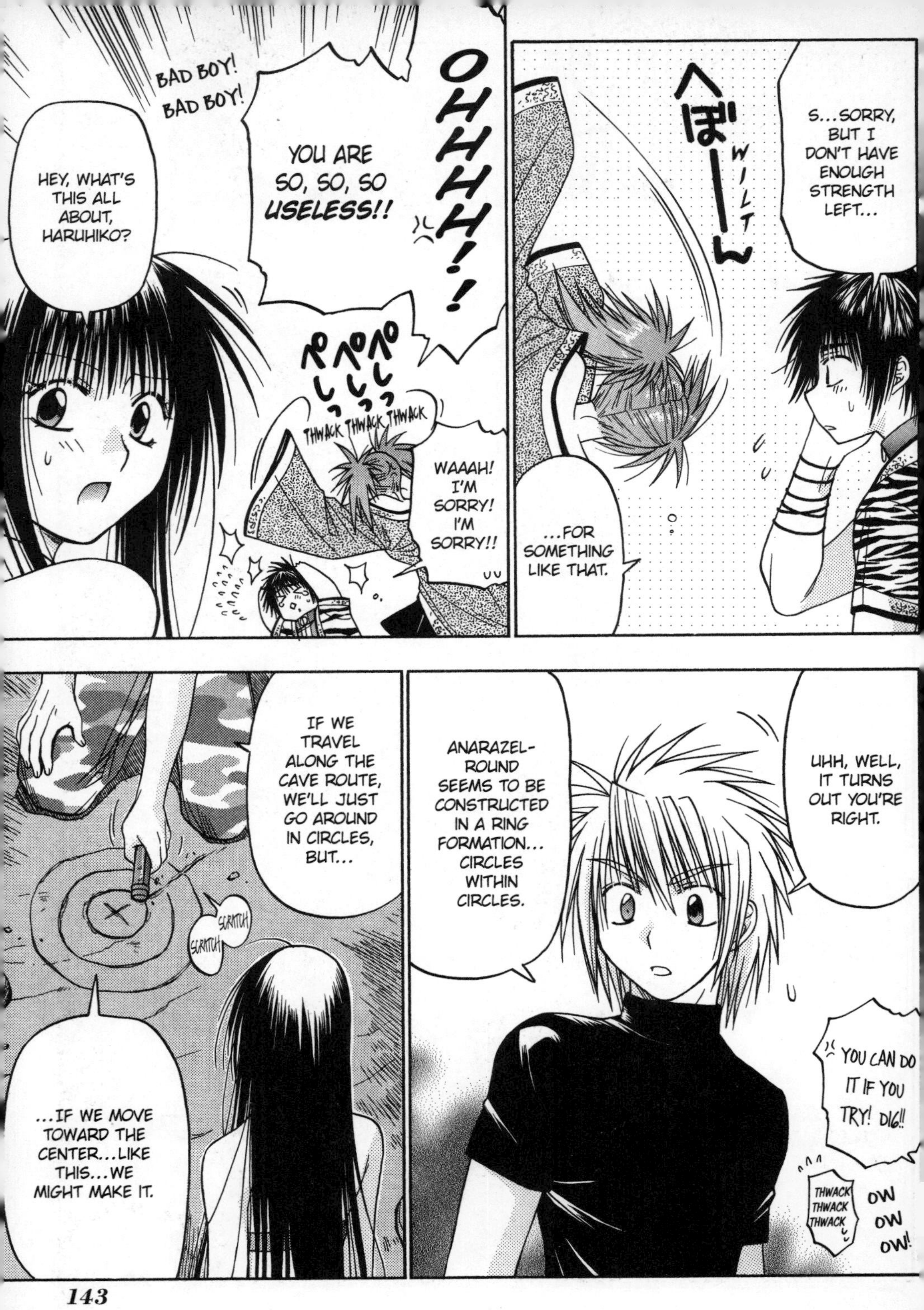
S...SORRY, BUT I DON'T HAVE ENOUGH STRENGTH LEFT...
へぼーーん
WILT
...FOR SOMETHING LIKE THAT.
OHHHHH!!
YOU ARE SO, SO, SO **USELESS!!**
BAD BOY! BAD BOY!
HEY, WHAT'S THIS ALL ABOUT, HARUHIKO?
ぺしっぺしっぺしっ
THWACK THWACK THWACK
WAAAH! I'M SORRY! I'M SORRY!!
UHH, WELL, IT TURNS OUT YOU'RE RIGHT.
ANARAZEL-ROUND SEEMS TO BE CONSTRUCTED IN A RING FORMATION... CIRCLES WITHIN CIRCLES.
YOU CAN DO IT IF YOU TRY! DIG!!
THWACK THWACK THWACK
OW OW OW!
IF WE TRAVEL ALONG THE CAVE ROUTE, WE'LL JUST GO AROUND IN CIRCLES, BUT...
SCRATCH SCRATCH
...IF WE MOVE TOWARD THE CENTER...LIKE THIS...WE MIGHT MAKE IT.

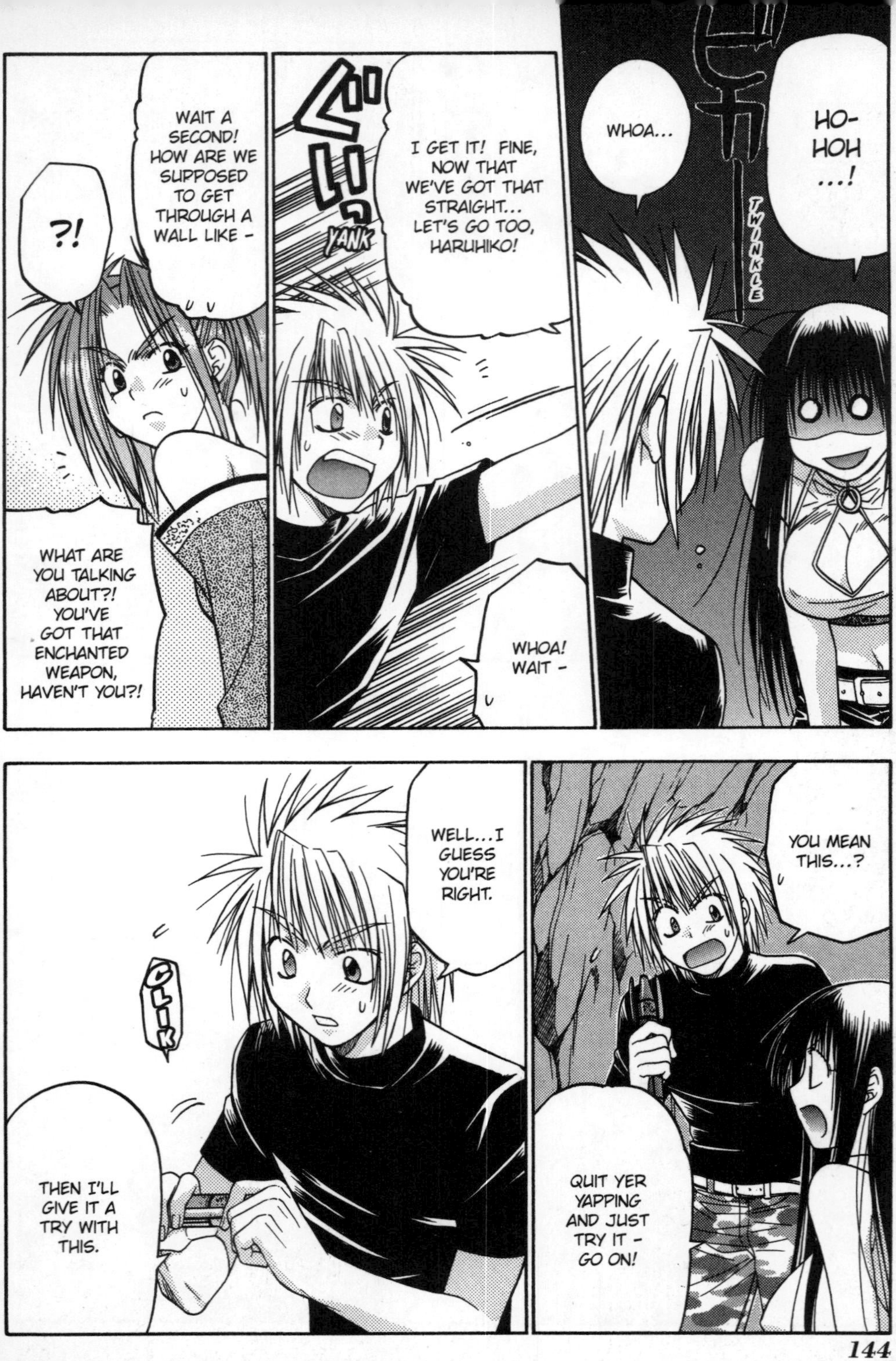
HO-HOH ...!
WHOA...
TWINKLE
I GET IT! FINE, NOW THAT WE'VE GOT THAT STRAIGHT... LET'S GO TOO, HARUHIKO!
YANK
WHOA! WAIT -
WAIT A SECOND! HOW ARE WE SUPPOSED TO GET THROUGH A WALL LIKE -
?!
WHAT ARE YOU TALKING ABOUT?! YOU'VE GOT THAT ENCHANTED WEAPON, HAVEN'T YOU?!
YOU MEAN THIS...?
QUIT YER YAPPING AND JUST TRY IT - GO ON!
WELL...I GUESS YOU'RE RIGHT.
CLIK
THEN I'LL GIVE IT A TRY WITH THIS.

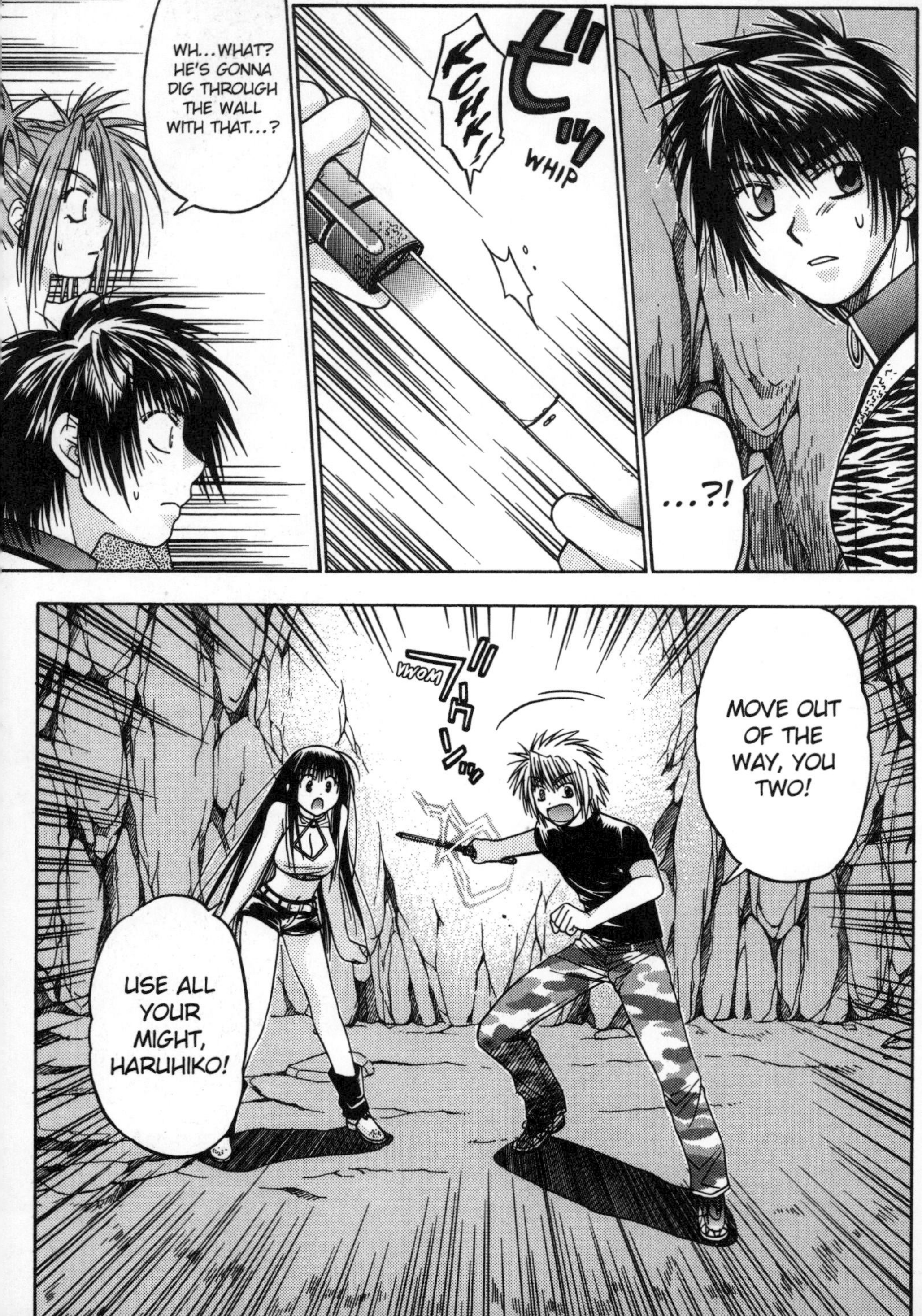
...?!
KCHH!
WHIP
WH...WHAT? HE'S GONNA DIG THROUGH THE WALL WITH THAT...?
MOVE OUT OF THE WAY, YOU TWO!
USE ALL YOUR MIGHT, HARUHIKO!

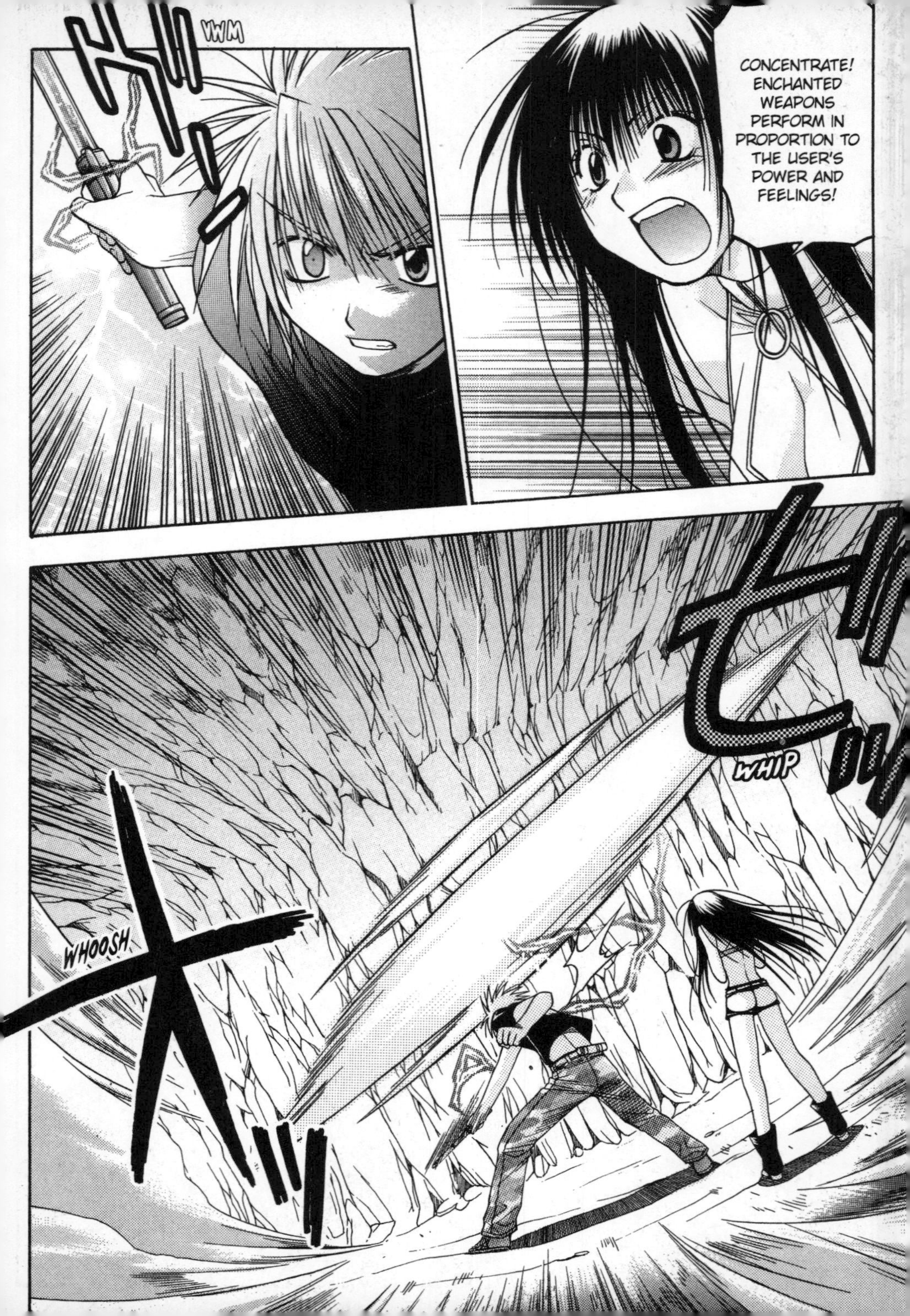
CONCENTRATE! ENCHANTED WEAPONS PERFORM IN PROPORTION TO THE USER'S POWER AND FEELINGS!
VWM
WHIP
WHOOSH

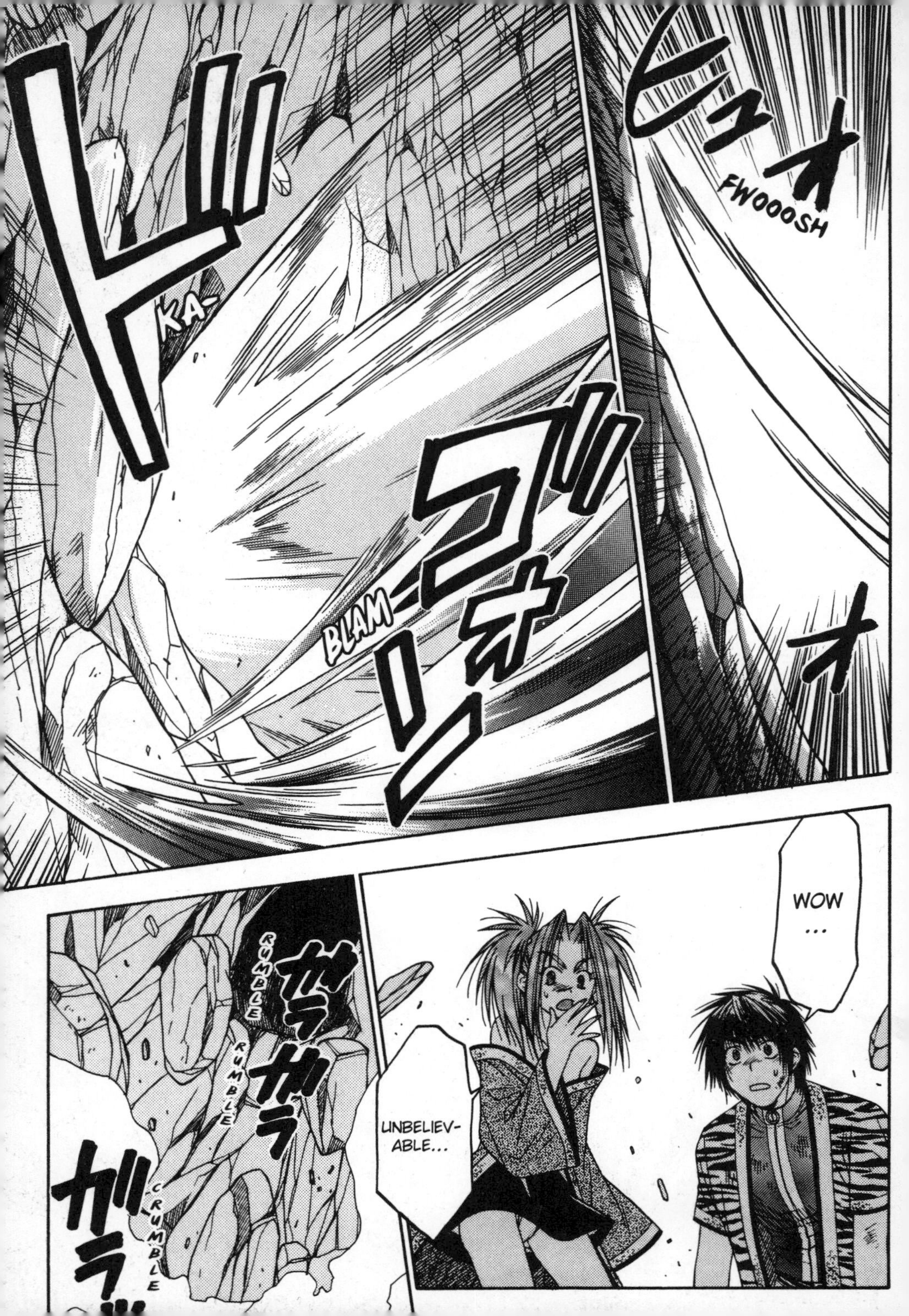
FWOOOSH
KA-
BLAM
WOW...
UNBELIEV-ABLE...
RUMBLE
RUMBLE
CRUMBLE

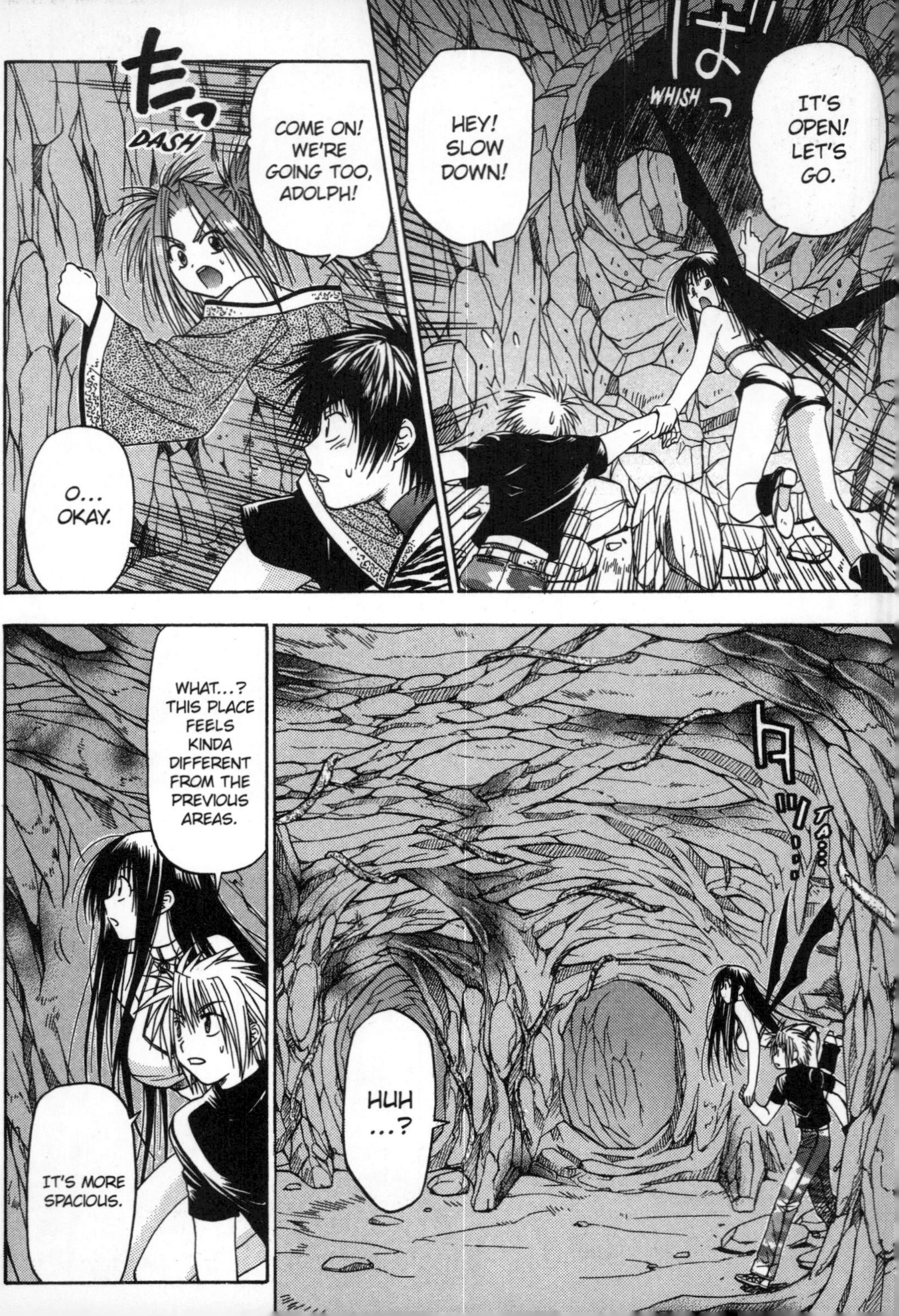
ばっ
WHISH
IT'S OPEN! LET'S GO.
HEY! SLOW DOWN!
たっ
DASH
COME ON! WE'RE GOING TOO, ADOLPH!
O... OKAY.
TA...
HUH ...?
WHAT...? THIS PLACE FEELS KINDA DIFFERENT FROM THE PREVIOUS AREAS.
IT'S MORE SPACIOUS.

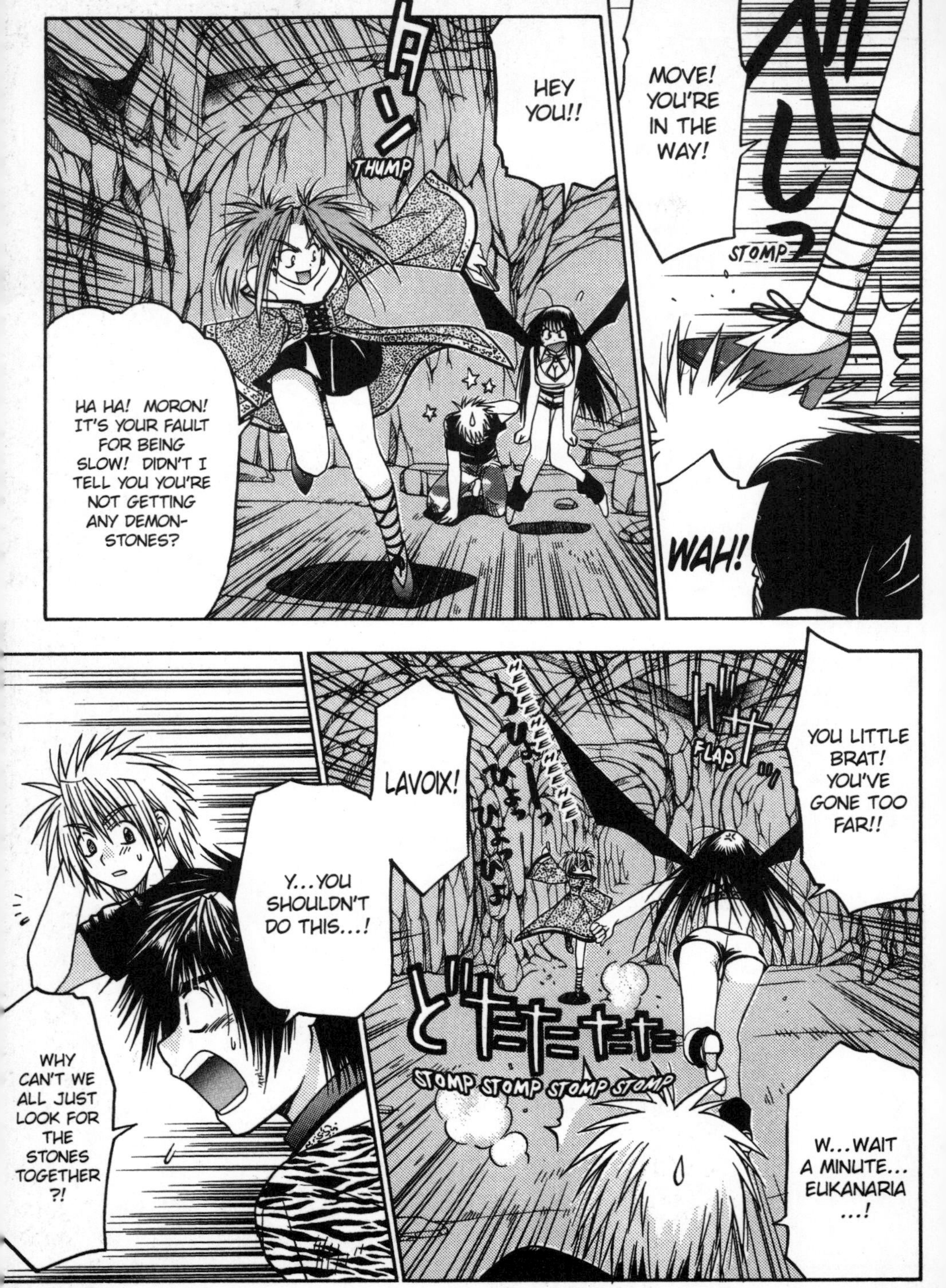

MOVE! YOU'RE IN THE WAY!
STOMP
WAH!
HEY YOU!!
THUMP
HA HA! MORON! IT'S YOUR FAULT FOR BEING SLOW! DIDN'T I TELL YOU YOU'RE NOT GETTING ANY DEMON-STONES?
YOU LITTLE BRAT! YOU'VE GONE TOO FAR!!
FLAP
HEEHEEHEEHEEHEE
LAVOIX!
STOMP STOMP STOMP STOMP
W...WAIT A MINUTE... EUKANARIA ...!
Y...YOU SHOULDN'T DO THIS...!
WHY CAN'T WE ALL JUST LOOK FOR THE STONES TOGETHER ?!

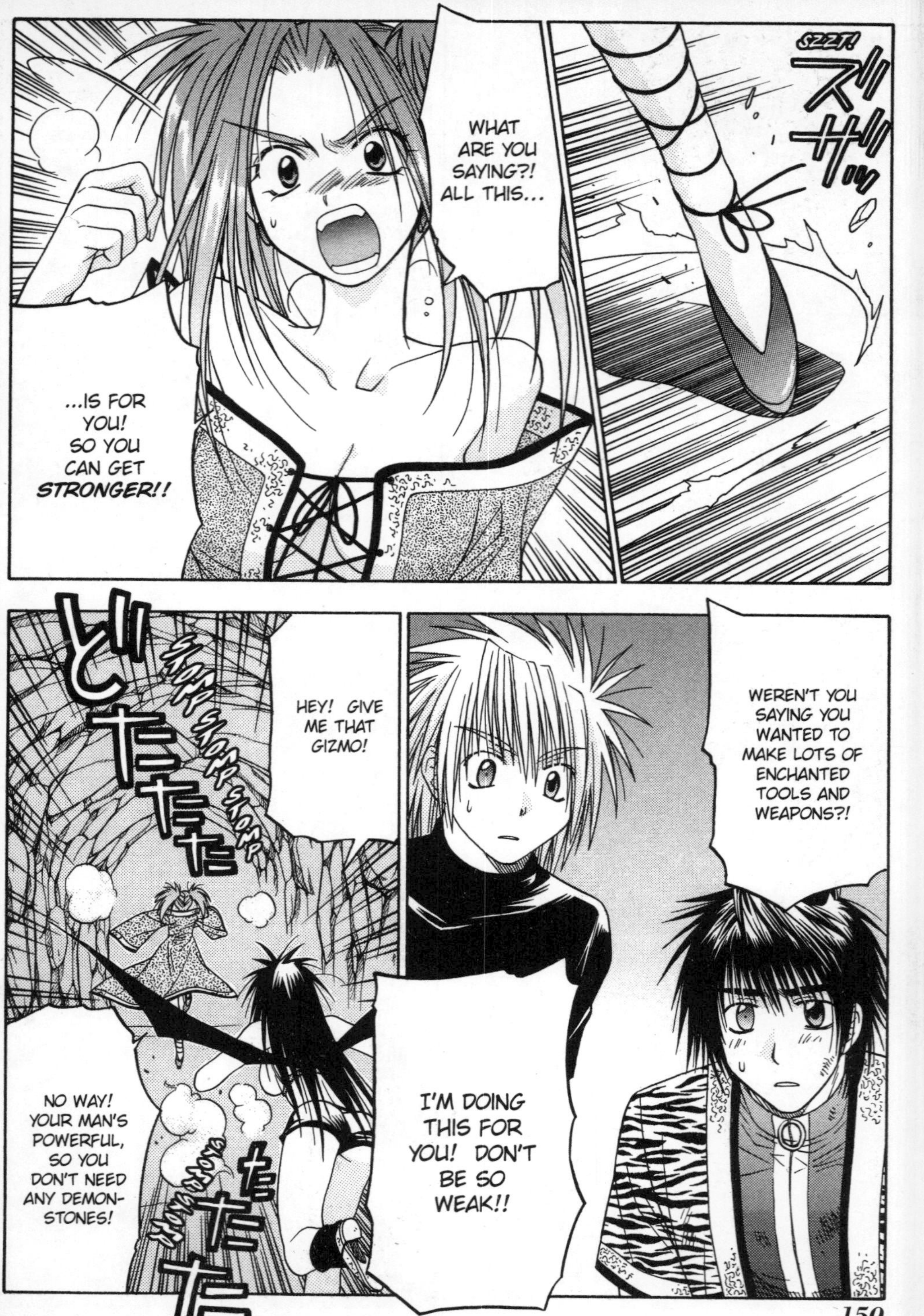
SZZT!
ズザザッ
WHAT ARE YOU SAYING?! ALL THIS...
...IS FOR YOU! SO YOU CAN GET STRONGER!!
WEREN'T YOU SAYING YOU WANTED TO MAKE LOTS OF ENCHANTED TOOLS AND WEAPONS?!
I'M DOING THIS FOR YOU! DON'T BE SO WEAK!!
HEY! GIVE ME THAT GIZMO!
どたたたた
STOMP STOMP STOMP
NO WAY! YOUR MAN'S POWERFUL, SO YOU DON'T NEED ANY DEMON-STONES!
たたた
STOMP STOMP

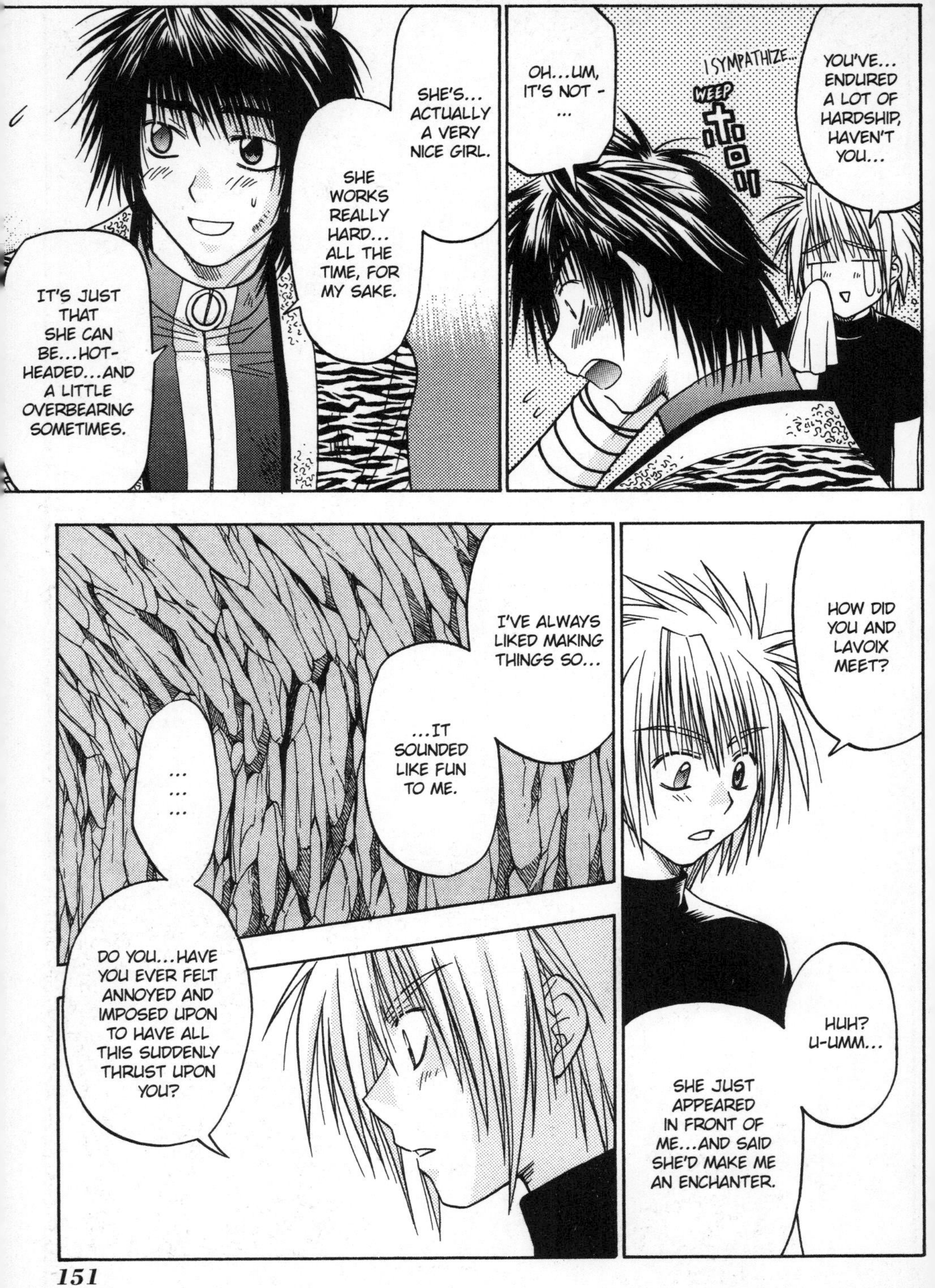
YOU'VE... ENDURED A LOT OF HARDSHIP, HAVEN'T YOU...
I SYMPATHIZE...
WEEP
OH...UM, IT'S NOT - ...
SHE'S... ACTUALLY A VERY NICE GIRL.
SHE WORKS REALLY HARD... ALL THE TIME, FOR MY SAKE.
IT'S JUST THAT SHE CAN BE...HOT-HEADED...AND A LITTLE OVERBEARING SOMETIMES.
HOW DID YOU AND LAVOIX MEET?
HUH? U-UMM...
SHE JUST APPEARED IN FRONT OF ME...AND SAID SHE'D MAKE ME AN ENCHANTER.
I'VE ALWAYS LIKED MAKING THINGS SO...
...IT SOUNDED LIKE FUN TO ME.
... ...
DO YOU...HAVE YOU EVER FELT ANNOYED AND IMPOSED UPON TO HAVE ALL THIS SUDDENLY THRUST UPON YOU?

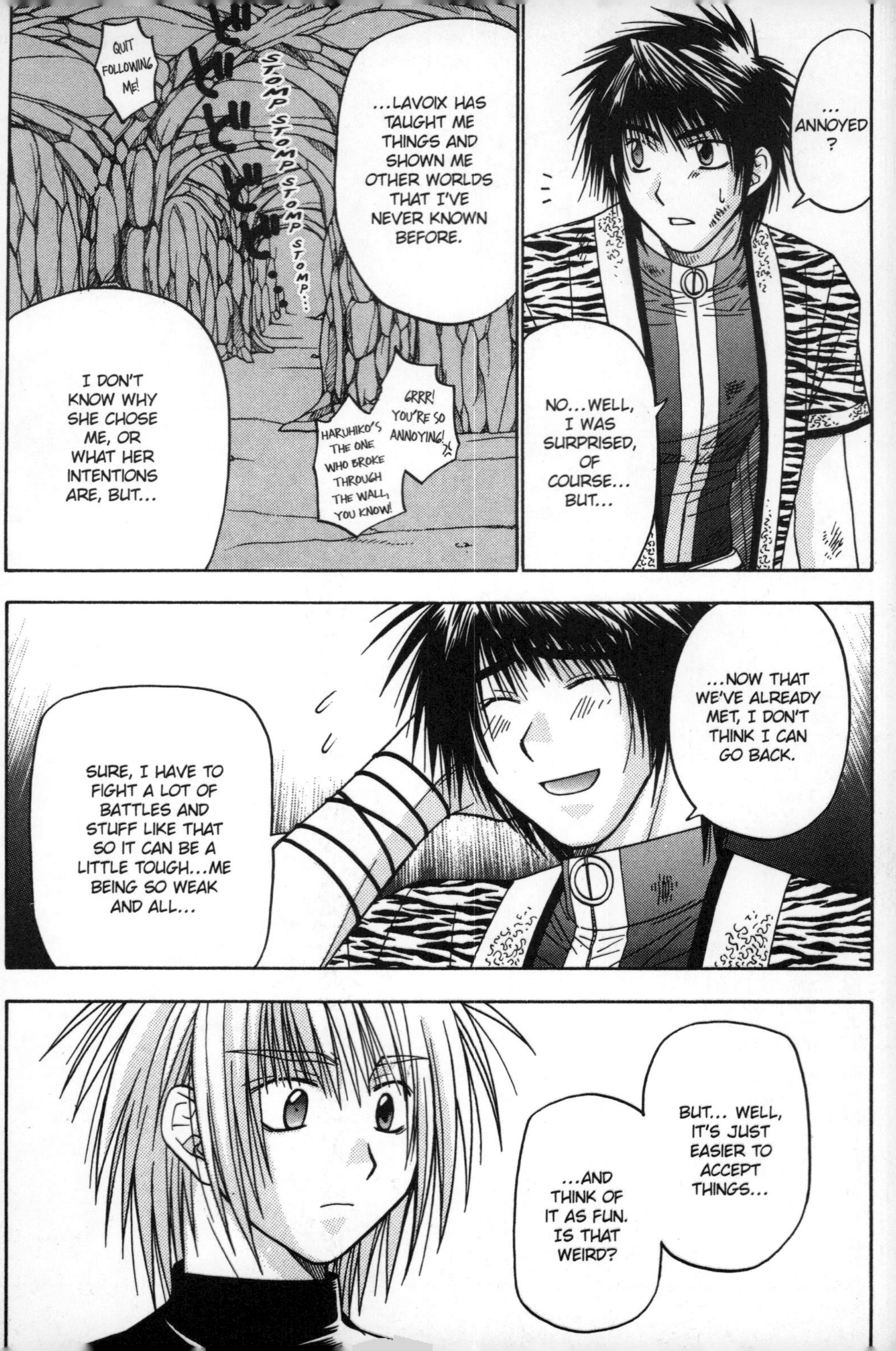
... ANNOYED?
NO... WELL, I WAS SURPRISED, OF COURSE... BUT...
...LAVOIX HAS TAUGHT ME THINGS AND SHOWN ME OTHER WORLDS THAT I'VE NEVER KNOWN BEFORE.
QUIT FOLLOWING ME!
STOMP STOMP STOMP STOMP STOMP...
GRRR! YOU'RE SO ANNOYING!
HARUHIKO'S THE ONE WHO BROKE THROUGH THE WALL, YOU KNOW!
I DON'T KNOW WHY SHE CHOSE ME, OR WHAT HER INTENTIONS ARE, BUT...
...NOW THAT WE'VE ALREADY MET, I DON'T THINK I CAN GO BACK.
SURE, I HAVE TO FIGHT A LOT OF BATTLES AND STUFF LIKE THAT SO IT CAN BE A LITTLE TOUGH...ME BEING SO WEAK AND ALL...
BUT... WELL, IT'S JUST EASIER TO ACCEPT THINGS...
...AND THINK OF IT AS FUN. IS THAT WEIRD?

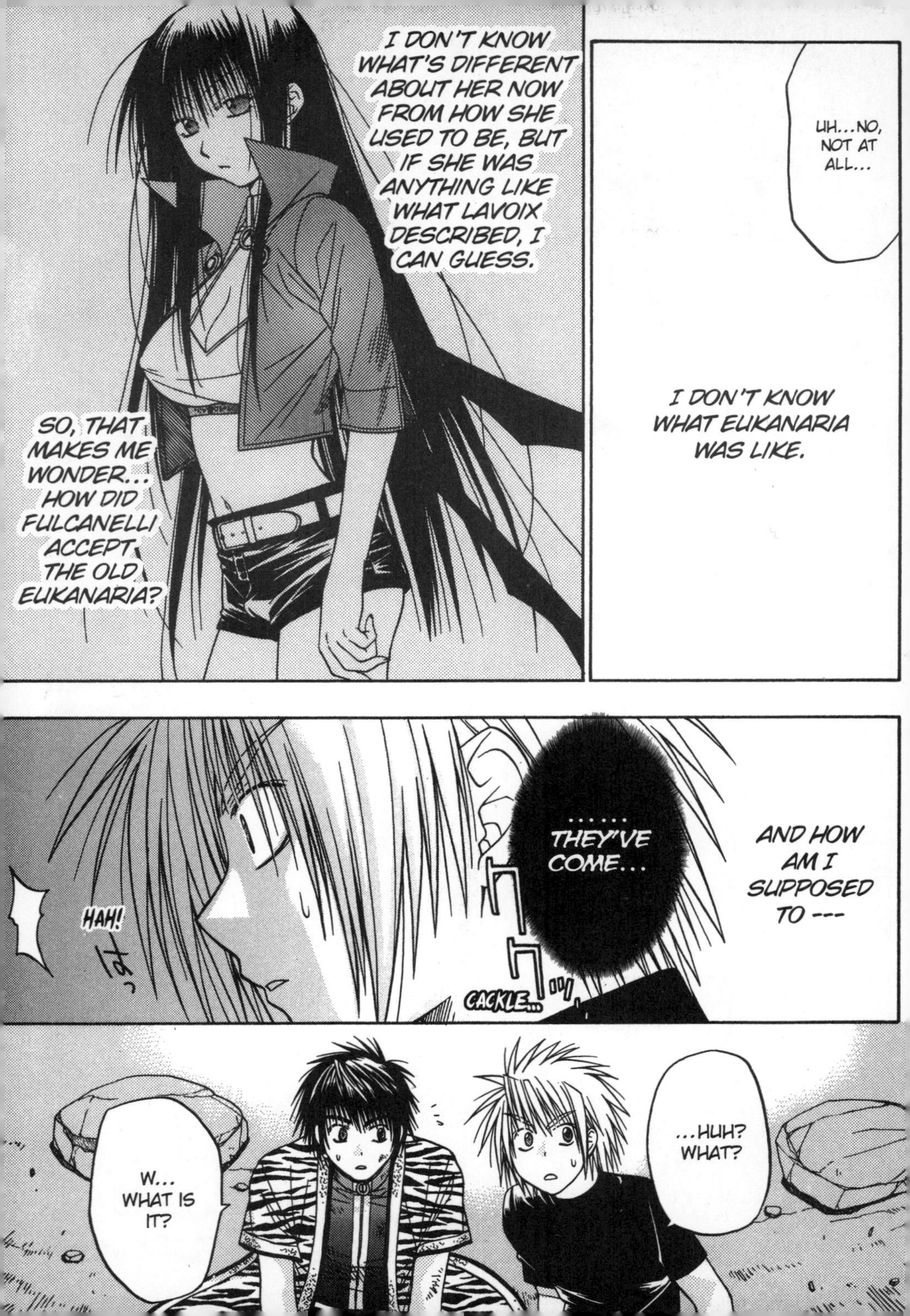
UH...NO, NOT AT ALL...
I DON'T KNOW WHAT EUKANARIA WAS LIKE.
I DON'T KNOW WHAT'S DIFFERENT ABOUT HER NOW FROM HOW SHE USED TO BE, BUT IF SHE WAS ANYTHING LIKE WHAT LAVOIX DESCRIBED, I CAN GUESS.
SO, THAT MAKES ME WONDER... HOW DID FULCANELLI ACCEPT THE OLD EUKANARIA?
AND HOW AM I SUPPOSED TO ---
...... THEY'VE COME...
CACKLE...
HAH!
...HUH? WHAT?
W... WHAT IS IT?

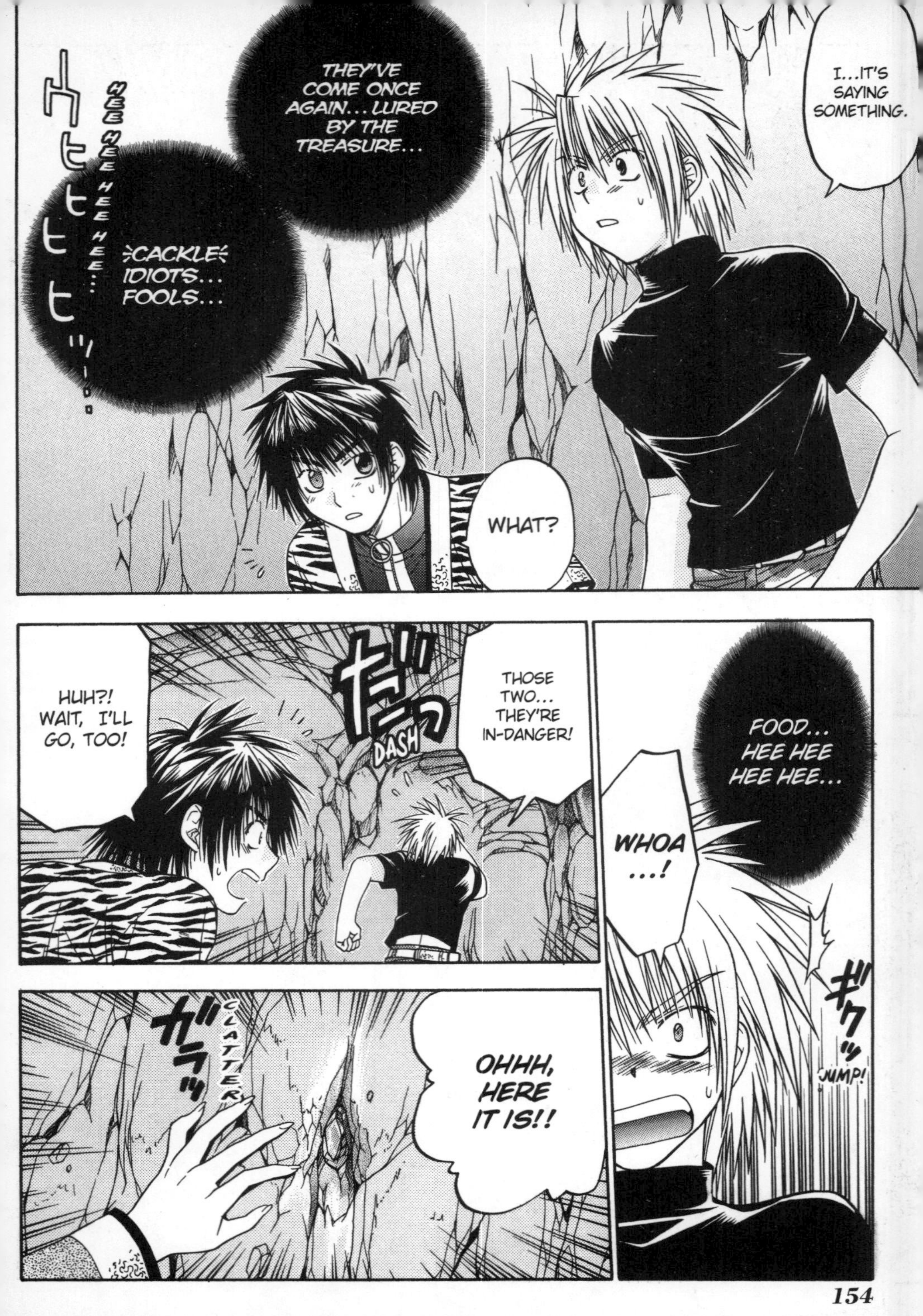
I...IT'S SAYING SOMETHING.
THEY'VE COME ONCE AGAIN...LURED BY THE TREASURE...
HEE HEE HEE HEE...
ウヒヒヒヒッ
CACKLE IDIOTS... FOOLS...
WHAT?
FOOD... HEE HEE HEE HEE...
WHOA ...!
JUMP!
THOSE TWO... THEY'RE IN-DANGER!
DASH
HUH?! WAIT, I'LL GO, TOO!
OHHH, HERE IT IS!!
CLATTER

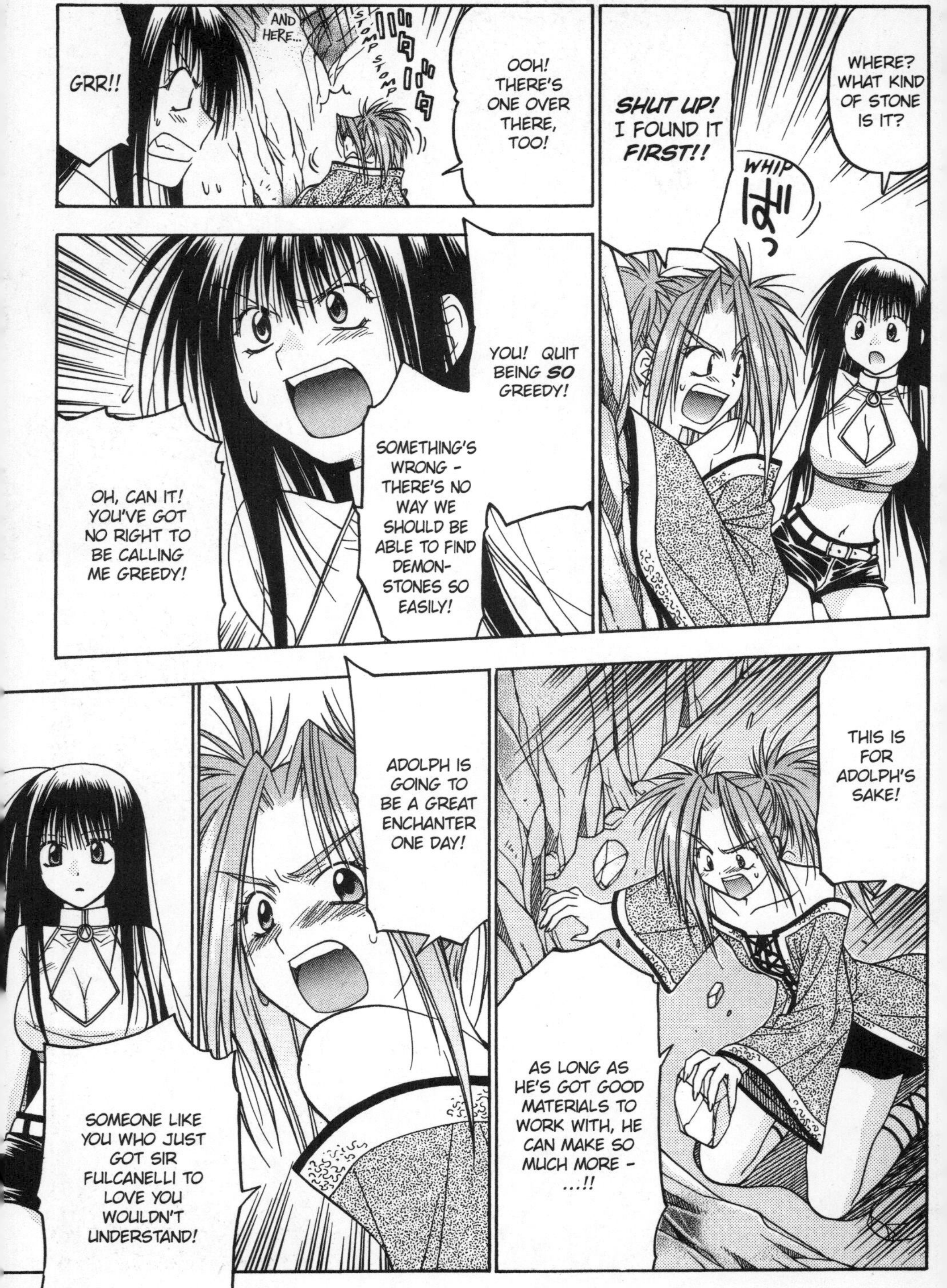
WHERE? WHAT KIND OF STONE IS IT?
SHUT UP! I FOUND IT FIRST!!
WHIP
OOH! THERE'S ONE OVER THERE, TOO!
STOMP STOMP
AND HERE...
GRR!!
YOU! QUIT BEING SO GREEDY!
SOMETHING'S WRONG - THERE'S NO WAY WE SHOULD BE ABLE TO FIND DEMON-STONES SO EASILY!
OH, CAN IT! YOU'VE GOT NO RIGHT TO BE CALLING ME GREEDY!
THIS IS FOR ADOLPH'S SAKE!
AS LONG AS HE'S GOT GOOD MATERIALS TO WORK WITH, HE CAN MAKE SO MUCH MORE - ...!!
ADOLPH IS GOING TO BE A GREAT ENCHANTER ONE DAY!
SOMEONE LIKE YOU WHO JUST GOT SIR FULCANELLI TO LOVE YOU WOULDN'T UNDERSTAND!

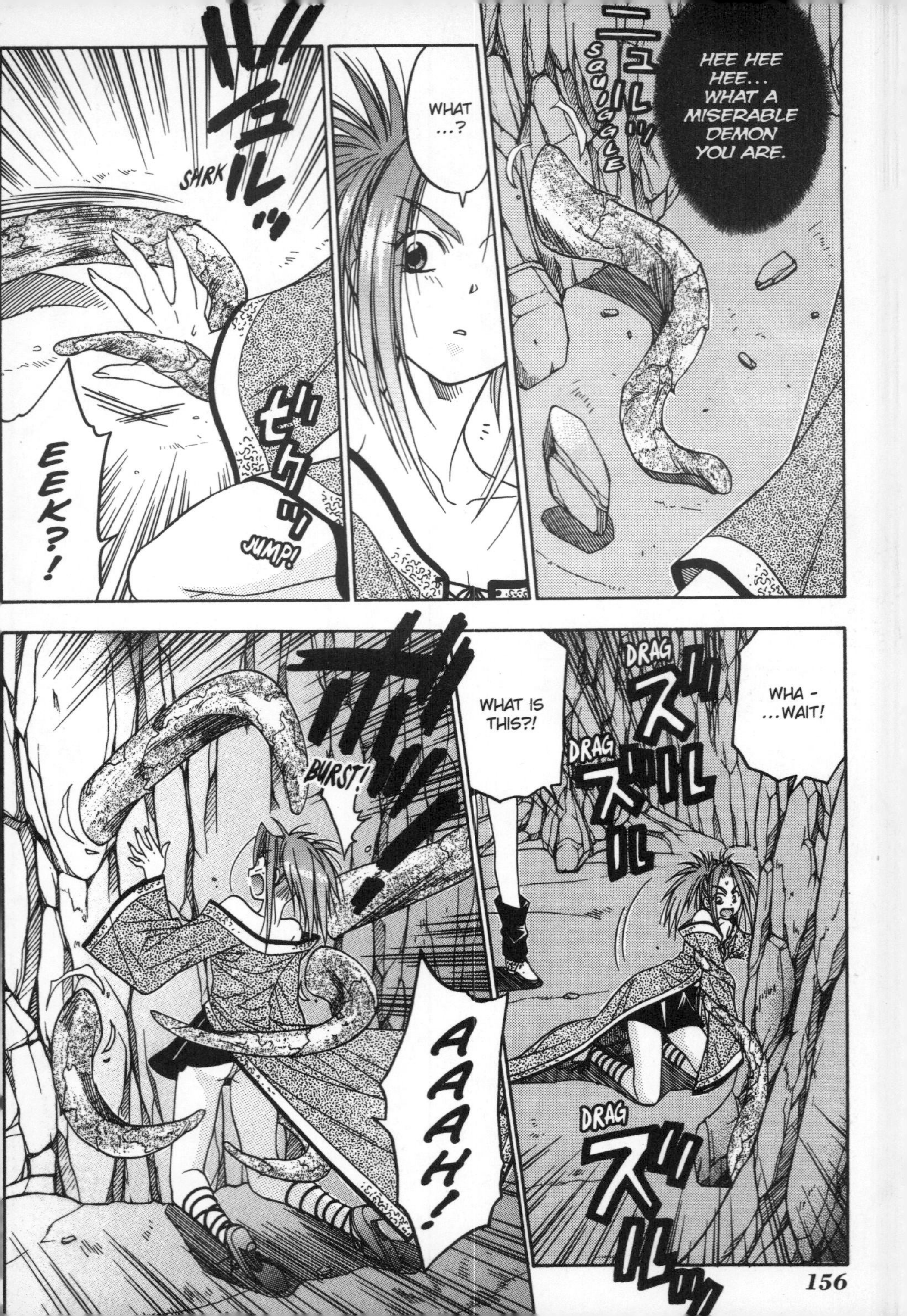
HEE HEE HEE... WHAT A MISERABLE DEMON YOU ARE.
SQUIGGLE
WHAT ...?
SHRK
JUMP!
EEK?!
WHA - ...WAIT!
DRAG
DRAG
WHAT IS THIS?!
DRAG
BURST!
AAAAH!

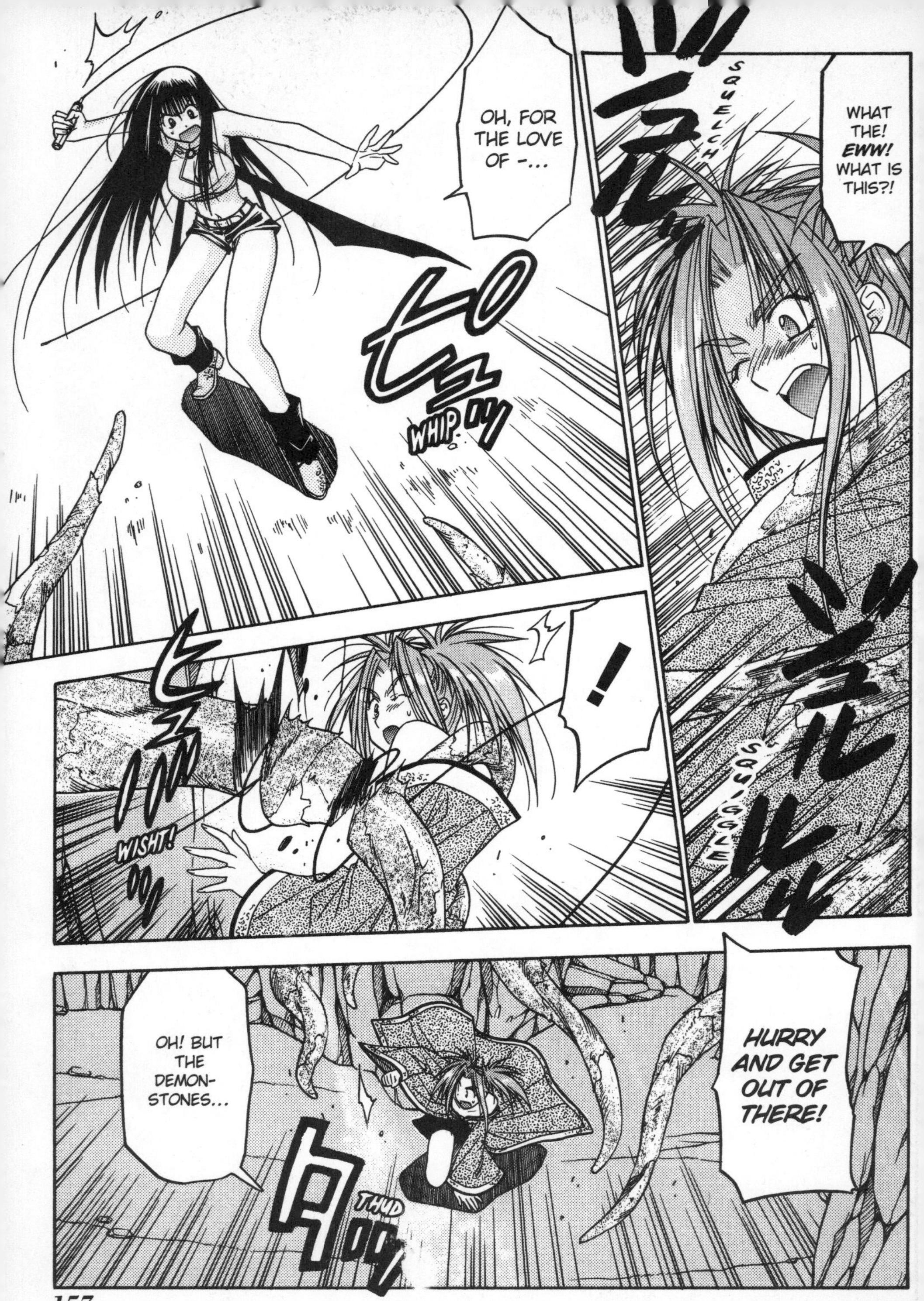
SQUELCH
WHAT THE! ***EWW!*** WHAT IS THIS?!
SQUIGGLE
OH, FOR THE LOVE OF -...
WHIP
!
WISHT!
HURRY AND GET OUT OF THERE!
OH! BUT THE DEMON-STONES...
THUD

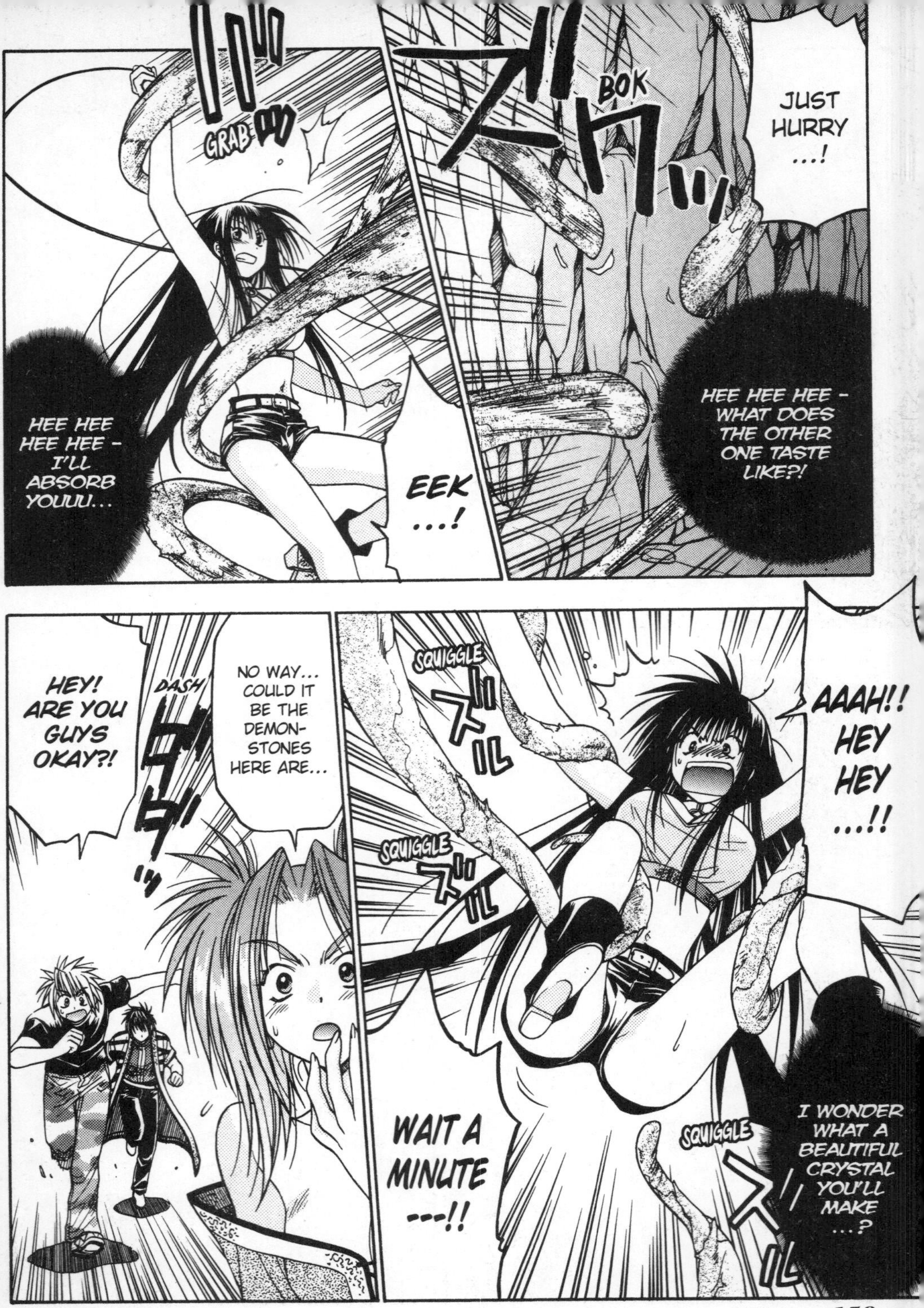
BOK
JUST HURRY ...!
HEE HEE HEE - WHAT DOES THE OTHER ONE TASTE LIKE?!
GRAB
HEE HEE HEE HEE - I'LL ABSORB YOUUU...
EEK ...!
SQUIGGLE
AAAH!! HEY HEY ...!!
SQUIGGLE
WAIT A MINUTE ---!!
I WONDER WHAT A BEAUTIFUL CRYSTAL YOU'LL MAKE ...?
SQUIGGLE
NO WAY... COULD IT BE THE DEMON-STONES HERE ARE...
DASH
HEY! ARE YOU GUYS OKAY?!

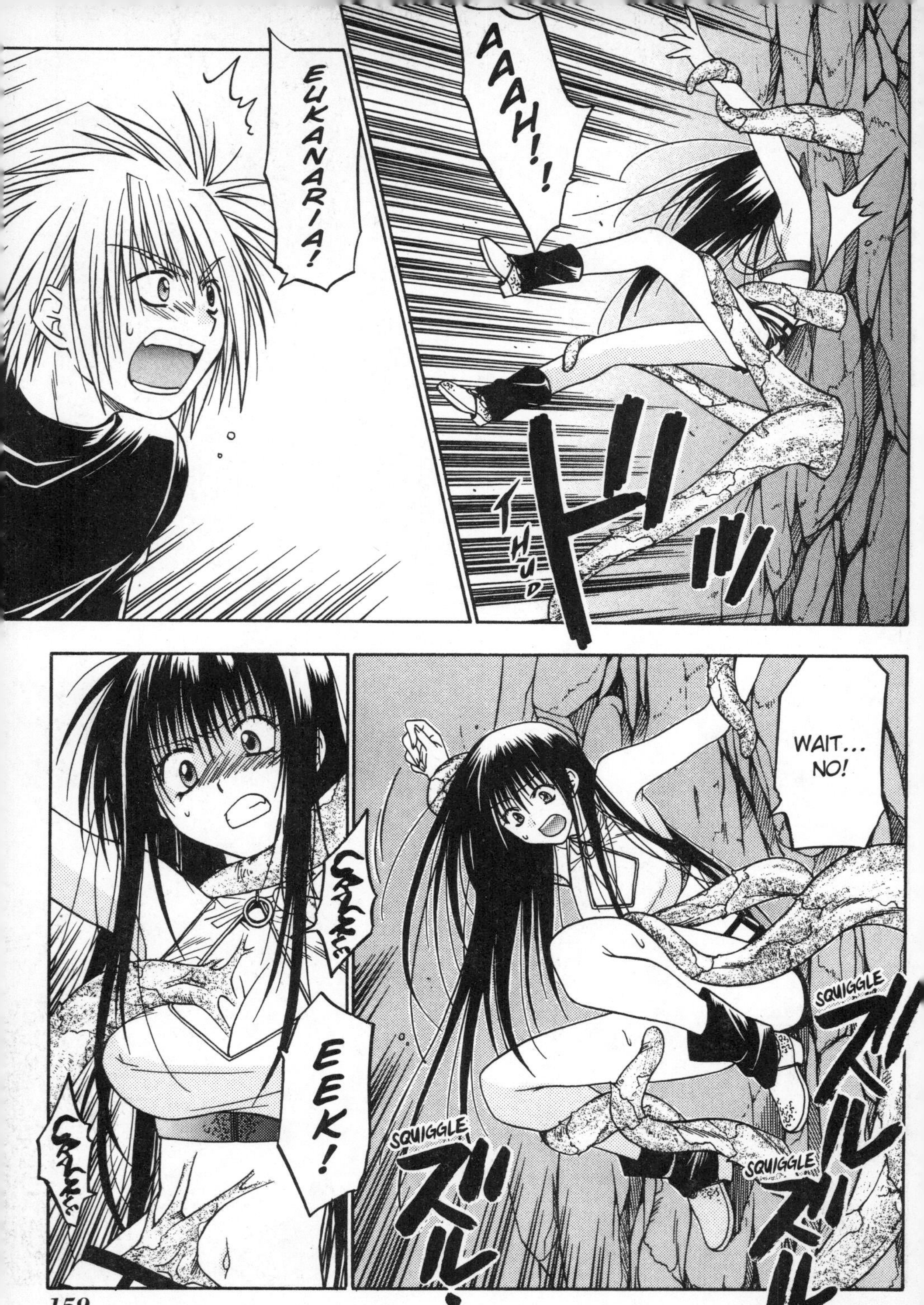
AAAH!!!
THUD
EUKANARIA!
WAIT... NO!
SQUIGGLE
SQUIGGLE
SQUIGGLE
EEK!

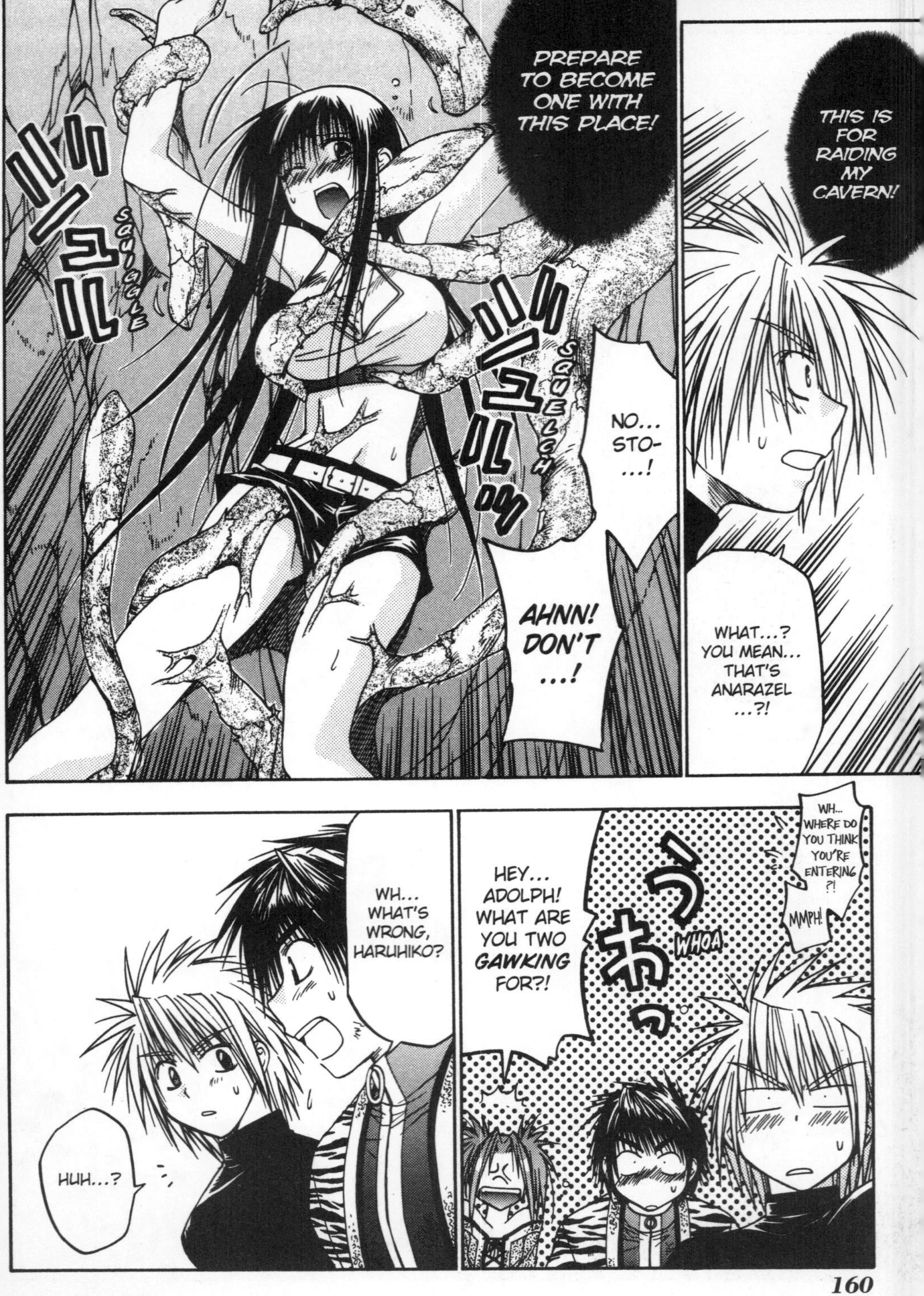
THIS IS FOR RAIDING MY CAVERN!
WHAT...? YOU MEAN... THAT'S ANARAZEL...?!
PREPARE TO BECOME ONE WITH THIS PLACE!
SQUIGGLE
SQUELCH
NO... STO-...!
AHNN! DON'T ...!
WH... WHERE DO YOU THINK YOU'RE ENTERING?!
MMPH!
うおっ
WHOA
HEY... ADOLPH! WHAT ARE YOU TWO GAWKING FOR?!
WH... WHAT'S WRONG, HARUHIKO?
HUH...?

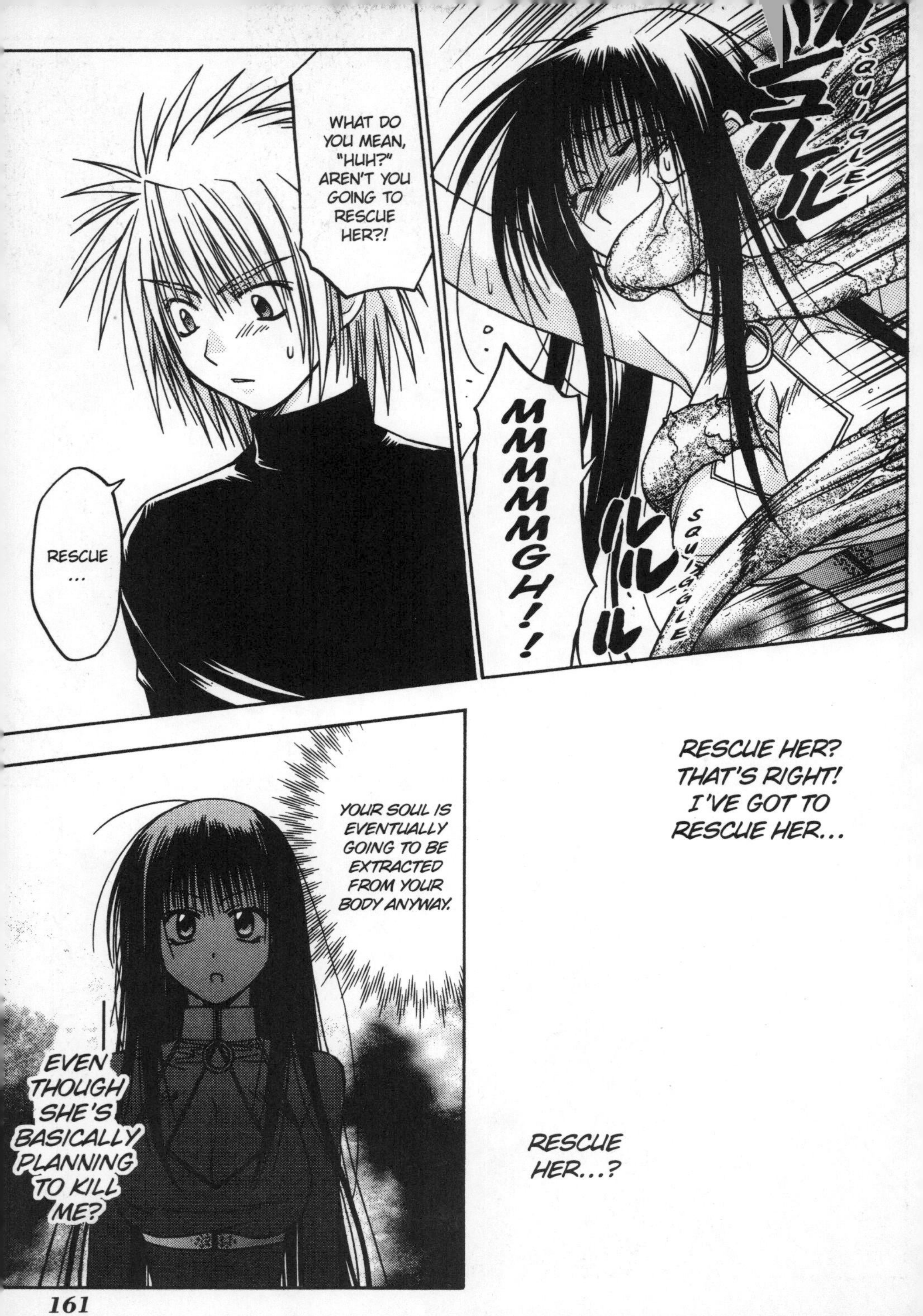
SQUIGGLE
MMMMMGH!!
SQUIGGLE
WHAT DO YOU MEAN, "HUH?" AREN'T YOU GOING TO RESCUE HER?!
RESCUE ...
RESCUE HER? THAT'S RIGHT! I'VE GOT TO RESCUE HER...
RESCUE HER...?
YOUR SOUL IS EVENTUALLY GOING TO BE EXTRACTED FROM YOUR BODY ANYWAY.
EVEN THOUGH SHE'S BASICALLY PLANNING TO KILL ME?

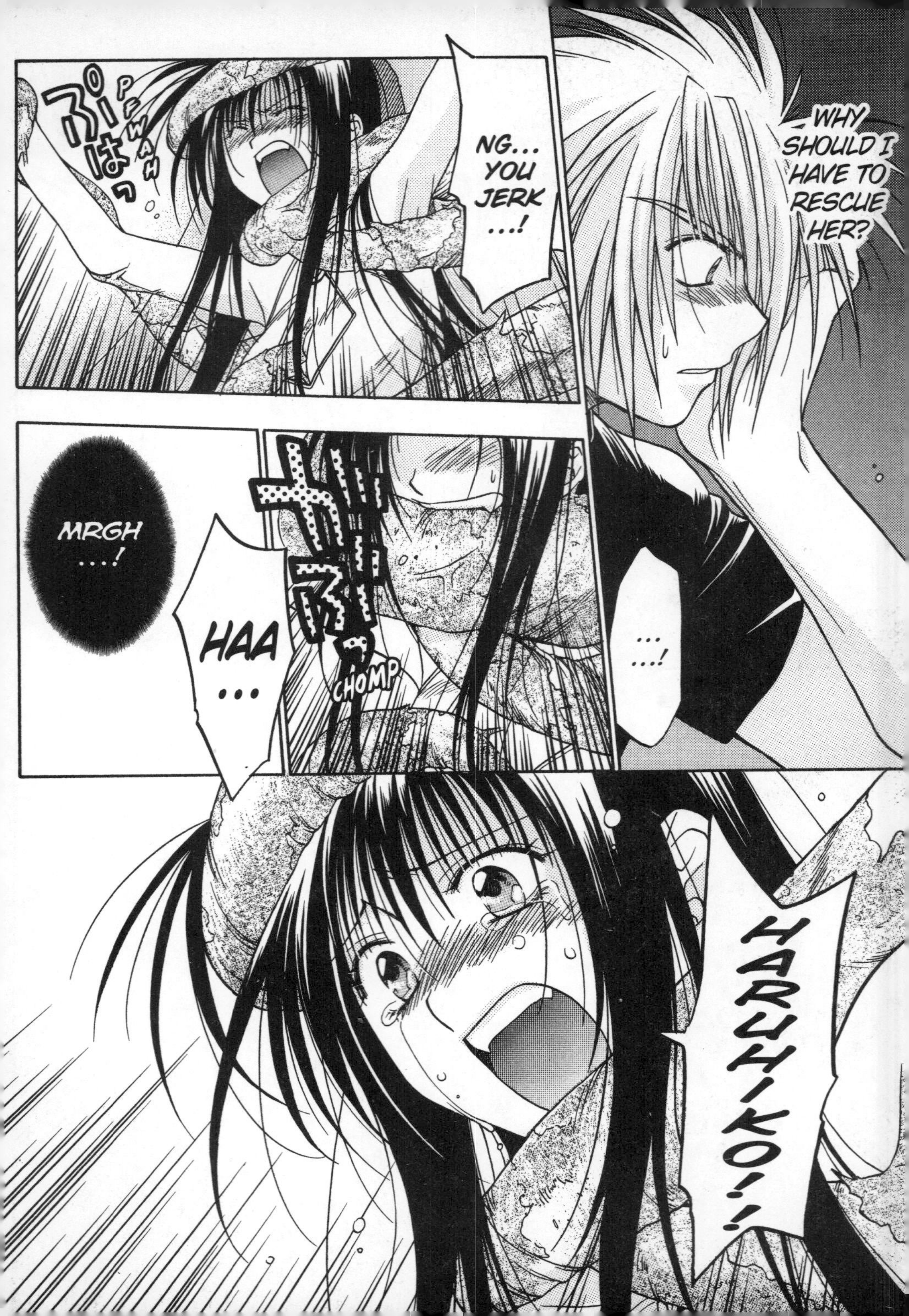
WHY SHOULD I HAVE TO RESCUE HER?
... ...!
NG... YOU JERK ...!
ぷはっ
PFWAH
ガぶっ
CHOMP
HAA ...
MRGH ...!
HARUHIKO!!

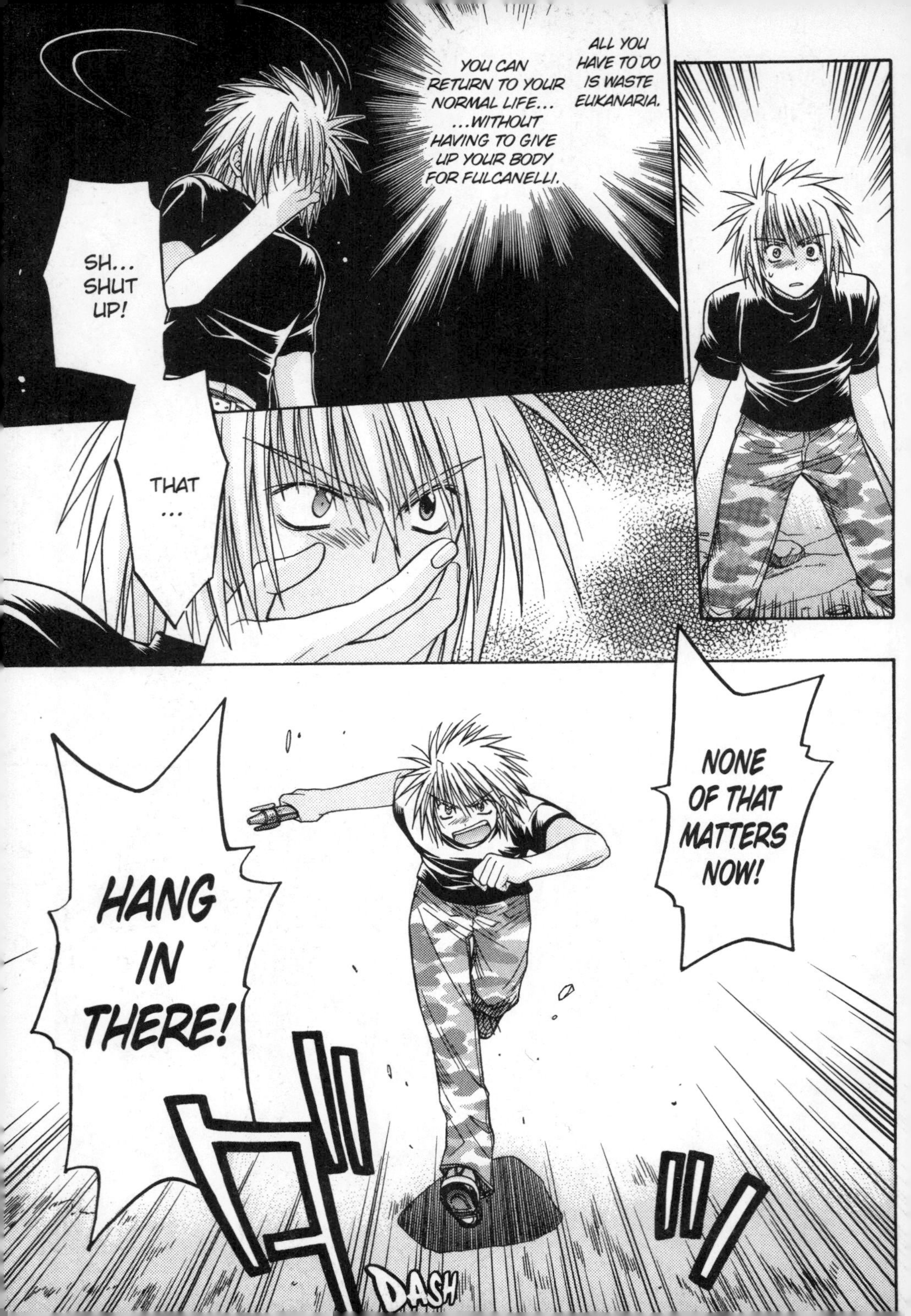
ALL YOU HAVE TO DO IS WASTE EUKANARIA.
YOU CAN RETURN TO YOUR NORMAL LIFE... ...WITHOUT HAVING TO GIVE UP YOUR BODY FOR FULCANELLI.
SH... SHUT UP!
THAT ...
NONE OF THAT MATTERS NOW!
HANG IN THERE!
DASH

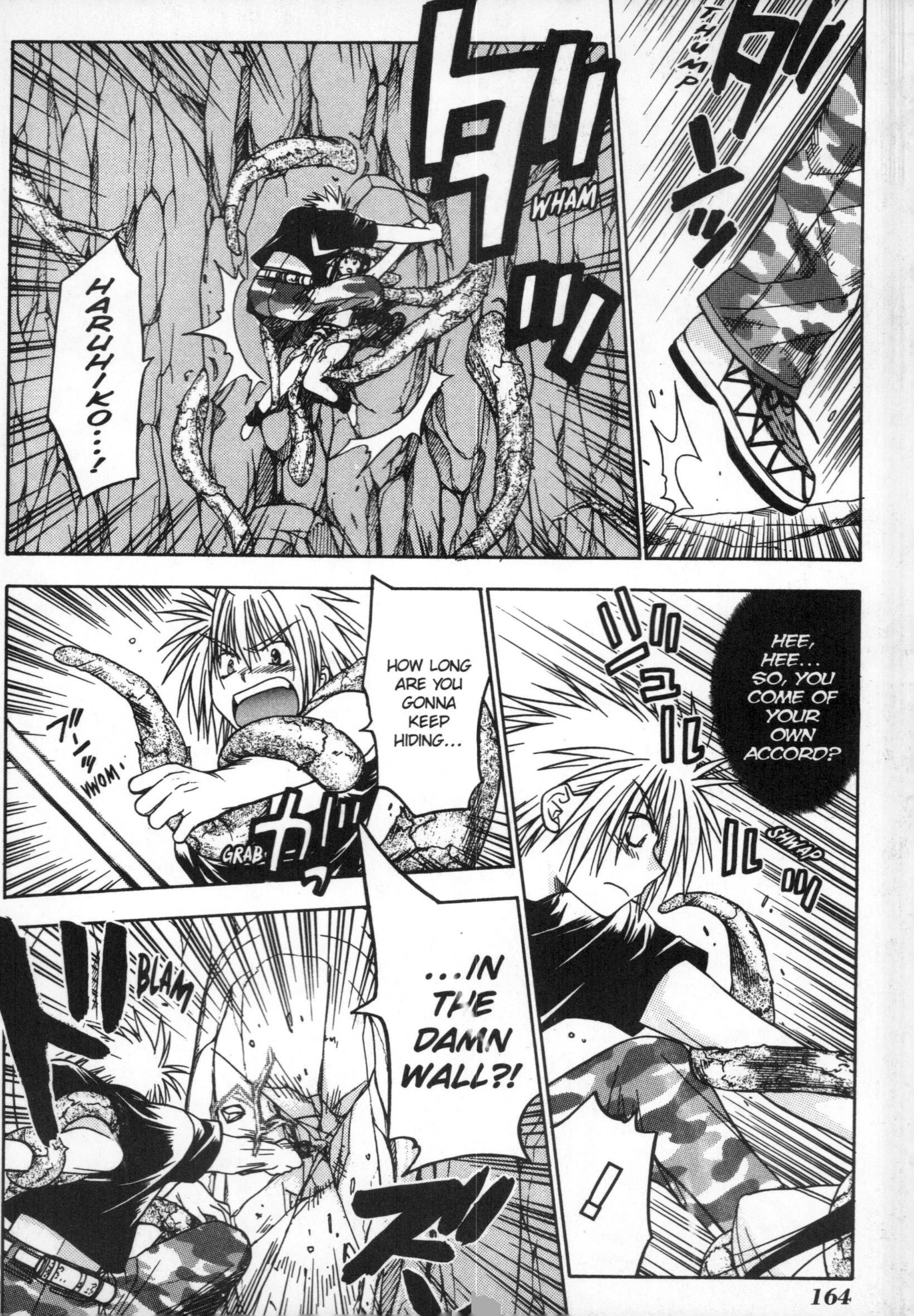
THUMP
WHAM
HARUHIKO...!
HEE, HEE... SO, YOU COME OF YOUR OWN ACCORD?
SHWAP
!
HOW LONG ARE YOU GONNA KEEP HIDING...
WOM
GRAB
BLAM
...IN THE DAMN WALL?!

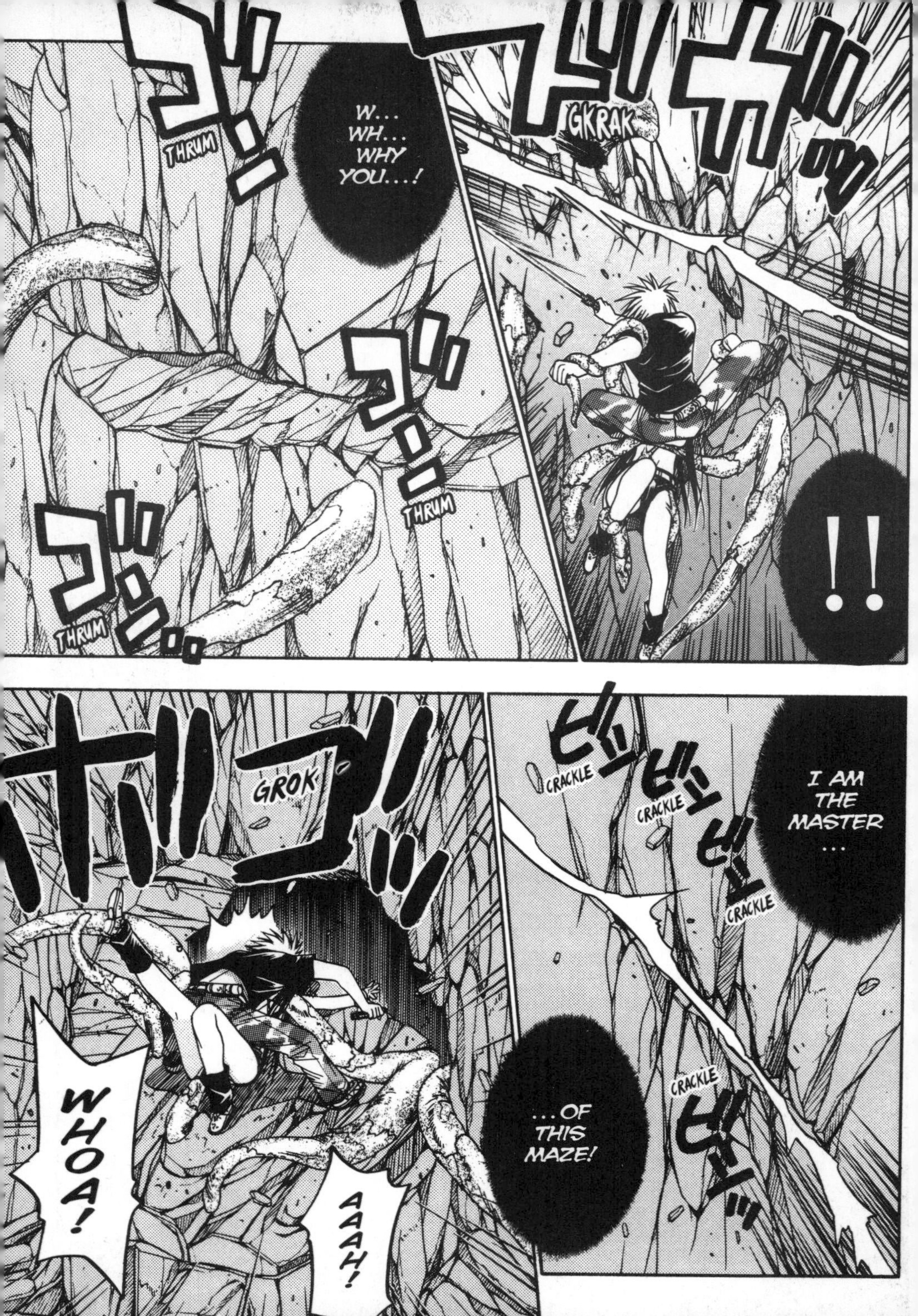
GKRAK
!!
W... WH... WHY YOU...!
THRUM
THRUM
THRUM
CRACKLE
CRACKLE
I AM THE MASTER ...
CRACKLE
CRACKLE
...OF THIS MAZE!
GROK
WHOA!
AAAH!

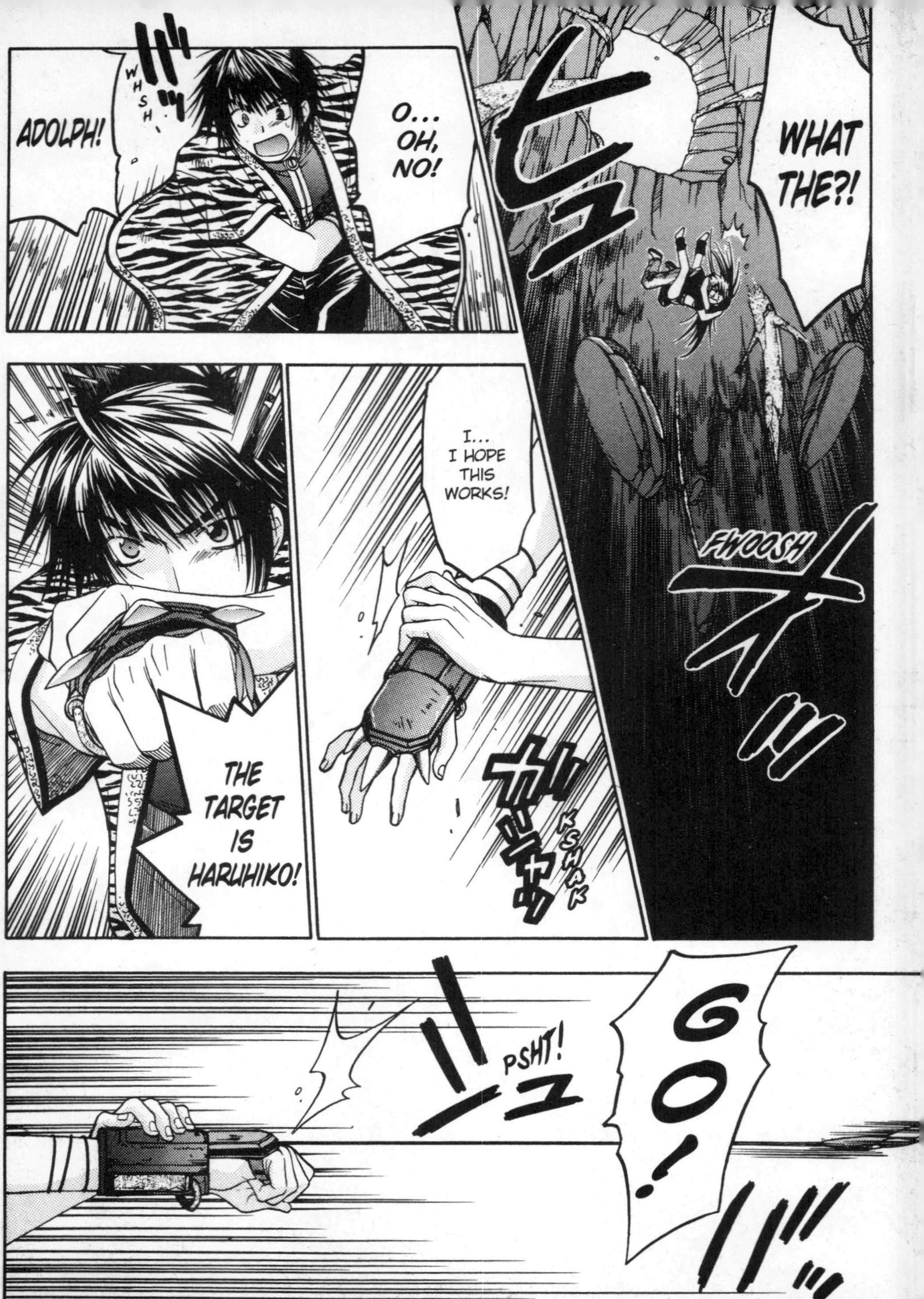
WHAT THE?!
FWOOSH
WHSH
O... OH, NO!
ADOLPH!
I... I HOPE THIS WORKS!
KSHAK
THE TARGET IS HARUHIKO!
GO!!
PSHT!

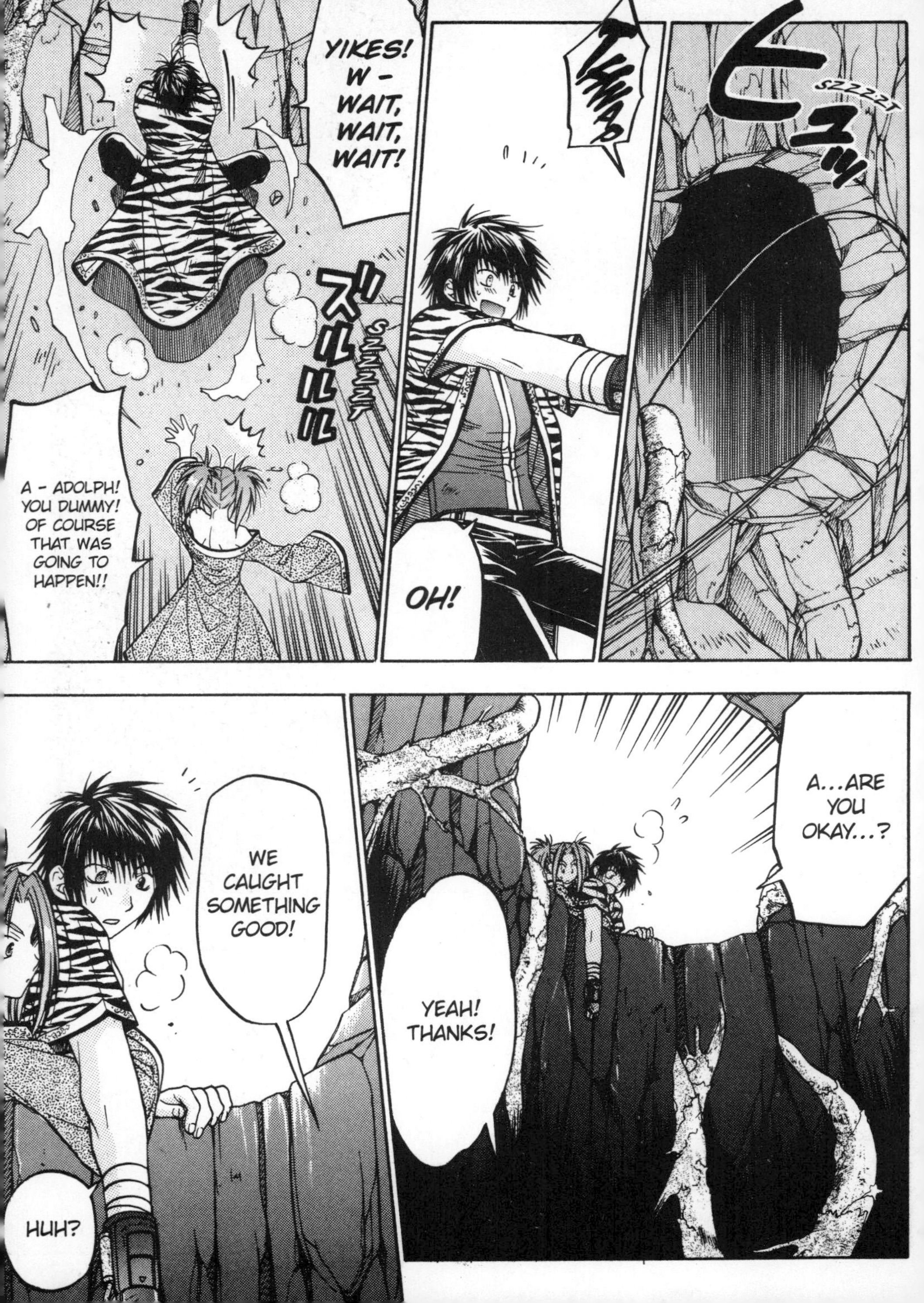
ヒュッ
SZZZZT
THWAP
OH!
YIKES! W - WAIT, WAIT, WAIT!
ズルルル
SNNNNT
A - ADOLPH! YOU DUMMY! OF COURSE THAT WAS GOING TO HAPPEN!!
A...ARE YOU OKAY...?
YEAH! THANKS!
WE CAUGHT SOMETHING GOOD!
HUH?

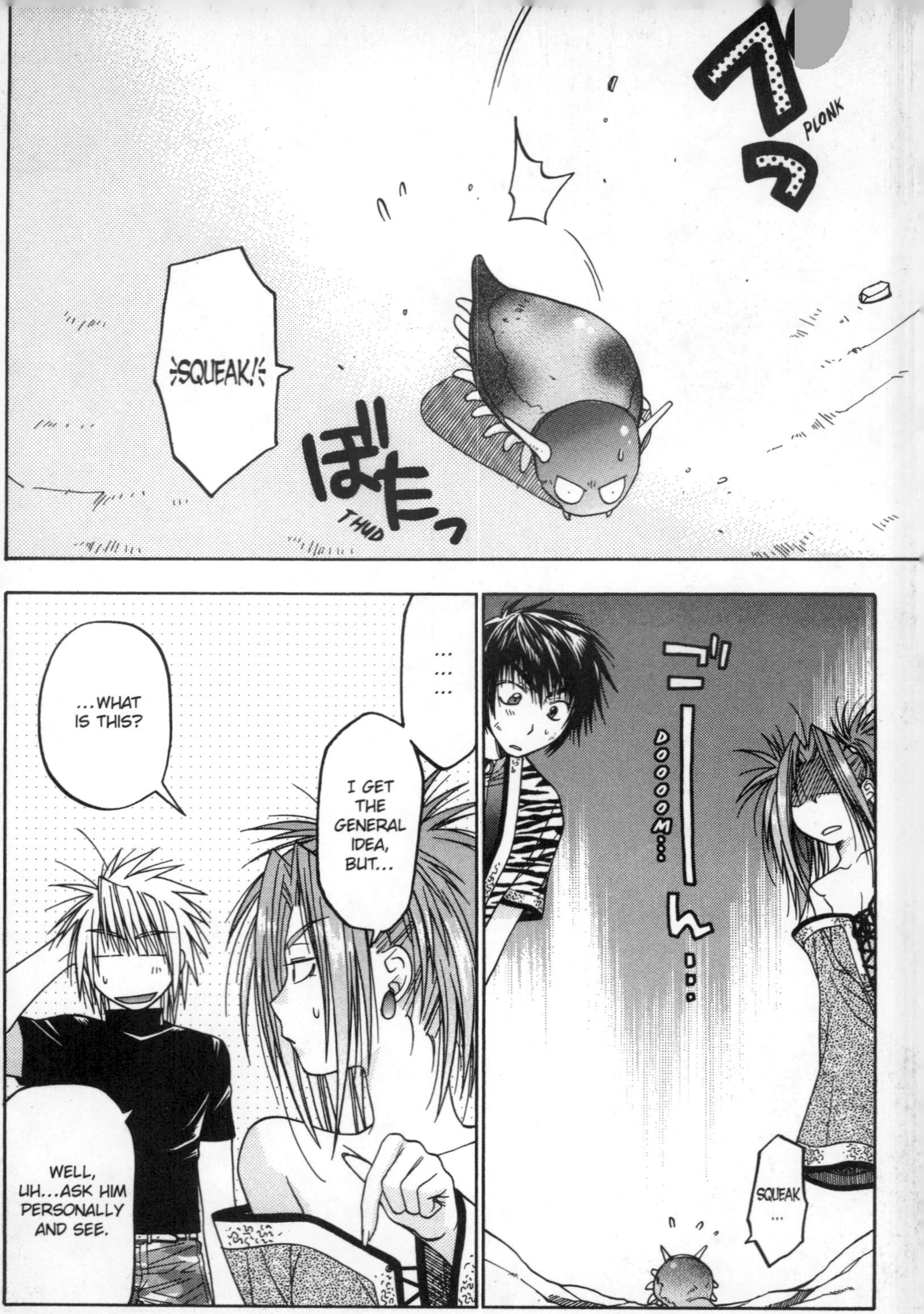
PLONK
SQUEAK!
THUD
DOOOOOM...
SQUEAK...
......
I GET THE GENERAL IDEA, BUT...
...WHAT IS THIS?
WELL, UH...ASK HIM PERSONALLY AND SEE.

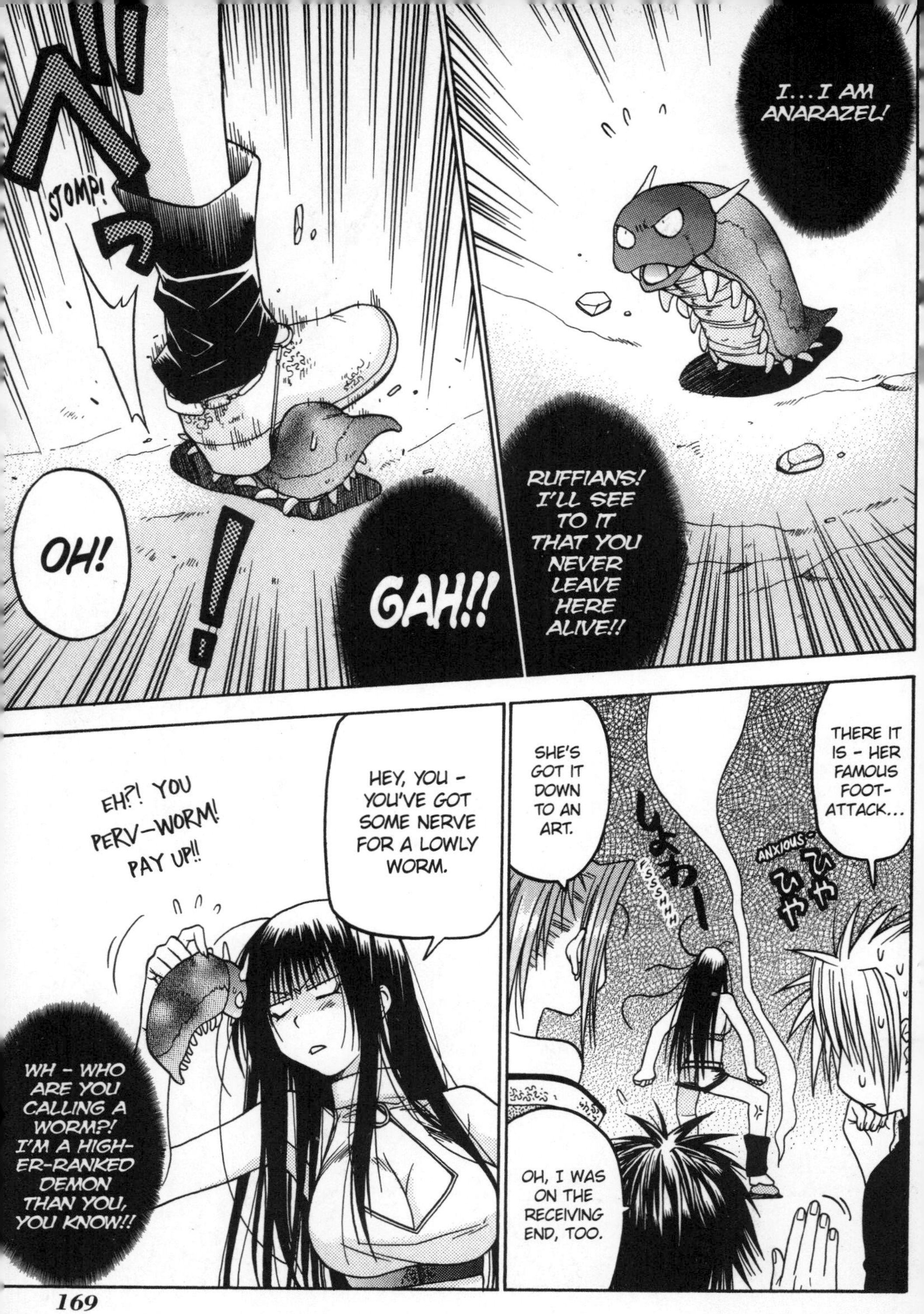
I...I AM ANARAZEL!
RUFFIANS! I'LL SEE TO IT THAT YOU NEVER LEAVE HERE ALIVE!!
STOMP!
GAH!!
OH!
THERE IT IS - HER FAMOUS FOOT-ATTACK...
SHE'S GOT IT DOWN TO AN ART.
ひやひや
ANXIOUS
しょわー
FSSSHH
OH, I WAS ON THE RECEIVING END, TOO.
HEY, YOU - YOU'VE GOT SOME NERVE FOR A LOWLY WORM.
EH?! YOU PERV-WORM! PAY UP!!
WH - WHO ARE YOU CALLING A WORM?! I'M A HIGHER-RANKED DEMON THAN YOU, YOU KNOW!!

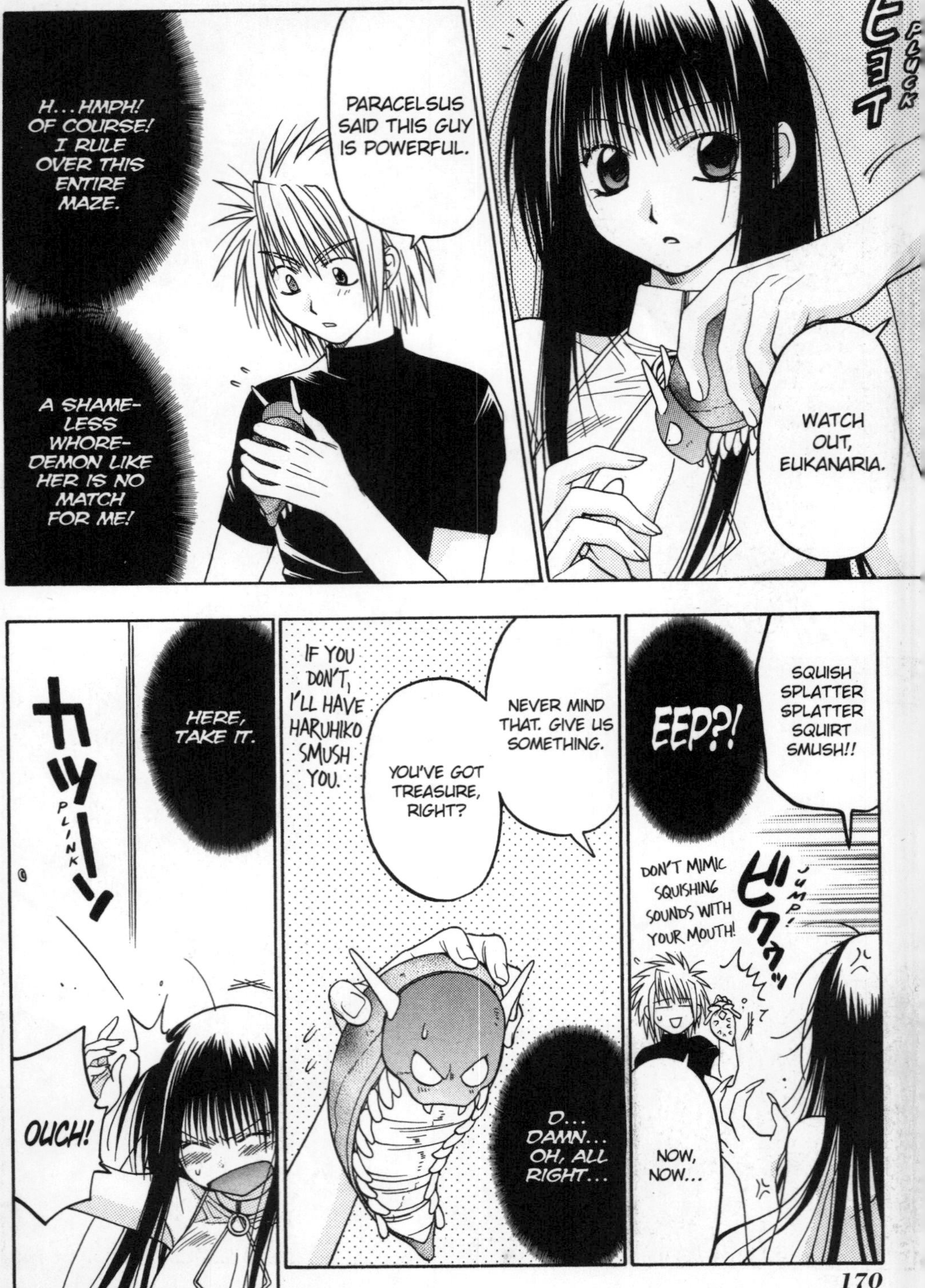
ヒョイ
PLUCK
WATCH OUT, EUKANARIA.
PARACELSUS SAID THIS GUY IS POWERFUL.
H...HMPH! OF COURSE! I RULE OVER THIS ENTIRE MAZE.
A SHAME-LESS WHORE-DEMON LIKE HER IS NO MATCH FOR ME!
SQUISH SPLATTER SPLATTER SQUIRT SMUSH!!
EEP?!
ビクッ
JUMP!
DON'T MIMIC SQUISHING SOUNDS WITH YOUR MOUTH!
NOW, NOW...
NEVER MIND THAT. GIVE US SOMETHING.
YOU'VE GOT TREASURE, RIGHT?
IF YOU DON'T, I'LL HAVE HARUHIKO SMUSH YOU.
D... DAMN... OH, ALL RIGHT...
HERE, TAKE IT.
カツーン
PLINK
OUCH!

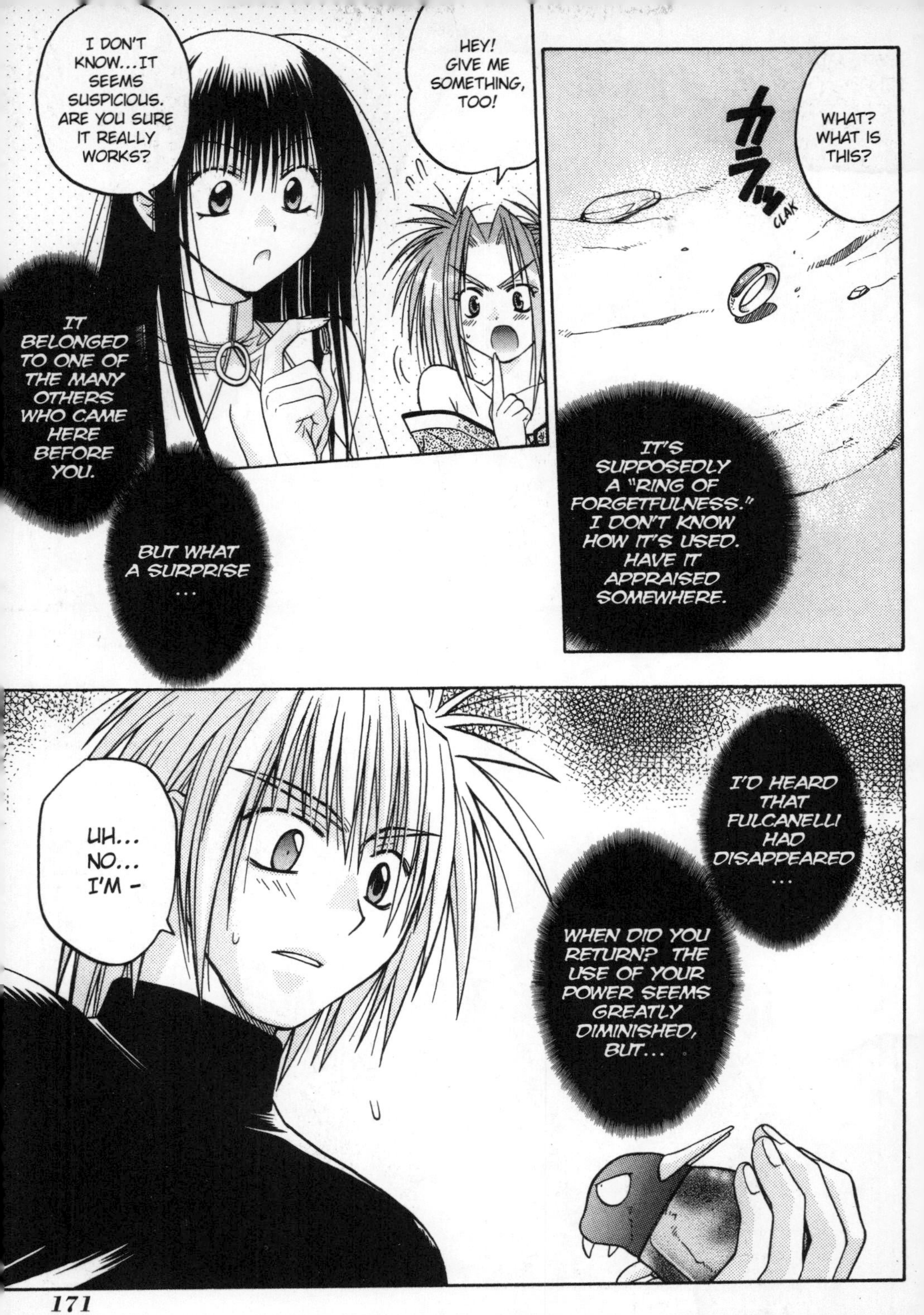
WHAT? WHAT IS THIS?
CLAK
IT'S SUPPOSEDLY A "RING OF FORGETFULNESS." I DON'T KNOW HOW IT'S USED. HAVE IT APPRAISED SOMEWHERE.
HEY! GIVE ME SOMETHING, TOO!
I DON'T KNOW...IT SEEMS SUSPICIOUS. ARE YOU SURE IT REALLY WORKS?
IT BELONGED TO ONE OF THE MANY OTHERS WHO CAME HERE BEFORE YOU.
BUT WHAT A SURPRISE...
I'D HEARD THAT FULCANELLI HAD DISAPPEARED...
WHEN DID YOU RETURN? THE USE OF YOUR POWER SEEMS GREATLY DIMINISHED, BUT...
UH... NO... I'M -

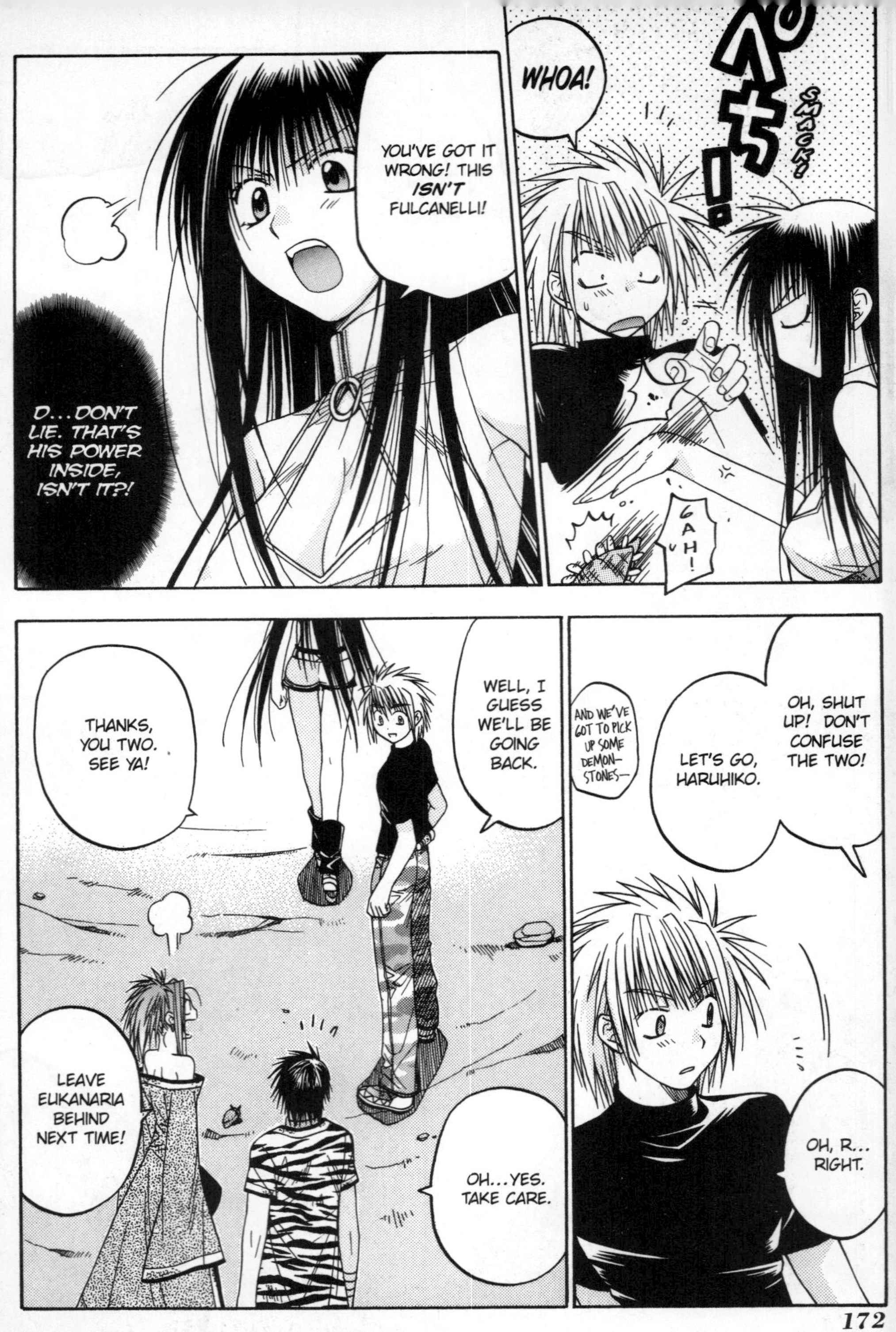
WHOA!
SMACK!
GAH!
YOU'VE GOT IT WRONG! THIS ISN'T FULCANELLI!
D...DON'T LIE. THAT'S HIS POWER INSIDE, ISN'T IT?!
OH, SHUT UP! DON'T CONFUSE THE TWO!
LET'S GO, HARUHIKO.
AND WE'VE GOT TO PICK UP SOME DEMON-STONES—
OH, R... RIGHT.
WELL, I GUESS WE'LL BE GOING BACK.
THANKS, YOU TWO. SEE YA!
OH...YES. TAKE CARE.
LEAVE EUKANARIA BEHIND NEXT TIME!

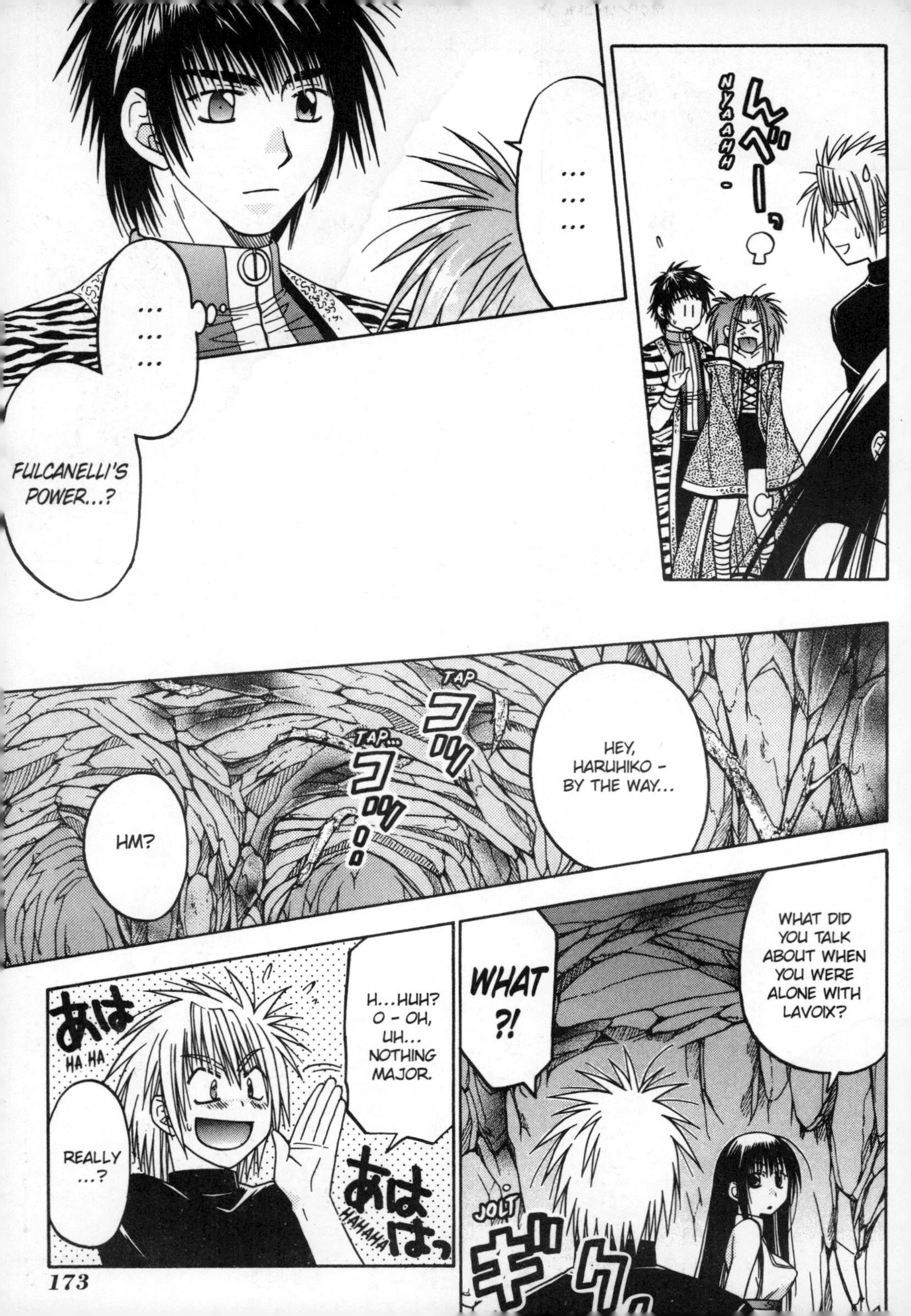

NYAAAHH.
...
...
...
...
...
...
FULCANELLI'S POWER...?
HEY, HARUHIKO - BY THE WAY...
TAP
TAP...
HM?
WHAT DID YOU TALK ABOUT WHEN YOU WERE ALONE WITH LAVOIX?
WHAT ?!
JOLT
H...HUH? O - OH, UH... NOTHING MAJOR.
あは
HA HA
REALLY ...?
あははっ
HAHAHA

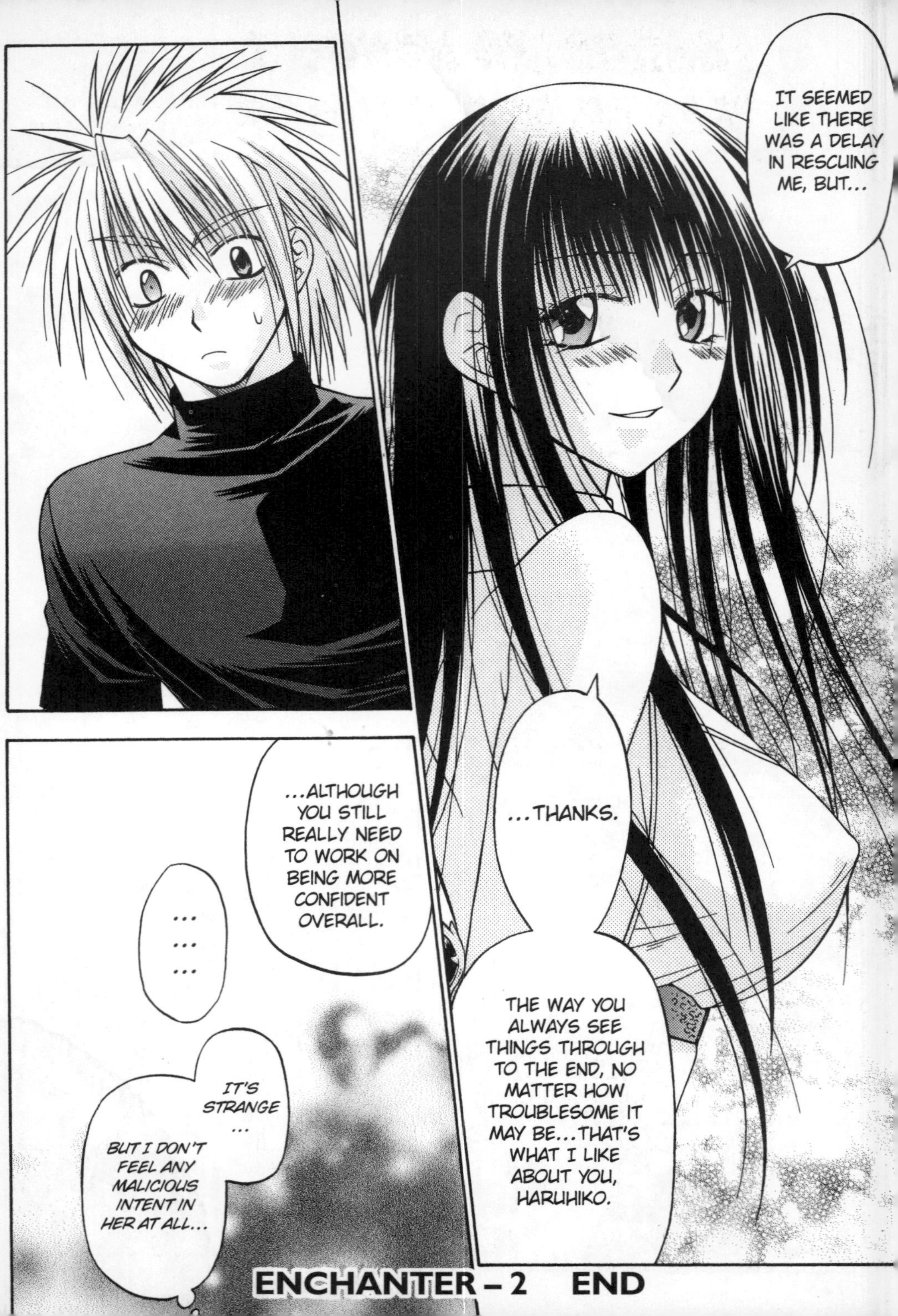
IT SEEMED LIKE THERE WAS A DELAY IN RESCUING ME, BUT...
...THANKS.
THE WAY YOU ALWAYS SEE THINGS THROUGH TO THE END, NO MATTER HOW TROUBLESOME IT MAY BE...THAT'S WHAT I LIKE ABOUT YOU, HARUHIKO.
...ALTHOUGH YOU STILL REALLY NEED TO WORK ON BEING MORE CONFIDENT OVERALL.
... ...
IT'S STRANGE... BUT I DON'T FEEL ANY MALICIOUS INTENT IN HER AT ALL...
ENCHANTER – 2 END

HARUHIKO KANOU'S "FRANKLY, IT'S TIRING"

CONCEPT TIME: 3 SECONDS
PRODUCED: WHILE WATCHING O.S.A.M.

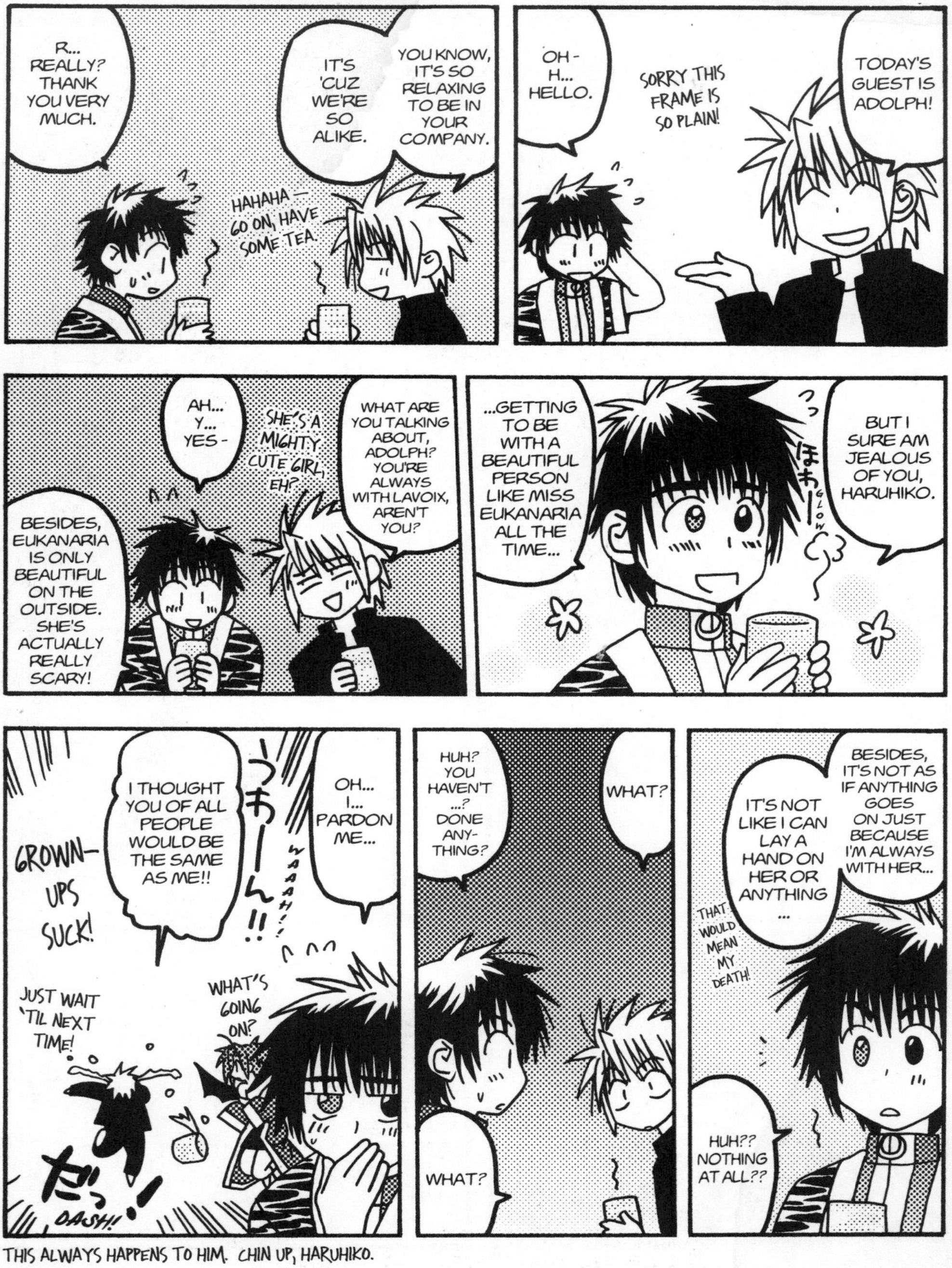
TODAY'S GUEST IS ADOLPH!
SORRY THIS FRAME IS SO PLAIN!
OH - H... HELLO.
YOU KNOW, IT'S SO RELAXING TO BE IN YOUR COMPANY.
IT'S 'CUZ WE'RE SO ALIKE.
HAHAHA— GO ON, HAVE SOME TEA
R... REALLY? THANK YOU VERY MUCH.
BUT I SURE AM JEALOUS OF YOU, HARUHIKO.
...GETTING TO BE WITH A BEAUTIFUL PERSON LIKE MISS EUKANARIA ALL THE TIME...
ほぉ～ GLOW
WHAT ARE YOU TALKING ABOUT, ADOLPH? YOU'RE ALWAYS WITH LAVOIX, AREN'T YOU?
SHE'S A MIGHTY CUTE GIRL, EH?
AH... Y... YES -
BESIDES, EUKANARIA IS ONLY BEAUTIFUL ON THE OUTSIDE. SHE'S ACTUALLY REALLY SCARY!
BESIDES, IT'S NOT AS IF ANYTHING GOES ON JUST BECAUSE I'M ALWAYS WITH HER...
IT'S NOT LIKE I CAN LAY A HAND ON HER OR ANYTHING ...
THAT WOULD MEAN MY DEATH!
HUH?? NOTHING AT ALL??
WHAT?
HUH? YOU HAVEN'T ...? DONE ANYTHING?
WHAT?
OH... I... PARDON ME...
うわーん!! WAAAAH!!
I THOUGHT YOU OF ALL PEOPLE WOULD BE THE SAME AS ME!!
GROWN-UPS SUCK!
WHAT'S GOING ON?
JUST WAIT 'TIL NEXT TIME!
だっ DASH!!

THIS ALWAYS HAPPENS TO HIM. CHIN UP, HARUHIKO.

NANIWA-JIN BATTLE DIARY

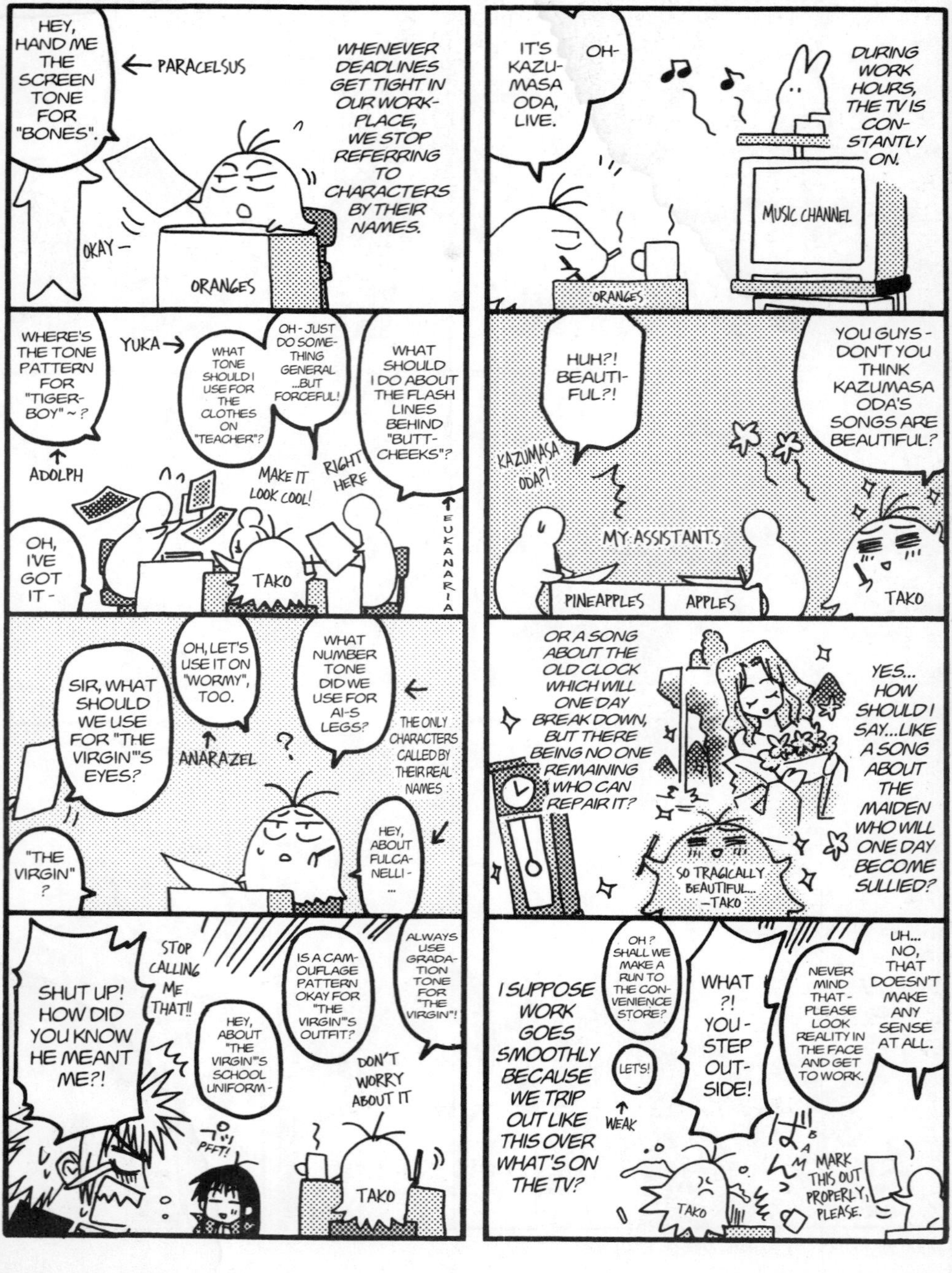
DURING WORK HOURS, THE TV IS CONSTANTLY ON.
OH-
IT'S KAZUMASA ODA, LIVE.
MUSIC CHANNEL
ORANGES
YOU GUYS - DON'T YOU THINK KAZUMASA ODA'S SONGS ARE BEAUTIFUL?
HUH?! BEAUTIFUL?!
KAZUMASA ODA?!
MY ASSISTANTS
TAKO
APPLES
PINEAPPLES
YES... HOW SHOULD I SAY...LIKE A SONG ABOUT THE MAIDEN WHO WILL ONE DAY BECOME SULLIED?
OR A SONG ABOUT THE OLD CLOCK WHICH WILL ONE DAY BREAK DOWN, BUT THERE BEING NO ONE REMAINING WHO CAN REPAIR IT?
SO TRAGICALLY BEAUTIFUL... -TAKO
UH... NO, THAT DOESN'T MAKE ANY SENSE AT ALL.
NEVER MIND THAT - PLEASE LOOK REALITY IN THE FACE AND GET TO WORK.
WHAT?! YOU - STEP OUTSIDE!
OH? SHALL WE MAKE A RUN TO THE CONVENIENCE STORE?
LET'S!
WEAK
I SUPPOSE WORK GOES SMOOTHLY BECAUSE WE TRIP OUT LIKE THIS OVER WHAT'S ON THE TV?
BAM
MARK THIS OUT PROPERLY, PLEASE.
TAKO
WHENEVER DEADLINES GET TIGHT IN OUR WORKPLACE, WE STOP REFERRING TO CHARACTERS BY THEIR NAMES.
PARACELSUS
HEY, HAND ME THE SCREEN TONE FOR "BONES".
OKAY—
ORANGES
WHAT SHOULD I DO ABOUT THE FLASH LINES BEHIND "BUTT-CHEEKS"?
EUKANARIA
RIGHT HERE
OH - JUST DO SOMETHING GENERAL ...BUT FORCEFUL!
MAKE IT LOOK COOL!
WHAT TONE SHOULD I USE FOR THE CLOTHES ON "TEACHER"?
YUKA
WHERE'S THE TONE PATTERN FOR "TIGER-BOY"~?
ADOLPH
OH, I'VE GOT IT -
TAKO
WHAT NUMBER TONE DID WE USE FOR AI-S LEGS?
THE ONLY CHARACTERS CALLED BY THEIR REAL NAMES
HEY, ABOUT FULCANELLI - ...
OH, LET'S USE IT ON "WORMY", TOO.
ANARAZEL
SIR, WHAT SHOULD WE USE FOR "THE VIRGIN"'S EYES?
"THE VIRGIN"?
ALWAYS USE GRADATION TONE FOR "THE VIRGIN"!
IS A CAMOUFLAGE PATTERN OKAY FOR "THE VIRGIN"'S OUTFIT?
DON'T WORRY ABOUT IT
HEY, ABOUT "THE VIRGIN"'S SCHOOL UNIFORM -
STOP CALLING ME THAT!!
SHUT UP! HOW DID YOU KNOW HE MEANT ME?!
PFFT!
TAKO

BONUS PAGE

★THIS IS ACTUALLY THE CORRECT VERSION OF THE TITLE PAGE FOR CHAPTER 5... BUT IT WAS REJECTED AT THE LAST MINUTE.

AS TO THE REASON WHY... WELL — FIGURE IT OUT. IT DOESN'T SEEM ALL THAT DIFFERENT TO ME, BUT...

★PERSONALLY, I'M GOING TO KEEP ON TRYING TO GET THE VERSIONS I WANT (LAUGH). SUPPORT ME, WON'T YOU?! (SUPPORT WHAT...?)

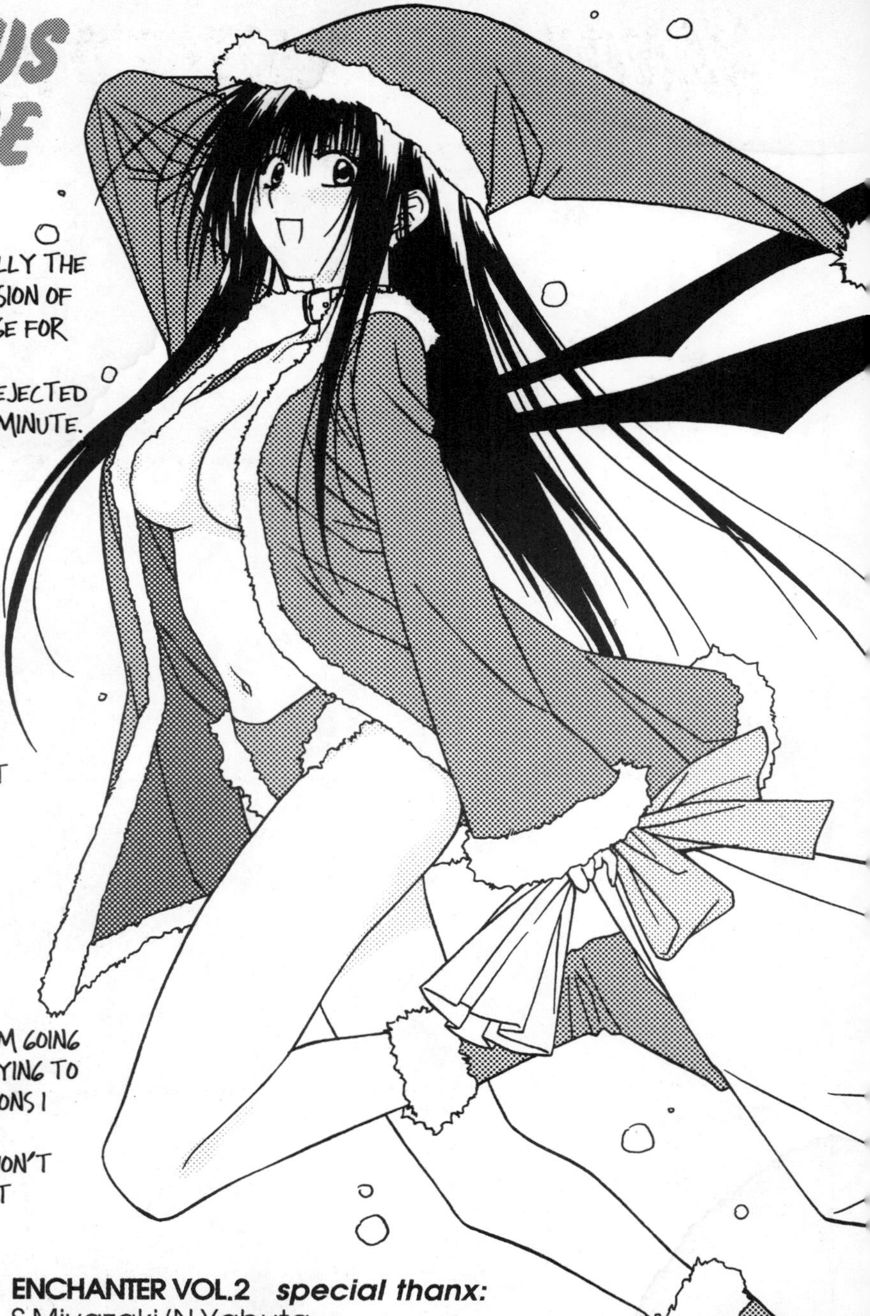

ENCHANTER VOL.2 ***special thanx:***
S.Miyazaki/N.Yabuta
H.Taninaka/T.Shimamoto/R.Takao
and:
K.Nakagawa

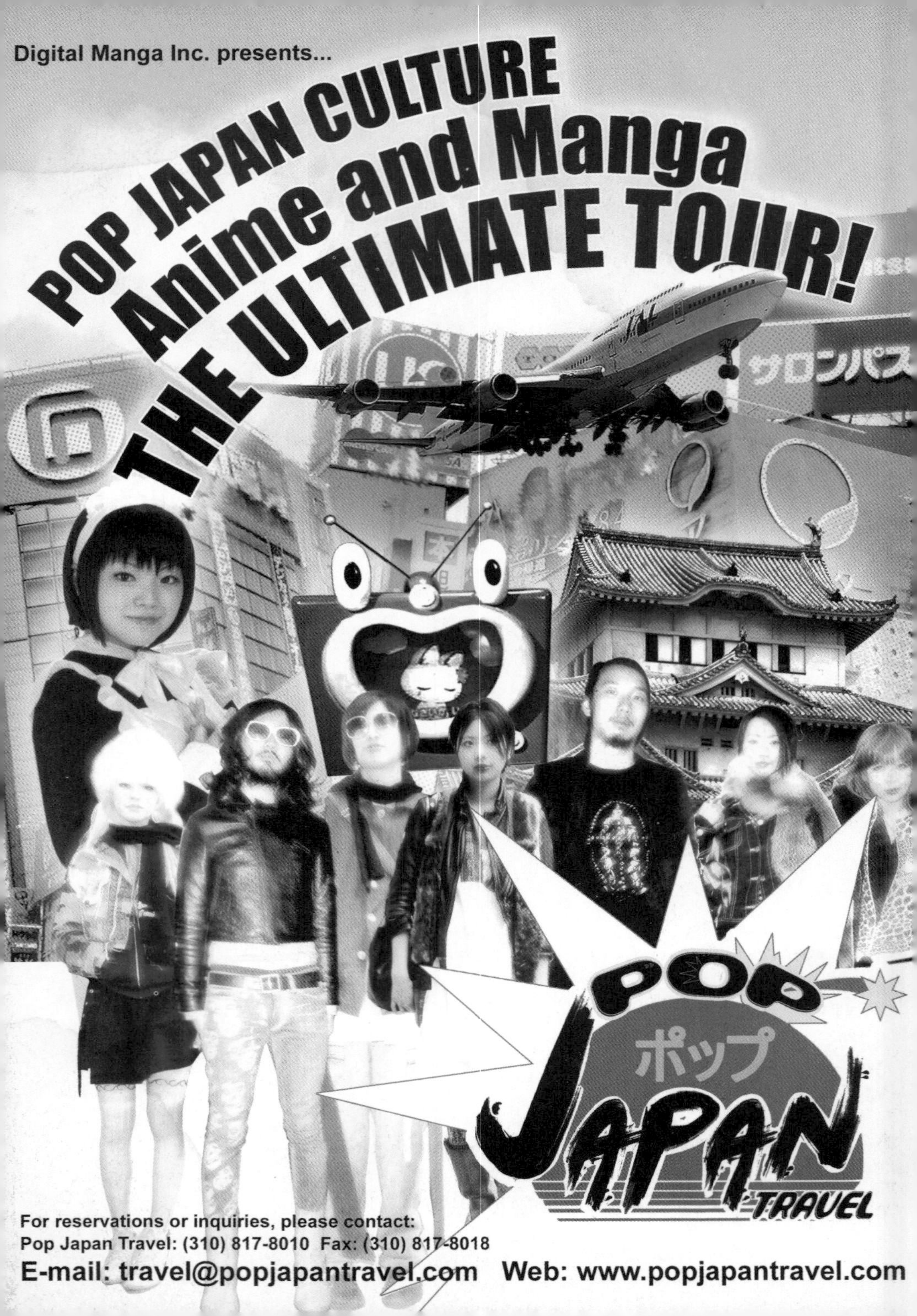
Digital Manga Inc. presents...
POP JAPAN CULTURE
Anime and Manga
THE ULTIMATE TOUR!
JAL
サロンパス
POP
ポップ
JAPAN
TRAVEL
For reservations or inquiries, please contact:
Pop Japan Travel: (310) 817-8010 Fax: (310) 817-8018
E-mail: travel@popjapantravel.com Web: www.popjapantravel.com

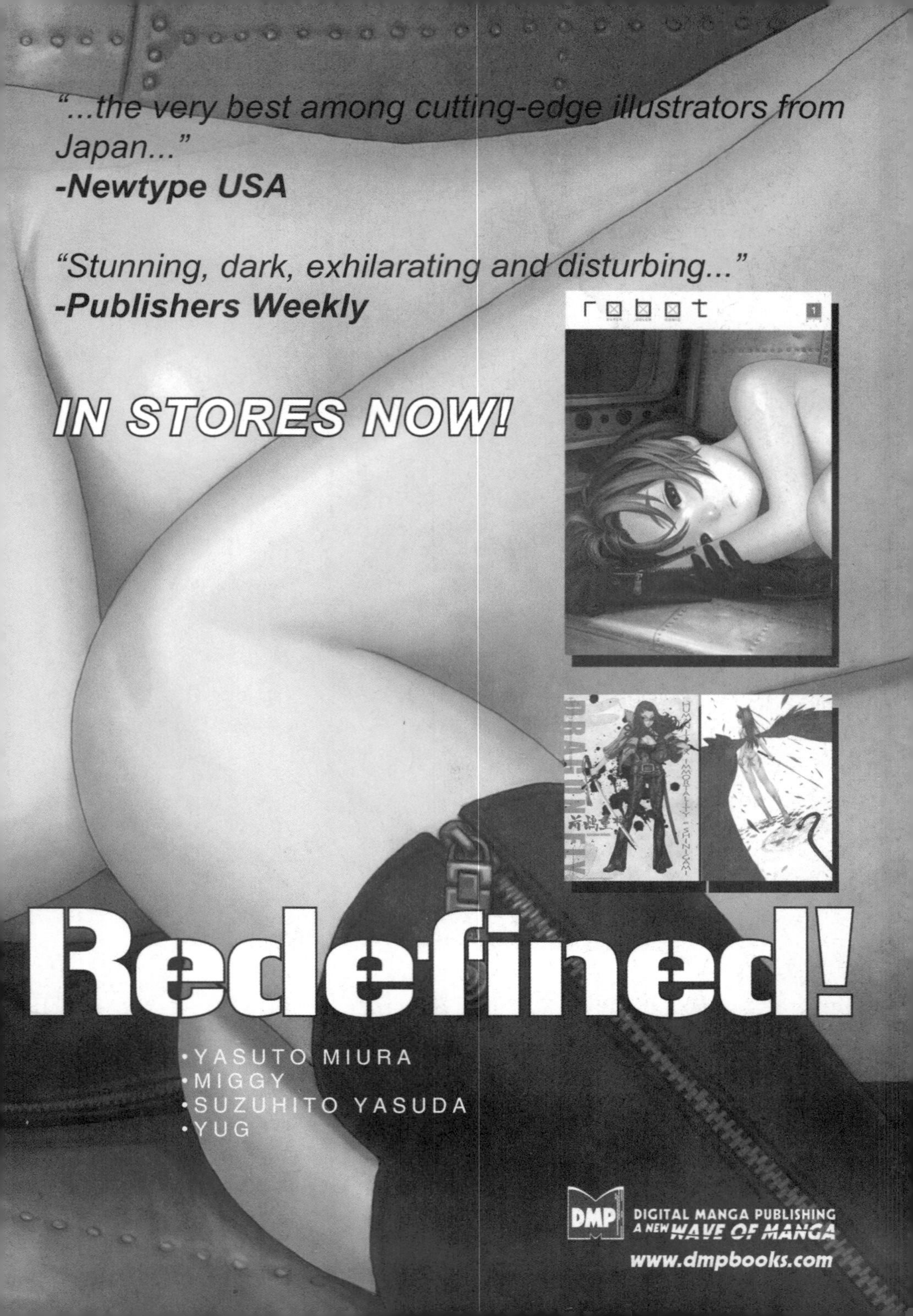
"...the very best among cutting-edge illustrators from Japan..."
-Newtype USA
"Stunning, dark, exhilarating and disturbing..."
-Publishers Weekly
robot
1
IN STORES NOW!
Redefined!
•YASUTO MIURA
•MIGGY
•SUZUHITO YASUDA
•YUG
DMP
DIGITAL MANGA PUBLISHING
A NEW WAVE OF MANGA
www.dmpbooks.com

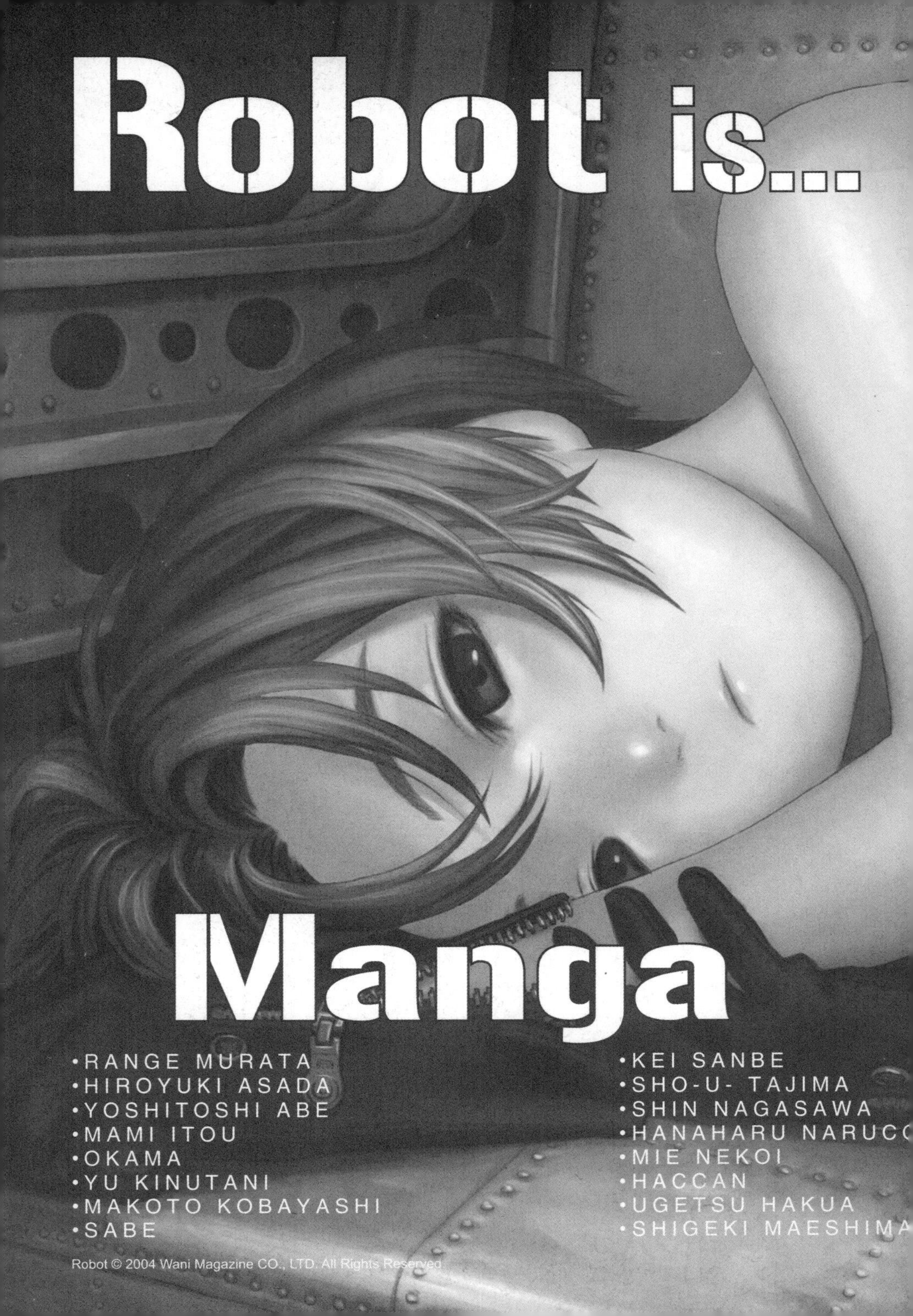
Robot is...
Manga
•RANGE MURATA
•HIROYUKI ASADA
•YOSHITOSHI ABE
•MAMI ITOU
•OKAMA
•YU KINUTANI
•MAKOTO KOBAYASHI
•SABE
•KEI SANBE
•SHO-U- TAJIMA
•SHIN NAGASAWA
•HANAHARU NARUC
•MIE NEKOI
•HACCAN
•UGETSU HAKUA
•SHIGEKI MAESHIMA
Robot © 2004 Wani Magazine CO., LTD. All Rights Reserved

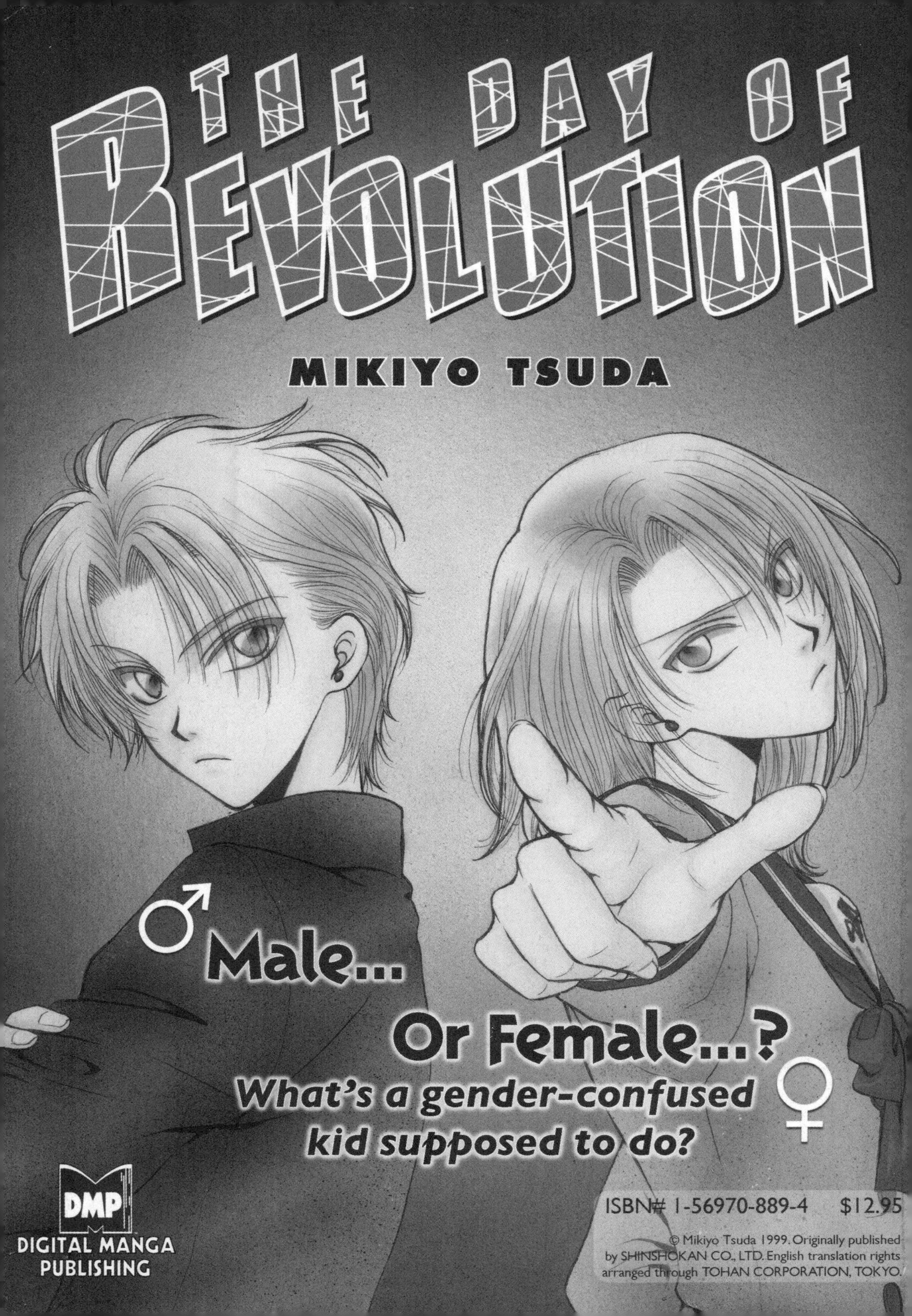

THE DAY OF REVOLUTION

MIKIYO TSUDA

♂ Male...

Or Female...?♀
What's a gender-confused
kid supposed to do?

DIGITAL MANGA
PUBLISHING

ISBN# 1-56970-889-4 $12.95

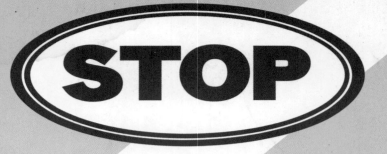

STOP

This is the back of the book!
Start from the other side.

NATIVE MANGA readers read manga from *right to left*.

1
1
2
2
3
3
4
5
4
5
6
6
7
8

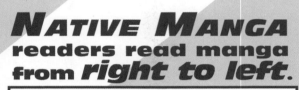

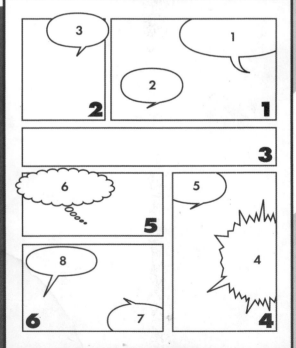

*If you run into our **Native Manga** logo on any of our books... you'll know that this manga is published in it's true original native Japanese right to left reading format, as it was intended. Turn to the other side of the book and start reading from right to left, top to bottom.*

Follow the diagram to see how its done.
Surf's Up!

NATIVE MANGA
READ RIGHT TO LEFT

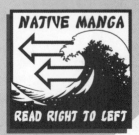